MW00528304

EPICUREAN ETHICS IN HORACE

Epicurean Ethics in Horace

The Psychology of Satire

SERGIO YONA

OXFORD
UNIVERSITY PRESS

OXFORD
UNIVERSITY PRESS

Great Clarendon Street, Oxford, OX2 6DP,
United Kingdom

Oxford University Press is a department of the University of Oxford.
It furthers the University's objective of excellence in research, scholarship,
and education by publishing worldwide. Oxford is a registered trade mark of
Oxford University Press in the UK and in certain other countries

First Edition published in 2018

Impression: 1

Published in the United States of America by Oxford University Press
198 Madison Avenue, New York, NY 10016, United States of America

British Library Cataloguing in Publication Data

Data available

Library of Congress Control Number: 2017944153

ISBN 978-0-19-878655-9

Printed and bound by
CPI Group (UK) Ltd, Croydon, CR0 4YY

Acknowledgements

This book, which is an expanded and revised version of my Ph.D. dissertation (University of Illinois at Urbana-Champaign 2014), would not have been possible without the help and generosity of a number of scholars and friends. First and foremost I owe many thanks to my committee members Ariana Traill, Kirk Sanders, and Kirk Freudenburg, who were a constant source of support throughout the writing process and whose guidance is greatly appreciated.

I owe special thanks to my dissertation director, mentor, and friend Antony Augoustakis, whose patience and advice over the years has made all the difference. To David Armstrong, whose generosity, insight, and support every step of the way have contributed enormously to the improvement of the project, I am profoundly grateful. I also wish to thank Elizabeth Asmis, who was kind enough to look at a portion of the manuscript.

My interest in Horace began at Queen's University at Kingston, where I had the great pleasure of learning from the late Professor Ross S. Kilpatrick. To him I will always be thankful, not only for having introduced me to the joys of Horace (as well as Lucretius) but also for his genuine interest in my progress and kind support early on.

I also wish to thank the editorial staff at Oxford University Press, Charlotte Loveridge, Catherine Owen, and Georgina Leighton, whose assistance has made the publication process a truly pleasant one. Many thanks are also due to the Press readers, whose feedback and recommendations have been invaluable.

Finally, to my wonderful family: to Angela, my loving wife, to our children, and to my parents, whose unconditional support and encouragement over the years has been a greater source of inspiration to me than they will ever know. To all of them I dedicate this book.

Contents

List of Abbreviations

ANRW	*Aufstieg und Niedergang der römischen Welt.* 1972– . Berlin
Arr.	Arrighetti, G., ed. and trans. 1962. *Epicuro: Opere.* 2nd edn. Turin: Einaudi
CIL	1863– . *Corpus Inscriptionum Latinarum.* Berlin
DK	Diels, H. and Kranz, W., eds. 1951–2. *Die Fragmente der Vorsokratiker.* 3 vols. Berlin: Weidmann
DL	Diogenes Laertius
Hdt.	Epicurus, *Letter to Herodotus*
KD	Epicurus, *Principal Doctrines* (Κύριαι Δόξαι)
LSJ	Liddell, H. G. and Scott, R., rev. H. S. Jones 1925–40. *Greek–English Lexicon.* Oxford: Oxford University Press
M	Marx (Lucilius)
Men.	Epicurus, *Letter to Menoeceus*
OCD	Hornblower, S., Spawforth, A., and Eidinow, E. 2012. *Oxford Classical Dictionary.* Oxford: Oxford University Press
OLD	Glare, P. G. W., ed. 2012. *Oxford Latin Dictionary.* Oxford: Oxford University Press
PCG	*Poetae Comici Graeci*
PHerc.	Papyrus Herculanensis
Pyth.	Epicurus, *Letter to Pythocles*
RE	Wissowa, G. et al. eds. 1893–1980. *Paulys Realencyclopädie der classischen Altertumswissenschaft.* Munich–Stuttgart
SV	Epicurus, *Vatican Sayings* (*Sententiae Vaticanae*)
SVF	Von Arnim, H., ed. 1905 (vols. 1–3), 1924 (vol. 4). *Stoicorum Veterum Fragmenta.* Leipzig: Teubner
TrGF	Snell, B., Kannicht, R., and Radt, S., eds. 1977–2004. *Tragicorum Graecorum Fragmenta.* 5 vols. Göttingen: Vandenhoeck & Ruprecht
U	Usener, H., ed. 1887. *Epicurea.* Leipzig: Teubner

Introduction

Horace, in describing the unreservedness of his predecessor Lucilius, notes that he "entrusted his secrets to his books as if they were faithful companions" (*S.* 2.1.30–1: *ille velut fidis arcana sodalibus olim | credebat libris*), with the result that the poet's whole life "is open to view, as if painted on a votive tablet" (33: *votiva pateat veluti descripta tabella*).[1] The self-revelatory expression of what appear to be one's inner thoughts and convictions, which is at the heart of Roman satire,[2] continues in Horace's *Satires* but with one important shift regarding intention: whereas the revelation of Lucilius' character and disposition is a by-product (cf. 32: *quo fit, ut omnis...*) of his criticism of contemporary society, Horatian satire is consciously introspective and, as such, revolves almost entirely around the poet's reflections—whether explicit or made through implied contrast—concerning his own development and presentation in the context of satiric observations of Roman society. One would be justified in assuming that such intimacy should ultimately reveal substantial information about the author's own life, but the fact that both Horace, his predecessor, and all Roman satirists chose to disclose autobiographical details through poetry rather than prose suggests otherwise.[3] Many have referred to Horace's self-presentation as

---

[1] The Latin text is taken from Klingner's 1970 Teubner edition and translations of Horace are those of H. R. Fairclough (1991) with occasional modifications. Unless otherwise noted, all other translations are my own. Citations of the *Satires* will henceforth be given by book, poem, and line number(s), e.g. *S.* 1.2.1–3.

[2] Philippson (1911) 77 points to this very parallel between Horace and Lucilius at the outset of his study. Cf. Lejay and Plessis (1915) xxxiii: "Le fond des Satires et des Épîtres est identique. Horace en est le principal sujet" ("The content of the *Satires* and *Epistles* is identical: Horace is their chief subject").

[3] Anderson (1982) 3–6.

a persona, which is informed by and responds to various literary traditions,[4] often without staking any real claims or expressing the serious convictions of the man behind the mask. Kirk Freudenburg, for instance, who is part of a tradition beginning with Alvin Kernan's 1959 *The Cankered Muse* and continuing with W. S. Anderson, regards any autobiographical information "not as documentary evidence for who [Horace] was, but as the first moves of a back-and-forth game played between reader and writer."[5] As the carefully crafted expression of poets, Roman satire first and foremost incorporates and often plays with the elements of many other traditions: there are comic situations and characters, parodies of epic poetry, literary criticism, and frequent engagement with philosophical teachings at every turn. Of course, the fact that not everything Horace says about himself is true—take, for example, his dubious claim in *Epistles* 2.2.51 to have been forced by *paupertas audax* to compose verses for survival, or his insistence that virtue rather than poetry was the cause of his successful encounter with Maecenas in *Satires* 1.6—further confirms that there is indeed an important theatrical or artistic component to his works. On the other hand, while persona theory has undoubtedly contributed to a more sophisticated or at least less naive understanding of Horace as poet, its over-application has often contributed to the view that satire is little more than an author's entertaining but learned and intergeneric *jeu d'esprit*. According to this view, Horatian satire is disjointed, inept, and even schizophrenic at times, with the author employing different "masks" for different purposes without any real underlying connection.[6]

In order to restore balance by tipping the scales toward a more serious reading of the *Satires* but without denying the presence of fictional autobiography and humor, this study argues that Horace

---

[4] Perhaps the most comprehensive examination of the confluence of various literary, stylistic, and philosophical aspects of the *Satires* is still that of Freudenburg (1993).

[5] Freudenburg (2010) 271, although he is keenly aware of the fact that persona theory has been "used in over-confident and self-congratulatory ways by critics" (p. 272). For the significance of the work of Alvin Kernan and others, see also Anderson (1982) 9–10 and Freudenburg (2005) 27–9.

[6] Lee (2008), in the introduction to his translation of Catullus (p. xx), points to this tendency in modern scholarship: "In literary studies, as in most other departments of life, fashion swings from one grotesque extreme to the other. In the nineteenth century many scholars took poetic statements as too literally related to real life; in the twentieth many have believed that poetry has no relation at all to life but exists in a self-referential vacuum or self-contained world of literary allusion."

portrays this poetic persona as consistently and competently engaged with Epicurean ethics throughout the entire collection. Its purpose is not to reveal definitively who the "real" Horace was or to uncover exactly what his convictions, philosophical or otherwise, were in life, which admittedly would be a fruitless attempt and one that any prudent scholar would consider misguided.[7] Nor does it go to the extreme of claiming that Epicureanism is the only element in the *Satires*. Rather, it aims to show that in his earliest works Horace creates a coherent persona whose observations, criticisms, and views are perfectly consistent with Epicurean teachings regarding ethics, and that this engagement reveals a profound understanding of and interest in the intricacies of ethical doctrines that were a topic of polemical debate at the time. The notion that Horace's persona is unified and communicates a coherent message is similar to the interpretation of Suzanne Sharland, who posits the predominant role of a "second self," which is the "overriding persona who is there in a sense throughout the *Satires*."[8] More specifically, this examination will suggest that it is possible to identify in these poems certain themes that, as will be shown in the following chapters, pervade most of the *Satires* and therefore provide overall unity,[9] such as the poet's self-proclaimed disposition as *purus et insons* (*S*. 1.6.69), his relationship with Maecenas, his attitude regarding wealth and his place in society, and the correct approach to applying criticism.[10] These themes also determine the manner in which individual poems will be examined in this study and how this

---

[7] As Graziosi (2009) 156–60 shows, even Suetonius' biography of Horace contains anecdotes that "mirror the poet's work," which itself contains many stories "shaped by literary motifs, narrative patterns and generic conventions." Rather than being a completely reliable source regarding the "real" Horace, then, Suetonius' *Life* most likely transmits bits of fact mingled with fiction inspired by the corpus of the poet's work, while at the same time carefully considering "the expectations set by the *Lives* of the Greek poets" in the Hellenistic tradition. There are certain details regarding the historical Horace, however, that cannot be doubted: that he received a good education, that he was a Roman knight who had served as a military tribune, and that he was on good terms with Maecenas as well as the poets who associated with him.

[8] Sharland (2009b) 63.

[9] The presence of Epicurean ethics is admittedly less prominent in *Satires* 1.7 and 1.8, although the latter includes a parody of divine intervention, which is consistent with Epicurean doctrine (cf. *S*. 1.5.101).

[10] It is unclear to what degree considerations regarding, for example, the acquisition of wealth or land, its confiscation, and the limitations on frankness in light of a new form of government are Horace's reflections on the political climate of the day. The best study of this is DuQuesnay (2009) 42–101.

4   *Epicurean Ethics in Horace*

organization contributes overall to Horace's self-portrayal as an Epicurean moralizer: the strong views in *Satires* 1.1–3 regarding money, sex, and friendship, all of which rely heavily on the Epicurean calculus of pleasure and pain, are justified by the portrayal of his quasi-philosophical upbringing in *Satires* 1.4. This poem, which is at the heart of the first collection, also looks ahead to *Satires* 1.6 and explains, from a philosophical and moral point of view, how the poet's persona made a positive impression on Maecenas, which is appropriately followed by the negative portrait of the pest in *Satires* 1.9 and the revelation of the members of Maecenas' circle of friends in the last satire.[11] In Book 2, *Satires* 2.1 and 2.5 revisit the topic of friendship in connection with frankness and flattery before turning once again to a positive description of Horace's healthy relationship with Maecenas in *Satires* 2.6. Following this description of idealized friendship and philosophical discussion in the country, which is facilitated by the gift of the Sabine estate, is that of Ofellus in *Satires* 2.2, a rustic who resembles Horace's persona but has recently experienced financial misfortune. Finally, in contrast to Ofellus' Epicurean equanimity in the face of a crisis and his useful moral advice concerning how to live happily, Horace introduces *Satires* 2.3 and 2.7, which parody two Stoic novices' misguided approach to what Horace's persona does so well, namely, the offering of frank criticism that is generally cheerful and useful.[12] One will immediately recognize that all of these topics and descriptions easily fall within the realm of ethics, which is not surprising given that Horace is often distinguished from other satirists by his significant concern with moral correction.[13] Insofar as the *Satires* are largely introspective and deal with ethical issues, moreover, one may be justified in speaking of the "psychology of satire" with respect to Horace's critical examinations, which are largely about his persona's mental health (ψυχή; cf. *S.* 1.4.128–9: *teneros animos . . . ego sanus*) as

---

[11] For Epicureanism in *Satires* 1.5, see Welch (2008) 47–74.

[12] Keane (2006) 116 views the satires of Book 2 in the same order. Hicks (2013) 200–50 examines at length the role of Epicureanism in the "food satires," especially *Satires* 2.4 and 2.8. For the argument that Horace intended the *Satires* to be read in the order in which they were published, see Zetzel (2009) 17–41 and Knorr (2004).

[13] Philippson (1911) 77 makes a vivid observation regarding Horace's portrayal of himself (emphasis mine): "Und die Lebensanschauung, die er zur Darstellung bringt, *ist getränkt mit Gedanken*, die er der griechischen Philosophie, vor allem der epikureischen entnommen hat" ("And Horace's portrayal of his approach to life *is drenched with ideas* he has taken from Greek philosophy, above all Epicureanism").

considered through prolonged and repeated conversations (λόγοι; cf. *S.* 2.6.71: *sermo oritur*) that function as a kind of therapeutic antidote to contemporary vices. Although his informal, and, especially in Book 2, dialectical style has been linked to that of Plato,[14] most commentators recognize the predominant role of Hellenistic ethics in Horatian satire.[15] By highlighting the role of Epicurean ethics in particular in the *Satires*, this study also attempts to demonstrate how Horace shows consistency in developing a persona throughout the collection that is not only concerned with "saving face," as Ellen Oliensis argues,[16] but with actively justifying his *virtus* and defending his place in society. The poet accomplishes this goal not only by engaging closely with the works of Lucretius and Cicero, but by working largely within the framework of Epicurus' moral doctrines as Philodemus of Gadara presents them in his treatises.

The idea that in the *Satires* Horace constructs a coherent persona whose observations and criticisms are constantly engaged with Epicurean doctrine begs the question: to what end, or, on a related note, for whom did the poet intend such a persona? This leads to the question of audience, with which many scholars have grappled over the years and which has led to a variety of interesting theories. In reading *Satires* 1.1, Barbara Gold posits four layers of audience, including an internal one consisting of Maecenas and the addressee within the satire, and an external one consisting of upper class Romans and anyone else who might have had access to the poems.[17] Frances Muecke similarly identifies two main groups, one fictitious (i.e. the nameless interlocutors) and the other actual (i.e. those actually hearing or reading the poems).[18] Randall McNeill, on the other hand, suggests that there are five "rings" of possible audiences, with Maecenas in the middle (first ring), then Horace's close friends and fellow poets (second ring), followed by the social elite (third ring), outsiders in general (fourth ring), and finally, those who "have no contact with the poet

---

[14] Anderson (1982) 414–19. Horace highlights the shift from monologue to dialogue that occurs between the two collections in *Satires* 2.3.11–12, where the names of Plato, Menander, Eupolis, and Archilochus appear (cf. *S.* 1.4.1 for a different list of names). See Kiessling and Heinze (1910) 219 (henceforth Kiessling–Heinze) and Lejay (1966) 392–3. Plato was an admirer of the mimes of Sophron and his dialogues show traces of this influence. See Greene (1920) 63–123.

[15] See e.g. Kiessling–Heinze (1910) xv–xix, Lejay and Plessis (1915) xxxiv–xxxv, Muecke (1993) 6–8, and Gowers (2012) 20–1.

[16] Oliensis (1998).   [17] Gold (1992) 161–71.   [18] Muecke (1993) 34–47.

and no hopes of advancing in his society but who read and respond to his poetry all the same" (fifth ring).[19] Denis Feeney regards Horace as making a distinction between "aristocratic Romans who are his ideal readers," such as those named at the end of *Satires* 1.10 (81–6), and "the babel of hybrid lowlife professionals who are also his readers, but his 'unideal' readers," although he cautions against regarding this division as a "real state of affairs."[20] Although all of these theories contribute something to the understanding of audience in Horace's earliest works, the following study adopts the view of Benjamin Hicks, who identifies the list of names in *Satires* 1.10 as the inner reading circle of his friends, who would have appreciated the convictions of an Epicurean persona (as opposed to outsiders, who may "fail to grasp the subtleties of satire"[21]). He states the following:

> Satire is characterized by its moral critique of human behaviors, not merely by the jokes and parodies. Some behaviors are inappropriate or inconsistent, but the implication of critiquing behavior is that a recognizably appropriate behavior does exist. This appropriate behavior stems from one's culturally derived worldview, of which philosophical preferences are a part. Horace's reading circle shows strong connections to Epicurean philosophy: Many of Horace's friends were trained by Philodemus, and many other upper-class Roman males studied Greek philosophy extensively enough to engage in sophisticated arguments over the correct moral actions of their lives. Thus, philosophy and the debates between schools become focal points of intellectual sparring.[22]

With the interests and philosophical proclivities of this inner circle of friends in mind, Horace creates a persona for himself that tackles the moral depravity of his day as an Epicurean moralizer, as someone whose views and understanding of such doctrines would have been wholeheartedly appreciated by the likes of Varius, Vergil, and the rest. These are the readers Horace hopes to impress, whereas the protection and support of powerful friends like Maecenas and Octavian, to say nothing of the poet's own artistic standards, suggest that he was far less concerned about reception beyond this group. Plotius, in other words, can laugh at Horace's feigned concern regarding outside readers' criticisms regarding the soft nature of his *Satires*, since such individuals will never quite understand his persona's Epicurean

[19] McNeill (2001) 36–8.   [20] Feeney (2009) 24–5.
[21] Hicks (2013) 49–59.   [22] Hicks (2013) 54–5.

approach to frank criticism. Varius can similarly grin at these out-siders' complaint that Horace's attacks, particularly those against the Stoics, are too severe, since he would have sympathized with his persona's strong disapproval of their doctrines.[23] The fact that Hor-ace successfully incorporates philosophical doctrines into his perso-na's observations, specifically for the purpose of sophisticated entertainment directed toward a select readership, suggest that he was more knowledgeable and better acquainted with Epicureanism than others have been willing to admit. And while it certainly does not prove that the historical Horace was a devoted follower of Epicurus, it does indicate that he was indeed sympathetic to his friends' views and perhaps even shared many of their philosophical convictions.[24]

The degree to which scholars have investigated the presence of Philodemus in Horace's works has fluctuated over the decades, although interest was first aroused after the discovery of papyri in the under-ground ruins of a Herculaneum villa in the eighteenth century.[25] The first editions to make any impact appeared in the 1860s, but it was Alfred Körte who initially considered the fragmentary evidence con-necting Philodemus to Augustan authors through a dedication in one of his treatises.[26] This inspired Robert Philippson, himself a scholar of and expert on Philodemus, to examine in more detail Horace's relationship to Epicureanism in two publications.[27] Such a connection was made by Richard Heinze in his revision of Adolf Kiessling's commentary,[28] and Giorgio Pasquali went further by connecting fragments of Philodemus

---

[23] The same could be said about Horace's tongue-in-cheek self-portrayal as a "porker from Epicurus' herd" and a "fat Phaeacian" in *Epistles* 1.4 and 1.15 respect-ively, which Epicurean readers would immediately recognize as the language used by those wishing to denigrate followers of the sect.

[24] Hicks (2013) 42: "[I]n using a persona that reflects the real man, there is something of the real man that cannot be removed from the text, not matter how hard he tries. Somehow that persona occupies the double standard of being Horace, yet not being Horace."

[25] Armstrong (2004b) 5–9 includes a similar review of literature but dealing more broadly with the Augustan poets in general. A more detailed overview of the discov-ery, restoration, and publication of the Herculaneum papyri will be given in the first chapter.

[26] Körte (1890a) 172–7.

[27] Philippson (1911) 77–110 and (1929) 894–6. He wrote a dissertation on Philode-mus' treatise *On Signs* (1881) and contributed an *RE* article detailing the philosopher's life and works (1938: 2444–7). Philippson also devoted a large portion of his textual work to proposing supplements to new texts from Herculaneum.

[28] Kiessling–Heinze (1910) xv, referring in the introduction to Horace's "Bekanntschaft mit Philodemos" ("acquaintance with Philodemus"), which, for

to Horace's views on sexual vice in *Satires* 1.2.[29] As Teubner editions of Philodemus continued to be published and consequently made his philosophical and poetic works readily available, they inspired articles dealing specifically with the role of his poetry in Horace. One of the earliest of these articles is that of G. L. Hendrickson, which, drawing from Georg Kaibel's 1885 edition of Philodemus' epigrams, investigates their possible presence in *Satires* 1.2, in which the philosopher is mentioned by name (121).[30] Although determining that the original epigram of Philodemus to which Horace refers is no longer extant, he expresses restrained yet enthusiastic support of Körte's identification of Horace as one of the dedicatees of the aforementioned Philodemean treatise, even asserting that "we are justified in concluding that a personal relationship of friendship existed between the two men."[31] This important article was followed a few years later by F. A. Wright's short piece, which responds to Hendrickson's thesis that the original source had been lost by proposing that Horace was in fact alluding directly to one of Philodemus' surviving epigrams, thus strengthening the connection between the two.[32] Around this time, the evidence regarding Philodemus' poetic theory in general was being studied by Augusto Rostagni, who consideres its influence on and challenges for Horace and other poets.[33] As the scholarship tradition clearly shows, in the early twentieth century many Horatian scholars interpreted the evidence from Herculaneum as proof that the Augustan poets associated with Philodemus, an interpretation which is further confirmed by Clayton Hall in his short article supporting the view that these men, including Horace, were involved in the Epicurean school at Herculaneum.[34] In the same year, classicist and philosopher Norman DeWitt published a study that deals specifically with the influence of Philodemus on Horace. This piece, along with the work of Philippson, is one of the earliest attempts to show the influence of Philodemean ethics, specifically the role of Epicurean παρρησία, in the works of Horace.[35] DeWitt, although perhaps relying too much on texts that were not as accessible then as they are now, attempts to show how the therapeutic application

---

Philippson (1911) 78 n. 1, was too brief an observation and inspired his much longer study.

[29] Pasquali (1920) 235.   [30] Hendrickson (1918) 27–43.
[31] Hendrickson (1918) 37.   [32] Wright (1921) 168–9.
[33] Rostagni (1923–4) 401–34.   [34] Hall (1935) 113–15.
[35] DeWitt (1935) 312–19.

of frank criticism, which is not mentioned by Epicurus but expounded upon in Philodemus' treatise *On Frank Criticism*, is employed by Horace in the *Odes* and *Epistles*. Four years later, DeWitt published another study in which he lists parallels relating Horatian poetry to various Epicurean doctrines, many of which appear in the writings of Philodemus but cannot be identified as distinctively his.[36] Along with DeWitt's findings regarding παρρησία in Horace, one may include the study of Agnes Michels, which expounds on the former's thesis and provides more supporting details.[37] Perhaps one of the most significant achievements in the area of Philodemus' influence on the Augustan poets during this time, however, is Jane Tait's 1941 dissertation, which examines the importance of Philodemus' literary theory on Horace's *Odes*. Related to this are the 1955 dissertation of Nathan Greenberg, which provides a detailed and systematic consideration of Philodemus' poetic theory, and the article of Quintino Cataudella, in which *Satires* 1.2 is read in the light of evidence from Philodemus' ethical treatises and epigrams.[38]

The following years witnessed important advancements in the appreciation of both the sophistication and artistic value of the *Satires* as well as Horace's engagement with the Epicurean tradition. This was undoubtedly facilitated by the monumental studies of Eduard Fraenkel, and, perhaps to a greater degree considering its more focused approach, that of Niall Rudd.[39] Both acknowledge the role of philosophy in Horace's satiric criticisms and were followed by more in-depth studies in this area, such as the article by Aroldo Barbieri, which examines the role of Epicurean ethics in *Satires* 2.6,[40] and the monograph of C. O. Brink, whose study of literary debates in the Hellenistic period and their significance for Horace draws heavily from Philodemus' criticisms in *On Poems*.[41] Along with these studies should be included those of Alberto Grilli on *Satires* 1.3 and R. L. Hunter on the importance of friendship and free speech.[42] In the 1970s, however, shortly before these essays appeared, major breakthroughs in the organization and promotion of the Herculaneum papyri (and therefore of Philodemus' works) were made under the guidance of Marcello Gigante, who, in addition to revitalizing the Centro Internazionale dei Papiri Ercolanesi (CISPE) in Naples, also provided scholars with access

[36] DeWitt (1939) 127–34.　　[37] Michels (1944) 173–7.
[38] Cataudella (1950) 18–31.　　[39] Fraenkel (1957); Rudd (1966).
[40] Barbieri (1976) 479–507.　　[41] Brink (1963).
[42] Grilli (1983b) 267–92; Hunter (1985a) 480–90.

to advanced technology and specialized venues for their scholarship, such as the *Cronache Ercolanesi* and *La Scuola di Epicuro*, both of which are series devoted to the publication of new scholarship and editions of Herculaneum fragments. These newer and more accessible editions continue to provide translations and insightful commentaries on difficult texts, thus inspiring scholars to revisit the literary climate in which poets like Horace lived and wrote. The fruits of such research are already visible in Gigante's contribution, published at the outset of these advancements, of various papers dealing with Philodemus and his connection to authors including Cicero and Horace.[43] This work, which includes a chapter that explores Philodemus' role in *Satires* 1.2, was followed by a full-length treatment of the same poem that explores further the connections between Horace and Epicurean ethics.[44] In the same year, scholars like Kirk Freudenburg began to emphasize the complexity of Horace's *Satires* by underscoring the importance of persona theory and recognizing that "the speaker who delivers his criticisms in the first person is not the poet himself but the poet in disguise."[45] The main contribution of this study lies in its emphasis on the importance of interpreting the content of the *Satires*, whether philosophical or otherwise, as relating to a largely fictional and self-consciously elusive persona that is not always to be taken seriously.[46] Along similar lines, Rolando Ferri, whose study focuses on connections between Lucretius' didactic poem to Memmius and Horace's intimate and philosophical discourse in the *Epistles*, recognizes parodic treatments of Epicureanism in the *Satires*.[47] Around the same time, Pierre Grimal similarly attempted to highlight Horace's philosophical eclecticism by pointing to the presence of distinctively anti-Epicurean sentiments in his iambic poetry.[48]

Some scholars, however, continued to demonstrate the presence of Philodemus' literary theory in Horace's works in light of newer fragments of his treatise *On Poems*. These studies include David Armstrong's long article on the dedicatees of the *Art of Poetry* and Anastasia Tsakiropoulou-Summers' 1995 dissertation on Philodemean poetic theory in the same work.[49] This research was

---

[43] Gigante (1983).   [44] Gigante (1993).   [45] Freudenburg (1993) 3.
[46] The impact of this theory, which was later expanded on in Freudenburg (2001), is easily detected in subsequent studies of Horace's persona, especially those of Braund (1996), Oliensis (1998), Gowers (2003) 55–92, and Turpin (2009) 127–40.
[47] Ferri (1993) 33–40.   [48] Grimal (1993) 154–60.
[49] Armstrong (1993) 185–230.

subsequently consolidated and expanded on in a volume edited by Dirk Obbink, which features chapters looking at the role of Philodemus' theory concerning the interconnectivity of poetic syntax with regard to Lucretius' epic and Horace's *Satires* 1.4.[50] To all of these advancements must be added the pioneering efforts of various Philodemean scholars who contributed their findings to a 2004 volume entitled *Vergil, Philodemus and the Augustans*. Among these individuals are Giovanni Indelli (103–10) and Jeffrey Fish (111–38), who examine Philodemus' sophisticated understanding and treatment of anger and explain how it relates to Vergil's *Aeneid*, F. M. Schroeder (139–58), who considers the role of Epicurean pictorial imagery within the context of frankness in the works of Vergil, and David Armstrong (2004a: 267–99), who draws connections between various Philodemean ethical treatises and Horace's *Epistles*. Returning to Horace's earliest work, an essay by William Turpin appeared five years later that, perhaps misapplying or rather over-applying persona theory, considers Horace's self-portrayal as a buffoon and morally bankrupt parasite in *Satires* 1.1–3.[51] This piece was met with a response in Jerome Kemp's balanced articles, reminding scholars not to overemphasize humor and self-parody to the complete exclusion of serious content.[52] Soon afterwards there came a brief examination of the same scholar, this time dealing specifically with the influence of Philodemus' fragmentary treatises *On Flattery* and *On Frank Criticism* on Horace's *Epistles* as well as *Satires* 2.5 and 2.8.[53] More recently, Jeffrey Fish and Kirk Sanders have edited a volume entitled *Epicurus and the Epicurean Tradition*, which engages rigorously with Philodemus' ethical works and their influence on authors such as Cicero and Seneca. The newest scholarship on the topic of Philodemus and Horace, moreover, includes two essays by David Armstrong on the "Epicurean diatribe" and friendship, along with an article by Jerome Kemp on *Satires* 1.2.[54] Nevertheless, Horatian scholarship continues to lack a full-length study that systematically investigates Philodemus' moral presence in the *Satires* as a whole. The following considerations will attempt to fill this gap, not by forcing parallels from an Epicurean

[50] Oberhelman and Armstrong (1995) 233–54.
[51] Turpin (2009) 122–37, to which cf. the similar thesis of Labate (2005) 47–63.
[52] Kemp (2009) 1–17, Kemp (2010a) 59 and, more recently, Kemp (2016) 132.
[53] Kemp (2010b) 65–76.
[54] Armstrong (2014a) 91–127 and (2016) 182–208; Kemp (2016) 130–46.

point of view that pretend to unlock the historical Horace, but rather by considering the relevance of his teachings for a Roman author dealing with difficult issues such as property loss, wealth administration, the corrupt patronage system, and the proper manner to discuss these issues tactfully and frankly with one's friends.[55]

Although the general content of the following chapters has been alluded to above, a more detailed summary here may be useful before proceeding. The first chapter of this study provides a preliminary consideration of the life and works of Philodemus, as well as an overview of how his doctrines align with but also expand and slightly adjust Epicurus' views in light of the concerns of his Roman audience. Chapter 2 is an examination of *Satires* 1.1–3, also known as the "diatribe satires," and how Philodemus' observations concerning economic administration, the pleasure calculus, frankness, and anger contribute to Horace's critiques of Roman society. Chapter 3 looks at certain Epicurean aspects of Horace's upbringing and moral formation as described in *Satires* 1.4. It attempts to show how the poet justifies the moral credentials of his persona by establishing connections to Epicurean ethical and methodological doctrines, which, given the programmatic nature of this satire, has implications for the rest of the *Satires*, especially the introductory ones. Having established the *virtus* of his literary persona in terms of the Epicurean tradition, this chapter next examines how Horace attempts to portray his relationship with Maecenas within the framework of Epicurean patronage. Beginning with the encounter scene between the two in *Satires* 1.6, it shows how he promotes himself as an Epicurean client-friend and economist, whose moral expertise is communicated through salubrious, ethical advice, which, in the case of Horace, takes the form of satirical conversations shared with Maecenas. Chapter 4 considers how Horace attempts to further promote himself as *purus et insons* by distinguishing himself from the typical flatterer through character portraits such as the one in *Satires* 1.9, which incorporates details also found in Philodemus' *On Flattery*. An integral part of this effort is his self-promotion as a lover of frankness, which is the hallmark of the Epicurean sage and

---

[55] Of course, the fragmentary state of some of Philodemus' ethical treatises, especially the fragments that make up the work *On Flattery*, will inevitably affect to a degree the reliability of certain connections. Often one must depend on conjectures that are based on the context of a particular treatise or on that of other works by the same author.

helps the poet to confirm his identity as a true and honest friend, which is reinforced at the end of *Satires* 1.10. This chapter next looks at the manner in which Horace dedicates himself to frankness in *Satires* 2.1 before exposing the flatterer's arts in *Satires* 2.5, which again testifies to his candor and willingness to invite comparison in the eyes of Maecenas. At the same time, however, his concern for genuine friendship and willingness to be content with little does not preclude his acceptance of greater wealth from a grateful patron, as he shows in *Satires* 2.6. In fact, his acceptance of the Sabine estate is perfectly in harmony with Philodemus' economic recommendations, since its bestowal makes possible the kind of philosophical withdrawal among friends advocated in his treatise *On Property Management*. Chapter 5, the final chapter, continues to investigate Horace's self-portrayal as a sage economist who accepts greater wealth but observes a proper measure in that regard and recognizes the requirements of nature. As a result, he is prepared to bear the loss of property with equanimity, just like his surrogate interlocutor Ofellus in *Satires* 2.2, which gives the poet an opportunity to consider how to respond to such a crisis like an Epicurean sage. It also allows him to showcase, through Ofellus, the proper way to deliver frank but useful advice, which stands in stark contrast to the much less considerate approaches of Damasippus and Davus in *Satires* 2.3 and 2.7. All the while, the poet cleverly recapitulates his humility through self-imposed and self-deprecatory examinations at the hands of these social inferiors, thus illustrating—at the expense of the Stoics—how not to conduct frank criticism and further endorsing his own portrayal as a tactful critic and a man of integrity.

1

Philosophical Background to Epicureanism in the *Satires*

BRIEF OVERVIEW OF PHILOSOPHICAL INFLUENCES

One finds a complex blend of ethical doctrines in the *Satires*, although, in addition to expressing more general views such as Aristotle's extremely influential concept of the virtuous mean (cf. *S.* 1.1.106: *est modus in rebus*, "there is a measure in things" and 1.2.24: *dum vitant stulti vitia, in contraria currunt*, "in avoiding some vices, fools run into their opposites"), Horace also engages with the more specific teachings of other philosophical schools.[1] Quite prominent among these teachings, specifically in poems attacking the Stoics and their doctrines, are various ethical paradoxes attributed to Chrysippus: the conviction that all offenses are equal, as expressed in *Satires* 1.3 (96: *quis paria esse fere placuit peccata*) and the notion that everyone except for the sage is mad, which is expressed in both *Satires* 2.3 and 2.7. The poet also dwells on the importance of decorum and consistency as emphasized by Panaetius (*S.* 1.3.9: *nil aequale*; cf. also 2.3.307–13 and 2.7.22–42) and alludes to Stoic physics as well as to Plato's *Phaedo* (83d) in a passage in Book 2 rife with parody (*S.* 2.2.77–9: *corpus . . . adfigit humo divinae particulam aurae*, "the body . . . fastens to earth a fragment of the divine spirit"). In the introductory satires Horace draws from the Hellenistic, or, more specifically, the Cynic tradition of street-preaching in the diatribe style, although he also seems to avoid carefully this sect's infamous predilection for overly harsh criticism (cf. *Ep.* 1.17.18: *mordacem Cynicum*, "snapping Cynic" and 1.18.1–8 for a

---

[1] Mayer (2005) 146–59.

negative description of Cynic frankness) and he spurns their rejection of useful conventions such as money (*S.* 1.1.73: *nescis, quo valeat nummus, quem praebeat usum?*, "don't you know what money is for, what end it serves?"). From Plato he borrows not only certain phrases, such as "this is not my story" (*S.* 2.2.2: *nec meus hic sermo est*, quoting *Sym.* 177a) and "earn your sauce with hard exercise" (20–1: *tu pulmentaria quaere | sudando*; cf. Cic. *On Ends* 2.90: *Socratem . . . audio dicentem cibi condimentum esse famem, potionis sitim*, "I listen to Socrates . . . when he says that hunger is the best sauce for food and that the best flavor for drink is thirst"), but also, as W. S. Anderson demonstrated decades ago, the practice of using constructive irony in the context of philosophical dialogue, which is especially prominent in the poems of Book 2.[2] Most important of all philosophical influences, however, is undoubtedly that of Epicurus and his followers in Italy, including Philodemus. Among the many Epicurean themes that play a role in almost all the *Satires* is the insistence on withdrawal from public affairs (cf. *S.* 1.6.18: *nos . . . a volgo longe longeque remotos*, "we . . . who are set far, far above the vulgar" and 2.3.5: *huc fugisti*, "you fled here for refuge") and the importance of philosophical gatherings in the countryside with friends, which is emphasized in the central passage of *Satires* 2.6 (59–76). One may add to this Epicurus' well-known teaching regarding the benefits of meager fare (cf. *S.* 1.6.114–15: *inde domum me | ad porri et ciceris refero laganique catinum*, "then I go home to my dish of leeks and peas and fritters," and 2.2.1: *vivere parvo*, "frugal living") and, perhaps most fundamental of all, his doctrine of the pleasure calculus and its crucial role in terms of making ethical decisions responsibly and to one's own advantage (cf. especially *S.* 1.2.78–9: *desine matronas sectarier, unde laboris | plus haurire maliest quam ex re decerpere fructus*, "cease to court matrons, for thence one may derive more pain and misery than enjoyment in the reality").[3] Of course, scholars have long since recognized the presence of these doctrines not only in the *Satires* but also in Horace's entire corpus. What may make the connection more profound and meaningful, however, is a consideration of the manner in which Philodemus expands on and streamlines these teachings with a view to the concerns

---

[2] Anderson (1982) 3–49.

[3] To these Epicurean doctrines should be added Horace's claim to have "learned that the gods lead a care-free life" (*S.* 1.5.101: *namque deos didici securum agere aevom*), which is taken directly from Lucretius (5.82). See Welch (2008) 62–63.

of his Roman audience and friends, among whom were the likes of Vergil and, very likely, Horace.

It is the purpose of the following investigation to enhance the traditional appreciation of Horace's engagement with Hellenistic philosophy by examining the influence on the *Satires* of Philodemus' ethical views, specifically as they pertain to the administration of wealth, the challenge of distinguishing flattery from genuine friendship, and, closely related to this, the therapeutic application of frank criticism. There are various reasons for investigating such a connection, which has not received the attention in modern scholarship that it truly deserves. One of the main reasons justifying this kind of study is both historical and social: not only was Philodemus a contemporary of Horace as well as his neighbor to the south of Rome, but he was also familiar and on demonstrably friendly terms with the poet's intimate friends Plotius, Varius, and Vergil, all of whom Horace identifies as part of his audience in *Satires* 1.10 (81): *Plotius et Varius...Vergiliusque*. Körte's well-known and frequently cited article from 1890 presents the fragmentary evidence from two of Philodemus' treatises dealing with flattery (PHerc. 1082) and avarice (PHerc. 253),[4] in which the names of Varius and Quintilian are legible (quoting here Körte's reconstruction of the second fragment): ['Ορά]τιε καὶ Οὐάρι[ε καὶ Οὐεργίλιε] καὶ Κοϊντίλι[ε].[5] Regarding the ending -τιε, Körte's restoration as it appears here obviously connects it to the name of Horace, although, as Francesco Della Corte has argued and as Marcello Gigante and Mario Capasso confirmed decades later using more advanced technology,[6] it in fact refers to that of Plotius Tucca, who coedited the *Aeneid* along with Varius after Vergil's death. This confirmation of Tucca's name and also of the three other Romans actually comes from another likely belonging, like PHerc. 1082, to Philodemus' treatise *On Flattery* (PHerc. Paris. 2.21–3): ὦ Πλώτιε καὶ Οὐάρ[ι]ε καὶ Οὐεργ[ί]λιε καὶ Κοϊντ[ί]λιε.[7] The list is an interesting one, particularly because, as David Armstrong observes, it recurs centuries later in the *Life of Probus* (fifth to sixth century AD), which confirms the quartet's

---

[4] For the identification of this and four other fragments as belonging to a Philodemean treatise probably entitled *On Avarice* (a heading that does not appear in the evidence from Herculaneum) see Dorandi and Spinelli (1990) 53–60.

[5] Körte (1890a) 172–7.

[6] Della Corte (1969) 85–8, Gigante and Capasso (1989) 3–6.

[7] For more details, see Sider (1997) 19–20 and Armstrong (2014a) 97.

devotion to Epicureanism: *Vixit [Vergilius] pluribus annis... liberali in otio, secutus Epicuri sectam, insigni concordia et familiaritate usus Quintilii, Tuccae et Vari* ("Vergil lived for many years... in the leisure of a free man; he was a follower of the Epicurean sect and enjoyed the remarkable solidarity and intimacy of Quintilian, Tucca, and Varius").[8] Returning to Horace, one may recall that, in addition to the passage from one of his satires quoted above and featuring this same list under consideration, there is another one in *Satires* 1.5 (40: *Plotius et Varius... Vergiliusque*). The point of all this is that, given the fact that a list of dedicatees appearing in three separate fragments of Philodemus' ethical treatises also appears, in the same exact order,[9] in two of Horace's satires, there is a strong possibility that the Roman poet was well acquainted with these very writings. Of course, that he was familiar with Philodemus' epigrams is indisputable (cf. *S.* 1.2.121), but it is not unreasonable to think that the philosopher was similarly aware of Horace's early poetry. In fact, the mutual bonds of friendship discussed above led Marcello Gigante to conclude that "although [Philodemus] does not mention Horace explicitly, nevertheless he was a reader of his satires."[10] It is highly likely, therefore, especially given Horace's playful fondness for Epicureanism (cf. *Ep.* 1.4.15–16: *me... Epicuri de grege porcum*, "me... a porker from the Epicurean herd"[11]), that, in addition to being familiar with Philodemus' poetry, he would likewise have been familiar with and rather partial to his philosophical insights. And despite the playful tone of this and other passages in which Horace appears to identify with the ethical teachings of this sect, it is worth noting that a formal connection between Horace and Epicureanism was made by the ancients themselves, as Porphyrio reveals in his commentary on *Odes* 1.34 (*ad* 1): *hac ode significat, se paenitentiam*

---

[8] Armstrong (2014a) 98.

[9] See Welch (2008) 64–65. Horace speaks highly of Quintilian in *Odes* 1.24 and *Art of Poetry* 438–44.

[10] Gigante (1998) 48: "[Filodemo] che non cita mai espressamente Orazio, fu lettore delle sue satire."

[11] The pig appears to have had important significance for Epicureans, as evidence from the Villa of the Papyri suggests. Among the artifacts that have been discovered there is a statue of a pig, which might have played a role in the building's sculptural program. There is also the Boscoreale cup, which features an image of Epicurus, pig at his feet, debating with other philosophers. See Warren (2002) 129–49 and Sider (1997) 16 n.13 for more.

agere, quod Epicuream sectam secutus, "In this ode he indicates his remorse for having been a follower of the Epicurean sect" (cf. pseudo-Acro, *in Serm.* 1.5.101, in which Horace's "theology" is compared to that of Vergil, whom the commentator explicitly identifies as an Epicurean). Aside from positing a significant connection between Horace and Philodemus based on historical and papyrological evidence (or at least the implications thereof), there is also another, perhaps more compelling reason to do so, and one that involves Horace's uniquely Philodemean engagement with certain ethical issues. His expression of the mean regarding wealth is, of course, inevitably linked to Aristotle's *Nicomachean Ethics.* In his treatises, however, Philodemus develops Epicurean economic theory, which, along with promoting a similar doctrine of the "measure of wealth" (πλούτου μέτρον) that is better suited to the context of many of Horace's satires, also includes specific advice about patronage and poverty that plays an important role in the poet's creation of his philosophical and ethical persona. Furthermore, Horace's concern with disassociating himself from flatterers and emphasis on his persona's trustworthiness is directly linked to his relationship with Maecenas, which also reflects the concern of Epicurean clients such as Philodemus, who, much like the poet, met accusations of flattery by attempting to distinguish the sage's disposition from that of the self-serving adulator. Finally, Horace's approach to frankness, which he frequently differentiates from the harsher invective of the Stoics and Cynics, features many of the elements discussed by Philodemus in his methodological treatment of therapeutic criticism. These include the importance of criticizing in a cheerful manner and acknowledging one's own shortcomings, both of which are characteristic features of Horatian satire. The nature of these treatments and the specific contributions of Philodemus will be discussed below, but it may be helpful first to acknowledge his presence in Italy and give an overview of the editions and scope of his works.

LIFE AND WORKS OF PHILODEMUS

Little is known about Philodemus' philosophical training in Greece and subsequent activity on the Italian peninsula, most of which is gleaned from references in his own treatises or the works of contemporary—although often hostile—Romans such as Cicero.[12] Born around the beginning of the first century BC in the Syrian town of Gadara, which was also the home-town of the epigrammatist Meleager (*c*.100 BC) as well as of a number of other, lesser-known poets,[13] Philodemus was probably of Greek extraction or at least heavily influenced by Hellenic literature and culture. Like many of his contemporaries he soon left home and traveled to Athens, where he began to study under the Epicurean scholarch and his fellow easterner Zeno of Sidon as well as with Demetrius of Laconia, another leader of the Epicurean sect at the time. Cicero, who states that he had heard Zeno's lectures in 79/80 BC, describes his style as "clear, weighty, and beautiful" (*On the Nature of the Gods* 1.59: *distincte graviter ornate*) and elsewhere refers to him as "a testy old man" and the "sharpest of all the Epicureans" (*Tusculan Disputations* 3.38: *ille acriculus me audiente Athenis senex Zeno, istorum acutissimus*), a description which likely owes something to the fact that he was often involved in logical disputes with the Stoics, even going to court with them (cf. *On the Nature of the Gods* 1.93: *Zeno quidem etiam litigabat*). His research interests appear to have ranged from physics and geometry to ethics (Diogenes Laertius at 10.26 refers to him as a "prolific author," πολυγράφος ἀνήρ), and although little of his output has survived in the form of a fragmentary collection,[14] more extensive insight regarding his teachings may be derived from the recorded lectures of Philodemus dealing with various ethical topics. Some time after his formal training in philosophy under Zeno, which lasted from 110 to 75 BC, Philodemus came to Italy, although the exact date of his arrival has been the subject of some scholarly controversy. Relying on a reference in Cicero to Lucius Calpurnius Piso Caesoninus (cos. 58 BC) as an *adulescens* when he met the Greek immigrant (*Pis.* 68: *Is* [sc. Philodemus] *cum istum*

[12] For sources detailing the life and works of Philodemus, see first and foremost the important *RE* study of Philippson (1938) 2444–7. This may be supplemented by Tait (1941) 1–23, who includes a useful overview that links Philodemus to the Augustan poets, and Gigante (1995), who examines his presence in Italy and, more specifically, his work at the library in Herculaneum. Most modern editions of his treatises similarly contain biographical information: see e.g. De Lacy and De Lacy (1978) 145–55, Sider (1997) 3–24, Konstan et al. (1998) 1–3. There is also the *ANRW* article of Asmis (1990) 2369–406, which contains a summary of his life and works.

[13] See Sider (1997) 3–4 for the evidence.

[14] Preserved in Angeli and Colaizzo (1979) 47–133.

adulescentem . . . vidisset, non fastidivit eius amicitiam, "After Philodemus had met Piso as a young man . . . he did not spurn his friendship"), some have placed this event in the 70s.[15] In any event, he
settled in southern Italy and established an Epicurean community
in the vicinity of Naples, possibly along with his colleague Siro,
whom Vergil fondly remembers for his "learned sayings" (*Cat.* 5.9:
magni . . . docta dicta Sironis) and modest living conditions (8.1–2):
Villula, quae Sironis eras, et pauper agelle, | *verum illi domino
tu quoque divitiae,* "O small villa and poor field, you who belonged
to Siro, although to your master even you were rich indeed." While
living in Italy, Philodemus appears to have formed a special relationship with Piso, the aristocrat and politician mentioned above, whom
Cicero, in a speech denigrating the latter's character and drawing from
comic stereotypes in order to do so, portrays as the patron of flattering
Greeks and the recipient of lascivious poetry:

> In quibus [carminibus], si qui velit, possit istius tamquam in speculo
> vitam intueri; ex quibus multa a multis et lecta et audita recitarem, ni
> vererer ne hoc ipsum genus orationis quo nunc utor ab huius loci more
> abhorreret; et simul de ipso qui scripsit detrahi nihil volo. qui si fuisset
> in discipulo comparando meliore fortuna, fortasse austerior et gravior
> esse potuisset; sed eum casus in hanc consuetudinem scribendi induxit
> philosopho valde indignam, si quidem philosophia, ut fertur, virtutis
> continet et offici et bene vivendi disciplinam.   (*Pis.* 70–1)

> It is possible, for anyone wishing to do so, to peer into Piso's life as if
> reflected in a mirror by reading Philodemus' poetry. And from it
> I would recite many verses that a number of people have read and
> heard, if I were not wary of the fact that the manner of speaking I am
> currently employing is itself already averse to the usual way of address-
> ing people in this place (nor do I want to detract anything from the
> author). But if he [Philodemus] had had better luck in terms of acquir-
> ing a fitting disciple, perhaps he would have turned out to be a more
> austere and dignified man himself; the misfortune of having met with
> Piso, however, led him to become accustomed to compose poetry in a
> manner that is very undignified for a philosopher indeed, if in fact
> philosophy entails, as they say, learning about virtue, responsibility, and
> the good life.

---

[15] See e.g. Sider (1997) 6. Cichorius (1922) 296, however, had proposed a later date
that was based on another reference in Cicero to Piso as *imperator* in Macedonia
(*Pis.* 70), which would have occurred in the 50s.

Based on this kind of evidence from the speech, along with one of Philodemus' epigrams (27), which is an invitation poem addressed to Piso, it is quite probable that the Roman aristocrat and politician was in fact the philosopher's patron, although some have vigorously argued against this connection.[16] What is not uncertain is the fact that, as Cicero suggests and as surviving evidence confirms, Philodemus is the author of a collection of epigrams that were preserved in the *Greek Anthology*, a conglomeration of sixteen books of epigrams originally preserved in two separate manuscripts but ultimately derived from the same source.[17] As David Sider acknowledges, these poems are interesting because, like Horace's *Satires*, they have a strong connection to the σπουδαιογέλοιον style or serio-comic tradition, with the result that "some of the philosophical point of his poetry has been obscured by their light-hearted tone."[18] On the other hand, in contrast to Cicero's attack on Piso and negative description of Philodemus as a writer of salacious poetry and a subservient *graeculus*, all of which is nothing more than a means of discrediting his political opponent, in his much more serious work *On Ends* (composed in 45 BC) he is not shy about praising both Philodemus and Siro by name (2.119): *Sironem dicis et Philodemum, cum optimos viros, tum homines doctissimos*, "You mean Siro and Philodemus, the best of men and most learned of human beings."[19] This laudatory description, which for centuries had lacked any real justification, was finally confirmed in the eighteenth century by the discovery of a dilapidated villa that unearthed the remains of Philodemus' works.[20]

---

[16] See especially Allen and De Lacy (1939) 59–65. For Cicero's portrayal of Philodemus in the speech *Against Piso*, see Gigante (1983) 35–53.

[17] It is uncertain exactly how many of the thirty-six poems actually belong to Philodemus, since the anthologies do not always agree on this issue. See Sider (1997) for an edition, translation, and commentary of these poems as well as for the question of authorship (46–7).

[18] Sider (1997) 4.

[19] For the possibility that Piso was given to a kind of overindulgence condoned by certain Epicureans in Rome, but then changed his ways after joining with Philodemus and his more sober companions in Naples, see Sider (1997) 16–19. See also Hutchinson (2013) 73 for Philodemus and Siro as a philosophical pair.

[20] Sedley (1998) has a useful discussion of Philodemus in Italy (65–8) and the discovery of the Herculaneum papyri, with particular emphasis on fragments of Epicurus' *On Nature* (94–8). See also Dorandi (2015) 15–52.

This villa, which is located in Herculaneum and probably belonged to the Pisones (although based on the archaeological evidence and epigrammatic remains there is no conclusive link between the two[21]), houses the only library to have survived from antiquity. The contents were immediately carbonized and thus preserved by the eruption of Mount Vesuvius in AD 79, but were discovered by accident in 1709 due to the digging of a well and tunneling, under the direction of the Swiss engineer Karl Weber excavations and explorations decades later, which had originally begun as something of a treasure hunt for ancient artifacts, eventually led to the unearthing of the actual papyri in carbonized form in the 1750s, around 1,800 in number including fragments.[22] Unfortunately, early attempts to unroll these fragile relics, which had been further damaged and warped over the centuries by rain and mud, resulted in significant damage to the texts, (not surprising if one considers that "tools" such as knives, mercury, and gas were used for this purpose). Significant progress was finally made, however, when in 1793 Father Antonio Piaggio, the inventor of a contraption designed to unroll papyrus scrolls, applied his machine for the purpose of opening the charred lumps very carefully and slowly. It was eventually revealed that, although most of the recovered texts were written in Greek, a few are in Latin.[23] The occurrence of texts in both languages, along with the fact that certain rooms in the villa have not yet been explored, may suggest that, as epigraphic evidence reveals was the case in the temple of Palatine Apollo,[24] there were in fact two separate libraries for Greek and Latin scrolls (one may also recall Trimalchio's description in *Satyricon* 48: *duas bybliothecas habeo, unam Graecam, alteram Latinam*, "I have two libraries, one Greek and the other Latin"). Fragments of Lucretius' didactic epic have turned up in the villa and were

---

[21] Mommsen (1880) 32–6. See also Allen and De Lacy (1939) 63.

[22] The original excavator was Roque Joaquín de Alcubierre, who in 1750 put the more competent Weber in charge.

[23] See Longo Auricchio and Capasso (1987) 37–47 and Sider (2009) 305–14 for the discovery in general. Sider (1997) 13 n. 2 lists the Latin texts. Gigante (1995) 1–60 has copious references to works dealing both with the architectural characteristics of the villa as well as the contents of its library.

[24] The following descriptions appear on monuments between the Via Appia and the Via Latina: AB · BYBLIOTHECE · GRAECA · TEMPLI · APOLLINIS (*CIL* 6.5188), A · BYBLIOTHECE · LATINA · APOLLINIS (*CIL* 5189; cf. 5884). Sider (1997) 13 also discusses this division and its connection to the villa.

deciphered in 1988, which is surprising since many have long maintained that this poet had no contact with contemporary Epicureans.[25] Given this recent connection, it is not unreasonable to speculate about the presence, as yet undiscovered in the villa, of the works of Horace and Vergil as well as other associates and friends of the Epicurean school at Herculaneum.[26] At any rate, after efforts to decipher these texts on the part of British and then Italian scholars there was the publication of two series of *Volumina Herculanensia* from 1820 to 1860, which inspired tentative editions of German scholars like Theodor Gomperz. In the early twentieth century a number of Teubner editions appeared, of which the most notable for this study are those of Christian Jensen (*On Property Management*), Alessandro Olivieri (*On Frank Criticism*), and Karl Wilke (*On Anger*). These editions elicited a response from scholars on the other side of the Atlantic, as evidenced by the studies of Hendrickson, DeWitt, Michels, and Tait, all of which made important connections between Philodemus and Latin authors as discussed in the Introduction.

For the next twenty years or so there was little progress in the field of Philodemean studies strictly speaking, until in 1970 Gigante slowly began to usher in a new and more fruitful era. Aside from creating important venues for the publication of articles and texts dealing with the Herculaneum papyri, Gigante attempted to organize the various treatises Philodemus authored, the range of which is rather surprising. His literary output encompasses works on various topics including intellectual history, rhetoric, literary theory, music, logic, theology, and of course, ethics. Major studies on his treatises are ongoing and include efforts to detail their content, as far as this is possible, as well as categorize them according to subject matter. Since their discovery, Gigante, along with Mario Capasso and Gianluca Del Mastro, have been the source of much progress in terms of providing bibliographic information and systematically cataloguing surviving rolls and fragments, which, in accordance with a certain organizational method, are designated by the abbreviation PHerc. (*papyrus herculanensis*) and followed by a number. To this end, the *Catalogo dei Papiri Ercolanesi* (often referred to as *CatPErc*), which has been supplemented twice, is monumental in that it

---

[25] For more, see Kleve (1989) 5–27 and, more recently, Obbink (2007) 33–40.
[26] See Sider (1990) 539.

gives detailed profiles of the scrolls that have been unrolled and examined, complete with inventory numbers, dates of unrolling, states of preservation, references to editions, indices of fragment titles, extensive bibliographies, and more.[27] As a result of all this, the following decades saw the participation of international scholars who continue to make excellent contributions to the study of Philodemus and the publication of better critical editions of his works. In this regard, more recent developments in technology in the twenty-first century, such as multispectral imaging (MSI), has made it possible for scholars to decipher, translate, and comment on previously inaccessible portions of many of Philodemus' treatises. This in turn has led to even better editions of ethical treatises such as *On Frank Criticism*, *On Property Management*, *On Death*, and *On Anger*.

Most of the ethical treatises that contribute evidence linking Philodemus' philosophical thought to much of the content of Horace's *Satires* come from three collections, produced between 75 and 50 BC, and dealing with various ethical issues. According to the *subscriptio* of a large fragment,[28] one of these collections examines important pedagogical and social aspects of the Epicurean community and bears the heading *Compendium on Characters and Ways of Life from the Lectures of Zeno* (ἐπιτομὴ περὶ ἠθῶν καὶ βίων ἐκ τῶν Ζήνωνος σχολῶν). The second collection of books is devoted to considering virtues and vices and, according to the evidence from the end of a fragment identified as Book 9 of the ensemble,[29] is entitled *On Vices and their Corresponding Virtues and the People in whom they Occur and the Situations in which they are Found* (περὶ κακιῶν καὶ τῶν ἀντικειμένων ἀρετῶν καὶ τῶν ἐν οἶς εἰσι καὶ περὶ ἅ).[30]

---

[27] Gigante (1979) 65–400 as well as the supplements of Capasso (1989) 193–264 and Del Mastro (2000) 57–241 with expanded bibliography.

[28] The title in PHerc. 1471, *On Frank Criticism*, appears as follows: Φιλοδήμου τῶν κατ᾽ ἐπιτομὴν ἐξειργασμένων περὶ ἠθῶν καὶ βίων ἐκ τῶν Ζήνωνο[ς σχο]λῶν... ὅ ἐστι περὶ παρρησίας.

[29] Cf. the title of PHerc. 1424, *On Property Management*: Φιλοδήμου περὶ κακιῶν καὶ τῶν ἀντικειμένων ἀρετῶν καὶ τῶν ἐν οἶς εἰσι καὶ περὶ ἅ θ᾽.

[30] When the word "virtues" occurs within the context of Epicureanism ethics it refers to, as Tsouna (2007) 26 explains, "inner states worth cultivating for the benefits that they procure, rather than for their own sake" and also "dispositions to act for certain reasons and/or perform certain kinds of actions." "Vices," of course, would entail opposite inner states that are not worth cultivating because they are detrimental to one's physical and mental health, which is an "evil." This is the way in which such

The third of these collections is concerned with and involves clinical observations of harmful emotions such as fear (specifically the fear of death), lust, and anger, and is appropriately entitled *On Passions* (περὶ παθῶν). Assigning particular books or treatises to these collections is sometimes easy, as when a legible *subscriptio* has survived, and sometimes a matter of conjecture or an educated guess, as when the *subscriptio* is partially legible or when too little of the treatise itself has survived to make a sure connection.[31] With this in mind, one may assign to the first collection, *On Characters and Ways of Life*, PHerc. 1471, entitled *On Frank Criticism*, which was originally edited by Olivieri in his 1914 Teubner version but has recently been republished by David Konstan et al. (1998). More recently, however, and largely through the efforts of papyrologists like Daniel Delattre, Dirk Obbink, Richard Janko, Michael White, and Jeffrey Fish among others, certain problems regarding the organization and layout of this text have been resolved.[32] The availability of advanced technology and a reconsideration of Olivieri's original methods have led to significant advancements: in addition to being able to read more of the text itself, it is now known that about half of the fragments printed by Olivieri (from 45 to 94) are actually the tops and bottoms of columns in random order. The final twenty-four columns of the treatise were far better preserved, because they were unrolled in 1808 using Father Piaggio's special machine, whereas the first half appears to have been cut in half, thus resulting in later confusion regarding their proper order. Also to this first collection (but possibly to the ensemble *On Vices*) may belong PHerc. 1414, entitled *On Gratitude* (according to the surviving *subscriptio* after col. 19), which is edited by Adele Tepedino Guerra (1977), and PHerc. 873, probably entitled *On Conversation*, which has an edition, translation, and commentary of the existing, partly legible fragments by Filippo Amoroso (1975).

words as "virtue," "vice," and "evil" are used in this study in connection with ethics and the *Satires*.

[31] See the table in White (2004) 125–5 for the possible relationships between these fragments and the three collections. Capasso (2001) 392 has a helpful bibliography of Philodemus' works and corresponding editions, old and new.

[32] See White (2009) 29–70 for the latest state of the text. A new critical edition is necessary, although thanks to David Armstrong I now have an updated translation with the fragments from 45 on rearranged in White's order, which I employ throughout the following chapters.

To the second collection, *On Vices*, one may safely assign PHerc.
1424, a very readable text entitled *On Property Management*, of which
the best critical edition continues to be that of Jensen (1907), although there is also the recent commentary and translation of Tsouna
(2012). There is a good chance that PHerc. 163, entitled *On Wealth*,
which is edited with a translation and commentary by Tepedino
Guerra (1978) and has been expanded recently by the publication of
a substantial number of new fragments without a *subscriptio* (PHerc.
1570) in Armstrong and Ponczoch (2011), belongs to this group as
well.[33] To these two one may add a third treatise, *On Flattery*, which is
dispersed among various fragments, including PHerc. 222 (Gargiulo
1981), PHerc. 223 (Gigante and Indelli 1978), PHerc. 1082 (Caini
1939), PHerc. 1089 (Acosta Méndez 1983), PHerc. 1457 (originally
edited by Bassi (1914) but later revised by Kondo 1974), and finally,
PHerc. 1675 (De Falco 1926).[34] The work *On Envy* (PHerc. 1678),
edited by Tepedino Guerra (1985), either belongs to this collection or
to the third one mentioned above. PHerc. 182, entitled *On Anger*,
which was edited by Wilke (1914) but has been superseded by the
edition, translation, and commentary of Indelli (1988) and has a
forthcoming edition by Armstrong and McOsker,[35] likely belongs to
the third group of treatises *On Passions*, in accordance with Indelli's
conjecture of the damaged *subscriptio* under col. 49 (Wilke had
assigned it to *On Characters and Ways of Life*). Aside from these
fragments dealing with ethical topics, among which must be included
On Choices and Avoidances (PHerc. 1251, which was named the
"Comparetti Ethics" after the original editor but has been recently
superseded by the edition, translation, and commentary of Indelli
and Tsouna-McKirahan 1995), the following study will also draw
from Philodemus' methodological treatise PHerc. 1965, entitled *On
Signs* and edited by De Lacy and De Lacy (1978). It will also take into
consideration a few aspects of his literary theory as expounded in
PHerc. 1425 and 1538, the fifth book of a treatise entitled *On Poems*
and edited by Christian Jensen (1923),[36] as well as his political work *On*

---

[33] See also Ponczoch (2009) 141–59.
[34] For differing views regarding the proper organization of these fragments, see the
back-to-back arguments of Capasso (2001) 179–94 and Monet (2001) 195–202.
[35] I am very grateful to David Armstrong and Michael McOsker for having
generously shared their forthcoming edition, translation, and commentary with me.
[36] There is also the newer edition of Mangoni (1993), which includes a helpful
introduction, translation, and commentary.

the Good King According to Homer (PHerc. 1507), edited by Dorandi (1982) and currently being supplemented by Fish (2011b).[37] Finally, some passing references will be made to Philodemus' works on philosophical history, specifically PHerc. 1418 and 310, entitled *On Epicurus* and edited by Militello (1997), PHerc. 1021 and 164, entitled *History of the Academics* and edited by Dorandi (1991), and PHerc. 1018, entitled *History of the Stoics*, also edited by Dorandi (1994). Of course, some of the treatises described above, especially *On Property Management*, *On Frank Criticism*, and *On Anger*, to name a few, are particularly relevant to the social and philosophical contexts of Horace's *Satires* and will therefore receive more attention than others. Before looking more closely at the nature of the relationship between Epicurean ethics and Horatian satire, it may prove fruitful to explore not only how the content of these Philodemean treatises fits into the Epicurean tradition as established by the Master himself, but also to consider their potential significance for contemporary Roman culture.

EPICURUS: ECONOMICS AND PATRONAGE

According to the little evidence that survives regarding Epicurus' views about wealth management, there seem to be a few general characteristics that define what may be called Epicurean economics. One of these involves forethought on the part of the sage in the sense that, being mindful of the future, he will make provisions for the purpose of acquiring goods (DL 10.120a): καὶ κτήσεως προνοήσεσθαι καὶ τοῦ μέλλοντος, "[Epicurus said that the sage] will provide goods for himself and be mindful of the future." Two noteworthy observations concerning this precept are possible: first, by condoning this kind of financial preparation Epicurus implicitly condemns begging for one's daily bread like a Cynic (cf. DL 10.119: οὐδὲ κυνιεῖν, "[he said that the sage] will not be a cynic" and οὐδὲ πτωχεύσειν, "nor will he beg"; see SV 25 for the distinction between πτωχεία and Epicurus' concept of πενία). Second, the inclusion of the term κτῆσις is ambiguous, but in the context of the rest of Epicurus' teachings it probably means something like "bare necessities" such as shelter, food, and water (cf. *Men.* 130–1). It is interesting to note, however, that in his

---

[37] Fish is also working on a new edition that will be published in separate installments in *Cronache Ercolanesi*.

correspondence with Menoeceus he does not condemn more extravagant pleasures, stating that growing accustomed to plain fare makes one better prepared to enjoy luxuries when they become available (*Men.* 131): καὶ τοῖς πολυτελέσιν ἐκ διαλειμμάτων προσερχομένοις[38] κρεῖττον ἡμᾶς διατίθησι, "This makes us better disposed toward the occasional extravagance when it becomes available." Nevertheless, such extravagance and luxury are by no means necessary for health of body and soul, which, according to Epicurus, is maintained by the satisfaction of necessary desires:

> ἀναλογιστέον δὲ ὡς τῶν ἐπιθυμιῶν αἱ μέν εἰσι φυσικαί, αἱ δὲ κεναί, καὶ
> τῶν φυσικῶν αἱ μὲν ἀναγκαῖαι, αἱ δὲ φυσικαὶ μόνον· τῶν δ' ἀναγκαίων αἱ
> μὲν πρὸς εὐδαιμονίαν εἰσὶν ἀναγκαῖαι, αἱ δὲ πρὸς τὴν τοῦ σώματος
> ἀοχλησίαν, αἱ δὲ πρὸς αὐτὸ τὸ ζῆν. τούτων γὰρ ἀπλανὴς θεωρία πᾶσαν
> αἵρεσιν καὶ φυγὴν ἐπανάγειν οἶδεν ἐπὶ τὴν τοῦ σώματος ὑγίειαν καὶ τὴν
> τῆς ψυχῆς ἀταραξίαν, ἐπεὶ τοῦτο τοῦ μακαρίως ζῆν ἐστι τέλος.
>
> (*Men.* 127–8 = KD 29 = SV 20)

We must also consider that regarding desires some are natural and others are empty, and that of the natural ones some are necessary while others are simply natural. Of the former some are necessary for happiness, others for the body's well-being and still others for survival itself. One who soberly considers these distinctions knows how to direct every choice and avoidance toward health of body and tranquility of mind, and on this depends the achievement of a happy life.

Epicurus, for example, regards desires for food, clothing, and friendship as "necessary" for slightly different reasons, such as survival, basic comfort, and safety respectively, but he also considers such things easy to come by (*Men.* 130: τὸ μὲν φυσικὸν πᾶν εὐπόριστόν ἐστι; cf. KD 15). All decisions made to fulfill these desires are fundamentally driven by the innate desire to live without pain, which is pleasurable in itself (cf. *Men.* 128) and explains why Epicurus calls pleasure the "measuring stick" of choices and avoidances:

> ταύτην γὰρ ἀγαθὸν πρῶτον καὶ συγγενικὸν ἔγνωμεν, καὶ ἀπὸ ταύτης
> καταρχόμεθα πάσης αἱρέσεως καὶ φυγῆς, καὶ ἐπὶ ταύτην καταντῶμεν

---

[38] Following the text of Arr. in reading προσερχομένοις, which appears in a number of prominent MSS (**B**, **P**, **Co**, and **f**). Usener has προσερχομένους, which also appears in Diogenes, but suggests that the sage is actively seeking or drawing near such luxuries rather than enjoying them as they become available. Cf. Philodemus' statement that the sage accepts wealth, he does not seek for it (*On Property Management*, col. 16.44–6, quoted below).

ὡς κανόνι τῷ πάθει πᾶν ἀγαθὸν κρίνοντες. καὶ ἐπεὶ πρῶτον ἀγαθὸν τοῦτο καὶ σύμφυτον, διὰ τοῦτο καὶ οὐ πᾶσαν ἡδονὴν αἱρούμεθα, ἀλλ' ἔστιν ὅτε πολλὰς ἡδονὰς ὑπερβαίνομεν, ὅταν πλεῖον ἡμῖν τὸ δυσχερὲς ἐκ τούτων ἕπηται· καὶ πολλὰς ἀλγηδόνας ἡδονῶν κρείττους νομίζομεν, ἐπειδὰν μείζων ἡμῖν ἡδονὴ παρακολουθῇ πολὺν χρόνον ὑπομείνασι τὰς ἀλγηδόνας. πᾶσα οὖν ἡδονὴ διὰ τὸ φύσιν ἔχειν οἰκείαν ἀγαθόν, οὐ πᾶσα μέντοι αἱρετή· καθάπερ καὶ ἀλγηδὼν πᾶσα κακόν, οὐ πᾶσα δὲ ἀεὶ φευκτὴ πεφυκυῖα. τῇ μέντοι συμμετρήσει καὶ συμφερόντων καὶ ἀσυμφόρων βλέψει ταῦτα πάντα κρίνειν καθήκει· χρώμεθα γὰρ τῷ μὲν ἀγαθῷ κατά τινας χρόνους ὡς κακῷ, τῷ δὲ κακῷ τοὔμπαλιν ὡς ἀγαθῷ. (Men. 129–30)

For we recognize this [i.e. pleasure] as our first and inborn good: we begin with and return to it in making every choice and avoidance, determining the goodness of every other thing by means of our feeling, as if it were a measuring stick. But although pleasure is our first good and it is born with us, we do not on account of this choose every single pleasure. Rather, there are times when we choose to pass over many pleasures if, as a result of them, more trouble will follow.[39] In a similar way we consider many pains preferable to certain pleasures whenever we see that, by enduring those pains for an extended period of time, a greater pleasure will come to us. Therefore, although all pleasure is by nature akin to us and good, not all pleasure is choice worthy; similarly, although all pain is evil, not every pain is to be avoided. One must base decisions regarding all these things on the measurement and examination of advantages and disadvantages, for sometimes we regard what is good as if it were evil and, in turn, what is evil as if it were good.

This practice of basing decisions on foreseeable results in terms of pleasure and pain, and the importance of ensuring that the former always outweighs the latter, is commonly referred to as the hedonic or pleasure calculus.[40] It is absolutely fundamental to Epicurean ethics and informs all such decisions, including those relating to economic matters, both for Epicurus as well as for his followers and sympathizers. For example, in the passage quoted earlier (Men. 131),

---

[39] Cf. KD 8 (= SV 50): Οὐδεμία ἡδονὴ καθ' ἑαυτὴν κακόν· ἀλλὰ τὰ τινῶν ἡδονῶν ποιητικὰ πολλαπλασίους ἐπιφέρει τὰς ὀχλήσεις τῶν ἡδονῶν, "No pleasure at all is evil in itself, but the effects of certain pleasures bring much more trouble than pleasure." Cicero ridicules this teaching often in his works, especially in Laws 1.39: Sibi autem indulgentes et corpori deservientes atque omnia quae sequantur in vita quaeque fugiant voluptatibus et doloribus ponderantes, "The Epicureans, moreover, indulge themselves and are subservient to their bodies, since all of their choices and avoidances are based on a measurement of pain and pleasure." See Hanchey (2013) 119–34 for other examples.

[40] See the explanation of this teaching in Roskam (2007) 35.

Epicurus asserts that the sage may more fully enjoy luxuries when they become available because he realizes that they are not necessary for survival, which can easily be achieved through the acquisition of readily available fare.

Consequently, he will not make the mistake of striving after such luxuries (which ultimately leads to more anxiety and pain than pleasure) nor will he be troubled if—or when—they disappear, which is a disposition Epicurus calls αὐτάρκεια (*Men.* 130): καὶ τὴν αὐτάρκειαν δὲ ἀγαθὸν μέγα νομίζομεν, οὐχ ἵνα πάντως τοῖς ὀλίγοις χρώμεθα, ἀλλ᾽ ὅπως, ἐὰν μὴ ἔχωμεν τὰ πολλά, τοῖς ὀλίγοις ἀρκώμεθα, "And we regard self-control or independence to be a great good, but not in order that we may subsist on meagre fare exclusively; rather, it is a good because, if we are not in possession of abundance, it allows us to be content with little."

A further observation concerning Epicurus' convictions regarding economics is that the financial planning and forethought he enjoins upon his followers seems to be related to rural life, since the precept immediately following his observation about the importance of making provisions for the future is that "[the sage] will be fond of the countryside" (DL 10.120a: φιλαγρήσειν; cf. KD 14: ἡ ἐκ τῆς ἡσυχίας καὶ ἐκχωρήσεως τῶν πολλῶν ἀσφάλεια, "the security that comes from peace and withdrawal from the masses").[41] This statement likely reflects the Master's preference for gathering outside of the city limits of Athens in a place called the Garden, where members of the sect spent significant amounts of time together exploring philosophical topics, as Diogenes says (DL 10.10–11): τοὺς φίλους... οἳ καὶ πανταχόθεν πρὸς αὐτὸν ἀφικνοῦντο, καὶ συνεβίουν αὐτῷ ἐν τῷ κήπῳ, "His friends... came to him from all over and lived with him in the Garden." Epicurean economics, then, closely relates to daily life in a rural setting and among members of a household or community, neither of which can exist, as one of Epicurus' *Vatican Sayings* reveals, without cheer, friendship, and philosophical discussion (SV 41): Γελᾶν ἅμα δεῖ καὶ φιλοσοφεῖν καὶ οἰκονομεῖν καὶ τοῖς λοιποῖς οἰκειώμασι χρῆσθαι καὶ μηδαμῇ λήγειν τὰς ἐκ τῆς ὀρθῆς φιλοσοφίας φωνὰς ἀφιέντας, "One must laugh while practicing philosophy and managing wealth; one must also engage in other private affairs and never abandon philosophical discussions about what is true." From

---

[41] Regarding the first of the passages quoted above, see U 570 with the following comment: *amabat Ep. rusticationem aeque atque Horatius et Vergilius* ("Epicurus loved the countryside as much as Horace and Vergil").

the above description, which perfectly describes life in general in the
Garden, one may conclude that Epicureans combined wealth management with philosophical discussion and a sense of merriment,
most likely connected to intimate friendship as an indispensable
element of community life (cf. SV 52: Ἡ φιλία περιχορεύει τὴν
οἰκουμένην, "Friendship dances around the world"; but cf. the distinction Seneca makes between community life and the Epicurean
sect in *Ep.* 6.6: *Metrodorum et Hermarchum et Polyaenum magnos
viros non schola Epicuri sed contubernium fecit,* "It was conviviality
and not the school of Epicurus that made Metrodorus, Hermarchus,
and Polyaenus great men").[42] Indeed, although Epicurus makes
provisions for economic wellbeing, he emphatically states that one
cannot purchase friendship (DL 10.120a: φίλον τε οὐδὲν κτήσεσθαι,
"[Epicurus said that the sage] will not buy friendship"), which implies
that friendly relations require cultivation, becoming stronger and
more intimate over time and through frequent interaction between
members of the community, even if they begin with a concern for
protection (cf. SV 23: ἀπὸ τῆς ὠφελείας; cf. KD 28). Perhaps the most
striking evidence regarding Epicurus' views on wealth acquisition,
however, has to do with the issue of acceptable sources and its
possible connection to friendship: for the Master, patronage is the
only acceptable means of acquiring wealth in order to provide for the
necessities of life. In his biography Diogenes succinctly expresses this
as follows (DL 10.121b): χρηματίσεσθαί τε, ἀλλ' ἀπὸ μόνης σοφίας,
ἀπορήσαντα. καὶ μόναρχον ἐν καιρῷ θεραπεύσειν, "[Epicurus said that
the sage] will be ready to make money, but only when he is in straits
and by means of his philosophy. He will pay court to a king as
occasion demands."[43] In other words, the sage, who refuses to beg
like a Cynic, will be mindful of his future needs and be willing to
satisfy these, but only through the exchange of philosophical wisdom
for benefits (if necessary) and only in the context of good cheer and
the cultivation of intimate friendship, preferably in the countryside.

Epicurus' statement regarding acceptable sources of income for
the sage reflects a system of patronage that fully developed in

    [42] For an exposition of the passage from Epicurus and more, see Armstrong (2011)
105–28. For Epicurus and society, see especially Asmis (2004) 134–43; for communal
celebrations during the time of Epicurus, Clay (1983) 255–79.
    [43] Cf. Stob. *Ecl.* 2 (= *SVF* 3.686) and Plut. *On Common Conceptions* 1043e (= *SVF*
3.693) for the Stoic description of the three acceptable ways of life as "royal"
(βασιλικόν), "political" (πολιτικόν), and "intellectual" (ἐπιστημονικόν).

the Hellenistic period and involved the exchange of benefits for political advice or moral instruction (i.e. λόγοι, *consilia*), usually offered to a monarch or wealthy potentate. Of course, at the time that Epicurus lived the practice of poetic or literary—not necessarily philosophical—patronage had already existed for centuries, as Homer's depictions of Demodocus and Phemius in *Odyssey* 8 and 22 respectively suggest,[44] and as the relationship between poets such as Anacreon and Ibycus and their patron Polycrates of Samos (and later on Pindar, Bacchylides, and Hieron II of Syracuse) likewise demonstrates. This practice continued into the Hellenistic period with the activity of poets like Theocritus, who composed pastoral poetry for Ptolemy II, himself somewhat of a literary connoisseur.[45] These examples, however, involve literary rather than philosophical patronage, which, aside from certain relationships such as that of Solon and Croesus, Plato and Dionysius I of Syracuse, and Aristotle and Alexander the Great at the court of Philip II of Macedon, appears to have developed fully via the mobile *consilium* of companions that followed Alexander and later advised his royal Successors in various parts of the Hellenistic world.[46] Antigonus Gonatas, for example, famously surrounded himself with philosophers like Bion of Borysthenes, whose acceptance of money in exchange for wisdom, which would have been unacceptable to so-called "hard" Cynics like Diogenes of Sinope, is due to his eclecticism (cf. DL 4.47: σοφιστὴς ποικίλος).[47] One fragment shows that the Cynic offered his royal patron advice in exchange for financial benefits:

καὶ σὺ μὲν εὔπορος γενόμενος δίδως ἐλευθερίως, ἐγὼ δὲ λαμβάνω εὐθαρσῶς παρὰ σοῦ οὐχ ὑποπίπτων οὐδὲ ἀγεννίζων οὐδὲ μεμψιμοιρῶν.

You give freely out of your wealth, and I cheerfully accept without suspicion, boorishness, or complaints about my lot.[48]

---

[44] Phemius also appears at the beginning of the epic (*Od.* 1.346–7), where Penelope asks him to change his mournful song and is immediately rebuked by Telemachus, who defends the bard's right to sing as he pleases: "μῆτερ ἐμή, τί τ' ἄρα φθονέεις ἐρίηρον ἀοιδὸν | τέρπειν ὅππῃ οἱ νόος ὄρνυται;" "Dear mother, why do you forbid this faithful bard from pleasing us in whatever way his mind urges him?".

[45] For a more detailed overview, see Gold (1987) 15–35.

[46] See Plaumann's *RE* article s.v. Ἑταῖροι, 1374–80. Other important sources are conveniently listed by Allen and De Lacy (1939) 59 n. 1 and Gold (1987) 35–7.

[47] See also Desmond (2008) 33–6. For Cynics as court-philosophers, see Dudely (1974) 69.

[48] Kindstrand (1976) F16A.

Zeno of Citium likewise had a close relationship with Antigonus, as Philodemus shows in his *History of the Stoics* (coll. 8–9), although, according to Diogenes' *Life of Zeno* (6–8), the philosopher declined an invitation to spend time at his court "because of old age" (διὰ γῆρας). With regard to Epicurus, Diogenes briefly mentions his relationship with a wealthy landowner and officer of Lysimachus named Mithres (DL 10.4–5): Μιθρῆν τε αἰσχρῶς κολακεύειν τὸν Λυσιμάχου διοικητήν... Παιᾶνα καὶ ἄνακτα καλοῦντα, "[They say that] he shamelessly flattered Mithres, the financial advisor of Lysimachus... calling him 'Savior' and 'Lord.'"[49] The contemptuous tone of this passage is explained by the fact that Diogenes is reporting the rumors of Stoics who were dedicated to "calumniating Epicurus most bitterly" (DL 10.3: πικρότατα αὐτὸν διαβέβληκεν), as the series of similar examples of name-calling that follows in the biography confirms. On the other hand, Philodemus couches the practice of addressing members of the school with affectionate terms, like those applied by Epicurus to Mithres, in the context of frank communication, the sting of which can be softened by such tenderness (*On Frank Criticism*, fr. 14.5–10). To Philodemus is also attributed the treatise *On Epicurus and Others* (PHerc. 1418), which further reveals that the Master received substantial aid from Mithres since it contains records of his correspondence (mostly involving annual requests for financial support and gifts) with members and associates of the Garden, especially Mithres, whose name appears more frequently in the work than that of Epicurus himself.[50] Such charitable gifts were connected with celebrations and semi-private communal meals and gatherings,[51] which, as mentioned above, offered opportunities for philosophical discussion that in turn strengthened the bonds of friendship. Since Epicurus dedicated to Mithres a treatise entitled *Opinions on Diseases* (DL 10.28: Περὶ νόσων δόξαι πρὸς Μιθρῆν), one may assume that the two engaged in such discussions with one another. Plutarch preserves anecdotes relating how at one point Epicurus went so far as to ransom Mithres from

[49] For further consideration of the identity of Mithres, see Beloch (1926) 331–5. Castaldi (1928) 299–300 considers this description as "molto esagerata" ("very much exaggerated") and maintains that Epicurus viewed his patron as a "vero amico" ("a true friend"). See also Roskam (2007) 50, 55, 68, and 75.

[50] Castaldi (1928) 293–9 presented the evidence from the treatise early on. For more recent evidence, see the edition of Militello (1997).

[51] See DeWitt (1936) 55–63, Clay (1983) 255–79, and Asmis (2004) 139.

the hands of Crates, a Macedonian general related to Antigonus Gonatas, which further confirms that a close bond existed between them.[52] Epicurus' contempt for the masses and avoidance of public speaking (cf. SV 6.29 and DL 10.120), his encouragement of semi-private gatherings, and high regard for philosophical communication through literary works and discussions, which deepens and strengthens friendship (cf. KD 27), all suggest that his frequent exchanges with Mithres contributed to the formation of a relationship that went beyond the strictly political and military expectations of Hellenistic patronage. Indeed, it became the model for future Epicureans and their sympathizers living in Rome, like Philodemus and Horace, who were tied to the less rigidly political and more literary and personal social phenomenon of *amicitia* in the late Republic.

PHILODEMUS: ECONOMICS AND PATRONAGE

Before looking at Philodemus' own relationship to his friend and probable patron Piso, as well as its role in interpreting certain passages from the *Satires* regarding the interaction between Horace and Maecenas, something must be said about his general views on economics and how they relate to or interact with those of Epicurus. Philodemus preserves the substance of Epicurean economic theory in his treatises *On Property Management*, which is made up of twenty-eight columns along with a few fragments, and *On Wealth*, which includes seven pieces (numbered 1, 2, 3, 4, 5, 6a, and 6b, with each one from 3 to 6a containing approximately three to five columns of text for a total of twenty) that do not bear his name but are probably his.[53] Both of these works involve a critical analysis of rival economic practices,

---

[52] See Plut. *Against Colotes* 1126e and *According to Epicurus it is Impossible to Live Pleasantly* 1097b for the accounts. Philodemus might have referred to this event in *On Epicurus and Others* (coll. 28–39), for which see Militello (1997) 37–9. Beloch (1926) 331–5 considers the evidence in more detail.

[53] See Ponczoch (2009) 141–59 as well as Armstrong and Ponczoch (2011) 97–9 for the state of this work and its attribution to Philodemus. For Philodemus' presentation of economic theory in general, see Castaldi (1928) 287–308, Laurenti (1973), Tsouna (1996) 701–14, Natali (1995) 95–128, Indelli and Tsouna-McKirahan (1995) 213–26, Asmis (2004) 133–76, Balch (2004) 177–96, Tsouna (2007) 163–94, Tsouna (2012) along with the very helpful review of Armstrong (2014b), and Swain (2013) 208–24.

especially *On Property Management*, in which Philodemus reviews
the theories expounded in Xenophon's *Oeconomicus* and pseudo-
Theophrastus' *Oeconomica* (he is the only ancient source to ascribe
this Aristotelian treatise to Theophrastus, although the identification is
problematic[54]). In responding to the views of these authors as well as
those of others, like the Cynics, Philodemus reproduces, defends, and
carefully modifies the traditional doctrines of the founders Epicurus
and Metrodorus of Lampsacus, while also mentioning in passing
Hermarchus (*On Property Management*, col. 25.1) and Polyaenus
(*On Wealth*, coll. 34.14 and 40.8). According to ancient practice,
treatises on economics appear to fall into two categories with regard
to audience: first, those written for the expert manager (δεσπότης),
such as the works of Xenophon and pseudo-Theophrastus, and
second, those intended for the sage or philosopher, as in the case of
Philodemus' *On Property Management* (cf. col. 12.16: φιλοσόφωι).[55]
The main purpose of this treatise is to explain how the Epicurean
sage manages wealth, which is prefaced by an extended criticism
of the views of his Greek rivals. Aside from specific criticisms regarding, for example, Xenophon's intentional blurring of the ordinary
meanings of terms (col. 4.1–16), such as when his version of Socrates
calls the rich Critobulus "poor" because of the many demands and
responsibilities attached to his estate (coll. 4.29–5.4) or refers to the
rich man's enemies as "possessions" (fr. 1.19–21),[56] and his understanding of the role of wives in property management (col. 2.1–36),
Philodemus' fundamental concern is with their understanding of
the purpose of economics and how they think property should be
administered. He quotes a passage from Xenophon's *Oeconomicus* in
which the main function of economics is equated with "managing
one's own estate well" (1.2: εὖ οἰκεῖν τὸν ἑαυτοῦ οἶκον), which, as a
later passage from the same work shows, allows for the unlimited

[54] See Laurenti (1973) 21–95 for a detailed treatment of these criticisms, as well as
Natali (1995) 102. Renate Zoepffel's 2006 commentary on ps.-Theophrastus is also
helpful (pp. 206–9), as is the examination of Philodemus' criticisms of Xenophon in
Angeli (1990) 45–51. Jensen's introduction to his 1907 edition includes a general but
useful outline of Philodemus' criticisms (18): coll. 1–7.37, *de Xenophontis oeconomico*;
coll. 7.37–12.2, *de Theophrasti oeconomico*; coll. 12.2–28.10, *de propriis scholae praeceptis*. For a different organization, see Angeli (1990) 43–5.
[55] See Natali (1995) 101–2.
[56] But cf. SV 25 (quoted below), in which Epicurus makes a very similar point
involving a shift in the usual meanings of the words "poverty" and "wealth," and see
Asmis (2004) 146–7.

acquisition of wealth so long as this is done legally (7.15): ἀλλὰ σωφρόνων τοί ἐστι καὶ ἀνδρὸς καὶ γυναικὸς οὕτως ποιεῖν, ὅπως τά τε ὄντα ὡς βέλτιστα ἕξει καὶ ἄλλα ὅτι πλεῖστα ἐκ τοῦ καλοῦ τε καὶ δικαίου προσγενήσεται, "But it is prudent, you see, for a husband and wife to act in such a way that their goods will be disposed in the best manner and that as many other goods as possible will be added to them properly and justly."[57] In order to accomplish this more effectively, four activities traditionally considered essential parts of wealth management are introduced (cf. On Property Management, coll. 10.28–11.3): acquisition (κτῆσις), preservation (φυλακή), organization (κόσμησις/διακόσμησις), and use (χρῆσις). Additionally, Xenophon (4.4–25) and pseudo-Theophrastus (1344b29–34) praise the methods of other nations, especially the Persian custom of personally watching over, examining, and visiting one's land and the goods associated with it. Philodemus, with a touch of humor, rejects these views on the grounds that the toil involved in the acquisition of limitless wealth as well as the effort required to safeguard it personally and at all times violates the hedonic calculus and is therefore unfit for the Epicurean manager:

ταλαίπωρον δὲ καὶ ἀνοί[κε]ιον φιλοσόφου τὸ πρότ[ερ]ον τῶν οἰκετῶν
ἐγε[ίρεσθ]αι καὶ καθεύδειν ὕστερο[ν· φα]νερὸν δὲ καὶ το[ἶ]ς τυχοῦσ[ιν
τὸ μ]ηδέποθ᾽ ὅλην οἰκία[ν] ἀφ[ύλα]κτον εἶναι, πάνυ δ᾽ ἐ[πί]πονον τὸ
δ[ιαν]ίστασθαι νύκτωρ εἰωθέναι· ζ[η]τῶ δ᾽ ε[ἰ] καὶ πρὸς ὑγίειαν καὶ
φιλοσοφ[ί]α[ν] ἐν ταῖς μικραῖς συμφέρει νυξίν.

(On Property Management, col. 11.30–41)

It is wretched, however, and also unfitting for the philosopher to rise out of bed before the house servants and to go to sleep after them. Also, it is clear to just about anyone that one's property should never be completely unguarded, but it is extremely toilsome to have to become accustomed to get up in the middle of the night. In fact, I wonder if doing this in the short nights of the year is beneficial to one's health and to the practice of philosophy.

[57] Cf. On Property Management, col. 1.1–14: [Εἰ μὲν ὑπελάμβανεν] ὅτι τῆς συν[ήθως νοουμένης] οἰκον[ομ]ίας ... τὸ πορίζειν πολλὰ χρήματα καὶ φυλάττειν πῶς διαμενεῖ τὰ πορισθέντα καὶ προϋπάρχοντα, "if he [Xenophon] supposed that the purpose of property management, as it is understood conventionally, is ... to acquire many riches and to consider how what has been acquired as well as one's original possessions may be preserved ..." Cf. Cic. On Duties 2.87, where Cicero explains this and even says that he has translated Xenophon's work into Latin.

Philodemus, like Epicurus (*Men.* 130-1 and SV 67), does not regard money as an evil in itself (cf. *On Property Management*, col 14. 5-9), but he realizes that limitless wealth is not necessary for survival and that the cares it brings are not worth the effort required to pursue it. As a general rule, he views the goal of wealth administration as one's own benefit (συμφέρει, in the above passage; cf. also col 13.20-2: [π]ολλὰ τῶι συμφ[έ]ροντι κα[ὶ ἀ]συμφόρωι δ[ιορ]ίζων) in terms of the avoidance of discomfort and the enjoyment of pleasurable conveniences,[58] both of which money is able to afford to some degree. Unlike the professional manager (col. 17.2-3: τεχνίτης), however, who goes to every length in order to amass wealth and safeguards it by keeping vigil as well as a careful inventory, Philodemus urges the Epicurean sage to observe the hedonic calculus in making decisions regarding, above all, the acquisition and preservation of wealth.[59]

Absolutely central to the discussion in *On Property Management* is Philodemus' careful explanation of the sage manager's disposition or "attitude toward the sources of wealth and its preservation" (col. 12.7-9: ὡς ἵστασθαι δεῖ περὶ χρημάτων κτήσεώς τε καὶ φυλακῆς). Voula Tsouna and Giovanni Indelli provide a succinct and accurate definition of this attitude and its relevance for these two functions, on which Philodemus seems to focus most of his attention:

"The behavior of the Epicurean towards money and property consists in abstaining from the extremes of penury and amassed wealth, in using the hedonic calculus to examine the sources of his income, and in preserving his equanimity and his self-sufficiency with regard to the actual task of managing his property."[60]

To be sure, the philosopher's disposition toward sources of income and preservation must always be characterized by the observation of a proper "measure of wealth" (*On Property Management*, col. 12.17-19: φι[λοσό]φωι δ' ἐστὶ πλούτου μέ[τρ]ον), which is a concept that closely relates to the hedonic calculus but that also owes something to Aristotle's notion of limited or "natural wealth" (cf. *Pol.* 1257b17-1258a14

---

[58] See Angeli (1990) 48-9 and Indelli and Tsouna-McKirahan (1995) 217.

[59] Tsouna (1996) 714 notes that, by making a clear distinction between the sage manager, who is concerned with happiness but may successfully acquire and maintain wealth, and the professional and skilled businessman, who cares primarily for financial profit as accomplished through systematic organization and use, Philodemus anticipates the modern concept of economics.

[60] Indelli and Tsouna-McKirahan (1995) 213.

38   *Epicurean Ethics in Horace*

for ὁ πλοῦτος κατὰ φύσιν within the context of economic theory).
The Epicurean understanding of natural wealth presupposes a firm
comprehension of the division of desires explained above: as Epicurus says, wealth may be called "natural" in the sense that nature
has made it easy to obtain whatever revenue is needed to satisfy
necessary and natural desires (KD 15 = SV 8): Ὁ τῆς φύσεως
πλοῦτος καὶ ὥρισται καὶ εὐπόριστός ἐστιν, ὁ δὲ τῶν κενῶν δοξῶν
εἰς ἄπειρον ἐκπίπτει, "Natural wealth is both limited and easy to
acquire, but the wealth of empty opinions goes on into infinity."
Just as Epicurus warns against using wealth to satisfy desires that
cannot be satisfied (because they are unnatural and unnecessary),[61]
he also prohibits the sage from living in destitute poverty (DL
10.119: οὐδὲ πτωχεύσειν). That is to say, there is a measure of
wealth based on the limits or requirements of nature, a measure
that both unlimited affluence and barefaced poverty seem to violate.
In addressing the problems associated with a life of penury, Philodemus draws heavily from a lost treatise of Metrodorus (*On Property
Management*, col. 12.27: Μ[ητρ]οδώρου). This mention of Metrodorus'
teachings, which also occurs in *On Wealth* (col. 37.11–15), has led to an
ongoing discussion concerning the originality of Philodemus' contribution and also the origin of this part of *On Property Management*,
which some have considered to be an extended quotation from the
former's treatise on the same topic (although there are also good
reasons supporting a different view).[62] In any case, the columns following this section, which are extremely important for the present
study, must coincide with or reflect Philodemus' own views regarding
economics. In both *On Property Management* and *On Wealth*
Philodemus—with the help of Metrodotrus—makes an important distinction between the Cynic practice of begging daily (*On Property
Management*, col. 12.40–1: [τὸ κ]αθ᾽ ἡ[μέραν π]οριζόμε[νον]; cf. *On
Wealth*, col. 43.1: [πτω]χείαν), which is necessitated by their complete

[61] Asmis (2004) 144–5.
[62] Sudhaus (1906) 45, for example, refers to coll. 12.45–21.35 as "ein . . . Abschnitt,
der nach Sprache und Stil unmöglich aus der Feder des Philodem stammen kann"
("an excerpt that, given its language and style, cannot possibly have been written by
the hand of Philodemus"). Another scholar who views this section as a verbatim copy
of Metrodorus' earlier treatise is Laurenti (1973) 108. Tsouna (1996), on the other
hand, does not consider details such as the presence of hiatus significant enough to
rule out Philodemean authorship or at least interpretation (n. 6). See also Asmis
(2004) 149–61. Körte (1890b) contains the fragments of Metrodorus.

rejection of all goods (*On Wealth*, col. 45.16–17: στέρ[ησιν] ... πάν[-των]), and the Epicurean understanding of poverty, which entails having and enjoying the few possessions required by nature (cf. *On Wealth*, col. 49.10–12).[63] Philodemus, here again taking his cue from Metrodorus, expands on Epicurus' criticism of the Cynics' utter rejection of all conventions and their consequent penury, but this expansion takes on another level of importance given the nature of the views of his contemporaries. The Roman audience of *On Property Management* and *On Wealth* would also have rejected Cynicism, but because their shamelessness, as William Desmond explains, was "incompatible with Roman *gravitas*; Cynic irreverence with Roman *pietas*; Cynic contempt for custom with Roman respect for the *mos maiorum*."[64] Furthermore, as Cicero demonstrates in *On Duties*, the Cynic way of life in general violates an important sense of social decorum:

> Nec vero audiendi sunt Cynici, aut si qui fuerunt Stoici paene Cynici, qui reprehendunt et inrident quod ea quae re turpia non sint verbis flagitiosa ducamus, illa autem quae re turpia sint nominibus appellemus suis. Latrocinari fraudare adulterare re turpe est, sed dicitur non obscene; liberis dare operam re honestum est, nomine obscenum; pluraque in eam sententiam ab isdem contra verecundiam disputantur. Nos autem naturam sequamur et ab omni quod abhorret ab oculorum auriumque approbatione fugiamus; status incessus sessio accubitio vultus oculi manuum motus teneat illud decorum. (1.128)

> Nor should one listen to the Cynics or any Stoics who resemble them, since they criticize and ridicule us for thinking that it is indecent to name certain things that are not in fact base, whereas we freely name other things that are in fact base. To steal, lie, commit adultery are morally base, but we may speak of them without being indecent; to beget children in wedlock is an honorable thing, but we think that speaking about it is indecent. And the same men, employing that very line of thought, argue about many other things against what is true. We, however, should follow Nature and avoid everything that is offensive to the approval of the eyes and ears: let a sense of propriety govern our standing, walking, siting, reclining, our expressions, our eyes, and how we move our hands.

---

[63] Cf. also SV 25: Ἡ πενία μετρουμένη τῷ τῆς φύσεως τέλει μέγας ἐστὶ πλοῦτος· πλοῦτος δὲ μὴ ὁριζόμενος μεγάλη ἐστὶ πενία, "Poverty measured by the limits of nature is great wealth, but wealth that is not limited is great poverty." Also Asmis (2004) 151–2 and Balch (2004) 177–96.

[64] Desmond (2008) 45.

40 Epicurean Ethics in Horace

It is perhaps no accident that this Roman sensitivity to Cynic shame-lessness or ἀναίδεια, which contradicts the rule of propriety and so is repugnant to the ideal of social tact (cf. S. 2.2.53–64), is compatible with Philodemus' description of the ideal manager.

As Epicurus states, the requirements of natural wealth are "easily met" (εὐπόριστος), which is a teaching Philodemus echoes in *On Property Management* when he emphasizes that the sage is "not bad at finding what suffices for himself" (col. 16.6–8: οὔτε κ[α]κὸς εὑρέσθαι τὰ πρὸς αὑτὸν ἱκανά), with the result that he never fears poverty (coll. 15.45–16.4; cf. *On Wealth*, col. 36.11–12: οὐ [γὰ]ρ ἄξιον φόβου).

On the other hand, whereas Epicurus' concept of natural wealth imposes strict limits on the acquisition of goods, Philodemus, either adopting the view of Metrodorus or responding to the sensi-tivities of his Roman and aristocratic dedicatees, many of whom, like Piso, were wealthy landowners, carefully notes that the sage "inclines in his wishes toward a more affluent way of life" (*On Property Management*, col. 16.4–6: ῥέπει δὲ τῆι βουλήσει μᾶλλον ἐπὶ τὴν ἀφθονωτέραν [δίαιταν])[65] and that he "should accept more, whenever it comes easily and without harm" (44–6: τὸ [δὲ π]λεῖον, ἃ[ν ἀ]βλ[α]βῶς καὶ [εὐ]πόρως γίνηται, δεκτέ[ον]). One may compare this to Epicurus' saying that the sage should grow accustomed to having little, not because having more is itself an evil, but because this kind of disposition will guard against making the easy mistake of regarding more extravagant and unnecessary things as indispensable for happiness and contentment, which will inevitably lead to extreme toil and anxiety (*Men.* 131). Philodemus does not necessary depart from this teaching, since he clearly states that the sage should be satisfied with what suffices (*On Property Management*, coll. 16.6–8 and 35–9) and should never fear the state of poverty as if it were evil (*On Wealth*, col. 36.11–14, partially quoted above). But he makes an additional and very important observation regarding the sage man-ager's understanding of ἀφθονωτέραν δίαιταν or "affluence" (perhaps

---

[65] There is a crucial distinction between merely "leaning towards" wealth, as communicated by ῥέπει, and the negative consequences of actively desiring or feeling the *need* for large amounts of it, which the sage economist will not do (cf. *On Choices and Avoidances*, col. 21.2–4: [οὐ] δὲ [χρ]ήζει τοῦ [πολλ]ὰ χ[ρή]ματ᾽ ἐπ[ισωρ]εύειν, "nor will the sage feel the need for heaping up great wealth"). The need to heap up mounds of cash is felt by, e.g., the Horatian miser in *Satires* 1.1 (41: *argenti pondus et auri*; cf. 51: *magno . . . acervo*).

Philosophical Background to Epicureanism   41

comparable to Epicurus' τοῖς πολυτελέσιν in the passage cited above⁶⁶)
and its connection to the hedonic calculus that is missing from the
fragments of Epicurus:

ἡ γὰρ ἐπιμέλεια καὶ τήρησις, ὅση πρέπει τῶν κατὰ τρόπον αὐτοῦ
προεστῶτι, παρέχει μέν τιν' ἐνίοτ' ὄχλησιν, οὐ μὴν πλείω γε τοῦ κατὰ
τὸν ἐφήμερον [πο]ρισμόν, ἂν δὲ καὶ πλείω, τῶν ἄλ[λ]ων ὧν ἀπαλλάττει
δυσχερῶν [ο]ὐ πλείον', ἂν μ[ὴ] δείξῃ τις ὡς οὐκ ἀποδί[δω]σιν ὁ φυσικὸς
πλοῦτος [πο]λλῷ[ι] μείζους τὰς ἐπικαρπίας ἢ τοὺς πόνους τῆς ἀπ'
[ὀ]λίγων ζωῆς, ὃ πολλοῦ δεήσε[ι παρ]ιστάνε[ιν].

(On Property Management, col. 14.9–23)

For the concern and vigilance fitting for one who takes proper care of
his things do at times bring a certain amount of trouble, but certainly not
more than the trouble that comes with the acquisition of daily needs; but
even if it did, this trouble would not be greater than the other difficulties
from which it frees us, unless anyone can prove that natural wealth does
not in fact result in greater benefits by far than the hardships of a life of
little means, a thing which he will be far from demonstrating.

This is without a doubt a remarkable yet carefully worded claim,
although, despite its boldness, it is entirely faithful to and dependent
on the specific conditions that Epicurus' pleasure calculus imposes.
Philodemus basically asserts that the sage manager may accumulate
great wealth, so long as the trouble involved in the process is less than
the benefits afforded by the same wealth. In this sense, even a state of
affluence may be identified as "natural wealth," which is an expression he borrows from Epicurus but uses in a slightly new way.⁶⁷

A simple example may help to illustrate the significance of this claim
as well as its relevance for Philodemus' Roman audience. According
to Epicurus, in order to survive and be healthy and happy a human
being requires simple foods, simple clothes, and the companionship of
others who share the same basic (philosophical) convictions. All of this
requires toil to some degree, but the pleasure derived in the end
is greater than this and therefore justifies the effort.⁶⁸ Philodemus

⁶⁶ The adjective Philodemus uses, which is the comparative of ἄφθονος, is used by
earlier authors in connection with the bounty of Mother Earth, especially during the
Golden Age, as well as with wealth in general, actual gold, the wealth of cities and
men, land or property, and the richness of speech. See LSJ 2 and 3 for citations.
⁶⁷ Asmis (2004) 156–7.
⁶⁸ See On Property Management, col. 13.8–11 (and cf. Men. 129): Πολλὰ γὰρ τῶν
πραγμάτων ἐνποεῖ μέν τινας λύπας ὑπάρχοντα, πλείω δ' ὀχλεῖ μὴ παρόντα, "For many
things cause certain pains when they are present, but result in even more trouble when

employs the same exact logic but on a different level: the toil involved in managing and preserving significant wealth, which may include owning an expanse of land and a luxurious estate in the country like the Villa of the Papyri,[69] may be greater than what is required for mere survival, but it also means that the owner will be freed from the many obligations and responsibilities that come with earning one's daily bread. Furthermore the management of such wealth may not in fact require more effort, especially, as Philodemus states elsewhere, if it is acquired as a gift from a grateful friend (cf. *On Property Management*, col. 23.27–8: εὐχάριστο[ν]) and if one has fieldworkers and servants who are well treated (col. 9.32–8) to do the physical labor (col. 23.7–11: ταλαίπωρον δὲ καὶ τὸ "γεωργο[ῦν]τ" αὐτὸν οὕτως ὥστε αὐτο-υργεῖν· τὸ δ' "ἄλλων, ἔχοντα γῆν" κατὰ σπουδαῖον, "but 'cultivating land oneself so as to be actively involved' is wretched, whereas 'having others do the work on the land one owns' is appropriate"). This negative view of the physical labor involved in agriculture undoubtedly would have been appreciated by Philodemus' Roman friends and associates, among whom Horace, who received the Sabine estate as a gift from Maecenas and leaves the manual work on it to his bailiff, may be counted:

> et tamen urges
> iampridem non tacta ligonibus arva bovemque
> disiunctum curas et strictis frondibus exples;
> addit opus pigro rivus, si decidit imber,
> multa mole docendus aprico parcere prato. (*Ep.* 1.14.26–30)

And yet you toil over fields long untouched by the hoe, you care for the ox after he is unyoked and you fill him up with fodder you have stripped; when you are dead tired, the brook brings fresh work, for if rain has fallen, it must be taught by many a mounded dam to spare the sunny meadow.

This passage is a description, from the poet's point of view, of his bailiff's complaints about his responsibilities regarding the property, which would have included supervising the other workers (cf. *S.* 2.7.118: *opera agro nona Sabino*, "the ninth worker on my Sabine

---

they are not present." Reflecting upon this passage, Armstrong (2016) 196 says that "[t]he trouble would survive the 'utilitarian calculus' and be worth it."

[69] For the luxury of this villa, see Deiss (1985) 60–82 and Wojcik (1986) 129 in general with plates and illustrations detailing statues, busts, frescos, floor decorations, and other artifacts. See also the beautiful color photographs in Guidobaldi and Esposito (2012) 89–117.

estate").[70] This avoidance of physical labor on the part of the land-owner is very much at odds with Roman tradition, as Cicero makes clear in his praise of agriculture in *On Duties* (1.151): *Omnium autem rerum ex quibus aliquid adquiritur, nihil est agri cultura melius, nihil uberius, nihil dulcius, nihil homine libero dignius,* "Of all the things, however, that serve as a means of financial gain, none is better, more profitable, sweeter or more worthy of a freeman than agriculture." For his part, Horace, perhaps in response to Philodemus' recommenda-tions, seems to prefer to leave the work to his slaves so that he can meet with friends and enjoy conversations about what really matters (cf. *S.* 2.6.72–3: *quod magis ad nos pertinent . . . agitamus*). The same holds true, according to Philodemus, for the sage manager, who, being freed from the "daily grind" by a certain amount of wealth, will have much more time for philosophical conversation with friends as well as other intimate exchanges (cf. *On Property Management,* col. 23.11–18, to be discussed in more detail in the following paragraph), all of which will result in much greater pleasure than whatever toil the property may require. Therefore, the state of affluence Philodemus alludes to in the passage above still, technically speaking, falls under the category of "natural wealth." The difference is that Philodemus, as Elizabeth Asmis points out, argues for having more wealth over having little wealth, whereas Epicurus is in favor of little wealth over destitute poverty.[71] It is difficult to disassociate this encourage-ment of affluence from the financial status of his Roman audience, many of whom, in the longstanding tradition of landownership, were wealthy property-owners like Piso or had country villas outside the city like Cicero and Horace, both of whom viewed their rural get-aways as perfect venues for philosophical conversation.

---

[70] At *Epistles* 1.14.39 Horace says that his neighbors laugh "as I move sods and stones" (*glaebas et saxa moventem*), which appears to suggest that he was just another worker. Bowditch (2001) 237, however, puts this scene into perspective: "[T]he vision of Epicurean freedom presented in the textual snapshot of Horace's body—napping, working up a mild sweat in a capricious rearrangement of stones—in part responds to the political rather than the spiritual status of the slave. The politically, historically, and economically contingent fact of the bailiff's slave status is the mirror reverse of Horace's freeborn status . . . despite the philosophical inconsistency that erratic phys-ical movement may signify for Horace, his is the political liberty to move to and from the country at will, whereas the slave, as much a *res* as the *saxa* or stones of the estate, can only be moved at the whims of his master."

[71] Asmis (2004) 156.

Along with recognizing that wealth has the power to remove difficulties and that it can provide the leisure necessary for philosophical study while noting, like an orthodox Epicurean, that its acquisition should not be motivated by empty fear or desire, Philodemus discusses generosity and the importance of sharing excess wealth with one's friends. This is communicated within the context of the advice of Hermarchus, the school's first scholarch after Epicurus' death:

αἱ φίλοις καὶ τῶν ἄλλων τοῖς οὐκ ἀτόποις γινόμεναι μεταδόσεις ἀφαιρέσεις [κ]αὶ τῆς ὑπάρξεω[ς] με[ιώ]σεις ἐνίοις εἶναι δο[κο]ῦ[σιν], εἰσὶν δὲ κτήσει[ς λ]υσιτελέστεραι κα[τὰ] τὸν Ἕρμαρχον ἐπιμέλειαι τ[ο]ιούτων ἀνδρῶν ἤπερ ἀγρῶν καὶ πρὸς τὴν τύχην ἀσφαλέστατοι θησαυροί... καὶ τῶν ἰδίων προΐεσθαί τι πολλάκ[ις], ὥ[σ]περ οἱ τὴν γῆν σπείροντες, ἐξ ὧν πρα[γμ]άτων (περὶ γὰ[ρ ἀ]νθρώπων ε[ἴ]παμεν) πολλαπ[λάσι]α καρπίζεσθαι γίνεται.

(On Property Management, coll. 24.41–25.4, 16–21)

To some people, the sharing that takes place with friends and, of one's other acquaintances, with those who are not offensive seems like a reduction and a diminution of their current wealth, when in fact, according to Hermarchus, the care we invest in such people becomes a more profitable acquisition than land and the most incorruptible treasure against the turns of fortune... and often [one must] send forth something of one's own, as if scattering seeds over the earth (we are speaking about people, of course), from which it eventually becomes possible to reap a much more bountiful harvest...

An important distinction is made in the above passage that strongly suggests that this portion of the text, even if influenced and dependent on Metrodorus' views, contains Philodemus' own contribution to economics based on his contact with Roman culture. In describing the benefits of sharing wealth he appears to speak of two different groups, namely, one's "friends" and "one's other acquaintances... who are not offensive." The second group likely refers to people with whom one shares wealth and to whom one shows a certain degree of kindness, chiefly in order that one may derive benefits from these individuals in the future (cf. DL 10.120 for the seed metaphor). Phildoemus expresses this sentiment clearly in another treatise on ethics:

καὶ προσέχει τοῖς ἰδίο[ι]ς ὡς ἔσ[τ]αι διοικεῖν· καὶ φροντίζει τῶν πρότερον ὡς τάχα πρὸς αὐτὸν ἐσομένων· καὶ πολυωρεῖ τε τῶν ἀνθρώπων ὅσους δύναται πλείστους [κ]αὶ τοῖς φιλοφρονησαμένοις εὐχα[ρ]ιστεῖ καὶ δι᾽

ἐλπίδας τιν[ῶ]ν αὐτοῖς μεταλήψεσθαι καὶ πάλιν ὑπὸ τῶν αὐτῶν εὖ τι
π[εί]σεσθαι   (*On Choices and Avoidances*, col. 22.12–21)

And [the sage] will mind his own assets in terms of how best to
administer them, and he will also consider how former decisions will
benefit him in the near future. In addition to this, he will treat with
much care as many people as possible and show gratitude to those who
are kind to him, with the hope that he will share some things with them
and receive something good from them in return . . .[72]

The expectation of future benefits in exchange for kindness is the
foundation of Epicurus' understanding of friendship as arising from
utility and the need for safety (cf. KD 28 and SV 23), which does not
merely entail protection from enemies but rather describes the agreeable condition afforded by positive interaction and the cultivation of
friendships, all of which extends to the development of communities.[73] David Armstrong describes three levels of Epicurean friendship, of which the first (F1) is based on utility and mutual benefit,
whereas the second (F2) is characterized by intense intimacy.[74]
According to his interpretation, these levels of friendship coincide
with the different classes of friends pertaining to the Roman practice
of patronage, which distinguishes "clients at large and other still
larger groups whose goodwill they cultivate for more general purposes"
from "one's personal friends among one's clients and equals."[75] The
former group would probably include a patron's prospective supporters and voters, who would reside in the city, whereas the friendship
of individuals in the second group, as Philodemus says, would be more
carefully cultivated over a longer period of time and, as he states
elsewhere in the same treatise, these would participate in a pleasant
life and a leisurely withdrawal along with his patron in a countryside
villa:

---

[72] Cf. *On Property Management*, col. 25.12–14: καὶ γὰρ νῦν εὐέλπιδας ποιεῖ (i.e.
προνοεῖν τοῦ μέλλοντος) καὶ παρὸν γινόμενον εὐφρ[αί]νει, "For providing for the future
produces good hopes in us and, when it arrives, makes us glad." This passage,
however, emphasizes forethought in the acquisition of property, whereas friendship
is not acquired in the same way by planning but rather cultivated over time (see DL
10.120b for the distinction).
[73] See Roskam (2007) 38 and Armstrong (2016) 183.
[74] Armstrong (2016) 182–4. The third level of friendship (F3), which the gods
experience, is completely separate from any consideration of utility. For the intimacy
of human friendship that seems to approach the intensely intimate and altruistic
nature of F3, cf. *On Frank Criticism*, fr. 28.1–12.
[75] Armstrong (2016) 198. Cf. Gold (1987) 65.

ἥκιστα γὰρ ἐπιπλοκὰς ἔχει πρὸς ἀνθρώπους, ἐξ ὧν ἀηδίαι πολλαὶ
παρακολουθοῦσι, καὶ διαγωγὴν ἐπιτερπῆ καὶ μετὰ φίλων ἀναχώρησιν
εὔσχολον (*On Property Management*, col. 23.11–16)

For it [i.e. being in the country with others working the land] brings the
least amount of involvements with men from whom many pains follow
and also affords a pleasant way of life, complete with a leisurely withdrawal with friends . . .

Armstrong draws another connection between this description of
peaceful living and Roman culture through the following observation:

First, it's obviously couched mainly for Romans. Athenian literature
does not deal in idyllic country properties as a setting for learned leisure.
But Romans in Philodemus's day had long entered a period when the
tide of prosperity had advanced until country villas (as in Cicero's
dialogues) could be settings for literary leisure and philosophical
study, rather than just income-producing farms.[76]

The significance of withdrawal to the countryside for Romans in
Philodemus' day in particular is demonstrated not only by the
country-estate setting of many of Cicero's philosophical writings (cf.
Tusculan Disputations), but also by the biographical evidence relating
to Vergil and Horace, which in both cases emphasizes the importance
of *secessus*.[77] The role of philosophical conversation, moreover, can
be seen, apart from Cicero, from Horace's famous description of
the conversation after dinner on his Sabine estate, where he and
his guests contemplate Epicurean questions about the true source of
happiness, the causes of friendship, and the nature of the highest good
(*S.* 2.6.73–6). Finally, in the course of his analysis of acceptable sources
of wealth, among which agriculture without personal labor is highly
ranked, Philodemus declares that the first and by far the best way to
make a living is to receive gratitude from a patron in exchange for
"philosophical conversations" (*On Property Management*, col. 23.24–5:
ἀπὸ λόγων φιλο[σό]φων), which echoes Epicurus' approval of patronage as appropriate for the wise man (DL 10.121b).

In the same treatise Philodemus advances views concerning
patronage that define it as a most acceptable source of income that

---

[76] Armstrong (2016) 199.
[77] Cf. Suetonius' *Life of Horace* (*in secessu ruris sui*) as well as the *Life of Donatus*
(13: *secessu Campaniae Siciliaeque uteretur*). But cf. Horsfall (1995) 1–25, who
considers some of the problems regarding the reliability of the latter account.

is strengthened and enriched by the bonds of friendship. In fact, friends are so important that they motivate economic decisions: the wise man administers his property in a spirit of generosity "because he has acquired and will continue to acquire friends" (col. 15.3–6: διοικεῖν γὰρ οὕτω ταῦτα τῶι κεκτῆσθαι καὶ κτᾶσθαι τὸν σοφὸν φίλους ἀκόλουθον), he makes economic sacrifices when necessary with his friends' best interests in mind (col. 26.1–9), and ensures that they will be financially stable after his death, "regarding them as his own children" (col. 27. 9: καὶ οἷα τ[έ]κνα θετέον).[78] Even the nature of the conversations that occur between members of the same community, or, more specifically, between a patron and his client, is described in terms of mutual respect, peace, honesty, and a certain informality, all of which consistently highlights the friendly tone of their interactions:

πρῶτον δὲ καὶ κάλλιστον ἀπὸ λόγων φιλο[σό]φων ἀνδράσιν δεκτικοῖς
μεταδιδομέν[ων] ἀντιμεταλαμβάνειν εὐχάριστο[ν ἅμ]α μετὰ σεβασμοῦ
παντ[ός], ὡς ἐγένετ᾽ Ἐπικο[ύ]ρωι, λο[ιπὸ]ν δὲ ἀληθινῶν καὶ ἀφιλο[ν]ε[ί]κων
καὶ [σ]υ[λ]λήβδη[ν] εἰπεῖν [ἀτ]αράχων, ὡς τό γε διὰ σοφ[ιστι]κῶν καὶ
ἀγωνιστι[κ]ῶν ο[ὐδέν] ἐστι βέλτιον τοῦ διὰ δη[μοκ]οπικῶν καὶ
συκοφαντικ[ῶν]. (*On Property Management*, col. 23.23–36)

It is superior and better by far to receive gratitude and respect in return for wise discussions shared with receptive men, which is what happened to Epicurus. Moreover, these discussions should be truthful, free from strife, and, in a word, peaceful, since holding discourse through sophistical and contentious speeches is no better than doing this through demagogical and slandering ones.

The primacy of philosophical discussion reflects Epicurus' aforementioned injunction to earn a living "from wisdom alone" (DL 10.121: ἀπὸ μόνης σοφίας),[79] but it also reflects Philodemus' awareness of Roman *amicitia* and perhaps the nature of his correspondence with the aristocrat and politician Piso.[80] The Roman system of patronage

[78] Cf. *On Choices and Avoidances*, col. 21.4–9 for the sage manager's devotion to his friends.
[79] See Laurenti (1973) 164–6. According to Diogenes' account, Chrysippus recommends making money from wisdom (7.188 = *SVF* 3.685: ἀπὸ σοφίας), although Plutarch further defines this source as "sophistry" (*Stoic Self-Contradictions* 1043e = *SVF* 3.693: ἀπὸ σοφιστείας), which suggests the more formal and contentious speeches criticized by Philodemus above. See also Natali (1995) 122–3.
[80] Tait (1941) 1–13 and Sider (1997) 5–14 (esp. 14 n. 7) discuss the evidence in favor of the identification of Piso as Philodemus' patron. Allen and De Lacy (1939)

manifests itself in different ways depending especially on the nature
of the exchange, the economic status of the client and the degree to
which both patron and client share the same interests, education, and
concerns.[81] As Peter White observes, the bond between poets or
literary men and their supporters often includes an important ethical
or even philosophical component that strengthens the friendship:

> Though far from equal to their great friends in wealth or dignity, they
> too generally belong to a social and economic upper class. They have
> had a similar education, engage in many of the same pursuits, and move
> in the same orbit. Sharing a similar background, they hold similar
> values. This convergence of values is implicit in the theme of choosing
> worthy friends that is so frequently sounded in our sources. Friendship
> as Roman authors present it is based not so much on personal chem-
> istry or economic parity as on ethical congruence: one chooses friends
> whose ideals and morals parallel one's own. The importance of a
> common background in creating friendships is evident also in the
> patterns of association one sees. Whereas upper-class Romans often
> befriend poets or philosophers, they rarely establish such connections
> with those artists and intellectuals whose origins and formation diverge
> radically from their own.[82]

This sharing of similar values is an essential prerequisite for true
friendship, as Cicero states in his treatise *On Friendship* (20, to which
cf. 74), in which he also discusses the sense of equality and mutual
respect such a congruence produces (69–73). Many passages in
Horace's *Satires* illustrate this, but perhaps the opening to 1.6, in
which the poet praises Maecenas for considering the quality of one's
life (11: *vixisse probos*) rather than one's upbringing (7–8: *quali sit
quisque parente | natus*), does so most clearly. After all, Horace's virtue
rather than his poetry was, as the poet describes it, what attracted
Maecenas in the first place (45–64). It is likely that the same kind
of congruence of values characterized and was fundamental to the

---

59–65, as mentioned already, question the view that Philodemus had successfully
become Piso's client, which is debatable, and note that there is no evidence linking the
latter to the Villa of the Papyri or even Herculaneum.

[81] For Roman patronage in general, see Saller (1989) 49–62 and Wallace-Hadrill
(1989) 63–88; for literary patronage, see White (1978) 74–92, Gold (1987) 111–72 and
especially Bowditch (2010) 53–74.

[82] White (1993) 13–14, who also discusses briefly the specifically Roman nature of
the possibility of congruence between people of unequal status and how this differs
from Aristotle's view of ideal friendship (274).

relationship between Philodemus and Piso, both of whom were devoted to—or, in the latter's case, at least interested in—the study of Epicureanism. It cannot be doubted that Philodemus shared an interest in politics and governance with his powerful friend, as his treatise *On the Good King According to Homer*, which was dedicated to Piso, clearly shows.[83] And although the evidence Cicero presents in his speech against the aristocrat must be taken with a grain of salt, it does suggest that the two spent almost all their time together and that Philodemus shared with his friend poetic compositions, which, since they have survived, may provide further evidence concerning the nature of their relationship.

In the collected epigrams of Philodemus the name of his close friend and possible patron appears three times, and each instance sheds some light on the quality of their relationship and the intimacy of their correspondence. It has been convincingly argued that, although Epicurus rejected poetry as a suitable medium for communicating philosophical doctrine (cf. DL 10.121b), in his epigrams Philodemus introduces certain philosophical *topoi* in a way that is pleasing qua poetry but incidentally, as an added bonus, faithful to basic Epicurean tenets.[84] One example of this is *Epigrams* 38, which, although most likely a clever imitation of the lost original, artfully and rather playfully communicates advice about romance in a Roman context that happens to be completely in line with the restrictions of the pleasure calculus.[85] It is easy to imagine an educated and socially connected man like Piso appreciating such advice and perhaps even engaging in conversation with Philodemus and his other companions regarding such an intimate subject as love. Piso's name also appears twice in *Epigrams* 27, in which the philosopher makes his friend the dedicatee of a poem that is more intimate on account of its intention. Here Philodemus addresses him as "dearest" (1: φίλτατε), refers to himself as a companion (2: ἕταρος), and personally invites him (1: Πείσων, repeated again at verse 7 in a kind of ring composition) to partake of the ritual festivities associated with "the Twentieth," a semi-private celebration held monthly in honor of Epicurus.[86]

---

[83] See Roskam (2007) 151.
[84] See Sider (1995) 42–57 as well as Sider (1987) 310–24.
[85] Sider (1997) 199. The connection between this epigram and *Satires* 1.2 will be discussed later.

The context is important, since it involves a communal gathering of members of the same philosophical sect, a gathering at which intimate and enjoyable conversations about important philosophical topics (cf., once again, *S.* 2.6.70–6), which one may associate with F2 friendship, undoubtedly would have taken place. As David Sider explains, the dynamics of their friendship is communicated partly by the vocabulary Philodemus employs, which describes Roman *amicitia* in terms of Epicurean friendship:

> Piso, the addressee of this poem, can be expected to understand the Epicurean connotation of friendship, but as a Roman statesman, he would know that the friendship alluded to in this poem could also evoke the patron–client relationship. For Philodemus quite clearly, if not shamelessly, is angling for reciprocal benefits from Piso in the future. In return . . . Piso will receive the combined pleasures of poetry and Epicurean friendship. Piso, that is, will provide patronage, while Philodemus will provide both Epicurean ambience and poetic delights: Piso and Philodemus will be both *amici*—i.e. patron and poet—and φίλοι, i.e. two members of an Epicurean friendship.[87]

Not all scholars would agree that, following the example of Epicurus according to his detractors, Philodemus "shamelessly angles for benefits" from his powerful friend, which in any case is a view that may be influenced by Cicero's political invective against his Roman rival. Indeed, in reading Philodemus' invitation poem Marcello Gigante states, perhaps with a different passage from Cicero's *On Friendship* in mind, that "the relationship is not that of subordinate to superior but one of friendship" and that "there is no flattery in the epigram."[88] As the future tense throughout Philodemus' invitation poem communicates, the philosopher has the expectation of enjoying quality time with Piso, which is consistent with his views in *On Property Management* and elsewhere concerning the importance of looking to the future and cultivating friendship as a treasure, not only because

[86] Sider (1997) 157 gives the text along with a translation and commentary. Allen and De Lacy (1939) 64 describe the language of this epigram as "an attempt to establish firmly the relation of *amicitia*." For Epicurean festival meals, see Clay (1983) 274–9. The use of superlative terms of endearment in the vocative within a philosophical context is characteristically Platonic; cf. e.g. *Crat.* 434e4 and *Sym.* 173e1 (ὦ φίλτατε).
[87] Sider (1995) 47–8. For the differences between φίλοι and *amici*, see Gold (1987) 36.
[88] Gigante (1995) 79, 85 respectively. Also Roskam (2007) 115.

this will result in benefits but because friends are like family members with whom one can speak openly and share "what is in one's heart and while listening when one responds" (*On Frank Criticism*, fr. 28.8–10: ὧι τά[γ]κάρδ[ι]ά τις ἐρεῖ καὶ λ[έγ]οντος ἀκούσεται). The pleasure of friendship and its expectation is famously expressed by Lucretius, who, with regard to his dedicatee Memmius, mentions "the expected delight of your pleasant friendship" (1.140–1: *sperata voluptas | suavis amicitiae*).[89] There is also a connection here with Horace, whose relationship to Maecenas, although based on the reception of benefits in exchange for literary production, some scholars have described in terms of true affection and as the expression of a real, personal friendship that developed and became stronger over time.[90] This is probably because, in addition to being of the same status, they also share the kinds of values mentioned above, as the content of the *Satires* reveals. Similar to the literary gifts of Philodemus to Piso, Horace's dedications to Maecenas contain observations about politics, love, and ethics in general, and he even takes his cue from the Epicurean philosopher in composing *Odes* 1.20, which is an invitation poem to his patron that closely resembles *Epigrams* 27.[91] As will become more evident in the following chapters, many of the characteristics of Horace's persona's relationship with Maecenas closely correspond to this pattern, thereby suggesting the influence of Epicurean patronage.

[89] See Bailey (1947) 597–8 for the evidence concerning Memmius. Also Gold (1987) 51–9. Allen (1938) 167–81 argues that Lucretius, like Catullus before him (cf. poem 28), failed to gain Memmius' patronage and that his use of *amicitia* more closely relates to Roman patronage than to Epicurean friendship.

[90] Gold (1987) 134–5 speaks of "true friendship" in a "personal sense," and states that Horace and Maecenas "had between them more than that [i.e. the element of utility]." Armstrong (1989) 21–5 calls Maecenas the poet's "intimate, lifelong friend" and points to the "language of filial affection" in his poetry. White (2007) 196–200 says that their relationship was an "association based ideally on sentiment" and that "nothing prevents a friend from occupying the position of a patron or a client at the same time."

[91] See Gigante (1995) 87–9. Hiltbrunner (1972) 177 mentions this ode's "purely Epicurean spirit" ("rein epikureischen Geist"). Catullus also wrote an invitation poem to Fabullus (13), which was probably inspired by Philodemus and was in turn certainly on Horace's mind when he composed *Odes* 1.20. For the possible relationship between Catullus and Epicureans like Memmius, Piso and Philodemus, see Fordyce (1961) 210–11 and the skeptical view of Shapiro (2014) 385–405. Landolfi (1982) 137–43 detects the influence of Philodemean literary theory in Catullus' poetry. Other invitation poems in Latin occur in Juvenal (11) and Martial (5.78, 10.48, and 11.52).

PHILODEMUS, FLATTERY, AND EPICUREAN
FRANKNESS

Although with respect to their patrons Epicurus and his followers
were often viewed as flatterers, the connection between patronage and
κολακεία most certainly pre-dates them. Perhaps one of the first
extended portrayals of this traditional association appears in the
fragments of Eupolis' comic play *Flatterers*, which contains references
to the sophist Protagoras of Abdera as a parasite in the house of his
wealthy Athenian patron Callias (*PCG* 5.157–8).[92] This portrait
undoubtedly influenced Plato's comic depiction of the same sophist
in his *Protagoras*, in which the eponymous sage enjoys suitable
lodging and philosophical leisure at Callias' expense (314d9–315b8).
Elsewhere, the two are described as being "drawn toward" one
another (*Theat.* 164e7–165a1: Οὐ γὰρ ἐγώ, ὦ Σώκρατες, ἀλλὰ μᾶλλον
Καλλίας ὁ Ἱππονίκου τῶν ἐκείνου ἐπίτροπος, "It is not I, Socrates, who
is drawn to Protagoras' teachings, but Callias the son of Hipponicus")
and in the *Gorgias* Plato twice makes a connection between rhetoric,
which is a distinctively sophistic skill, and flattery (517a6–7 and
522d9).[93] The charge of flattery, however, which in the case of the
sophists had been largely marginal, became a more prevalent and
serious problem as a result of societal changes in the Hellenistic period,
as David Konstan explains:

> In the altered ideological environment of the Hellenistic period, in
> which friendship between the powerful and their dependents was the
> focus of attention, the chief worry concerning the perversion of friend-
> ship was the possibility that a person motivated by narrow self-interest
> would insinuate himself into the coterie of a superior and, by a pretense
> of friendship, achieve his own gain at the expense of his master.[94]

Within this new social context, those closest to monarchs and wealthy
individuals, and therefore most susceptible to the charge of flattery,

---

[92] See Ribbeck (1884) 9–12 for a discussion of this fragment and for lists of
the Greek and Roman comic plays that involve flatterers or parasites (30–1).
A much more recent study on the fragments of Eupolis' *Flatterers* is Storey (2003)
179–97.
[93] See Longo Auricchio (1986) 81–2 for more examples from Plato. Millett (1989)
25–37 has a useful discussion of patronage and its avoidance in democratic Athens.
[94] Konstan (1996) 10. Also helpful is Konstan (1997) 93–108.

were typically advisors or literary figures.[95] The identification of frankness or παρρησία as the hallmark of a true friend also began to develop during this time, before which it generally referred to the public right of free speech within a democratic polis such as Athens.[96] With the political limitations consequent upon the formation of monarchical rule, frankness became more of a private or moral virtue and hence one that was of particular concern to Hellenistic philosophers, who in many cases were the very advisors and literary figures mentioned above. The importance of distinguishing flatterers from friends was a significant concern in contemporary philosophical literature, as evidenced by Aristotle's treatments in both the *Nicomachean Ethics* (1126b11–1127a12) and the *Eudemian Ethics* (1233b40–1234a3), not to mention Theophrastus' influential character portrait of the flatterer (*Char.* 2) and the Cynics' infamous insistence on unbridled frankness as the mark of the true sage.[97] The earliest reference to this more private, philosophically oriented understanding of παρρησία appears to come from the correspondence of Isocrates, especially in his letter *To Nicocles*, in which he mentions "frankness, as well as the privilege of friends to rebuke and of enemies to attack each other's faults" (3: ἡ παρρησία καὶ τὸ φανερῶς ἐξεῖναι τοῖς τε φίλοις ἐπιπλῆξαι καὶ τοῖς ἐχθροῖς ἐπιθέσθαι ταῖς ἀλλήλων ἁμαρτίαις). As mentioned already, in the case of Epicurus the situation is rather complicated: again, he sanctioned patronage as the only reputable source of income for the sage, which on occasion entails service to a king (DL 10.121b), and because early Epicureans understood friendship as primarily utilitarian, prominent figures of the sect were easily accused of shameless flattery. Even much later authors, such as Lucian of Samosata, made accusations about how Epicurus made parasitism into an art form and identified it as a "philosophical goal" (*On Parasites* 11: τέλος).[98] To make matters worse for Epicureans, there is little or no

[95] Ribbeck (1884) categorizes and lists the known flatterers of Alexander the Great (84–6), Demetrius Poliorcetes (86–8), and other Hellenistic rulers (88–92).

[96] See Scarpat (1964) 11–57, Momigliano (1973–4) 2.258, and Konstan (1996) 7–10.

[97] For Theophrastus' portrait, see especially the newer edition of Diggle (2004) 181–98, which includes an introductory note on the flatterer. Trapp (1997) 125 mentions lost treatises on flattery attributed to Simias, Speusippus, Xenocrates, Theophrastus, Theopompus, Clearchus, and Chrysippus. See Scarpat (1964) 62–9 for Cynic παρρησία.

[98] For the close relationship between parasites and flatterers, see McC. Brown (1992) 98–106 and Arnott (2010) 322–4.

evidence of any systematic treatment of παρρησία in the available fragments of Epicurus. One can imagine, of course, that honesty and candor are implicitly necessary for healthy friendships, and that the Master surely would have recognized and promoted this in his own life and writings. Nevertheless, the mention of frankness in his works appears to be exclusively connected with his concern for clear conversation and the explanation of doctrinal matters:

κέχρηται δὲ λέξει κυρίᾳ κατὰ τῶν πραγμάτων, ἣν ὅτι ἰδιωτάτη ἐστίν, Ἀριστοφάνης ὁ γραμματικὸς αἰτιᾶται. σαφὴς δ' ἦν οὕτως, ὡς καὶ ἐν τῷ Περὶ ῥητορικῆς ἀξιοῖ μηδὲν ἄλλο ἢ σαφήνειαν ἀπαιτεῖν. (DL 10.13)

Epicurus used conventional language in dealing with matters, which Aristophanes the grammarian criticizes as being one of his personal traits. And he was so concerned with being clear that in his treatise _On Rhetoric_ he regarded nothing worth searching for aside from clarity.[99]

Indeed, this concern for transparency is the fundamental reason for Epicurus' rejection of syllogistic reasoning and poetry as vehicles of philosophy. For Philodemus, however, providing an account of the importance and characteristics of frankness as it was understood by his Hellenistic contemporaries became necessary in connection with Roman patronage, and specifically as a response to how critics viewed his own relationship with Piso.

One of the difficulties immigrant philosophers like Philodemus had to overcome or at least address was the charge of flattery, which, in addition to being a vice the Romans generally associated with Greek clients (cf. Cic. _Pis._ 70: _ut Graeculum, ut adsentatorem_), was one that was also easily levelled against the Epicureans on account of their utilitarian view of friendship. Indeed, for Cicero such a view is not only wrong but also reprehensible, inhuman, and ultimately precludes the possibility of or even destroys an existing friendship:

---

[99] Apparently Epicurus was nevertheless misunderstood even in his own day because he was never willing to sacrifice philosophical truth, no matter how obscure to some, for popularity. Cf. SV 29: Παρρησίᾳ γὰρ ἔγωγε χρώμενος φυσιολογῶν χρησμῳδεῖν τὰ συμφέροντα πᾶσιν ἀνθρώποις μᾶλλον ἂν βουλοίμην, κἂν μηδεὶς μέλλῃ συνήσειν, ἢ συγκατατιθέμενος ταῖς δόξαις καρποῦσθαι τὸν πυκνὸν παραπίπτοντα παρὰ τῶν πολλῶν ἔπαινον, "For, to be quite frank, I would prefer while discussing how the world works to speak in oracles about what is beneficial to all mankind, even if no one would understand it, rather than to reap the mighty praise that comes from the masses by conforming to others' opinions."

ut igitur et monere et moneri proprium est verae amicitiae, et alterum
libere facere, non aspere, alterum patienter accipere, non repugnanter,
sic habendum est nullam in amicitiis pestem esse maiorem quam
adulationem blanditiam assentationem: quamvis enim multis nominibus
est hoc vitium notandum levium hominum atque fallacium, ad volupta-
tem loquentium omnia, nihil ad veritatem.   (*On Friendship* 91–2)

Therefore, just as it belongs to true friendship to advise and be advised,
and to do so rather freely in the first case without being harsh, and to
accept it patiently rather than reluctantly in the second, so also there can
be no greater detriment to friendship than adulation, obsequiousness,
and flattery. For indeed, this is collectively the vice of fickle and dishonest
men, and of those who will say anything for pleasure but not for the sake
of the truth. It must be censured no matter what we choose to call it.[100]

The distinction between "friend" (φίλος) and "flatterer" (κόλαξ) was
notoriously blurry in antiquity in general,[101] but it was perhaps even
more difficult to ascertain in Horace's or Plutarch's Rome, where the
stratifications of *amicitia* were many and the number of Greek sages
vying for their patrons' favor unsurprisingly elicited charges of flattery.[102] Cicero in particular considered the Greeks "truly deceptive in
general as well as fickle and knowledgeable in their constant dedication
to excessive flattery" (*Letters to his Brother Quintus* 1.5.19–20: *vero
fallaces sunt permulti et leves et diuturna servitute ad nimiam adsen-
tationem eruditi*),[103] which of course influenced his portrayal of
Philodemus in his attack on Piso. Despite the fact that Cicero's attack
involves the application of general stereotypes and stock qualities,
which, as mentioned above, suggest that it is more comic than
serious,[104] critical observations such as this likely motivated Philodemus to addresses the issue at length in the fragments of his
treatise *On Flattery*, in which he admits that there are certain

---

[100] Cf. *On Ends* 2.78–85. Glad (1996) 25 and Glad (1995) 111–13 discusses the
nature of this "anti-Epicurean polemic." See also Konstan (1997) 108–13.
[101] Hunter (1985a) 483: "In the Greek world φίλος was used as a court title, and so
a man who was φίλος (or ἑταῖρος) τοῦ βασιλέως was, from another point of view, a
flatterer and a slave." Later on the term ἑταῖρος comes to mean something like "count"
or "earl," the Latin equivalent of which is *comes* (see e.g. *LSJ* 7).
[102] Allen and De Lacy (1939) 61–3.
[103] Cf. *On the Orator* 1.22.102 for similar derogatory remarks concerning the
Greeks.
[104] See Gigante (1983) 44–7 and Corbeill (1996) 169–73. Maslowski (1974) 69–71
and, more recently, Griffin (2001) 95–7 note that Cicero actually portrays Epicureanism
favorably by stating that Piso had seriously misunderstood their doctrines (*Pis.* 69).

56   Epicurean Ethics in Horace

similarities between the flatterer and the sage (PHerc. 222, col. 2.1–2: ἔσονταί τινες ὁμοιότητες).[105] For instance, both look forward to the reception of gifts and honor, which, in the case of the sage, some mistakenly identify as the fruits of obsequiousness:

καὶ τῶν [ὑ]παρχόντων πόλλ᾽ ἀπολα[υ]στὰ διδόασιν αὐτῶι· κα[ὶ
σ]υ[γ]γενεῖς ἐνίων καὶ συνήθε[ις] π[ρ]οτιμώ[μ]ενον ὁρῶντες
[ἀποδιδ]όασιν αὐτὸν ὡς κόλα[κα].   (PHerc. 222, col. 2.16–22)

From their possessions they give to him [the sage] many pleasing things, and even the relatives and associates of some [of the patrons] will consider him a flatterer when they see him being honored more than themselves.

Both figures, moreover, are often drawn to wealthy or powerful patrons (PHerc. 222, col. 5.3–4: ἀνθρώπ[οις] μεγαλοπλούτοις), in whose presence they praise philosophical wisdom (PHerc. 222, col. 2.9–10: [τ]ῶν [ἀγα]θῶν ἐπα[ιν]ετικὸ[ς σοφίας]). Having briefly discussed such similarities, Philodemus elucidates the differences between flatterers and sages by drawing inspiration from the comic tradition and Theophrastus' portraits of the flatterer (Char. 2) and the obsequious man (Char. 5), and he describes the various tactics, motives, approaches, and reactions typical of individuals who engage in the vicious practice of adulation.

According to Philodemus, the true difference between these two groups lies in their respective intentions or dispositions. The flatterer, who uses rhetorical charm with malicious intent, speaks only to please his victim (PHerc. 1457, col. 4.7: πρὸς χά[ρ]ιν λέγων) while slandering his competitors (PHerc. 222, col. 7.1–2: [μισεῖ δ᾽ ὁ κόλαξ] πάντας ἁπλῶς τοὺς [ἐπιτη]δείους τῶν κολακευ[ομένων], "But the flatterer hates without qualification all those close friends of the people who are flattered"), and his attraction to wealthy individuals is motivated by avarice alone (PHerc. 1457, col. 12.22: φιλαργυροῦσι).[106] Theophrastus includes a similar description of greed and self-interest in

---

[105] For flattery in Philodemus, see Longo Auricchio (1986) 79–91, Glad (1996) 23–9, Asmis (2001) 206–39, and Tsouna (2007) 126–42 in addition to the introductions of the various fragments cited above. There is also the comprehensive study of Ribbeck (1884) on flattery in antiquity, as well as the RE article of Kroll (1921) 1069–70 and the modern commentary on Theophrastus' Characters by Diggle (2004) 181–2. The topic of the similarity between flatterers and true friends is of course addressed at length by Plutarch in How to Tell a Flatterer from a Friend.
[106] Cf. Pl. Soph. 222e1–223a1 and Arist. Nic. Eth. 1127a8–10. Philodemus briefly discusses the dispositions of flatterers and sages in PHerc. 1089, coll. 1–2.

connection with flattery as a disposition or character, defining it as "the kind of converse which is dishonorable but profitable to the one flattering" (*Char.* 2.1: ὁμιλίαν αἰσχρὰν εἶναι, συμφέρουσαν δὲ τῷ κολακεύοντι).[107] In his initial discussion of the challenge of distinguishing adulatory charm from sage advice Philodemus includes mythology, as he so often does (*On the Good King According to Homer* is only one of other examples), when describing the wise man's "converse" as potentially similar to that of the flatterer:

ὁ δὲ σοφὸς ὅμοιον μ[ὲν] οὐδὲν προσοίσεται κόλα[κι], παρέξει δέ τισιν ὑπόνοιαν [ὡς] ἔστι τοιοῦτος, ὅτι κη[λεῖ φρέ]νας οὕτως ὃν τρόπον οὐδ' α[ἱ μυ]θικαὶ Σειρῆνες. (PHerc. 222, col. 2.2–7)

The sage will not at all behave like the flatterer, but he will offer some the suspicion that he is in fact such a one, precisely because he charms the mind in a way that not even the mythical Sirens can.

Despite this similarity, for the Epicurean philosopher one of the major differences—if not *the* major difference—between flatterers and sages vis-à-vis their benefactors is that the former rarely "speak frankly" (PHerc. 222, col. 3.27–8: παρρη[σιαζόμενον]), since, given that their main objective is to gain something by saying whatever will please their victims (PHerc. 1457, col. 1.9, similar to the passage quoted above: [ὁ λέγων πρὸ]ς χάριν), this would be counterproductive. The sage, on the other hand, engages in conversations that are, as Philodemus states in *On Property Management*, "truthful and not looking for quarrels" (col. 23.30–1: ἀληθινῶν καὶ ἀφιλο[ν]ε[ί]κων), nor does he imitate the flatterer's garrulity and rhetorical charm despite his Siren-like persuasiveness. Instead, he is particularly trustworthy because his conversation is not only frank but also pithy and beneficial to the recipient, since he, unlike the dishonest flatterer, uses his powers of persuasion in order to reveal to his friends their vices (PHerc. 222, col. 2.7–9). Elsewhere Philodemus describes others' response to the sage's companionship, which is pleasing without being obsequious,[108] as profound and genuine "gratitude" (*On Property Management*, col. 23.27–8: εὐχάριστο[ν]).

---

[107] Many scholars delete this opening observation, which Philodemus reproduces in his fragments but without connecting it to Theophrastus. The rest of this character portrait does not seem to expand on the idea that the flatterer speaks for his own benefit.

[108] For the distinction between "being obsequious" (ἀρέσκειν), which is a sign of flattery, and "being pleasing" (ἀνδάνειν), which is an acceptable characteristic of

For Philodemus frankness and honesty not only characterize the
sage's conversation with his supporters,[109] but they are also the most
important *sine qua non* of Epicurean communities and relationships
at all levels. As such, they closely relate to Philodemus' observations
in his economic treatises regarding patrons as sources of wealth as
well as the informal nature of his epigrammatic invitation to Piso.
It is fitting, then, that he should have given frankness extended consideration in his "class notes" of Zeno's lectures, which are presented in the
form of the treatise entitled *On Frank Criticism*. For later Epicureans
like Zeno and Philodemus, the application of frank criticism was
largely pedagogical or rather psychogogical, and, exercised within
the context of small communities consisting of pupils and sages, its
purpose was to foster virtue through the therapeutic and purifying
medicine of self-knowledge.[110] This, in accordance with a long tradition going back to Socrates' promotion of the traditional maxim
"know thyself," is viewed as a prerequisite for moral correction. In
his treatise *On Frank Criticism*, which is the only ancient tractate with
that name, Philodemus explains the nature of frank criticism as a
pedagogical method as well as its aims, the different kinds of pupils
and their respective challenges, and the proper disposition of the
sage.[111] As a method strictly speaking, frankness is conjectural
and based on the sage's extended observations of another's behavior
(cf. *On Frank Criticism*, fr. 1.8–9: στοχαζόμενος εὐ[λ]ογίαις), to which
he responds in a timely fashion (fr. 25.1: καιρόν) with a degree of harshness commensurate with the pupil's needs.[112] Although this is a communal affair, extreme harshness and public

Epicurean relationships, see Kondo (1974) 54–6 and Glad (1996) 28. This comparison
with ἀνδάνειν is based on PHerc. 1457, col. 10.8–9, which is partially damaged and
reads as follows in Bassi's 1914 edition: ἐ[ν] τοῖς ΠΕ . ΚΑ . Α . ΔΑΝΕΙΝ. Kondo,
following the plausible reconstruction of previous scholars, reads ἐν τοῖς πέλας
ἀνδάνειν ("in being pleasing to one's neighbors") and compares SV 67: εἰς τὴν τοῦ
πλησίον εὔνοιαν διαμετρῆσαι, "in order to win the good favor of one's neighbor."

[109] This appears in the fragments of his treatise *On Conversation*, which will be
discussed in later chapters.
[110] Philodemus employs medical imagery throughout *On Frank Criticism*, for
which see Gigante (1975) 53–61 and Konstan et al. (1998) 20–3. The pedagogical nature
of Epicurean frankness, which Glad (1995) examines in terms of communal psychagogy
(101–60), is also treated by Gigante (1974) 37–42. Cf. *On Anger* coll. 2–8.
[111] For the structure and an overview of the treatise, see Konstan et al. (1998) 8–20.
As mentioned already, White (2004) 1031–127 notes there are still significant problems regarding the order of the fragments.
[112] See Gigante (1983) 55–113.

embarrassment are avoided at all costs and, instead, constructive and well-intentioned—even cheerful—criticism is encouraged. A good example of this appears in fragments 37 and 38 (of which only the second is truly readable) as well as in fragment 79, in which Philodemus notes that criticism should not be given against every single error, nor in the hearing of people who should not be there, nor in a manner that is malicious and full of spite (1–12). The proper application of frankness requires a certain measured response to vice that ultimately depends on the pleasure calculus. That is to say the pain caused by the "goad of frank criticism" (fr. 17.10: π[αρρ]ησίας κ[έντ]ρον), which is employed for the same purpose that a surgeon uses a scalpel, is outweighed by the healing that follows (cf. col. 2a–b). And although Philodemus rejects the Cynic and Stoic practice of censuring for its own sake, he also acknowledges that there are real benefits in employing a harsher form of frankness that, like other schools, makes use of vividness and pictorial imagery.[113] In accordance with the traditional practice of the Hellenistic diatribe, he recommends the use of a technique he calls "placing before the eyes" (On Frank Criticism, fr. 26.4–5: τιθῶμεν δὲ πρὸ ὀμμάτων; cf. On Anger, col. 1.23 quoted below), which is particularly effectual with certain students and especially with those suffering from an irascible disposition.

The different levels of frankness required and their possible effects depend ultimately on the pupil's disposition, which Philodemus categorizes in terms of sex (On Frank Criticism, coll. 21b.12–22b.9), age (coll. 24a.7–24b.12), social status (coll. 22b.10–24a.7), and above all, "strong" and "weak" tempers (fr. 7.1–3: τοὺς μᾶλλον τῶν ἀπαλῶν ἰσχυρούς).[114] All of these different types of pupils require different strategies in terms of the application of frank criticism, which

---

[113] On Anger col. 1.12–27 (spoken in the diatribe style in question!): εἰ μὲν οὖν ἐπετίμα τοῖς ψέγουσι μ[ό]νον, ἄλλο δὲ μηδὲ ἓν ποιοῦσιν ἢ βαι[ό]ν, ὡς Βίων ἐν τῶι Περὶ τῆς ὀργῆς καὶ Χρύσιππος ἐν τ[ῶ]ι Πε[ρ]ὶ παθῶν Θεραπευ[τι]κῶι, κἂν μετρίως ἵστατο. νῦν δὲ τ[ὸ] καθόλ[ο]υ τὰ παρακολουθοῦν[τ]α κακὰ τιθέναι πρὸ ὀμμάτων καταγέλασ-τ[ο]ν εἶναι καὶ ληρῶδες ὑπολαμβάνων, αὐ[τός ἐστι ληρώ]δης καὶ κα[ταγέλαστος], "If then he [Timasagoras] had rebuked those who merely blame [anger] without accomplishing anything else or little else, like Bion in his On Anger and Chrysippus in the Remedy for Anger of his On Emotions, then he would have done so reasonably. But as things are, in claiming that it is wholly ridiculous and raving to place before the eyes of one the evils that result from his vices he himself is raving and ridiculous." For Philodemus' restrained approval of certain beneficial elements of the diatribe, see Armstrong (2014a) 105–6. Also Glad (1995) 117–20 and Tsouna (2007) 202–5.

[114] See Glad (1995) 137–52.

underscores the importance for the Epicureans of understanding their dispositions and therefore has much to do with the role of careful observation. Old men and those involved in politics, for instance, will require a harsher form of correction: for the former, on account of their age and corresponding view that they are particularly wise and so deserve to be honored (cf. col. 24a–b, where the description includes the phrase διὰ τὸν χρόνο[ν]); for the latter, on account of their ambition and keen awareness of their own personal importance and influence (cf. col. 18b for the phrase διὰ δὲ δοξοκοπίαν). The same point is made in connection with frankness as applied to women (col. 22a–b) as well as the rich and powerful (coll. 23b–24a). Either way, the sage will carefully observe his pupils and select the best manner of criticism, whether more or less gentle, but always with a view toward achieving healing and progress in the philosophical life within the community. With regard to the sage, Philodemus emphasizes the importance of moral strength, perseverance, careful observation, patience, and especially humility: the reason why sages do not criticize harshly, for example, is that they see their own faults and recognize their imperfections (fr. 46.7–9: γινώσκω[ν] αὐτὸν οὐκ ὄντα τέλε[ι]ον). This recognition is remarkable when compared to the Stoic conviction regarding the sage as perfect in every way and not subject to any emotion whatsoever, least of all anger. Overall, Philodemus' observations regarding both flattery and the proper application of true and honest criticism shed light on the social and historical context in which Horace composed the *Satires*. As will be shown in the following chapters, it becomes evident from various poems that literary men of some ambition envied Horace on account of his intimate relationship with the wealthy Maecenas. Accusations appear to have been made that, as with Philodemus, inspired Horace to give an account of the nature of his friendship with his patron. In fact, the topic of flattery in the context of patronage is not only relevant to *Satires* 1.6, it is also the central concern in *Satires* 2.5 as well as *Epistles* 1.17 and 1.18, all of which reveals a real concern on the poet's part regarding the distinction between flattery and friendship. In response to such accusations and in an attempt to confirm his own status as a true and honest client friend of Maecenas, Horace appears to draw heavily from Philodemus' views on frank criticism. He avoids, for example, the harsh invective of the Cynics and the unrestrained *libertas* of his predecessor Lucilius, which, given the political context of his day and the growing power of Octavian in Rome, was perhaps too risky an approach to social commentary. Instead, Horace's *Satires* seem to

communicate frank advice in a critical yet cheerful manner to a private
audience that consists of close friends and acquaintances, much like
the practice, according to Philodemus, in Epicurean communities
around the Bay of Naples. Finally, the poet's typical employment of
self-deprecation and public confession admittedly serves to disarm the
attacks of his enemies, but such candor also reinforces his own self-
awareness and consequent qualification as a critic of Roman society's
faults, all of which, as any good Epicurean would know, are necessary
first steps toward the therapeutic healing of vice.

EPICURUS, PHILODEMUS, AND METHODOLOGY

An essential prerequisite for the successful application of frank criticism, not to mention the correct diagnosis of a vicious disposition
in general, is the close observation of visible behavior. Of course, the
sage's ability to cure (or at least treat) moral imperfections depends
not only on careful observation but also on his consistent exposure to
such behavior, which is possible within the context of small communities like those of the Epicureans. It goes without saying that living in
close proximity with others fosters a keener awareness of individual
personalities and habits, which, when discussed openly and in a spirit
of genuine concern for improvement, as Philodemus describes in *On
Frank Criticism*, leads to progress and ultimately happiness. The investigation of invisible realities through sensory evidence and observation,
however, is also an important component of Epicurus' methodology
in general, and therefore merits some attention. For the Master, philosophical investigation presupposes the ability to communicate clearly
by using the acceptable and readily understood terms for concepts that
are common to all human beings (*Hdt.* 37–8).[115] In addition to being
able to understand one another, Epicurus emphasizes the importance
of observing the world around us, stating in his *Letter to Herodotus*:

εἶτα κατὰ τὰς αἰσθήσεις δεῖ πάντα τηρεῖν καὶ ἁπλῶς τὰς παρούσας
ἐπιβολὰς εἴτε διανοίας εἴθ᾽ ὅτου δήποτε τῶν κριτηρίων, ὁμοίως δὲ καὶ
τὰ ὑπάρχοντα πάθη, ὅπως ἂν καὶ τὸ προσμένον καὶ τὸ ἄδηλον ἔχωμεν οἷς
σημειωσόμεθα, ταῦτα δὲ διαλαβόντας συνορᾶν ἤδη περὶ τῶν ἀδήλων.

(*Hdt.* 38)

---

[115] The term πρόληψις is used in connection with these concepts, for which see DL
10.33. Asmis (1984) 19–80 and Tsouna (2016) 160–221 offer much more detailed
examinations.

Whence it is necessary to observe everything in accordance with sensation and attendant contacts, whether of concepts or of the senses, and
in accordance with the present affections, in order that we may be able
to infer from signs what will become clear but is currently invisible, and
then, after having considered these things carefully, to have an understanding about what is invisible per se.[116]

The denseness of this passage threatens to obscure the doctrine itself,
but the general notion is that perceptions depend or rely on the senses
as well as the mind, and that through this it is possible to draw
inferences regarding invisible realities. As Elizabeth Asmis explains,
"In Epicurus' terminology, the perceptions and feelings are activities
of the 'criteria,' the senses and the mind, which judge, by an immediate
act of apprehension, what is real."[117] Through the careful consideration
or "observation" (τηρεῖν) of these perceptions and feelings, one may
"infer from perceptible signs what is imperceptible" (DL 10.32: καὶ περὶ
τῶν ἀδήλων ἀπὸ τῶν φαινομένων χρὴ σημειοῦσθαι).[118] Inferences
regarding what Epicurus calls τὸ προσμένον or "what is expected to
appear" (for example, an object blurred by distance) may be verified by
comparing the information from subsequent, more reliable perceptions
to the initial expectation: one's opinion about what is seen at a distance,
for example, is verified by the subsequent "witness" or presentation of
what was expected to be true and rejected by the lack of confirmation
or a "counter-witness." With regard to a theory or opinion about τὸ
ἄδηλον or "what is invisible per se" (for example, atoms and the void),
it is true whenever it is "not counter-witnessed" by other phenomena
(since in this case there can be no perceptible confirmation of
the thing itself), so that the theory about what is invisible "follows"
(ἀκολουθία); on the other hand, such a theory is false whenever it is

---

[116] For this section in general, see Verde (2010) 80–7.

[117] Asmis (1984) 100, who discusses the difference between Epicurus' identification of κριτήρια as "senses and the mind" and Diogenes' later association of them with
"sensation, preconceptions, and feelings" (DL 10.31), which "does not involve a
distortion of [Epicurus'] doctrine, but was designed to bring it in conformity with
the conceptual framework that was used also by other Hellenistic philosophers."

[118] As Asmis (1984) 23 notes, Diogenes description of inference from signs pre-
cedes his definition of "preconceptions," whereas Epicurus, in laying out his methodology, takes the opposite approach. I follow Asmis (1984) 84–6 in translating
Epicurus' τηρεῖν as "observe," thus distinguishing it from mere perception and linking
it to this inferential method.

Philosophical Background to Epicureanism 63

"counter-witnessed" by something else.[119] Additionally, with reference to what is too remote to be perceived, Epicurus has recourse to a process of making inferences by calculating similarities between the observable and the invisible, as words like ἀναλογίζειν, ἀναλογία, and ἀνάλογος indicate (cf. *Hdt.* 58).

In one passage he states: "And so one must investigate the causes involving celestial matters and all that is not apparent by comparing in how many ways a similar thing happens in our experience" (*Hdt.* 80: ὥστε παραθεωροῦντας ποσαχῶς παρ' ἡμῖν τὸ ὅμοιον γίνεται, αἰτιολογητέον ὑπέρ τε τῶν μετεώρων καὶ παντὸς τοῦ ἀδήλου).[120] It is unclear to what extent Epicurus was willing to rely on such similarities when making inferences about what cannot be perceived. What is certain, however, is that Philodemus goes to great lengths to defend this method in his treatise *On Signs*, which offers a more detailed account and may be of relevance for Horace's own colorful descriptions of vicious behavior in the *Satires*. In any case, the technique always involves reflection and contextualization of new experiences in the light of what one already knows from one's own and others' observations.

Although both the removal and similarity methods of investigation result in confirmation, there is a difference between them in that the first involves a causal connection whereas the second relies purely

---

[119] *Hdt.* 51-2 (cf. 50-1): ἐὰν μὲν μὴ ἐπιμαρτυρηθῇ ἢ ἀντιμαρτυρηθῇ, τὸ ψεῦδος γίνεται· ἐὰν δὲ ἐπιμαρτυρηθῇ ἢ μὴ ἀντιμαρτυρηθῇ, τὸ ἀληθές, "if, on the one hand, a witness is not forthcoming or there is a counter-witness then the opinion is false; if, on the other hand, there is in fact a witness or the lack of a counter-witness, then the opinion is true." See Asmis (1984) 145 and 178-9. As Sextus Empiricus explains (*Against the Grammarians* 7.213-14), a claim about a non-apparent entity like "there is no void" would require the "removal" (referred to as ἀνασκευή) of the phenomenon of motion. But the fact that there is motion in the universe "counter-witnesses" the claim and makes it false. Lucretius uses the method of witnessing and counter-witnessing frequently in his proofs, e.g. the teaching "nothing comes from nothing" is confirmed by the lack of counter-witnessing, since one never observes "all things being produced out of all things" (1.159-60: *ex omnibu' rebus | omne genus nasci posset*). Alternatively, the claim "something comes from nothing" would involve a removal of the orderly, systematic generation of things according to their kind. The phenomenon of production *generatim* "counter-witnesses" this claim and makes it false. It is worth noting that terms like ἀνασκευή and ἀκολουθία do not appear in Epicurus' works but are used by later authors like Sextus and Philodemus in the context of logical disputes.
[120] Cf. Lucr. 2.112-24 and the famous example of motes in a sunbeam, which are described as a "similitude" (*simulacrum*) always present before the eyes and a "small thing that can give an analogy of great things" (*rerum magnarum parva potest res | exemplare dare*).

on empirical observation. As Philodemus explains in his treatise *On Signs*,[121] in order to infer something about an imperceptible reality with consistent accuracy one must first gain experience by frequently "attending to the manifold variety of visible signs that accompany the phenomena" (col. 33.11–13: τὸ παντοδαπὸν ποίκιλμα τῶν φαινομένων κατοπτεύσας). One then appraises or "calculates the phenomena" (col. 27.22–3: ὁ τῶν φαινο[μένων] ἐπ[ιλογισμό]ς), and, noting that these have similarly coincided on many occasions and that there is no evidence to the contrary (the term he uses is ἀντιπίπτειν), one uses this as a basis for making the actual inference. Although uses of this term in Epicurus' extant remains are somewhat ambiguous,[122] Philodemus consistently describes ἐπιλογισμός and ἐπιλογίζεσθαι as the rational process by which an observer makes calculations on the basis of similarities or differences.[123] An example of this method in *On Signs* involves his favorite proof (cf. coll. 2.25–4.10), based on the observed similarity, that all men are mortal:

[ο]ὔτε μὴν τοὐναντίον τῶι προκειμένωι προλήψομαι, καταντήσω δὲ
διὰ τοῦ τῶν φαινομένων ἐπιλογισμοῦ [ἐπὶ] τὸ καὶ κατ᾽ αὐτὸ δεῖν τὴν
ὁμοιότητα ὑπάρχειν. ἐπεὶ γὰρ τοῖς παρ᾽ ἡμῖν ἀνθρώποις τοῦτο παρέπεται
τὸ σύμπτωμα, πάντως ἀξιώσω πᾶσιν ἀνθρώποις τοῦτο παρακολουθεῖν,
ἐπιλογισμῶι συνβιβάζων ὅτι καὶ κατὰ τοῦτο δεῖ τὴν ὁμοιότητ᾽ εἶναι.

(coll. 22.35–23.7)

Nor shall I assume in advance the opposite of this statement [i.e. that all men are mortal]; but by empirical inference from appearances I shall arrive at the view that similarity must exist in this respect also. For since this property follows on the man among us, I shall assuredly judge that it follows on all men, confirming by empirical inference that the similarity must exist in this respect also.

[121] As Sedley (1982) 239–72 argues, this treatise is largely devoted to addressing criticisms from Stoic adversaries, against which Philodemus defends the method of drawing conclusions based on similarity. For a more detailed analysis of the importance of the similarity method, see Asmis (1984) 197–211 and Allen (2001) 208–41. Translations of the following quotations of this treatise are those of De Lacy and De Lacy (1978).

[122] See Asmis (1984) 176–8.

[123] For the meaning of ἐπιλογισμός, see the contrasting views of Arrighetti (1955), De Lacy (1958), De Lacy and De Lacy (1978), Sedley (1973), Asmis (1984) 205 n. 23, Schofield (1996) 221–38, and Tsouna (2007) 55. The reconstruction of this term in the passage quoted above is that of Philippson, and is justified by the same, better-preserved expression in *On Signs*, col. 22.37–9, quoted below.

Here Philodemus comes to the conclusion that all men everywhere are mortal solely on the basis of empirical observation, a calculation of its relevance, and the lack of contrary evidence. This proof does not depend on "removal" since there is no clear physical connection (as with the reality of motion and the consequent necessity of empty space), but rather a careful consideration of similarities and the application of inductive reasoning. That is to say, the relationship between motion and void is that of causal dependence, whereas the idea that some men are not mortal is absurd or "inconceivable" (col. 21.29: ἀδιαν[όητον]) precisely because it defies one's own constant experience through observation.[124] Philodemus goes even further in stating elsewhere that all investigation is ultimately inductive, even if it can in fact be expressed as an inference from removal, such as the argument regarding motion and void:

τὰ γοῦν παρακολουθοῦντ[α πά]ντα τοῖς παρ' ἡμῖν κινουμέν[οις, ὧ]ν
χωρὶς οὐδὲν ὁρῶμεν κ[ινούμ]ε[νον,] ἐπ[ιλογι]σάμενοι, [τούτ]ωι πά[νθ'
ὅσα κι]νεῖται κατὰ π[ᾶ]ν πρὸς [τὴν ὁμοι]ότητ' ἀξιοῦμε[ν κιν]εῖσθαι,
[καὶ] τῶι τρόπωι τούτωι τὸ μ[ὴ] δυνατὸν εἶναι κίνησιν ἄνευ κενοῦ
γίν[εσ]θαι σημε[ι]ούμεθα.   (*On Signs*, coll. 8.32–9.3)

Thus we first determine empirically (ἐπ[ιλογι]σάμενοι) all the conditions attendant on moving objects in our experience, apart from which we see nothing moved; then by this method we judge that all moving objects in every case are moved similarly (πρὸς [τὴν ὁμοι]ότητ' ἀξιοῦμε[ν]); and this is the method by which we infer (σημε[ι]ούμεθα) that it is not possible for motion to occur without void.

The point here seems to be that even if one has recourse to the removal method, reasoning that if void is removed than so too is motion, the obvious existence of the latter provides a counter-witness that leads to induction based on similarity, in that one extends particular observations of motion to all objects everywhere, even those one cannot observe. What is more interesting about this method, however, is how Philodemus extends it to the realm of ethics and the observation of symptoms of vicious dispositions, which he considers in other treatises that are more relevant to the present study.

This process of identifying external, perceptible signs as manifestations of invisible realities bears striking resemblance to the empirical

---

[124] Cf. similar proofs regarding observations such as "If Plato is a man, Socrates is also a man" (col. 11.19–31) and Asmis (1984) 199–200.

methodology of ancient Greek medicine. Phillip and Estelle De Lacy
note the following:

> In observing and recording the similarities and uniformities of perceptible
> phenomena, the early empirical physicians used appearances as signs
> of imperceptible things. The physicians found that relatively few diseases
> can be observed directly. The majority of diseases, being internal and
> unobservable, are known only by auxiliary means.[125]

This tradition significantly influenced the ethical approach of Epicurus'
followers, who considered the perceptible signs of vice analogous to
the visible symptoms of a hidden disease, namely, the underlying
disposition. This method is of particular importance for Philodemus,
whose ethical treatises often begin with a clinical description of the
symptoms and signs that accompany certain vicious dispositions.[126]
In his treatise *On Anger* in particular he relies on evidence that is
perceptible (cf. col. 3.26–7: [ἄ]π[ασιν] φ[ανε]ρώτερον) in order to make
inferences about individuals with irascible dispositions, and other
terms that appear in *On Signs*, such as ἐπιλογισμός and ἀδιανοησία,
also occur in this work.[127] He observes, for instance, that the presence
of an individual vice such as anger can be inferred through the
observation of signs that have regularly and similarly coincided with
certain other phenomena:

[ν]υνεὶ [δ' ἐροῦμεν τὰ τῆς ὀργῆς συμπτώ]μα[τ' ε]ῖναι[ί πως ὁ]μο[ιότατα],
κἂν περι[ττότερόν τινες] καταφρον[ούμενοί πως] ἐπὶ πᾶσιν [ὀργίζωνται],
καὶ τὰ συμ[πτώματα τοῦ πάθους] εἶναι [πᾶσι κοινὰ οὔτε] νέοις
οὔ[τε γέρουσιν οὖσ]ῶν εὐ[λαβειῶν.]   (*On Anger*, coll. 7.26–8.8)

But now we say that the symptoms of anger are very similar, even if
some, being exceedingly scornful, get angry with everyone, and that the

---

[125] De Lacy and De Lacy (1978) 122, who also mention the important influences
of Aristotle and the Empirical School of medicine (pp. 165–82). Asmis (1984)
180–90 discusses other Hellenistic theories of signs, including that of the Stoics,
Skeptics, and Rationalist physicians. See especially the study of Allen (2001) 89–97
for the medical background of sign-inference. For a definition of Epicurean διάθεσις
as the arrangement of soul atoms and hence an imperceptible reality, see Konstan
(1973) 62–3. For the relationship between the Epicurean and Aristotelian tradition
regarding this concept, see Furley (1967) 228, Grilli (1983a) 93–109, and again
Konstan (1973) 62–3.

[126] See Tsouna (2007), who discusses this method with regard to several treatises,
including *On Flattery* (127–32), *On Arrogance* (145–51), and *On Anger* (210–17).

[127] De Lacy and De Lacy (1978) 153–4.

symptoms of this passion are common to all, there being safeguards for neither the young nor the old.[128]

This method is described in *Epidemics* 6 (3.12), and Galen says that it was further developed by the Empiricist physicians, who made diagnoses by relying on the careful and frequent observation (ἐμπειρία) of visible symptoms (συμπτώματα) that often appear simultaneously in a syndrome (συνδρομή).[129] In his examination of anger, Philodemus describes, in a strikingly colorful manner reminiscent of Cynic character portraits, the symptoms of an irascible disposition in much detail (col. 8.21–38). This method of "marking" imperceptible vices by means of drawing inferences based on similarity, which Philodemus consistently employs in his ethical treatments, was apparently a topic of heated debate in the first century BC, as the polemical tone of *On Signs* and certain passages from Cicero reveal.[130] It is not unreasonable to suggest, therefore, that such controversies might have contributed something to Horace's approach to moral investigation in his satiric poetry, especially, as will be seen presently, the portrayal of his father's pedagogical method in *Satires* 1.4 (105–15). In other words, the training of Horace's persona, which to some degree appears to combine elements of the Epicurean criteria of sense perception and feelings for the purpose of moral guidance, also involves exposure to and observation of the patterns of perceptible behavior that reveal his contemporaries' vicious dispositions. All of this, combined with his father's rather Epicurean application of frankness for the purpose of correction, indicates, as Marcello Gigante observes, that for Horace as a satirist Philodemus was "someone who suggested instructional methods and images, which did not conflict with his conscience as a subtle educator and refined artist."[131]

In addition to reflecting an educational strategy traditionally employed by both Greeks and Romans, Horace's father's training

---

[128] The damaged state of this passage, which Philippson (1916) 444 inserted after col. 7, draws from the conjectures of Wilke (1914) and appear to be consistent with Philodemus' language and methodology in other ethical treatises. On the other hand, it should be noted that the reconstruction itself is highly problematic and that Armstrong and McOsker reject it in their forthcoming edition.

[129] See Deichgräber (1930) 48–9.

[130] Cf. Cic. *On the Nature of the Gods* 1.87–8 for criticisms of the Epicurean preference for empirical inference. De Lacy and De Lacy (1978) 206–30 discuss "logical controversies" of Epicureans, Stoics, and Skeptics.

[131] Gigante (1995) 27.

may also engage with contemporary methods of sign-inference as elucidated by Philodemus in his ethical and methodological treatises.

The use of visible examples for the purpose of moral instruction has a long history in Greek literature, especially Old Comedy,[132] but it also appears in the philosophical dialogues of Plato. The sophist Protagoras describes this very method in passing in the work that bears his name:

διδάσκοντες καὶ ἐνδεικνύμενοι ὅτι τὸ μὲν δίκαιον, τὸ δὲ ἄδικον, καὶ τόδε μὲν καλόν, τόδε αἰσχρόν, καὶ τόδε μὲν ὅσιον, τόδε δὲ ἀνόσιον, καὶ τὰ μὲν ποίει, τὰ δὲ μὴ ποίει.   (*Protagoras* 325d2–5)

By teaching and instructing them, saying that "this is just, that is unjust," and "this is admirable, that is shameless," and "this is pious, that is impious," and "do this, avoid that."

This deictic style of education or rebuke became commonplace among the Cynics and was also widely popular with later Greek comic playwrights as well as their Roman counterparts, as a passage from Terence's *Brothers* involving Demea's pedagogical tactics (414–19), which has been closely connected to Horace's father's approach, demonstrates. In his treatise *On the Education of Children*, moreover, Plutarch identifies the use of "examples" (παραδείγματα) as one of the most basic and effective methods of child-rearing,[133] which resembles Philodemus' use of the verb παραδείκνυμι in reference to the "manifestations," "proofs," or "showings" of perceptible phenomena (*On Signs*, col. 27.16–17: [τ]ὰ φα[ι]νό[μενα π]αρέδειξ[ε]; cf. col. 28.33–4: αὐτὰ τὰ φαινόμενα παρέδειξεν). With regard to the practice of Horace's father, a similar introduction of paradigms of manifest behavior may serve as the proof or basis for an inference by similarity at *Satires* 1.4(106). More specifically, his father conducts ethical investigations by inferring (*notando*) each of the vicious dispositions (*quaeque vitiorum*) by means of manifest patterns of observable behavior (*exemplis*). The verb *notare*, aside from establishing a connection to the Greco-Roman tradition of branding, whether in the genre of comedy or as practiced by the Roman censors (cf. *S.* 1.3.24: *notari*), may also mean "to infer by a sign."[134] In this way,

---

[132] Cf. Gowers (2012) 176–7 and especially Ferriss-Hill (2015) 5–7.

[133] Cf. 16c–d, which bears many similarities to Horace's father's method: Plutarch mentions "threats" (ἀπειλοῦντας), "prayers" (δεομένους), and the "fear of punishment" (φόβος τιμωρίας).

[134] *OLD* s.v. *noto* (8) lists the following: "to indicate by a sign; to be a sign or token of, mark."

one may infer the time of year by observing the stars (cf. Sen. *Ben.* 7.31.4: *notant*), just as Caesar inferred the Ides of March by means of the constellation Scorpio (Plin. *Nat.* 18.237: *notavit*), and the sun is wreathed in heat which cannot be inferred through visible signs (Lucr. 5.612: *notatus*).[135] Returning to Horace's training, inferences about hidden dispositions are made based on certain "manifestations of visible phenomena," which, as Philodemus and Plutarch demonstrate, are expressed by the Greek παραδείγματα and closely correspond to the Latin *exempla*. These phenomenal paradigms are "proofs" or "showings" of the observable symptoms and consequences that accompany particular vices, and which Philodemus identifies as being "very similar" and "common" in all victims (*On Anger*, coll. 7.26–8.8, quoted more fully above: [ὁ]μο[ιότατα] ... [κοινά]). The paradigms to which Horace's father refers, therefore, may be understood to correspond to the visible symptoms of individuals like Baius and Scetanus, who are "copies" or "patterns" (i.e. παραδείγματα or *exempla*) in the sense that their actions show them to be typical representatives of their class. On the basis of similarity, Horace's persona learns to expect (or, more accurately, to infer) that other individuals, who, like them, suffer from lust or prodigality, will invariably display the same symptoms. Again, as Philodemus explains, such an inference is based on the careful observation of phenomena, which, unless contradicted in some way by other evidence, is a true and reliable conclusion:

ἀπὸ τούτων τεκμηριοῦσθαι περὶ τῶν ἀφανῶν, μήτ' ἀπιστεῖν τοῖς δι' αὐτῶν κατὰ τὴν ὁμοιότητα παραδεικνυμένοις, ἀλλ' οὕτω π[ισ]τεύειν ὡς καὶ τοῖς ἀφ' ὧν ἡ [σημείωσι]ς. (*On Signs*, fr. 2.1–6)

[One ought not to stop with evident things] but from them make inferences about the non-apparent, and one should not mistrust the things exhibited through them by analogy but trust them just as one trusts the things from which the inference was made.

---

[135] Horace clearly associates marks (*nota*) with signs (*signa*) in reference to conventionally accepted language at *Art of Poetry* 58–9: *licuit semperque licebit | signatum praesente nota producere nomen*, "It has ever been, and ever will be, permitted to issue words stamped with the mint-mark of the day." Cf. also [Cic.] *Rhet. Her.* 4.65, where he refers to the positive moral function of *notationes*, which are descriptions of another's inner nature (*natura*) by means of clear and perceptible signs (*certis signis*), and Ter. *Brothers* 821–2: *multa in homine, Demea, | signa insunt ex quibu' coniectura facile fit*, "There are many signs in a man, Demea, based on which one may easily make inferences."

A careful inference based on similarity, then, is as trustworthy as the initial sensory data, which is presented (in the case of ethical investigations) to the keen observer by manifest behavior and consequences. Based on his frequent exposure to his father's empirical method, Horace can successfully "diagnose" avarice whenever he encounters a particular combination of "symptoms," among which are included excessive toil (*S.* 1.1.93: *labor*), universal abandonment (1.1.85: *odium*), squalor (2.2.53–69: *sordes*), envy (1.1.40: *invidia*), speechlessness (1.4.28: *stupor*), and greed (1.1.61: *cupido*).[136] In a similar fashion, individuals who suffer from a sexual addiction commonly place themselves in dangerous situations (*S.* 1.2.40: *pericla*), commit suicide (1.2.41: *se praecipitem tecto dedit*), suffer death (1.2.41–2: *flagellis | ad mortem caesus*), buy their own safety (1.2.43: *dedit hic pro corpore nummos*), ruin their reputations (1.2.61: *famam*), and undergo tremendous toil (1.2.78: *laboris*).[137] The irascible disposition is characterized by the inability to meet slight offenses with a calculated response (*S.* 1.3.78: *ponderibus modulisque*), which results in egregious acts of violence such as beatings (1.3.119: *horribili...flagello*) and executions (1.3.82: *cruce*); additionally, the irascible individual may be detected by means of physiological changes in voice and appearance (1.3.136: *rumperis et latras*). Finally, the flatterer shows signs of a vicious disposition through his social interactions with wealthy or influential figures, which include accosting them in the street (*S.* 1.9.3: *accurrit*), imitating or mimicking their usual behavior (1.9.23–5), constant and obsequious prattle (1.9.13: *garriret*), and a relentless desire to eliminate any competition for their victim's favor (1.9.48: *summosses omnis*). By having recourse

[136] Not all of the following citations are exact quotations from the *Satires*, but rather identifications, closely connected to the actual text, of the kinds of symptoms involved.

[137] Descriptions of the physical symptoms of love and their consequences abound in Latin poetry, especially in Vergil's portrayal of Dido's sufferings in *Aeneid* 4 and in many passages from Ovid's works and other elegiac poets. Also in later authors who were influenced by such depictions, for which see Apuleius' *Metamorphoses* (10.2): *pallor deformis, marcentes oculi, lassa genua, quies turbida et suspiritus cruciatus tarditate vehementior...Heu medicorum ignarae mentes, quid venae pulsus, quid coloris intemperantia, quid fatigatus anhelitus et utrimquesecus iactatae crebrior laterum mutuae vicissitudines!*, "unsightly pallor, languid eyes, weak knees, troubled sleep, and very intense sighing on account of the of the protracted torture... Alas, the unknowing minds of physicians! They cannot interpret what this means, the throbbing of veins, the changing complexion, the labored breathing, and the frequent tossing back and forth from side to side."

to the similarity method of sign inference as described above, Horace may safely conclude that such vicious behaviors will consistently accompany the presence of their corresponding dispositions in every instance and at all times. This is a method that the poet employs to a greater or lesser degree in many of his satirical observations, but above all in the introductory poems, which, aside from relying heavily on the serio-comic tradition, also reveal his frank engagement with the other ethical topics such as wealth administration, lust, and the proper management of emotions such as anger.

2

Epicurean Economic and Social Undertones of *Satires* 1.1–3

PHILODEMUS AND THE EPICUREAN DIATRIBE

The first verse of Horace's *Satires* showcases one of the most provocative and stunning openings in all of Latin literature. A loaded question bursting with energy and frustration communicates, through his persona, the poet's concerns regarding society as well as his willingness to share such thoughts with his patron Maecenas (*S.* 1.1.1: *Qui fit, Maecenas, ut nemo . . .*). These two seem to be on very good terms, given that Horace is apparently free to address his wealthy and powerful benefactor so directly and with impunity, both here as well as in *Satires* 1.3 (64: *tibi, Maecenas*).[1] The intentional directness and low register of his language reflects the informal style of discourse traditionally associated with philosophical sermons or diatribes. There has been some controversy regarding the identification of the "diatribe" as an ancient genre,[2] since, aside from a passing reference in Philodemus to "harsh censure in the writings and lectures . . . of philosophers" (*On Anger*, col. 35.33–7: ἔλεγχος ἀκριβὴς ἔν τε γραφαῖς καὶ διατριβαῖς τῶν . . . φιλοσόφων), the term does not appear to have been employed in antiquity to refer to a specific kind of literature. On the other hand, the fact that numerous philosophers employed extended, moral discourses in their writings and that whole sects came to be associated with this approach cannot be denied. If not an actual genre, then, the diatribe

---

[1] Cf. Freudenburg (2001) 21.
[2] As Moles indicates in his *OCD* article (s.v. "diatribe") and as other scholars have argued (see Sharland 2009b: 9–28 for the debate), the diatribe was first described as a genre by Usener. See also Oltramare (1926) 9–66, Kindstrand (1976) 97–9, and Indelli and Tsouna-McKirahan (1995) 53–61.

style was certainly an attractive tool for communication, criticism, or correction, and it will be worthwhile to explore briefly its characteristics within various philosophical sects, especially that of the Epicureans, before returning to *Satires* 1.1.

Perhaps the most exuberant diatribists in antiquity were the Cynics, who were rather infamous for their unbridled παρρησία, and who frequently relied on ridicule, obscene language, and harsh invective—often in public—for the purpose of making a moral point.[3] The diatribes of Cynics like Bion of Borysthenes are well known among Horatian scholars, especially since the poet seems to identify his satires with them in *Epistles* 2.2 (60: *Bioneis sermonibus*).[4] Not as familiar, however, are the less playful philosophical dialogues of the Stoics (hilariously parodied by Horace in *Satires* 2.3 and 2.7) as well as of the Epicureans, both of whom also employ the diatribe style of preaching for the sake of advancing their own ethical or philosophical doctrines.[5] Philodemus in particular takes full advantage of the diatribe's appeal in his treatise *On Anger*, in which, as David Armstrong has recently demonstrated, he acknowledges the potential of the diatribe technique and then launches into one himself. In an effort to engage with his audience more effectively Philodemus employs "a diatribic rant of his own against anger," which is "emotional, excited, incantatory and implying the loud voice and gestures of the professional reciter."[6] He vividly describes, in a strikingly colorful manner reminiscent of Cynic character portraits, the symptoms of an irascible disposition in much detail (col. 8.21–38): "flaring up" (ἐκπυρώσεως), "swelling" (διοιδή[σ]εως), "heaving of the lungs" (διάστασιν [τ]οῦ πλεύμονος), "redness" (διερεθισμοῦ), the "dreadful desire for revenge" (δεινῆς ἐπιθυμίας τοῦ μετελθεῖν), and "rapid breathing" (μετεωρότερον ἄσθμα) among others.[7] Philodemus' imitation of the Bionean style is so prominent in this and other passages of his treatises that Marcello Gigante has identified his writing style

---

[3] See Scarpat (1964) 62–9 and Kindstrand (1976) 263. A more recent study is that of Konstan (1996) 7–19.

[4] This connection was made early on by Heinze (1889).

[5] Ringeltaube (1913) 32 mentions that certain themes were so popular among diatribists that, even if they represent different traditions, the content of their attacks was often the same (*etsi nulla ratio inter eos intercedebat, eadem praeberent*). See also Moles (2007) 168.

[6] Armstrong (2014a) 105.

[7] Cf. also *On Anger*, coll. 7.6–26 and 8.20–41, for which see Armstrong (2014a) 106–7.

as more influenced by the Cynics than that of Horace: "So Bion . . . either openly or subtly leaves his mark on the works of Philodemus: indeed, perhaps some Philodemean treatises could more justly be considered Bionean than some of Horace's satires."[8] Despite the imitation, however, there is an extremely significant difference between the Cynic and Epicurean approaches to diatribe, namely, the emphasis on therapy and healing as the ultimate goals of frank criticism.

The corrective and therapeutic nature of Philodemus' style of criticism is easily detected in a technique, discussed briefly in the previous chapter, that was popular among philosophers such as Plato (*Gorg.* 471a8–d2 and 473c1–d2) and Aristotle, and figures prominently in Epicurean ethical treatises.[9] By colorfully describing the symptoms of anger, for example, Philodemus "places before the eyes" (*On Anger,* col. 3.13: τιθεὶς ἐν ὄψει; cf Arist. *Rhet.* 3.10.6: πρὸ ὀμμάτων ποιεῖν) of his audience the horrible consequences of submitting to one's rage, and as a result makes it possible to "flee more easily" (*On Anger,* col. 3.17–18: ἀποφυγεῖν ῥᾳδίως) from such a harmful indulgence. Lucretius similarly employs the diatribic style therapeutically in his lengthy criticisms of the fear of death (3.526–1094) and the consequences of erotic passion (4.1037–1287), which, rather than being pointless attacks on hot topics, are attempts to dissuade his audience from anxiety and therefore intended as helpful advice.[10] That the Cynic–Stoic tradition of pure invective was repulsive to Philodemus (and presumably to most Epicurean sympathizers, including Horace) can easily be demonstrated by his condemnation of harsh criticism for its own sake and emphasis on the importance of frankness as a therapeutic tool intended to prevent or correct moral deficiency:

δύνηται [δ'] αὐτὸς ἢ δι' ἡμῶν ἢ δι' ἄλλου τῶν σ[υ]σχολαζόντω[ν
θ]ε[ρ]απευθῆναι, μηδὲ συνεχῶς αὐτὸ ποιεῖν, μηδὲ κατὰ πάντων, μηδὲ

---

[8] Gigante (1992) 107–8: "Così Bione . . . lascia un'orma manifesta o segreta nell'opera di Filodemo: forse *Bionei sermones* possono essere considerati alcuni libri filodemei a maggior diritto che alcune satire oraziane." For some of the problems associated with claiming that specific passages from Philodemus's works, especially *On Anger,* were taken *directly* from Bion, see Ringeltaube (1913) 39.

[9] See Tsouna (2003) 243–7 and (2007) 204–9. Its application specifically within the context of therapeutic frankness may have been further developed by Zeno of Sidon and Philodemus. Schroeder (2004) 139–56 discusses the technique of "placing before the eyes" (which he calls *avocatio*) in Lucretius and Vergil.

[10] For Lucretius' exploitation of Bion and the Cynics, see Schmid (1978) 135–6. For Lucretius' use of the diatribe and satire, especially in the finale to Book 4, see Brown (1987) 137–9.

πᾶν ἁμάρτημα καὶ τὸ τυχόν, μηδ' ὧν οὐ χρὴ παρόντων, μηδὲ μετὰ
διαχύσεως, ἀλλὰ συνπαθῶ[ς] τ[ὰς ἁμαρ]τίας ὑπο[λαμβάνειν καὶ μὴ]
καθυ[βρίζειν μηδὲ λοιδορεῖ]ν (On Frank Criticism, fr. 79.1–12)

That he may be able through us or through some other of his school-
mates to be healed, and not (for the teacher) to practice correction
continually, nor against all, nor every error, even ones made by chance,
nor with people there (to listen) who ought not to be there, nor with
ridicule, but sympathetically . . . [11]

The point here is that Philodemus, as well as Lucretius and, as will
be seen presently, Horace, knows how to take advantage of the
diatribe style without becoming immersed in or even possessed by
it, like the Stoics or Cynics.[12] Indeed, it is noteworthy that Horace,
like Philodemus, also condemns this kind of παρρησία in his correspondence with Lollius Maximus in the *Epistles*:

> est huic diversum vitio vitium prope maius,
> asperitas agrestis et inconcinna gravisque,
> quae se commendat tonsa cute, dentibus atris,
> dum volt libertas dici mera veraque virtus. (*Ep.* 1.18.5–8)

There is a vice opposite of this [sc. flattery]—perhaps a greater one—a
clownish rudeness, awkward and offensive, which commends itself by
scraped skin and black teeth, while fain to pass for simple candor and
pure virtue.

The mention of "importunate rudeness" (*asperitas inconcinna*) when
blurting out offensive remarks in this poem establishes a link to
the bitter frankness of "biting Cynics" in *Epistles* 1.17 (18: *mordacem
Cynicum*), whom Horace similarly criticizes as "importunate" and
"inept" (29: *inconcinnus*, 32: *ineptus*). Contrary to the boorish
approach of Cynics like Bion, then, in his "diatribe satires" Horace
incorporates, like Philodemus and Lucretius, the effectiveness of the
diatribe but without losing sight of his chief objective, which is to offer
Maecenas and his reading circle entertaining but salubrious advice on
various moral issues including wealth administration, sexual appetite,

---

[11] Cf. also Philodemus' specific references to the Cynics at *On Frank Criticism*, col.
3b.4–5 (κυνώδη) and fr. 73.12–13 (κυνι[κω]τέραν).
[12] As Erler (2011) 14–28 clearly shows, the Epicurean practice of borrowing
language and techniques (like παρρησία) from other philosophical traditions so long
as they are helpful goes back to Epicurus himself, and Philodemus also sanctions this
practice in *On Property Management* (col. 27.12–18).

and mutual forbearance.[13] Horace's Epicurean approach to frank criticism in the introductory satires will be discussed in more detail after a fuller consideration of the nature of his advice concerning wealth in *Satires* 1.1 and its connection to Philodemus' economic treatises.

EPICUREAN ECONOMICS IN *SATIRES* 1.1

Horace's introductory address to his patron in *Satires* 1.1 establishes the literary setting of this poem as an informal conversation between friends who, in a manner perfectly consistent with Epicurean tradition, have separated from society in order to examine the causes of the general public's discontentment. The informal language his persona uses suggests, as Barbara Gold notes, that Maecenas is "a friend who is interested in philosophical disquisitions on contentment and greed and is the suitable recipient of a diatribe on these subjects."[14] Contrary to the Cynic tradition of public invective through street preaching, however, the opening lines of *Satires* 1.1 frame this "diatribe" within the context of a peaceful and private withdrawal:

> Qui fit, Maecenas, ut nemo, quam sibi sortem
> seu ratio dederit seu fors obiecerit, illa
> contentus vivat, laudet diversa sequentis?   (*S.* 1.1.1–3)

> How comes it, Maecenas, that no man living is content with the lot
> which either his choice has given him, or chance has thrown in his way,
> but each has praise for those who follow other paths?

The inclusion of the expression *qui fit* and the unpoetic *nemo* undoubtedly reflects Horatian satire's chatty tone,[15] but it also communicates the notion of intimacy, as if the poet has just granted his readers exclusive access to a very private conversation. This is a "privileged group of two, who are not quite included with the rest of mankind,"[16] and a kind of "splendid isolation from the rest of

---

[13] Cf. Armstrong (2014a) 113–14.

[14] Gold (1992) 164. Other primary recipients would include the poet's close friends, as he reveals at the end of *Satires* 1.10.

[15] See Lejay and Plessis (1915) 280, Axelson (1945) 76, and Gowers (2012) 62. Freudenburg (1993) 11 describes this language as consistent with "the popular moralist of Greek diatribe."

[16] Gold (1992) 168.

humanity,"[17] which resembles Lucretius' description of the temples of wisdom at the beginning of Book 2 of his didactic epic:

> sed nil dulcius est, bene quam munita tenere
> edita doctrina sapientum templa serena,
> despicere unde queas alios passimque videre
> errare atque viam palantis quaerere vitae,
> certare ingenio, contendere nobilitate,
> noctes atque dies niti praestante labore
> ad summas emergere opes rerumque potiri.   (2.7–13)

But nothing is sweeter than to possess towering and peaceful sanctuaries that are well fortified by the teachings of wise men. From here you may look down upon others and behold them far and wide, wandering abroad and seeking the path of life, striving with their wits and fighting for precedence, laboring night and day with surpassing toil to reach the height of wealth and to lay hold of power.

Both Lucretius and Horace intend to impart to their respective listeners advice that is not only philosophical and moral in nature, but also intended—or at least portrayed as intended—for their ears alone. One may contrast the power and authority of Horatian verse to communicate public *consilia* in the "Roman Odes" (*Odes* 3.1–6) with his persona's private *consilia* in the *Satires* (cf. *S.* 1.4.133: *consilium proprium* and 1.6.130: *me consolor*), which are shared directly with his patron in an intimate setting (cf. *S.* 1.6.18: *nos*). And although Horace's target audience in this poem extends beyond Maecenas to include intimate friends like Vergil, who would have been present at private recitations as suggested at *Satires* 1.10 (81–90), as well as the imaginary and avaricious interlocutor within the poem, it is evident that in the introductory satires his patron is the primary addressee.[18] Consequently, Maecenas is also the main beneficiary of his client's frank advice which, in the spirit of Epicurean patronage, is communicated to a receptive patron and within the context of a peaceful withdrawal from the anxieties of life.

This exclusive setting in *Satires* 1.1 between two friends, one of whom casually shares moral advice concerning the rest of humanity with his receptive patron, reflects in many ways Philodemus' description in *On*

---

[17] Gowers (2012) 59.
[18] For a more detailed discussion of Horace's audience in *Satires* 1.1, see especially Gold (1992) 161–71 and Hicks (2013) 119–20.

Property Management of the ideal economic state. One will recall that
the best source of income for an Epicurean sage is to receive "gratitude"—including financial benefits, no doubt—from an attentive and
grateful listener, just as the Master himself did:

> πρῶτον δὲ καὶ κάλλιστον ἀπὸ λόγων φιλο[σό]φων ἀνδράσιν δεκτικοῖς
> μεταδιδομέν[ων] ἀντιμεταλαμβάνειν εὐχάριστο[ν ἅμ]α μετὰ σεβασμοῦ
> παντ[ός], ὡς ἐγένετ᾽ Ἐπικο[ύ]ρωι.
>
> (*On Property Management*, col. 23.23–30)

It is superior and better by far to receive gratitude and respect in return
for wise discussions shared with receptive men, which is what happened
to Epicurus.

The context of this passage is, of course, related to Philodemus'
description of acceptable sources of income, the best of which he
identifies with philosophical patronage in accordance with Epicurus'
conviction that the wise man will make money but from wisdom alone
(DL 10.121b). The source of this financial "gratitude" is the receptive
patron, who welcomes critical observations that are "free from strife"
(*On Property Management*, col. 23.31: ἀφιλο[ν]ε[ί]κων) as opposed to
the "contentious" or "slandering" speeches expected from a typical
Cynic (col. 23.32–4: διὰ σοφ[ιστι]κῶν καὶ ἀγωνιστι[κ]ῶν). Regarding
these recommendations, one may reasonably consider Horace's critical
but ultimately well-intentioned presentation to Maecenas as an expression of Philodemus' "wise discussions" (λόγων φιλο[σό]φων), which
occur among friends and in isolation (cf. col. 23.15–16: μετὰ φίλων
ἀναχώρησιν). Of course, Horace's bluntness and his preference for
brevity owes much to the literary standards of Callimachus, who
famously championed the cause of γένος λεπτόν or, as Horace
puts it in *Odes* 2.16, "the slight inspiration of a Greek Muse" (38:
spiritum Graiae tenuem Camenae).[19] Additionally, however, it may
engage with the Epicurean tradition of short but useful instruction, as
in the *Principal Doctrines* and *Vatican Sayings*, and with Philodemus'
words in *On Property Management* regarding how some critics may
complain about the conciseness of his advice on a summarily useful
subject (col. 27.35–9): ἀ[λλ]ὰ δὴ καὶ [πι]θανώτερος ἂν [εἶ]ναι δόξ[ει]εν ὁ
παντελῶ[ς ὀ]λίγα φῆσ[ων] ἡμᾶς περὶ πρά[γ]ματος μ[ε]ιζόνως ὠφελή
[σ]οντος, "But that one would seem to have a more plausible argument,
who will say that on a whole we say very little about a subject that is of

---

[19] For this connection, see especially Mette (1961) 136–9.

greater benefit" (cf. *Art of Poetry* 2.2.335–6). What results is a setting in which Horace as pithy moralist and far removed from society as well as from the standards of older poets (similar to Callimachus in *Epigrams* 28.1–4, to which cf. *Odes* 1.1.30–2), imparts critical but therapeutic advice to his receptive patron, who in turn rewards his client-friend with financial benefits. Certainly, what we do *not* have here is Horace on a street corner shouting at passers-by, or "stopping his man-in-the-street, calling attention to himself, drawing a crowd."[20] This would be to place Horace in the same category as Cynic moralists, whom Cicero, like the poet, blames for their hypercritical and intentionally public tirades: *solent quocumque in loco, quoscumque inter homines visum est, de rebus aut difficillimis aut non necessariis argutissime disputare*, "They are accustomed to engage in strenuous arguments over the most inappropriate or trivial matters in all places and among anyone who seems suitable" (*Orat.* 2.18). Rather than joining in wholeheartedly with such a boorish lot, in *Satires* 1.1 Horace merely employs Cynic tradition as "flare" (cf. *S.* 1.1.25: *crustula*). Such an effect, which is undoubtedly an essential component of his poetry, serves to lighten the *Satires*' moralizing tone without trivializing or overshadowing their positive content.

From the point of view of two detached observers, then, Horace leads Maecenas through a philosophical investigation of the causes motivating people's choices and avoidances, which is a skill his father attributes to the instruction of an unnamed sage in *Satires* 1.4 (115: *sapiens*). The poet's scientific method is a reflection of his upbringing as programmatically described in the same poem,[21] and which involves close observation of the manifest behavior of generic examples of moral deficiency (*S.* 1.4.106: *exemplis vitiorum*; cf. 1.1.13: *cetera de genere hoc*).[22] In the case of *Satires* 1.1, Horace's persona's preliminary observation of the perceptible behavior and consequences of vice resembles the methodological approach of Philodemus in treatises like *On Anger*, which combines descriptions of the irascible disposition of a straw man with frank criticism regarding

---

[20] Freudenburg (1993) 12.

[21] See Schrijvers (1993) 59, Oliensis (1998) 25, and Gowers (2003) 70–1.

[22] Gowers (2012) 66, commenting on the significance of *genere hoc*: "draws attention not just to the type of examples used and rejected here but also to the unnamed genre that contains them." Cf. also Rudd (1966) 15: "[T]his poetry...is concerned entirely with the behavior of the individual in society." Horace's upbringing will be discussed in the next chapter.

how to overcome destructive anger. As mentioned earlier, both authors consciously imitate the Cynics' flamboyant technique for the sake of its shocking effectiveness, which Epicureans generally considered useful for communicating ethical truths.[23] Horace's incorporation of this technique becomes apparent immediately following the introductory address, as he launches into a popular theme of moral philosophy identified as μεμψιμοιρία or "the blaming of one's fortune,"[24] which, according to the evidence, was extremely popular among Cynics like Bion:

> "o fortunati mercatores" gravis annis
> miles ait, multo iam fractus membra labore;
> contra mercator navim iactantibus Austris:
> "militia est potior. quid enim? concurritur: horae
> momento cita mors venit aut victoria laeta."
> agricolam laudat iuris legumque peritus,
> sub galli cantum consultor ubi ostia pulsat;
> ille, datis vadibus qui rure extractus in urbem est,
> solos felicis viventis clamat in urbe.   (*S.* 1.1.4–12)

"O happy traders!" cries the soldier, as he feels the weight of the years, his frame now shattered with hard service. On the other hand, when southern gales toss the ship, the trader cries: "A soldier's life is better. Do you ask why? There is the battle clash, and in a moment of time comes speedy death or joyous victory." One learned in law and statutes has praise for the farmer, when towards cockcrow a client comes knocking at his door. The man yonder, who has given surety and is dragged into town from the country, cries that they only are happy who live in town.

Aside from the fragmentary evidence preserved by Teles, the character portrait of Theophrastus (*Char.* 17), passages from Cicero (*On Duties* 1.120, which involves approval of a *mutatio institutorum* when done carefully and for good reason) and Lucretius (3.1060–7), all of which likely influenced Horace's description, no particularly outstanding specimen of μεμψιμοιρία has survived from early antiquity.[25]

---

[23] For more on this connection, see Gigante and Indelli (1978) 124–31, Indelli (1988) 25, Schmid (1978) 135, and Gigante (1992) 107–8.

[24] Scholarship concerning the role of μεμψιμοιρία in *Satires* 1.1 is extensive: see e.g. Heinze (1889) 15–17, Fraenkel (1957) 90–7, Rudd (1966) 13–21, Herter (1970) 330–3, Fiske (1971) 219–28, Freudenburg (1993) 11–16, and Beck (2003) in general.

[25] For evidence concerning the Cynics, see Kindstrand (1976) F16A and Hense (1969) 9–10. Later examples are the seventeenth pseudo-Hippocratic letter and a

While the comparison of antithetical professions at the outset of *Satires* 1.1 is probably Cynic,[26] Horace's persona's clear emphasis on the mental and physical disturbances that result from their restlessness is suggestively Epicurean.[27] It bears a noteworthy resemblance, for instance, to the Lucretian passage cited above, but worth quoting here:

> exit saepe foras magnis ex aedibus ille,
> esse domi quem pertaesumst, subitoque revertit,
> quippe foris nilo melius qui sentiat esse.
> currit agens mannos ad villam praecipitanter,
> auxilium tectis quasi ferre ardentibus instans;
> oscitat extemplo, tetigit cum limina villae,
> aut abit in somnum gravis atque oblivia quaerit,
> aut etiam properans urbem petit atque revisit. (3.1060–7)

The man who is thoroughly tired of being at home goes out of his huge mansion and then, suddenly, returns home because he feels that it is no better to be abroad. Another man rushes headlong into town, driving his Gallic steeds as though bringing water to a house on fire; then, after his arrival, he immediately yawns or falls into a deep sleep or seeks to forget everything, or else makes haste to go back and see the city again.

Here, as in the opening passage from *Satires* 1.1, the author has borrowed from Cynic tradition in order to make an important Epicurean point regarding practical virtue. This point is that the unnecessary fear of death or poverty is exacerbated by the endless toil to overcome it, whereas only a proper understanding of the limits of nature can lead to tranquility of body and mind.[28] In Horace's satire, this is similarly communicated by the erratic behavior of individuals whose dissatisfaction breeds envy and results in the constant transgression of both natural (*S.* 1.1.6: *navim, Austris*; cf. *Odes* 1.3.9–26) and social boundaries (*S.* 1.1.9: *agricolam, legumque peritus*). Their anxiety contrasts starkly with the peace and *otium* associated with the author's "Epicurean day" as described in *Satires* 1.6

---

passage from the third-century AD sophist Maximus of Tyre, for which see Kiessling-Heinze (1910) 5 and Lejay (1966) 7–8.

[26] Heinze (1889) 17 considers Bion as the most likely influence on Horace, while Fiske (1971) 220–1 adds to the list the fragmentary evidence from Phoinix of Colophon, for which see Gerhard (1909) 4–7. Wimmel (1962) 12 is more cautious, agreeing that Horace's pairing of lives draws from an older source but that "there is no detectable source for this motif" ("es für dies Motiv keine Quellenvermutungen gäbe").

[27] Armstrong (2014a) 113.   [28] Cf. Juv. 10.356 and 14.316–19.

(111–31) and his poetic contentment as expressed in the priamel of
Odes 1.1.[29] Furthermore, on more than one occasion Horace emphatically calls himself "content" (e.g., *S.* 1.6.96: *contentus*), which is a
quality Cicero describes as distinctively Epicurean (*On Ends* 1.44–5):
ut sapiens solum, amputata circumcisaque inanitate omni et errore,
naturae finibus contentus sine aegritudine possit et sine metu vivere,
"And so only the wise man, after he has cut away and pruned all
vanity and error, can possibly live untroubled by sorrow and by fear,
content within the limits of nature." In contrast to this (cf. *S.* 1.1–3:
nemo . . . contentus vivat), the immense toil that the soldier and
farmer undergo preclude any possible enjoyment of bodily repose
(ἀπονία), while the constant anxiety that plagues the merchant and
politician render impossible the attainment of tranquility (ἀταραξία).
As Horace indicates a few lines later, the irrational willingness of these
individuals to endure such excessive *labor* only to blame their fortunes
afterwards is ultimately motivated not only by envy, but by their
underlying desire to accumulate great wealth.

In closely uniting discontentment and avarice as joint causes of the
toil associated with certain sources of income, Horace is following a
philosophical tradition of which Philodemus is an important part.
The connection between these two is worth exploring briefly, especially since many scholars have thought that the seemingly rough
transition from discontentment to avarice is evidence that Horace
had spliced these themes from two separate sources. Richard Heinze,
for example, uses the phrase *diversa componi* to refer to what he views
as an artificial union, Niall Rudd notes the "informal aspect" of *Satires*
1.1, and G. C. Fiske mentions Horace's "partially successful attempt"
to fuse the two themes.[30] This debate continues to the present day,
with a number of scholars recognizing that Horace was most likely
drawing from a single philosophical tradition according to which
these themes were closely related.[31] This tradition includes Theophrastus' sketch of the typical μεμψίμοιρος in his collection of moral

[29] For the relationship between the openings of *Satires* 1.1 and *Odes* 1.1, see the
contrasting opinions of Radermacher (1920–1) 148–51 and Wimmel (1962) 11–17.
[30] Heinze (1889) 15, Rudd (1966) 13, Fiske (1971) 219.
[31] See Fraenkel (1957) 92–5, Wimmel (1962) 11–16, Armstrong (1964) 88, Herter
(1970) 340–2, Brown (1993) 89, Dufallo (2000) 579–90, and especially Beck (2003),
whose extended introduction provides a detailed and useful summary of the debate
(with bibliography). Hubbard (1981) 305–21 argues for unity based on the poem's
"rhetorical mode."

essays, which implicitly identifies greed as the underlying cause of grumbling: the discovery of a coin, for instance, does not satisfy the desire for treasure (*Char.* 17.5: θησαυρόν).

The role of greed with regard to discontentment is also suggested by Bion, who warns against "desiring" the lot of others: μὴ οὖν βούλου δευτερολόγος ὢν τὸ πρωτολόγου πρόσωπον, "Do not, therefore, desire to be the star when you are but a supporting actor."[32] In her study of Philodemean ethics Voula Tsouna briefly discusses the damaged treatise PHerc. 1678, possibly entitled *On Envy* and most likely authored by Philodemus, in which the causes of envy are linked to the obsession with external goods such as wealth:

> Philodemus' recommendations and methods of therapy focus on the fact that both envy and malicious joy derive in part from the excessive value that people afflicted by them ascribe to external goods and evils. The envious person feels envy of the wealth, power, beauty, etc., of his neighbour and, on account of these goods, considers his neighbour more fortunate than himself.[33]

Such a conclusion, which is based on false reasoning and a lack of understanding regarding the requirements of nature, causes individuals "intense suffering" (*On Envy*, fr. 12.1: μάλιστα [πά]θειν) because of "self-inflicted pain" (5: λυπού[μενο]ι) as a result of "evil they have drawn to themselves" (4–5: ἐφ' αὑτοὺς [τ]ὸ [κα]κὸν ἕλκοντε[ς]), which Aristotle also mentions in connection with envy (*Nic. Eth.* 1108b5: λυπεῖται).[34] The truth, it seems, is that one will always encounter another who is more successful or has discovered an easier way to amass wealth, as Horace states in *Satires* 1.1.113: *sic festinanti semper locupletior obstat*, "in such a race there is ever a richer man in your way."[35] The reason for envy, then, is the painful and misguided realization that others are more efficient at acquiring wealth and thus better able to live securely, which points to avarice and fear of poverty as underlying causes.

In all of his ethical treatises Philodemus emphatically denounces vice, especially avarice, as an irrational evil (cf. *On Envy*, fr. 16.1:

---

[32] Kindstrand (1976) F16A.   [33] Tsouna (2007) 124.
[34] Cf. Arist. *Eud. Eth.* 1233b20 (τὸ λυπεῖσθαι) and Kindstrand (1976) F47A–48 on Bion and envy.
[35] Cf. S. 1.1.38–40 and Armstrong (1964) 88. A similar connection is made in Hippoc. [*Ep.*] 17.8: καὶ τούτων πάντων αἰτίη φιλαργυρίη, "Of all this [suffering], greed is the cause."

φιλαργυρίας δό[ξα] καί [τινων ὁμ]οίων ἄλογον τ[ίθησι] κακόν, "the reputation for avarice and similar things creates an irrational evil"), which in the context of wealth acquisition results in excessive toil that, as Horace's malcontents clearly demonstrate, violates the pleasure calculus. A case in point is the poet's description in *Odes* 1.1 of the restless *mercator*, whose willingness to undergo extreme danger (15: *luctantem Icariis fluctibus Africum*; cf. *S.* 1.1.6) originates in his refusal to live modestly (*Odes* 1.1.18: *indocilis pauperiem pati*). In other words, he is willing to experience fear (16: *metuens*) in order to become wealthy, but, as *Satires* 1.1 shows, if military service appears to offer similar wealth while involving less risks then he immediately feels the sting of envy and declares "military life is better!" (7: *militia est potior*). Neither his constant comparisons with others nor his insatiable desire for wealth will ever allow him to escape intense suffering, which of course he experiences at the expense of mental and physical repose. One may compare all this to Horace's subsequent description in this poem of certain individuals' irrational willingness to submit to extreme labor, even to the point of risking their lives, for the sake of acquiring wealth:

> ille gravem duro terram qui vertit aratro,
> perfidus hic caupo, miles nautaeque, per omne
> audaces mare qui currunt, hac mente laborem
> sese ferre, senes ut in otia tuta recedant,
> aiunt, cum sibi sint congesta cibaria.   (*S.* 1.1.28–32)

> That farmer, who with tough plough turns up the heavy soil, the lying innkeeper, the soldier, the sailors who boldly scour every sea, all say that they bear toil with this in view, that when old they may retire into secure ease, once they have piled up their provisions.

The busyness conveyed by this action-packed description, which is summed up by the phrase *laborem ferre*, may reflect the restless toil and pursuit of riches designated by the Greeks as πολυπραγμοσύνη. Aristotle associates continuous toil (διατριβή) with accumulating limitless wealth in his *Politics* (1258a1–15), and the same connection also appears in Teles' report of Bion: ἢ πάλιν οὐχ ὁρᾷς διότι οἱ μὲν πλούσιοι πλείω πράττοντες κωλύονται τοῦ σχολάζειν, "Or don't you see that the rich, on account of being overactive, are prevented from enjoying leisure?"[36] Aside from engaging with these sources, in the

---

[36] Fiske (1971) 221–2.

above passage Horace is likely drawing from the economic advice of Philodemus, who sanctions the gaining of wealth provided that it is not accompanied by excessive toil or anxiety:

[τ]ῶι γὰρ μὴ λυ[πε]ῖσθαι τ[ῶι] παραπολλυμέν[ωι] μηδὲ διὰ τὴν ἄκρατον σ[που]δὴν περὶ τὸ πλέον καὶ το[ὕλαττ]ον ὑφ' αὑ[τ]οῦ ζητρί[οις τισὶ]ν ἐ[γκ]εῖσθαι, τούτω[ι γ'] ὀ[ρ]θῶς οἰκο[νο]μεῖσθαι νομίζω τὸν πλοῦ[τ]ον· ὁ [γ]ὰρ κατὰ τὴ[ν κτῆ]σ[ι]ν π[όν]ος [κἂν] τῶι προ[σφορ]ὰν ἕλκειν ἑαυ[τῷ]³⁷ γίνετ[αι] κἂν τῶι περὶ τῶν ἐλαττ[ωμάτ]ων ἀγωνιᾶν ὡς εὐθέ[ως εἰ]ς ἀλγηδόν[α κ]α[τ]αστησόντων ἢ παροῦσαν ἢ προσδοκωμένην.

(On Property Management, col. 14.23–37)

For this is what I consider the proper administration of wealth to be: not to be grieved at the loss of revenue nor trapping oneself on treadmills because of the unconquerable zeal regarding profit and loss. For the toil involved in acquiring wealth involves increasing one's profit and agonizing over losses that will quickly result in pains, either present or expected.

Philodemus' observation is simple: the potential "toil" (πόνος) involved in wealth acquisition must not be more than the ultimate pleasure derived from it. Furthermore, unlike the individuals in Horace's itemized descriptions, whose broken limbs, calloused hands, and constant fear of death are the direct result of an active pursuit of wealth (cf. S. 1.1.38: quaesitis and 92: quaerendi), the sage economist is not obsessed with increasing profits at the expense of physical and mental health. Rather than become a slave to money, the Epicurean should passively "accept more wealth whenever it comes easily and without harm, but should not suffer on account of it . . ." (On Property Management coll. 16.44–17.2: τὸ [δὲ π]λεῖον, ἂ[ν ἀ]βλ[α]βῶς καὶ [εὐ]πόρως γίνηται, δεκτέ[ον, τὸ] δὲ κακοπαθ[ε]ῖν [κατ' α]ὑτὸ τοῦτο μή).³⁸

At the heart of this frenzied race for wealth is, according to Philodemus in On Choices and Avoidances, a fundamental misunderstanding of desires, which happens when people regard unnecessary and unnatural desires as the most necessary (col. 5.4–14).³⁹ Among these empty desires are those for "illustrious reputations, overabundant

---

³⁷ This is the reading in Tsouna's 2012 edition, whereas Jensen (1907) has πρὸ[s βί]αν ἕλκειν ἑαυ[τὸν] ("dragging oneself by force").

³⁸ Asmis (2004) 159: "Philodemus emphasizes that the rich person must not grab; he accepts." For the problems regarding this damaged passage, see Tsouna (2012) 96.

³⁹ See Lejay (1966) 3–4.

wealth, and such luxuries" (5.15–17: καὶ λαμπρᾶς δόξης καὶ π[ε]ριουσίας
ὑπεραγούσης καὶ τ[ρυ]φῶν τοιούτων), and the effort to acquire such
things generally results in more pain than pleasure. That is to say,
Philodemus recommends the pleasure calculus be applied to every
decision, especially economic ones:

> τοῦτο γὰρ δε[ῖ] καὶ ποεῖν τὴν χρείαν ἄλυπον καὶ τὸ διὰ ταύτης τέρπον
> ἀκέραιον τὸ μὴ προσεῖναι τῆι πλούτου κτήσει τοῖς σοφοῖς φροντίδα
> βαρεῖαν, πῶς δυνήσεται σώζεσθαι, μη[δ'] ὅταν οἱ σφαλερώ[τ]ατοι
> κ[αιρ]οὶ καθεστήκωσι[ν]·   (*On Property Management*, col. 15.37–45)

This is also necessary: to enjoy revenue without pain and make sure that
the pleasure derived from this revenue is pure and that its acquisition
does not render to the sage profound anxiety regarding how he will
preserve it or when difficult times will arrive.

In light of this advice, Horace's characters' pursuit of "leisure"
(*S.* 1.1.31: *otia*) by means of intense pain and prolonged suffering seems
all the more irrational. The Stoic and Epicurean association of vice
with madness seems to have left its mark on later authors like
Plutarch, who in his treatise *On Desire for Wealth* describes love of
money as "madness" (524 f.: μανικόν).[40] As mentioned already, such a
view is foundational in the works of Philodemus, in which references
to the irrationality of vice are ubiquitous: they occur in his treatments
of arrogance (*On Arrogance*, col. 16.15–27) anger (*On Anger*, col.
26.4–7), and economics (*On Property Management*, col. 14.23–30,
quoted above). All of these passages involve descriptions of great pain
caused by false opinions or, in the case of property management,
overwhelming toil, and it is possible that Horace, in a spirit of irony,
has deliberately constructed the introductory scenes of *Satires* 1.1 as
comic inversions of the Epicurean calculus with regard to wealth
administration.[41] This may be further confirmed by the poet's surprisingly negative description of the toil involved in agricultural
work, which, judging by Cicero's evaluation in *On Duties* (1.151)
and Livy's famous portrait of Cincinnatus (3.26.8–11), was traditionally accepted by Romans as perhaps the noblest source of income. For
Horace, however, it is inherently toilsome: the farmer's turning the

[40] Cf. Hippoc. [*Ep.*] 17.5: τίς ἡ κενὴ σπουδὴ καὶ ἀλόγιστος μηδὲν μανίης διαφέρουσα,
"What is this empty and irrational passion, no different from madness?."
[41] Gowers (2012) 64: "This looks more like a satire on human irrationality and the
ironies of *plus ça change* than deliberately incompetent logic on Horace's part."

weighty earth (S. 1.1.28: *gravem terram*) with a hard plough (28: *duro* . . . *aratro*) is strenuous labor, as the carefully chosen vocabulary, the rather convoluted interlocking word order and the ponderous succession of three spondees powerfully communicate. His criticism might have been influenced by a similar evaluation of Philodemus, who, in addition to condemning emphatically the active pursuit of wealth through military service (*On Property Management*, col. 22.17–28: πορισμὸν . . . δορίκτητον; cf. S. 1.1.29: *miles*) and political office (coll. 22.28–23.1: τοὺς πο[λ]ιτικούς; cf. S. 1.1.9: *legum peritus*), likewise rejects agricultural labor on the part of the property-owner (col. 23.8: γεωργο[ῦν]τ᾽ αὐτόν; cf. S. 1.1.9: *agricolam*) as wretched on account of the many pains it involves, which preclude the attainment of leisurely retirement (col. 23.15–16: ἀναχώρησιν εὔσχολον; cf. S. 1.1.31: *otia recedant*).[42]

Through his moralizing persona Horace subsequently compares the masses' obsession with accumulating wealth to the industrious ant, which, along with addressing issues related to Epicurean economic theory, also serves as an entertaining transition to the important topic of wealth limitation. According to Epicurus, and as discussed in the previous chapter, the proper administration of wealth is characterized by forethought and implies that the sage will not beg like a Cynic (DL 10.119: οὐδὲ κυνιεῖν . . . οὐδὲ πτωχεύσειν) but rather plan ahead (DL 10.120a: προνοήσεσθαι καὶ τοῦ μέλλοντος).[43] The same issue is dealt with by Philodemus, who in both of his economic

---

[42] See Laurenti (1973) 154–64, Tsouna (2007) 188–91, and Asmis (2004) 168–70 for these passages. According to Teles (Hense 1969: 42), Diogenes describes how people wish to grow up, but, as soon as they are grown, complain about having to engage in military service and politics (but no mention of agriculture), which prevent them from enjoying the leisure (σχολάσαι) they had taken for granted as youths. It is possible that, like Philodemus, Zeno of Citium rejected agriculture as an acceptable source of income, although positive evidence for this is restricted to an ambiguous line from Stobaeus (= SVF 1.312). Chrysippus omits agriculture from his list of ways of acquiring money in *On Vices*, for which see Natali (1995) 122–3. Cf. also Hippoc. [*Ep.*] 17.5, which includes a short description of farming as inherently toilsome: ἄλλοι δὲ τῶν περὶ γεωργίην ἀσχοληθέντων, "some [laugh] at those who practice [lit. have been deprived of leisure with regard to] farming." This last source betrays the influence of Epicureanism in various passages (e.g., the mention of ἀταραξία at 12 and 17.7, the atomic swerve at 17.7, and the implication that perception alone is sufficient for knowledge at 17.7). Like Philodemus, moreover, the author of this letter rejects mining from slave labor and horse-breeding as acceptable sources of income (17.5; cf. *On Property Management*, col. 23.1–7).

[43] See Asmis (2004) 148, Gigante (1992) 29–36, and Castaldi (1928) 291.

treatises condemns the Cynics' rejection of all possessions and their practice of begging daily as involving much "anxiety and torment" (*On Property Management*, col. 13.32–3: καὶ φροντίδ[α]ς καὶ [ἀγ]ωνίας), both of which cause much pain.[44] Instead, the sage economist recognizes the importance of forethought, as Philodemus explains:

> δεῖ δὲ τὸν μέλλοντα καὶ συνάξειν τι καὶ τὸ συναχθὲν φυλάξειν μὴ 'τὸ παρὸν
> εὖ ποιεῖν', κατ' Ἐπίχαρμον, οὐ μόνον δαπάνης ἀλλὰ καὶ τοῦ προφανέντος
> κέρδους ἁρπαστικὸν γινόμενον, προνοεῖν δὲ καὶ τοῦ μέλλοντος·
>
> (*On Property Management* col. 25.4–12)

And it is necessary to gather something as provision and to preserve what has been gathered ("lest one should live well for the moment," as Epicharmus says), and, making acquisitions not only with a mind towards actual expenses but also foreseeable profits, to be mindful of the future.

The importance of forethought and the recognition that wealth acquisition, even if accompanied by some toil, is preferable to mendicancy is communicated by Horace's *exemplum* from fable,[45] which emphasizes the ant's industry and prudence:

> sicut
> parvola—nam exemplo est—magni formica laboris
> ore trahit quodcumque potest atque addit acervo
> quem struit, haud ignara ac non incauta futuri. (*S.* 1.32–5)

Even as the tiny, hard-working ant (for she is their model) drags all she can with her mouth, and adds it to the heap she is building, because she is not unaware and not heedless of the morrow.

By introducing an entertaining fable for pedagogical purposes Horace is also tapping into another tradition that was popular among the Cynics, namely, the use of "sweeteners" in order to make critical observations more palatable. Diogenes, for example, preached extreme asceticism in a comic manner, which he compared to medicinal honey, while

---

[44] A longer discussion occurs at *On Property Management*, coll. 12.5–17.2. See Tsouna (2007) 177–80, Balch (2004) 184–6, Asmis (2004) 149–61, and Laurenti (1973) 97–149.

[45] Cf. the Aesopic version (Perry 373). Marchesi (2005) 310 (n. 11) notes, however, that the ant's laboriousness was so common in antiquity that it is difficult to connect Horace's passage specifically to Aesop. For fables as rhetorical and moral *exempla*, see Holzberg (2002) 1–38, who does not include the above passage in his list of Horace's references to fables (p. 32). For their role in Roman education, see Bonner (1977) 254–6, who mentions their popularity among children.

Bion reputedly stated that the only way to please the vulgar masses is to "transform oneself into a honeyed cake" (πλακοῦντα γενόμενον).[46] This awareness of the crowd-pleasing effect of entertaining language, which is communicated in Horace's earlier simile about "cookies" as incentives for learning (S. 1.25–6: *crustula*), is also prominent in Lucretius' famous description of the "Muses' honey" (1.936–8), as well as in Philodemus' colorful depictions of vice in treatises like *On Anger*. And although all three authors employ this technique in accordance with the conventions of their respective genres, they do so primarily for the purpose of transmitting healthy advice within the context of a unified, Epicurean understanding of ethics.

Translating the Greek epithet πολύμοχθος (cf. ps.-Phocyl. 170), Horace connects the ant to his previous characters by means of her "great labor," which she undergoes for the sake of financial stability.[47] In contrast to their restlessness and obsession with gain, however, the ant's toil is favorably described in terms of reserved caution (S. 1.1.35: *non incauta*) and passive awareness (35: *haud ignara*), which motivate her to plan for the future.[48] A similar description involving Horace's enjoyment of stores in accordance with moderation occurs in *Epistles* 2.2 (190–1: *utar et ex modico, quantum res poscet, acervo, | tollam*, "I shall use and from my modest heap take what need requires"), to which may be added Ofellus' approval of the wise man's economic prudence through the expression *metuens futuri* in *Satires* 2.2(110).[49] Unlike the shameless dog, whom the Cynics consider a pristine example of how to live according to nature,[50] Horace's persona and the ant live by calculated forethought and enjoy the benefits of their toil, just as the sage economist is "not unaware of the toil involved in such

[46] See Oltramare (1926) 15 and Kindstrand (1976) F18 respectively.
[47] For the ant as negatively characterized for its love of gain, see Gerhard (1909) 27 and Laurenti (1973) 103.
[48] See Wimmel (1962) 15–16 and Rudd (1966) 29. In his attack on women and their economic imprudence, Juvenal makes a reference to the ant in connection with men (6.360–2).
[49] Cf. Verg. G. 1.185–186, according to which the pesky ant is motivated by fear: *populatque ingentem farris acervum | curculio atque inopi metuens formica senectae*, "And the weevil ravages a huge heap of grain, or the ant, fearing a lack of resources in old age." But cf. 4.402–3. This kind of "fear," however, appears to be healthy and so different from the irrational fear of death as famously described in *Odes* 1.11 (1–2): *Tu ne quaesieris, scire nefas, quem mihi, quem tibi | finem di dederint, Leuconoe*, "Do not ask, Leuconoe, what kind of death the gods have assign to you or to me, for it is forbidden to know."
[50] See Gerhard (1909) 23–4, Oltramare (1926) 49 and 145, and Fiske (1971) 223.

possessions, nor of the enjoyment that comes from it" (*On Property Management*, coll. 18.45–19.1: οὔτε γὰρ ὁ πόνος ὁ καθ' ὁποιανοῦν κτῆσιν [ἄ]δηλος αὐτῷ[ι] δῆλον ὡς οὔθ' ἡ τέρψις ἡ διὰ τ[ὴν κτῆσι]ν). Along with rejecting Cynic mendicancy, which Horace scorns in *Epistles* 1.17 (13–32), in his economic treatise Philodemus also applies to the sage a measure of wealth (cf. *On Property Management*, col. 12.18–19), which, in accordance with a similar doctrine expressed by Aristotle in the *Politics* (1257b30–1258a14) and influenced by his description of the mean (*Nic. Eth.* 1107b5–10), places a certain limit to wealth acquisition within the context of household economics.[51] As mentioned above, Philodemus follows Epicurus in valuing wealth as a useful means of satisfying necessary desires (cf. DL 10.121b: ἀπορήσαντα), but places additional value on its ability to increase the general quality of life by removing difficulties, provided that this is not accompanied by more pain than pleasure (cf. *On Property Management*, col. 14.9–23). Under no circumstances, however, will the sage become a professional money-maker or view wealth acquisition as an end in itself:

τεχνίτης μὲν οὖν ἅμα καὶ ἐργάτης [κ]τήσεως πολλῆς καὶ ταχέως
συναγομένης οὐκ ἴσως ῥητέος ὁ σοφός· ἔστι γὰρ δή τις ἐμπειρία καὶ
δύναμις καὶ περὶ χρηματισμόν, ἧς οὐ κοινωνήσει σπουδαῖος ἀ[ν]ήρ.
(*On Property Management*, col. 17.2–9)

Let not the sage be called an expert or a practitioner at generating much wealth and collecting it efficiently, for there is indeed a certain expertise and ability concerning moneymaking in which the prudent man will not take part.

Philodemus means that the sage may freely acquire even great wealth, but that this must not be motivated by fear of poverty or a perverted understanding of the practical value of money. Above all, the sage's economic practices must not violate the pleasure calculus: he should be a good χρηματιστής but never a φιλοχρηματιστής.[52] This careful distinction does not appear in other economic treatises, such as Xenophon's *Oeconomicus*, in which spokesman Ischomachus defines economic "prudence" (σωφρόνων) as the ability to "add as much as possible to one's possessions" (7.15: ὅτι πλεῖστα . . . προσγενήσεται), or Cicero's statement in *On Duties* 1.25 that, even if one has an "insatiable

---

[51] See Tsouna (2007) 177–80, Asmis (2004) 165, Natali (1995) 111–12, and Laurenti (1973) 99 for the πλούτου μέτρον doctrine in Philodemus.
[52] See Tsouna (2007) 192–4 and Natali (1995) 112–14.

desire for wealth" (*infinita pecuniae cupiditas*), the only moral obligation is to "avoid its unjust acquisition" (*fugienda semper iniuria est*). In contrast to these views, Horace's ant appears to instantiate Philodemus' doctrine concerning the limits and necessary enjoyment of wealth, since her wisdom allows her to gather substantial stores with the ultimate goal of actually enjoying their benefits and providing for her needs. This is communicated in a critical passage immediately following the introduction of the ant simile that is centered on a relative pronoun having the force of an adversative conjunction:

> quae, simul inversum contristat Aquarius annum,
> non usquam prorepit et illis utitur ante
> quaesitis sapiens[53]   (*S.* 1.1.36–8)

Yet she, soon as Aquarius saddens the upturned year, stirs out no more but uses the store she gathered beforehand, wise creature that she is . . .

By means of the transitional *quae*, Horace effectively shifts the argument's focus from the toil involved in acquisition to the topic of wealth limitation, of which the ant suddenly becomes a primary exemplar. As one scholar has put it, the ant is a "counter-example that recoils on the discontents, introducing *quaesitis uti* as criterion of sensible behavior."[54] The importance of this transition is highlighted by Niall Rudd, who notes that "the innocent *quae* in v. 36 has actually the force of *at ea*. It represents the very thin end of the wedge which Horace is about to drive between the ant and the greedy man."[55] The tiny creature's "wisdom" is conveyed by the prudence and logic of her economic practices, which is supported by the fact that she is the only figure in the poem to merit the title *sapiens*.[56] Aside from observing the change in season and adapting accordingly, like the Hesiodic ant in *Works and Days* that "knowingly gathers its heap" (778: ἴδρις σωρὸν ἀμᾶται), her practices are clearly limited (*non usquam prorepit*) and adhere to the requirements of the pleasure calculus. That is, the previous toil involved in gathering stores

---

[53] The reading *sapiens*, which is given by Ψ and *Blandin(ian)us*, seems more appropriate than *patiens*, which appears in 𝔈. As Wimmel (1962) 16 n. 16 observes, however, the latter reading would still be consistent with Horace's portrayal of the ant's ability to "endure" a measure of wealth (cf. *S.* 1.1.106: *modus*).

[54] Mader (2014) 425. Beck (2003) 29 similarly describes the ant positively as a "counter-example" (*Gegenbeispiel*).

[55] Rudd (1966) 29.   [56] I owe this observation to Schlegel (2005).

(*illis ante quaesitis*) is outweighed by her present enjoyment (*utitur*),[57] as Philodemus recommends:

μετρήσει μὲν οὖν ἴσω[ς τὸ] συμφέρον καὶ κτήσει καὶ φυλακῆι πολὺ βέλτισθ᾽ οὗτος, ὥστε μὴ πλείω [π]ονεῖν διὰ τὰ χρήματ᾽ ἤπερ εὐπαθεῖν.

(*On Property Management*, col. 18.40–4)

[The sage] will better calculate what is beneficial for both the acquisition and preservation of things, so as not to engage in more labor for the sake of money than pleasure.

Horace's passage may also echo similar advice from a fragment of Lucilius (561 M), who states: "Thus should you also acquire such fruits as you may enjoy and delight in at home when adverse weather arrives" (*sic tu illos fructus quaeras, adversa hieme olim | quis uti possis ac delectare domi te*).[58] The ultimate goal of accumulating stores, therefore, is to be able to take comfort in them in times of adverse weather, as represented by Aquarius, which may even be understood as an Epicurean metaphor concerning virtue as a bulwark in the face of anxiety, fear, and other related "storms of life."[59] Either way, the ant's prudent behavior is an example of the proper balance between pleasure and pain, the observation of a limit of wealth, and the importance of enjoying it responsibly. As will soon become clear, this entertaining description is carefully opposed to Horace's portrayal of the miser, and as such provides the key to understanding his economic message.

Horace's extended description of the miser's irrational behavior and bizarre administration of wealth, which depend heavily on the Cynic and comic traditions without being engulfed by them, may also be interpreted as projections of his interlocutor's underlying false desires. This is comparable to Philodemus' description of the safe-guards necessary for financial security and prosperity, which include above all the responsible management of one's desires and fears:

---

[57] Cf. Mader (2014) 425 for the "good sense" implied by *usus*.

[58] Quotations of Lucilius are from the 1904 edition of Marx. See also Fiske (1971) 232.

[59] This metaphor is as old as Alcaeus (cf. fr. 107), although it became extremely popular in Epicurean ethics. Epicurus seems to have had a predilection for it, which, aside from being connected with the Epicurean *summum bonum* identified as ἀταραξία (lit. "a state of not being stirred up"), also appears in the expressions χειμάζει (DL 10.137) and χειμών (*Men.* 128). Cf. Horace's description of the Aufidus River in *Satires* 1.1.56–60 as bringing *turbatam aquam* and Lucretius 2.1: *mari magno turbantibus aequora ventis* ("on the great sea with the winds stirring up the waters"). See Kiessling–Heinze (1910) 73 for the "storm of life" motif.

ὧν δ' ἐπιτηδευτέον εἰς π[ρ]όσοδον καὶ τήρησιν ταύτης τε καὶ τῶν προϋπαρχόν[τ]ων τὸ μὲν συνέ[χ]ον ἡγητέον ἐν τῆι τῶν ἐπιθυμιῶν εὐσταλείαι καὶ τῶν [φ]όβων· (*On Property Management*, col. 23.36–43) Of the things that one must pursue for the sake of revenue and the protection of both this and the possessions one had before, one must regard that the principal one consists in the management of one's desires and fears.

In the lines following this passage he specifically identifies the desire for "admiration" (coll. 23.46–24.1: π[ε]ριβλέψε[ις]), which also suggests the competition inspired by envy, or, as commonly designated in Greek, πλεονεξία, as one of the primary causes of the mismanagement of wealth. One thinks of the relentless pursuit of riches vividly satirized by Lucretius, who, as quoted fully above, notes that the masses contend "night and day with ever-present toil in order to achieve the greatest wealth and possess property" (2.12–13: *noctes atque dies niti praestante labore | ad summas emergere opes rerumque potiri*). This ambition may also help to explain the Horatian miser's year-round pursuit of wealth and insatiable desire to become the Ebenezer Scrooge of ancient Rome:

> cum te neque fervidus aestus
> demoveat lucro neque hiems, ignis mare ferrum,
> nil obstet tibi, dum ne sit te ditior alter. (*S.* 1.1.38–40)

While as for you, neither burning heat, nor winter, fire, sea, sword, can turn you aside from gain—nothing stops you, until no other man be richer than yourself.[60]

Our first impression of the miser occurs within the context of his need to outstrip all others in financial prosperity and win universal

---

[60] The sudden reappearance of a seemingly present addressee at this point in the poem is striking, and one cannot help but wonder whether Horace's energetic sermon on the race for wealth has any implications for his millionaire patron (especially since the addressee's identity is obscured by his vague use of the personal pronoun). It is likely that the poet intends this critical observation for what Gold (1992) calls the "internal audience" as represented by the vicious miser (168–9). Lyne (1995) 139–43, on the other hand, supposes that *tu* refers to Maecenas himself. Oliensis (1998) 19 n. 6 disagrees with Lyne's interpretation on the basis that "Horace is in no position . . . to accuse his rich friend of being excessively devoted to wealth." But despite being filthy rich, Maecenas was anything but a hoarder of wealth (as revealed more than once by Horace himself, who had benefited enormously from his patron's generosity; cf. *Ep.* 1.7.15). See also Hicks (2013) 119.

admiration, although this is not explicitly revealed as a false desire until later. At the very heart of the poem Horace introduces the partial answer to his introductory question *Qui fit* in the following verses, seemingly spoken by the obstinate and deluded miser (*S.* 1.1.61–2): *at bona pars hominum decepta cupidine falso | 'nil satis est,' inquit, 'quia tanti quantum habeas sis'*, "But a good many people, misled by false desire, say 'You can never have enough: for you are worth as much as you have.'" The expression "worth as much as you have" appears to have been a commonplace in ancient literature, which influenced the Cynics as well as Lucilius, who in fragment 1119 M declares: "Gold and public approval both are virtue's ideal: you will be regarded and valued in accordance with how much you possess" (*aurum atque ambitio specimen virtutis utrique est: | tantum habeas, tantum ipse sies tantique habearis*).[61] As Pseudo-Acro noted long ago, Horace specifically roots this desire in a false or empty opinion (*ad* 61: *Falsa opinione, aut inepta et inani cupiditate*), which scholars have rightly connected to Epicurus' description of the exaggerated desire to fulfill a natural need as originating in idle imaginings (KD 30: κενοδοξίαν).[62] In the case of the miser, he incorrectly imagines that more wealth will result in more happiness (*S.* 1.1.72: *gaudere*) and tranquility (31: *otia*), which consequently urges him to amass limitless heaps of cash (70–3) in the boundless search for money and self-worth. It is for this reason as well that he will never observe a limit to his acquisitions (92: *sit finis quaerendi*) nor depart, as Lucretius says, from the table like a satisfied guest (3.935–9; cf. Lucr. 5.1431–3: *[hominum genus] semper et in curis consumit inanibus aevum, | nimirum quia non cognovit*

---

[61] It is expressed already in Alcaeus (fr. 360), Pind. *Isthm.* 2.11 and more explicitly by Bion (Fiske 1971: 237). Cf. Plut. *On Desire for Wealth* (526c): κέρδαινε καὶ φείδου, καὶ τοσούτου νόμιζε σεαυτὸν ἄξιον ὅσον ἂν ἔχῃς, "Make acquisitions and take care of them, and consider your worth as determined by your possessions." This appears to be a prose paraphrase of a lost work of tragedy (cf. *TrGF* Adespota 461), which Seneca translates in his correspondence with Lucilius (*Ep.* 115.4). Cf. also Juvenal's observation that "each person's credit corresponds to the amount of cash in his money chest" (3.143–4: *quantum quisque sua nummorum servat in arca, | tantum habet et fidei*) and Trimalchio's statement that "if you have a penny you're worth a penny" (*Sat.* 77: *assem habeas, assem valeas*). For the expression "nothing is enough" in Latin, cf. Lucil. 558 M: *stulto nil sit satis.*

[62] See Lejay (1966) 5, Fiske (1971) 236, Rudd (1966) 24, and Schlegel (2005) 22. Horace underscores the irrationality of the miser's false opinion concerning hoarded wealth by placing into his mouth the Lucretian phrase *suave est* (51), which originally refers to the tranquility of those who have withdrawn from the race for wealth (cf. Lucr. 2.1–2).

quae sint habendi | finis, "the human race continuously wastes life away with empty worries, because it does not know what is the limit of possessions").[63] Unlike the ant, who observes the proper *modus* by making calculated "expenditures" in accordance with her means (cf. *On Property Management*, col. 25.23–4: κατὰ τὰς ὑπάρξεις ἀναλίσκε[ι]ν) and rations wealth in order to satisfy both natural and necessary desires, the miser views wealth acquisition as an end in itself and refuses to enjoy its benefits (*S*. 1.1.73): *nescis, quo valeat nummus, quem praebeat usum?*, "Don't you know what money is for, what end it serves?"[64] As Epicurus states, the objects of limitless desires, such as wealth and admiration, cannot of themselves procure freedom from disturbances or result in true happiness and joy:

Οὐ λύει τὴν τῆς ψυχῆς ταραχὴν οὐδὲ τὴν ἀξιόλογον ἀπογεννᾷ χαρὰν οὔτε πλοῦτος ὑπάρχων ὁ μέγιστος οὔθ' ἡ παρὰ τοῖς πολλοῖς τιμὴ καὶ περίβλεψις οὔτ' ἄλλο τι τῶν παρὰ τὰς ἀδιορίστους αἰτίας. (SV 81)

The disturbance of the soul cannot be ended nor true joy created either by the possession of the greatest wealth or by honor and respect in the eyes of the mob or by anything else that is associated with unlimited causes.

The belief that substantial wealth cannot eliminate disturbances or contribute to happiness is associated with Epicurus' teaching that pleasure cannot be increased beyond the satisfaction of basic and necessary desires (KD 18). Philodemus likewise borrows Stoic terminology, stating that since the requirements of nature are easily satisfied, the loss of wealth is "indifferent" (*On Wealth*, col. 53.2: [ἀδιά]φορο[ν] and 56.7: ἀδιαφορίαν) and that one may derive "equal pleasures from wealth and poverty" (col. 56.4–6: [ἐ]κ τῆς πενίας τὰς ἴσ[ας] ἡδονὰς κομίζεται τὰς ἐκ πλούτου).[65] For this reason the sage economist is not disturbed or frightened by financial loss, which is certainly more than can be said of the miser.

---

[63] Cf. Cic. *On Ends* 1.45 (as well as KD 20): *inanium autem cupiditatum nec modus ullus nec finis inveniri potest*, "No measure or limit, moreover, can be found for empty desires." According to Teles (Hense 1969: 43), Bion similarly taught that the limitless desire for wealth pushes one into service like a slave.

[64] Gowers (2012) 76, commenting on *usum*: "'enjoyment,' in the Epicurean or financial sense."

[65] See Asmis (2004) 152 and Erler (2011) 9–28. Also Cic. *On Duties* 1.6.

Horace completes his moralizing persona's identification of the underlying reasons for economic vice by incorporating the negative consequences of fear into his description of false desire. According to the poet, it is the "fear of poverty" (cf. *S.* 1.1.93: *pauperiem metuas minus* and 76: *metu*), the "terror of evil theft" (77: *formidare malos fures*) and the "dread of being oppressed by scarcity of food" (98–9: *ne se penuria victus | opprimeret, metuebat*) that drives the miser to take drastic measures in order to guard his ever-growing wealth.[66] This exaggerated concern for his livelihood, for instance, scares him into thinking that any expenditure will result in the complete liquidation of his resources:

> quid iuvat inmensum te argenti pondus et auri
> furtim defossa timidum deponere terra?
> "quod, si conminuas, vilem redigatur ad assem."   (*S.* 1.41–3)

What good to you is a vast weight of silver and gold, if in terror you stealthily bury it in a hole in the ground? "But if one splits it up, it would dwindle to a paltry penny."[67]

Horace's mention of the miser secretly burying his gold closely resembles Plautus' description of Euclio's grandfather in the prologue to *Pot of Gold*, spoken by the household god (6–9), who states: "this man's grandfather as a suppliant secretly entrusted to me a hoard of gold, he buried it in the middle of the hearth" (*mi avos huius obsecrans concredidit | thensaurum auri clam omnis, in medio foco | defodit*).[68] For Cynics, the portrayal of animals as free from such practices was a standard theme and also appears in later works such as the pseudo-Hippocratic *Epistles* (17.8): τίς γὰρ λέων ἐς γῆν κατέκρυψε χρυσόν, "What lion ever hid gold in the ground?"[69] In the case of *Satires* 1.1, this theme primarily serves to distinguish the

---

[66] Cf. Lucr. 3.1076–94, where the empty fear of death is the underlying cause of people's "great desire for life" (*vitai tanta cupido*), which is projected by their discontentment and constant labor.

[67] Klingner and Gowers (2012) omit quotation marks and print a question-mark here, indicating that this is the narrator speaking and anticipating the miser's response. I follow the interpretation of others such as Wickham (1901) and Fairclough (1991), who view verse 43 as being spoken by the miser.

[68] Cf. also Theoph. *Ch.* 10.14: καὶ τὸ ὅλον δὲ τῶν μικρολόγων καὶ τὰς ἀργυροθήκας ἔστιν ἰδεῖν εὐρωτιώσας καὶ τὰς κλεῖς ἰωμένας, "In general, you may see the money-chests of the miserly covered in mold and their keys in rust." This passage, however, may be a later addition to the original text.

[69] For the Cynic tradition, see Heinze (1889) 18 and Fraenkel (1957) 93–4.

Horatian miser's hoarding from the wise ant's careful use of her stores. The inclusion of *timidum*, moreover, reveals his economic habits as influenced by the fearful equation of expenditures with poverty, which Philodemus associates with the wretched toil and anxiety avoided by the sage economist:

κτᾶσθαι μέντοι γ' οὐ δυνήσεται πλεῖστα καὶ τάχιστα καὶ διαθεωρεῖν, ὅθεν
ἂν μάλιστα τὸ πλεῖον αὔξοι[το], μηδὲν ἀπομετ[ρῶ]ν πρὸς τὸ τέλος, ἀλλὰ
πρὸς τὸ πλέον καὶ τοὔλαττον, καὶ τὰ προϋπάρχοντ' ἀεὶ φυλάττειν
ἐντόνως· πολὺς γὰρ ὁ πόνος ἤδη περὶ τοῦτο καὶ μετὰ φροντίδος σκληρᾶς
γιγνόμενος καὶ πᾶν τιθε[ίση]ς ἐν πενίαι τὸ δυσχερές
(*On Property Management*, col. 19.4–16)

[The sage] will not acquire as much as possible very quickly or examine closely whence his surplus may be increased most of all, measuring off nothing with regard to the ultimate purpose but with regard to the more and the less, and always striving to safeguard his possessions. For the toil associated with this is great and brings bitter anxiety, which equates every difficulty with poverty . . .

As Philodemus explains, the fear of poverty is completely unfounded, primarily because the requirements of nature are easily satisfied (col. 19.16–19): ἐναργῶς τῆς φύσεω[ς δει]κνυούσης, ἄν τις αὐτῆ[ι] προ[σ]έχ[ηι], διότι καὶ τοῖς ὀλίοις εὐκόλ[ω]ς χρήσεσθ', "although nature makes it clear, if anyone pays attention to her, since she is easily satisfied and requires few things." For this reason, worry about an economic fall is "not worthy of fear" (*On Wealth*, col. 36.11–12: οὐ [γὰ]ρ ἄξιον φόβου). One may, for example, quite easily fulfill necessary desires for food by purchasing basic foodstuffs, as Horace reminds the miser (*S*. 1.1.74–5): *panis ematur, holus, vini sextarius, adde | quis humana sibi doleat natura negatis*, "You may buy bread, greens, a measure of wine, and such other things as would mean pain to our human nature, if withheld." Porphyrio similarly links this passage to "necessary desires" (*ad* 75: *quae sunt necessariae*), which establishes a clear connection to Epicurean ethics as expressed in the *Principal Doctrines* (KD 29) and related by Horace elsewhere in the *Satires*.[70]

---

[70] Cf. *S*. 1.2.111–12 for similar advice: *natura . . . quid latura sibi, quid sit dolitura negatum*, "Nature . . . what satisfaction she will give herself, what privation will cause her pain." Cf. also *S*. 1.6.115.

98 Epicurean Ethics in Horace

Although Horace's advice concerning such meager fare may appear to have an ascetically Cynic flavor, a few distinctions should be made. First, the Cynics were (in)famous in antiquity for their rejection of all social conventions, which especially included money, as Diogenes' divinely inspired injunction to "deface the coin" demonstrates (DL 6.20–1).[71] Furthermore, even relatively less austere Cynics like Bion equated "independence" (αὐτάρκεια) with extreme "poverty" (πενία), which for them entailed the complete rejection of such basic conventions as beds, eating-utensils, and wine. The best evidence of Bion's asceticism is preserved in a passage of Teles, which involves a speech given by Poverty personified:

καὶ ἡ Πενία ἂν εἴποι... "ἀλλὰ μὴ τῶν ἀναγκαίων ἐνδεὴς εἶ; ἢ οὐ μεσταὶ μὲν αἱ ὁδοὶ λαχάνων, πλήρεις δὲ αἱ κρῆναι ὕδατος; οὐκ εὐνάς σοι τοσαύτας παρέχω ὁπόση γῆ; καὶ στρωμνὰς φύλλα;... ἢ πεινᾷ τις πλακοῦντα ἢ διψᾷ Χῖον;"

And Poverty would say: "Indeed, do you lack any of the necessities of life? Do not roads pass through the midst of wild greens, and are not the natural springs full of water? Do I not supply you with the earth as your bed and the leaves as your blanket?...Does one's hunger demand honeyed cakes or one's thirst Chian wine?" [72]

As mentioned already, Epicureans like Philodemus condemn the Cynics' view of poverty as entailing mendicancy (On Wealth, col. 45.15–17: πτωχεία[ν] ... [τὴ]ν στέρ[ησιν οὐ] πολλῶν, ἀλλὰ πάν[των]), which is an evil (43.4–5: κα[κὸν δὲ π]τωχεία), and instead emphatically define πενία as "the possession of few things" (col. 49.11 = 45.5: ὕπαρ[ξιν] τῶν ὀλίγων), "which is good" (col. 49.11–12: ὅ ἐστιν ἀγαθ[όν]). This is the context in which Philodemus asserts that the sage, though unwilling to engage in toilsome beggary, will be content with few possessions and not fear poverty:

[οὔ]τε [γ]ὰρ ἀσχαλᾶι σώφρων ἀνὴρ καὶ πρὸς τὸ μέλλ[ον εὐ]θ[α]ρρὴς τῆι ταπεινῆι καὶ πενιχρᾶι διαίτηι, τὸ φυσικὸν εἰδὼς καὶ ὑπὸ ταύτης διοικούμενον (On Property Management, coll. 15.45–16.4)

[The sage] is confident with regard to the future and the possibility of a poor and meager life, for he knows that the requirements of nature are satisfied even by this...

[71] See Desmond (2008) 98–103 for the Cynics' renunciation of money.
[72] Hense (1969) 7–8. See also Oltramare (1926) 51–2 and Kindstrand (1976) F17 with commentary (217–18).

Being poor means possessing "what suffices" (col. 16.7–8: τὰ...
ἱκανά) without being distressed by the unquenchable desire for
more (cf. *On Wealth*, col. 58.8–9: τῆς [ἐ]πιθυμίας τῆς π[ρ]ὸς πλοῦτον).
The same advice is offered by Horace's persona when he states the
importance of "requiring only what one needs" (*S.* 1.1.59: *at qui
tantuli eget quanto est opus*),[73] which is not the same as recommend-
ing that one live as a beggar. Horace makes this point himself in
Epistles 1.17, in which the pleasure-seeking Cyrenaic Aristippus
addresses a Cynic straw man, saying "I do service that I may have a
horse to ride and be fed by a prince, but you beg for paltry doles"
(20–1: *equos ut me portet, alat rex, | officium facio: tu poscis vilia*).
This is a statement the poet himself declares to be "better" (17:
potior), because Aristippus "aimed at higher things but was content
with what he had" (24: *temptantem maiora, fere praesentibus ae-
quum*). All of this is consistent with his careful distinction in *Satires*
1.1 between being "poor" (79: *pauperrimus*; cf. *Odes* 1.1.18: *pauperiem pati*) and living without any means whatsoever (*S.* 1.1.103–4):
non ego avarum | cum veto te, fieri vappam iubeo ac nebulonem,
"When I call on you not to be a miser, I am not bidding you become
a worthless prodigal." Above all, he reminds the miser that there is
"moderation in property management" (106: *est modus in rebus*),[74]
and that, rather than living like a Cynic beggar or fearfully hoarding
treasure, he should imitate the wise ant by acquiring and enjoying
wealth responsibly.

[73] Cf. *Ep.* 1.2.46: *quod satis est cui contingit, nihil amplius optet*, "Whoever lives
according to what is sufficient does not long for anything more." I disagree with
Fiske (1971) 224–5, who equates Horace's understanding of *satis* with the Cynic
teaching that the sage will live ἀρκούμενος τοῖς παροῦσι (see Hense 1969: 38). The
expression τοῖς παροῦσι seems to me to entail "that which is at one's immediate
disposal" (i.e. the earth, natural springs, wild barley, etc.) or what one presently has.
Horace's point, however, is not that the miser should get rid of his money and live
like a beggar, but that he should learn to administer it properly and enjoy its
benefits responsibly.

[74] This meaning of *res*, which is often equated with land (cf. *S.* 1.1.50: *iugera
centum*), is confirmed by the obvious parallel in *S.* 1.4.31–32: *nequid | summa deperdat
metuens aut ampliet ut rem* ("[the miser] fearful lest he lose aught of his total, or fail to
add to his wealth"); cf. also *S.* 1.4.110: *patriam rem*. Gowers (2012) 81 notes the
following: "Technically *modus* is a measured amount, sometimes of land... here,
connected with fixed boundaries (*certi fines*), it recalls physical images of plots of
land." Cf. also Lucil. (1331 M): *virtus quaerendae finem re scire modumque*, "Virtue is
knowing when to limit and control the search for wealth" and *S.* 2.6.1: *modus agri*, "a
measure of land..."

Towards the end of this ethical investigation Horace considers the detrimental consequences of overvaluing wealth, which, aside from the immense toil and anxiety already mentioned, includes universal abandonment. In his description of the many benefits associated with cultivating friendships Philodemus mentions that, far from being a financial burden, close friends are "a more profitable acquisition . . . than tilled land and a most secure treasure against the turns of fortune" (*On Property Management*, coll. 24.47–25.4: κτήσει[ς λ]υσιτελέστεραι . . . ἤπερ ἀγρῶν καὶ πρὸς τὴν τύχην ἀσφαλέστατοι θησαυροί).[75] One may recall that the cultivation of friendship is described as sowing seeds in the earth, from which it becomes possible to "reap the fruit many times over" (col. 25.20–1: πολλαπ[λάσι]α καρπίζεσθαι γίνεται). Part of this process involves philanthropy (col. 18.34: τὸ φιλάνθρωπ[ον]), which Aristotle describes as the expression of the natural bond that exists between members of the same species (*Nic. Eth.* 1155a17–21) and the safeguard of prosperity (1155a10–12): ἢ πῶς ἂν τηρηθείη καὶ σῴζοιτ' ἄνευ φίλων; ὅσῳ γὰρ πλείων, τοσούτῳ ἐπισφαλεστέρα, "Or how could such prosperity be safeguarded without friends, since the greater it is the greater its insecurity?" According to Philodemus, the sage is always concerned with sharing surplus wealth with his friends, whose companionship ultimately contributes to the preservation of suitably acquired wealth (*On Property Management*, col. 24.19–35). The greedy and acquisitive economist, on the other hand, hoards wealth, isolates himself from society, incurs the hatred of others, and consequently jeopardizes his revenue:

καὶ μὴν ἀφιλία δοκεῖ μὲν ἀναλωμάτων κουφίζε[ιν], ἀσυνεργήτους δὲ ποιεῖ καὶ ὑπὸ παντὸς καταφρονουμένους καὶ [ὑ]π' εὐνοίας ἀπολυωρήτους, ἐξ ὧν οὔτε πρόσοδος ἀξιόλογος οὔτε τήρ[η]σις ἀσφαλής, ὥστε ἂν φιλίαν περι-ποι[ῆ]ται, καθ' ἑκάτε[ρον] εὐτυχή[σ]ει. καὶ ἀφιλανθ[ρω]πία δὲ [κ]αὶ ἀνημερότης ζημιοῖ πολ[λ]ὰ καὶ ἀβοη[θ]ήτου[ς] ποιεῖ, πολ[λ]άκις δ' ἄρδ[η]ν ἀν[αρ]πάζεσθαι [τ]ὴν οὐσίαν.   (col. 24.19–33)

Indeed, traditional managers think that friendlessness procures relief from costs, but it isolates them and makes them despised by everyone and not highly esteemed with regard to people's favor, which does not lead to suitable revenue or secure preservation; consequently, if he should cultivate friendships then he would be fortunate in each of

---

[75] For the importance of φιλία in this treatise, see Laurenti (1973) 168–72, Asmis (2004) 173–6, and Tsouna (2007) 182–3.

these areas. But misanthropy and rudeness cause much suffering, make one helpless, and often cause one's property to be plundered entirely.

Perhaps a perfect example of this is afforded by our miser, whose overwhelming preference for money (cf. S. 1.1.86: *cum tu argento post omnia ponas*) is analyzed within the context of a hypothetical situation: in the case of a medical emergency, he would be completely abandoned and left alone helplessly to face the turns of fortunes (84–5): *non uxor salvum te volt, non filius; omnes | vicini oderunt, noti, pueri atque puellae,* "Your wife does not want you well, nor does your son: everyone hates you, neighbors and acquaintances, boys and girls." Contrary to the sage economist, the miser continues to lose friends and suffer more intensely on account of his perverted administration and understanding of wealth. Philodemus also notes that such reckless mismanagement and misanthropy runs the risk of incurring the envy or wrath of others, whose desire to "plunder wealth" (ἀν[αρ]πάζεσθαι [τ]ὴν οὐσίαν) often results in unspeakable deeds of violence (cf. *On Envy*, fr. 6.4–5: μοχθηρὰ πράτ[τειν]).[76] The relationship between wealth and envy, which was somewhat of a commonplace of moral philosophy,[77] affects even close friends and family members, as Horace's story about the fate of Ummidius at the murderous hands of his *liberta* clearly shows (S. 1.1.99–100): *at hunc liberta securi | divisit medium, fortissima Tyndaridarum,* "Yet a freedwoman cleft him in twain with the axe, bravest of the Tyndarid breed."[78] With this serio-comic warning Horace concludes his analysis of the empty desires and fears underlying the masses' discontentment (cf. 108–9: *nemo, ut avarus, | se probet*), which is closely related to avarice and manifests itself in the endless contest over wealth (cf. 113: *locupletior*) and the willingness to undergo unending and perpetual toil (cf. 112: *hunc atque hunc superare laboret*) in order to acquire it.

---

[76] Cf. also Arist. *Eud. Eth.* 1234a30: ὁ μὲν οὖν φθόνος εἰς ἀδικίαν συμβάλλεται, πρὸς γὰρ ἄλλον αἱ πράξεις αἱ ἀπ' αὐτοῦ, "Therefore envy results in injustice, for the actions that come from it are directed toward another person."

[77] See Gerhard (1909) 92–4 for the evidence. In *On Frank Criticism* Philodemus notes that the sage is "free of all envy" (col. 1b.6–7: φθόνου καθαρός).

[78] Gowers (2012) 80: "[T]he miser who occupies two poles of existence is split down the middle in a parody of the golden mean by an axe-wielding freedwoman."

EPICUREAN FRANKNESS IN *SATIRES* 1.1–3

Horace's incorporation into *Satires* 1.1 of a nameless interlocutor who creates opportunities for ethical platitudes is largely a Cynic technique, and it contributes an important sense of vigor and entertainment to this moral conversation. Indeed, in considering dialogue within the context of Cynic literature, André Oltramare calls the inclusion of a fictitious interlocutor "the most obvious of all the formal characteristics of the diatribe."[79] But, an approach that involves lively interrogation for the purpose of moral correction also would have been the perfect template for a literary representation of Epicurean frankness,[80] which, as Philodemus suggests, occurs in a private setting and is ultimately therapeutic but often requires multiple applications of criticism:

καὶ μηδὲν π[εράνα]ς πάλι χρή[σ]εται πρὸς [τ]ὸν α[ὐ]τόν. εἰ δ᾽ ἡμαρτηκὼς
οὐχ ὑπήκουσε τῆς παρρησίας, πάλι παρρησιάσεται· καὶ γὰρ ἰατρὸς ἐπ[ὶ]
τῆς αὐτῆς νόσου διὰ κλυσ[τῆ]ρος οὐδὲν περάνας, πάλ[ι κε]νοῖ. καὶ διὰ
τοῦτο πάλ[ι π]αρρησιάσεται, διότι πρότερον οὐδὲν ἤνυσε, καὶ πάλι ποήσει
τοῦτο καὶ πάλιν, ἵν᾽ εἰ μὴ νῦν ἀλλὰ νῦν [τελεσφορήσηι.]

(*On Frank Criticism*, fr. 64.1–13)

. . . and having accomplished nothing he will use it again on the same person; and if the student has erred or disobeyed the frank criticism, he will offer it again; and in fact if a doctor has accomplished nothing in the case of the same disease with a clyster, he will purge again. And just for that reason he (the teacher) will try frank criticism again, because he has accomplished nothing; and he will do it again and again, so that if not this time (he may succeed) at another . . .

Horace's persona's conversation with the nameless miser includes consistent exhortations that are directed toward a stubborn "pupil,"

---

[79] Oltramare (1926) 11: "le plus évident de tous les caractères formels de la diatribe." See also Fraenkel (1957) 92, Coffey (1976) 92, and Freudenburg (1993) 8–16. Schlegel (2005) 19–20, however, notes that the connection to popular philosophy does not define the function of Horatian satire in Book 1 as a whole, which is only related to "limitation in an ethical or experiential sense" in the introductory satires.

[80] Since, according to Philodemus (cf. *On Anger* col. 17), certain Epicureans practiced the diatribe and were criticized for their harshness, the "nameless interlocutor" motif would hardly have been new to members of the Garden. For the nature of the diatribes of Basilides and Thespis, who were Epicureans, see *On Anger*, col. 5 as well as Ringeltaube (1913) 41 and Armstrong and McOsker's note on the text (forthcoming).

whose repeated resistance to the poet's efforts eventually elicits a more potent form of treatment. Philodemus explains the reason for such persistence in relation to certain dispositions, which, in the case of stubborn or recalcitrant patients such as the Horatian miser, are described as being "strong and accepting change with difficulty" (*On Frank Criticism*, fr. 7.6–8: τοὺς ἰσχυροὺς καὶ μόλις . . . μεταθησομένους).[81] The first frank exchange in *Satires* 1.1 involves Horace's attempt to reveal to the miser the extreme wretchedness caused by his physical efforts to acquire wealth. Again, these efforts not only prevent him from the enjoyment of Epicurean "physical repose" (ἀπονία) but also force him to endure inclement weather (*S.* 1.1.38–9: *hiems*) as well as serious threats to his life (39: *ferrum*). Despite all of this, in response to the poet's criticism, which is initially centered on appealing to the miser's consideration for his physical health, the speaker effectively states that he prefers to ruin his body rather than risk his savings (43).[82] Instead of abandoning his "patient," however, Horace's Epicurean persona, like a good physician, meets this resistance by listening to his interlocutor's excuses, as Philodemus recommends (*On Frank Criticism*, fr. 51.1–4): ἀκ[ού]σει μᾶλλον, [ἅ]μα καὶ θεωρῶν ἡμᾶς κα[ὶ] ἑαυτῶν γινομένους κατηγόρους, "The teacher will rather listen while observing us becoming accusers even of ourselves, whenever we err." Having considered the miser's apprehension regarding the use of his wealth, he subsequently alters his focus in order to provide more effective criticism (*S.* 1.1.46): *non tuus hoc capiet venter plus ac meus*, "Your stomach will not hold more [grain] than mine." In his second application of frankness, Horace attempts to explain that the miser's desire to amass unlimited stores is unnecessary and overlooks the requirements of nature (50: *naturae finis*), thus appealing to the Epicurean doctrine of natural and necessary desires as easy to fulfill (*Men.* 127 and 130; cf. KD 29).[83] But once again, the poet's efforts

---

[81] See Glad (1995) 137–52 and Gigante (1974) 41.

[82] Codoñer (1975) 46 regards the speaker's comments here and elsewhere (e.g. 61) as serving a transitional purpose: "Its purpose is to bring about a change, to move from the specific to the general, which is something the 'transitional adversary' brings about," "Su función es operar un cambio, pasar del planteamiento concreto al general, y se encuentra en el adversario de transición." In this sense, the miser's complaints and excuses allow Horace to make more general connections to Epicurean ethics.

[83] Gowers (2012) 73 includes the belly, which is a popular organ in Roman satire, among the "host of vessels and containers used to measure capacity in the poem

are dashed by the miser's unwillingness to accept correction, which is expressed by his overpowering and misguided desire for "a huge heap" (S. 1.1.51: *magno . . . acervo*). In the face of such intransigence, Philodemus states that the sage will not give up but rather persevere in employing criticism, like a purgative medicine, even on a third occasion (*On Frank Criticism*, fr. 65.1–8): [εἰ δὲ παρρησί]αι χρήσεται π[άλιν], φανε[ῖται] οὕτως ἐφικέσθαι. πολλάκι δ' ἀντιστρόφως, ποτὲ δὲ καὶ ποήσας, ἢ ἑξῆς πρότερον ἡ δευτέρ[α], τάχα δ' ἡ τρίτη τελεσφορήσει, "and if he employs frankness again, he will be seen to succeed thus. And sometimes he is successful right after the first time, the second time; or maybe the third will do it." Perhaps in accordance with this statement Horace, for the third time, applies frankness by employing a weather metaphor in order to warn his patient that such reckless excess will inevitably cause psychological turbulence (S. 1.1.60: *turbatam . . . aquam*). This mental turbulence will in turn preclude "tranquility" (ἀταραξία), which complements his initial appeal to the preference for physical repose but is, alas, just as ineffective.

Unsurprisingly, the miser's continued obstinacy and deluded convictions finally drive him to declare that "nothing is ever enough!" (S. 1.1.62: *nil satis est*), which prompts an obviously frustrated Horace to underscore this stubbornness by throwing up his hands and asking: "What can you do with someone like this?" (63: *quid facias illi?*). The response, of course, is an application of harsher frankness through the series of vivid representations that immediately follows: the prospect of ending up like Tantalus (68–9: *Tantalus a labris sitiens fugientia captat | flumina*, "Tantalus, dying of thirst, chases the water as it escapes from his lips") and the pathetic portrait of the miser sprawled upon sacks of money, mouth gaping wide with admiration and religious awe (70–2: *inhians*; for *inhians* as a typical behavior for misers, cf. Plaut. *Pot of Gold* 194: *inhiat aurum ut devoret*, "He gapes at the gold as if to devour it").[84] These colorful images certainly owe

<hr>

(heaps, money-bags, jugs, bushels, plots of land)." See also Gowers (1993) 129: "This Epicurean tirade is also a literary polemic on the excessive consumption of words." So also Hicks (2013) 135.

[84] As Tarrant (2007) 68–9 notes, the idea that torture in the Underworld merely represents human misery on earth is Lucretian (cf. 3.978–1023). Cf. Hicks (2013) 137: "The task of the moral teacher is to create a mirror for the audience through historical or mythological examples in which they can recognize themselves."

much to the Cynic and comic traditions;[85] their main purpose, however, is to inspire a sense of horror and disgust in the patient, who, having come face to face with his own vice (cf. *On Frank Criticism*, frs. 26.4–5 and 42.1 for the phrase τιθέναι πρὸ ὀμμάτων), becomes better able "to flee from it more easily, having been reminded that this possibility exists within himself" (*On Anger*, col. 3.15–18: ὥ[σ]τε τοῦ παρ᾽ αὐτὸν εἶναι προσυπομνησθέντος ἀποφυγεῖν ῥᾳδίως). Perhaps the clearest example of this technique involves Horace's subsequent presentation of the hypothetical risks or consequences involved in preferring money to friendship: the miser would be abandoned and left alone in the face of adverse fortune:

> at si condoluit temptatum frigore corpus
> aut alius casus lecto te adfixit,[86] habes qui
> adsideat, fomenta paret, medicum roget, ut te
> suscitet ac reddat gnatis carisque propinquis?
> non uxor salvum te volt, non filius; omnes
> vicini oderunt, noti, pueri atque puellae.   (*S.* 1.1.80–5)

But if your body is seized with a chill and racked with pain, or some other mishap has pinned you to your bed, have you someone to sit by you, to get lotions ready, to call the doctor so as to raise you up and restore you to your children and dear kinsmen? No, your wife does not want you well, nor does your son: everyone hates you, neighbors and acquaintances, boys and girls.[87]

Once again, the vividness of this example creates space between the miser and his obsession and is designed, as Philodemus explains in *On Anger*, to cause the patient "great fear" (col. 3.14–15: μεγάλ[ην] . . . φρίκην; cf. the very similar context in *S.* 1.4.127: *metu*) as he comes face to face with his disease and reflects on it objectively. Of course, part

[85] As Herter (1970) 330 observes, the allegory involving Tantalus was probably inspired by Bion (for which, see Hense 1969: 34). Freudenburg (1993) 190–1 analyzes this passage (as well as *S.* 1.4.80–5) within the context of literary theory and Callimachean aesthetics. Mader (2014) 426–7 likewise considers the role of literary aesthetics in this poem, but also views binaries such as "large/small, excess/satiety" as "ethical markers."

[86] This is the reading in Fairclough's revised 1991 edition, although *adflixit*, which is in Kingner's text, appears in the many codices represented by *Ξ* and *Ψ*.

[87] Shackleton Bailey (1985), like Klingner, suggests that these are Horace's words, whereas Gowers (2012) and Fairclough (1991) read them as the miser's excuse for amassing wealth, which can provide for such resources. But would the miser be willing to spend money, even to save his own life? Probably not (cf. *S.* 2.3.91–4 as well as Juv. 14.135–7).

of the irony of this scene is that there is no conditionality: the miser *is* in fact gravely ill and in need of medical attention, but his is a moral disease that can only be cured by the philosopher acting as physician. The language Horace uses in this passage is wholly consistent with Philodemus' employment of medical analogies to describe the process of frank criticism: the obstinate patient needs a caring physician (ἰατρός = *medicum*) who will sit by his side (βοηθέω = *adsideat*; cf. Sen. *Ep.* 9.8: *dicebat Epicurus in hac ipsa epistula, "ut habeat qui sibi aegro adsideat"*, "As Epicurus said in this very letter, 'so that he may have someone who will sit by his side when he is sick'") and apply the necessary treatments (θεράπευσις = *fomenta*) in order to restore (ἀναπλάττω = *suscitet*) him back to health.[88] A similar description of frankness as medicine occurs in Plutarch's *How to Tell a Flatterer from a Friend* (55c–d):

δεῖ γὰρ ὠφελοῦντα λυπεῖν τὸν φίλον, οὐ δεῖ δὲ λυποῦντα τὴν φιλίαν
ἀναιρεῖν, ἀλλ' ὡς φαρμάκῳ τῷ δάκνοντι χρῆσθαι, σῴζοντι καὶ φυλάττοντι
τὸ θεραπευόμενον.

For one must harm a friend only to help him, and one should not by hurting him destroy the friendship, but use the stinging word as a medicine that restores and preserves that which is being treated.

These passages emphasize and reinforce the importance of stinging criticism for the sake of healing, which, again, is the hallmark of Epicurean frankness and sets it apart from the infamous παρρησία of the Cynics. The significance of this for the above passages from *Satires* 1.1 and even the poem as a whole, then, is that Horace's ethical persona, who has been trying to heal the miser all along and may properly be considered an *amicus sanus*, is in an important sense also a "physician" who will attempt (even if unsuccessfully) to cure vice through the frank criticism of his satiric verses.

In transitioning to *Satires* 1.2, traditionally regarded as Horace's earliest satire, the audience encounters the formidable consequences associated with sexual extremes, which, like the dangers of poor wealth administration, was a popular topic of moral philosophy. Perhaps one of the most salient features of this treatment is the complex *variatio*

---

[88] For medical terminology and imagery in *On Frank Criticism*, as well as citations of relevant passages, see Konstan et al. (1998) 20–3 and Gigante (1975) 53–61. Freudenburg (1993) 191–2 reads *frigus* as "designating bombast, the vice of the grand style," which is cured through "criticism" (*adsideat*) and "warmers" (*fomenta*).

Horace employs, which involves engagement with Roman comedy, elegiac poetry, Hellenistic epigram, and the Cynic diatribe, to name just a few genres and traditions.[89] The impressive and intentionally dizzying array of such influences, however, which successfully communicates the disorder and chaos of sexual imprudence, is not itself delivered in a "hackneyed" or "confusing" manner, as some scholars have asserted.[90] Rather, the poet, by means of textual and thematic parallels, coherently establishes various links between the importance of maintaining a careful balance regarding sexual and financial choices, thus connecting this satiric conversation to the preceding one. One may appreciate this more fully by noting that both poems employ the same sequence of arguments, and that the overall importance in *Satires* 1.2 of maintaining a sexual mean through ambiguous terms such as *pretium*, *nummus*, and *fructus* also has obvious financial applications.[91] Furthermore, there is an ethical approach holding all of these components together that is not just an abstract notion of balance or the vague application of Aristotle's mean, which is insufficient in itself as an explanation for Horace's description of the advantages and disadvantages associated with various types of ladies.[92] Rather than having recourse to the golden mean, in *Satires* 1.2 Horace consistently and clearly applies the Epicurean calculus, which, as in *Satires* 1.1, dictates that in all ethical decisions the pleasure derived must outweigh the pain involved in satisfying one's desires (cf. *Ep.* 1.2.55: *nocet empta dolore voluptas*, "pleasure procured with pain is harmful"). For the miser this means not hoarding wealth, which will result in bad physical health and emotional abandonment; similarly, for the sexual addict it means avoiding excessive pain by not courting matrons (*S.* 1.2.78–9): *desine matronas sectarier, unde laboris | plus haurire mali est quam ex re decerpere fructus*, "cease to court matrons, for thence one may derive pain and misery, rather than reap enjoyment in the reality." The

---

[89] Freudenburg (1993) 3–51 provides a most extensive examination of the many allusions to and parallels with Roman comedy. Fiske (1971) 251–74 considers the role of Cynic diatribe as well as of Epicureanism and the fragments of Lucilius, and Hendrickson (1918) 27–32, Tait (1941) 24–87, Schmid (1978) 181–3, Cataudella (1950) 18–31, Cody (1976) 108–19, Gigante (1983) 65–76, Freudenburg (1993) 193–8, and Gigante (1993) 86–8 all look at the presence and function of the Hellenistic epigrammatists Callimachus and Philodemus.
[90] See Fraenkel (1957) 79 and Rudd (1966) 11 respectively.
[91] See Armstrong (1964) 88–91, Bushala (1971) 312–15, and Dessen (1968) 200–8.
[92] Rudd (1966) 11.

centrality of the Epicurean calculus for this and other colorful descriptions is underscored by Marcello Gigante, who associates the many examples of pleasure gone awry with the "unifying theme" of the poem:

> The variety of these episodes and scenes helps to promote the unifying theme, which has an Epicurean foundation, namely, the purity of pleasure, the acquisition of uncompromised pleasure that is free of pain, all of which is based on the twofold doctrine of choices and avoidances as well as the distinction between correct desire and calculated rejection.[93]

The role of calculation is so prominent in *Satires* 1.2 that various scholars have identified it as the "main theme" of Horace's treatment, while some have called into question, on account of a lack of comparatively detailed evidence and proof of similar treatment, the alleged foundational influence of Bion and the Cynics.[94] This is not to say that the influence of non-Epicurean sources on this satire is negligible, but perhaps one may suggest that here, as well as in *Satires* 1.1, Horace flavors his persona's fundamentally Epicurean approach to frank criticism with a generous dash of Cynic wit.

The identification of the pleasure calculus as central to this poem is not only consistent with Horace's treatment of the dangers and anxieties associated with certain relationships, but it also clears up some of the confusion regarding the poet's moral stance. Some, for example, have correctly noted that nowhere in *Satires* 1.2 does his persona condemn adultery per se or any particular social status, but have incorrectly interpreted this as proof that the poem is "entirely satirical" and "innocent of any moral message."[95] Others, such as William Turpin, have gone so far as to assert that Horace is a voice that "we do not have to take seriously at all," while Niall Rudd states that the lack of a "firm Aristotelian framework" in this satire

---

[93] Gigante (1993) 23–4: "La varietà degli episodi o delle scene è in funzione della tesi unitaria, il cui fondamento epicureo è la purezza del piacere, il conseguimento della *voluptas* intatta, priva di dolore, che è basato anch'esso su un doppio, sulla dottrina della scelta e della fuga, del discrimine fra retto desiderio e calcolata ripulsa." Cf. Hicks (2013) 140.

[94] Kiessling–Heinze (1910) 26, Fraenkel (1957) 78, Lejay (1966) 32, Rudd (1966) 31, Curran (1970) 230, and Fiske (1971) 248–51. Cataudella (1950) 18–20 questions the role of Cynic doctrine in this satire.

[95] Baldwin (1970) 465, who is corrected by Gigante (1993) 19–20. Schlegel (2005) 28–9 is more careful, stating that this poem has no "overt moral content."

compromises its moral integrity.[96] In general, many commentators and scholars who do acknowledge a moral message in *Satires* 1.2 identify it as exclusively Aristotelian,[97] which is problematic because it does not account for the poet's unwillingness to identify particular social statuses as vicious or virtuous. Of course, one cannot overlook the influence of Aristotle's doctrine of the mean on Hellenistic thinkers like Epicurus; at the same time, however, Horace's understanding of virtue regarding sex does not exactly involve an identification of freedwomen as the unequivocal and virtuous *medium* nor of matrons, brothels, and prostitutes as vicious extremes in themselves (cf. Cato's advice at *S.* 1.2.31–5), as some have thought.[98] Instead it involves, as Eckard Lefèvre suggests, the ability to observe a proper measure—not of wealth as in *Satires* 1.1 but of sexual pleasure—in light of the perceived or imagined consequences of one's decisions.[99] In other words, it involves the consistent application of the Epicurean calculus of pleasure and pain, and not just in one or two passages but overall as an effective solution that provides ethical coherence to Horace's lively portraits. A more accurate interpretation of the poet's approach, therefore, would involve the realization that he condemns sexual affairs only when they violate the requirements of nature and result in disastrous consequences, such as public scandal or the loss of one's property (*S.* 1.2.61–2 ~ 1.4.118–19): *bonam deperdere famam,* | *rem patris oblimare malum est ubicumque,* "To throw away a good name, to squander a father's estate, is at all times evil." The moral message here is very similar to that of *Satires* 1.1, namely, that one should avoid overlooking the pleasure calculus, for

[96] Turpin (2009) 122 and Rudd (1966) 10–11. But cf. Kemp (2016) 132.
[97] Freudenburg (1993) 26, Mayer (2005) 142 and Gibson (2007) 21. Kemp (2016) 130–46 shows how in *Satires* 1.2 Horace plays with the elusiveness of the Aristotelian mean and slowly shifts his attention from that doctrine to Epicurean moderation in connection with desires.
[98] Rudd (1966) 11. Kemp (2016) touches on this point when he mentions how Horace has shown how "a mean can itself be a vice if not pursued in a moderate way" (143).
[99] Lefèvre (1975) 320–1, partly following Fraenkel (1957) 78–9. Courtney (2013) 76, following Dessen (1968) 202, rightly notes that the mean is to be identified with correct behavior rather than with freedwomen themselves. This important distinction had already been made by Cataudella (1950) 25. Cf. also Kemp (2016) 139. Here again, Horace's persona's condemnation of excessive and passionate lust and preference for love that is simple, honest, free of guile and even a prelude to friendship may be read in terms of Callimachus' approval of simplicity and elegance in terms of poetic composition. For sex as a symbol of style, see Freudenburg (1993) 193–8.

both hoarding wealth as a miser and squandering it as a profligate and shameless lover results in more pain than pleasure (cf. *S.* 1.2.78–9).[100] Another aspect of *Satires* 1.2 that has caused some confusion is the presence of obscene language throughout the poet's observations of harmful behavior. It is true that, in order to communicate this lesson to his audience, Horace employs rather shocking expressions that are charged with both sexual as well as moral meaning and recall to a certain degree the Cynics' provocative style. But despite this connection, it is somewhat of an oversimplification to declare that the entire satire is characterized by "a crudeness of speech, which recalls in every tone the somewhat brutal παρρησία . . . affected by the Cynics."[101] Such a view completely overlooks the generally protreptic nature of this poem and Horace's repeated emphasis on the Epicurean calculus for the sake of moral correction. Indeed, the poet's use of overt frankness and explicit words like *futuo* (*S.* 1.2.127), *cunnus* (36), and *mutto* (68), which recall the poetry of Catullus (cf. 16.1: *pedicabo*, 37.5: *confutuere*, and 41.1: *defututa*),[102] is not gratuitously offensive but ultimately intended to influence correct behavior and promote vigorously the importance of satisfying desires in accordance with nature. In this sense, such expressions endeavor to "make the strongest possible case for nature,"[103] which involves an application of practical and frank advice through concrete examples as well as graphic visualizations of the dire consequences of vice, all of which Horace, according to his account, learned from his father (cf. *S.* 1.4.109: *nonne vides?*).[104]

---

[100] Sharland (2009b) 122 states "not for any moral reasons, but simply because of the danger and inconvenience involved in adultery, any sexual partner is better than another man's wife." According to the Epicureans, this kind of calculation is directly related to practical ethics and the avoidance of pain, rather than to the attainment of virtue or oral perfection for their own sake.

[101] Fiske (1971) 251. Turolla (1931) 67 similarly states that Horace "è uno che ride malamente" ("someone who laughs maliciously").

[102] See Gigante (1993) 19. For the implications of such language for Horace's apparently sexist view of women, see Henderson (1999) 184–91, Oliensis (1998) 24, and Courtney (2013) 72.

[103] See Curran (1970) 230. For other descriptions of the language of *Satires* 1.2, see Lefèvre (1975) 311–12.

[104] Gigante (1993) 15: "The obscenity of the terms . . . serves to stir up a change regarding one's behavior in life, which is proof of the validity of a philosophical system. The obscenity of this language reflects the viciousness of others rather than that of the poet; it is a manifestation of the practical ethics his father had instilled in him, but it also points to the inefficiency and insufficiency of philosophical

The poet contextualizes his treatment of sexual vice by stating, in mock-epic fashion, the importance of observing the hedonic calculus before introducing a series of frank visualizations and examples. Manipulating an Ennian passage and thus suggesting the epic nature of the "struggle" (*S.* 1.2.38: *laborent*) between certain desires,[105] Horace announces the formidable "dangers" (40: *pericla*) of seeking "pleasure marred by much pain" (39: *multo corrupta dolore voluptas*). The idea that one's pleasure should be pure or unmixed with excessive pain is of course expressed by Epicurus (SV 51) and, in connection with sexual pleasure, by Lucretius, who like Horace warns against sexual delights that result in "care and certain pain" (4.1067: *curam certumque dolorem*; cf. *On Property Management*, col. 15.39–40: τέρπον ἀκέραιον).[106] In fact, the point of Lucretius' extended diatribe on love is precisely the same as that of *Satires* 1.2, namely, to incorporate vivid imagery for the purpose of advising against love affairs that bring "mixed" or "corrupt" pain:

> Nec Veneris fructu caret is qui vitat amorem,
> sed potius quae sunt sine poena commoda sumit.
> nam certe purast sanis magis inde voluptas
> quam miseris. (4.1073–6)

Nor does the one who avoids love lack the fruit of Venus, but rather he takes the advantages that are without penalty; for certainly a purer pleasure comes from this to the healthy than to those who are lovesick.

For both poets the prospect of truly enjoying the "fruits" of pleasure (*Veneris fructu*, cf. *S.* 1.2.79: *fructus*) depends entirely on maintaining a safe or "healthy" (*sanis*, cf. *S.* 1.4.129: *ego sanus ab illis*) distance from the consequences associated with risky relationships, such as those involving married women (cf. *S.* 1.4.113: *ne sequerer moechas*).

---

abstractions and outlines," "L'oscenità di termini . . . [ha] la funzione di suscitare una ripulsa nel comportamento, nella practica della vita che è il terreno di prova di validità di un sistema filosofico. È un aspetto—il linguaggio osceno—della malittia degli altri, non del poeta; è una manifestazione della concretezza di cui l'aveva formato il padre, ma anche l'indizio della persuasione dell'inefficacia di ogni astrazione, dell'insufficienza degli schemi."

[105] Cf. Enn. *Ann.* 494–5 Sk.: *audire est operae pretium, procedere recte qui rem Romanam Latiumque augescere voltis*, "It is worth the while to hear, you who wish to advance the Roman state and increase Latium." See Fraenkel (1957) 81–2, Gigante (1993) 63–4, Smith (2005) 122, and Gowers (2012) 100 for other views concerning the bathetic juxtaposition of Ennius' solemn expression to Horace's *moechis*.

[106] See Cataudella (1950) 18–20 and Gigante (1993) 17.

Luctrius' diatribe on love ends with criticism of excessive passion
and what appears to be praise for a stable relationship, in which a
stronger bond—even friendship—is formed over time and through
"obliging manners" (4.1281: *morigerisque modis*). Both poets'
approval or rejection of romantic affairs has nothing to do with social
status itself but with a calculation of potential pleasure derived in
relation to pain endured: the affair that provides the most pleasure
with the least risk is the best kind, regardless of status or position.
Again, neither Horace nor Lucretius recommends or advises against
any kind of relationship without having recourse to the pleasure
calculus, which explains why dealings with other men's wives are
generally discouraged and, as Lucretius observes, a long-term relationship based on good manners (that is, not one involving prosti-
tutes) can develop into a healthy love (cf. 4.1283: *consuetudo
concinnat amorem*).[107] For his part, Horace condemns the many
dangers and foolish risks associated with adultery (*S.* 1.2.38: *moechis*)
by means of vivid examples and pictorial imagery, which, as in *Satires*
1.1, helps to "place before the eyes" the frightening consequences of
such affairs:

> hic se praecipitem tecto dedit, ille flagellis
> ad mortem caesus, fugiens hic decidit acrem
> praedonum in turbam, dedit hic pro corpore nummos,
> hunc perminxerunt calones; (*S.* 1.2.41–4)

One man has thrown himself headlong from the roof; another has been
flogged to death; a third, in his flight, has fallen into a savage gang of
robbers; another has paid a price to save his life; stable-boys have pissed
all over another.

Like his father (cf. *S.* 1.4.126), Horace aggressively employs the
demonstrative combination *hic ... ille* in order to emphasize proximity and call attention to the ubiquitous consequences of sexual vice.
As Marcello Gigante notes, in *Satires* 1.2 Horace drowns his readers
in "situations and personages ... that represent the ghastly specter of
love's suffering."[108] He relies on examples that are practical and

---

[107] Brown (1987) 89: "The *amor* of the final paragraph grows slowly, on the basis of
compatibility, and seems free from anxiety or illusion; it belongs, moreover, to a
steady, long-lasting relationship rather than a temporary liaison."

[108] Gigante (1993) 25: "In realtà, Orazio svela un'arte intrisa di realtà, saporosa di
situazioni e di personaggi, affrancata e rovente, che raffigura lo spettro del pathos
d'amore, gli amori cittadineschi. Non astrazioni, ma concretezza di parole e di gesti ..."

immediately relevant to most people, which, apart from making them all the more shocking and therefore better able to deter his audience from a similar fate, also resembles Philodemus' frank use of pictorial imagery in *On Anger* (col. 3.13–18) as described above.

In the same work, Philodemus recommends that his followers assess the pure corruption associated with unnecessary sexual desires by observing their manifold consequences, which are regarded as symptomatic of this particular disposition. With regard to this assessment, he states the following:

οὕτω δὲ τὴν εἰλικρίνειαν ἐπιλογίσασθαι τοῦ κακοῦ, καθάπερ καὶ ἐπὶ
τῆς ἐρ[ωτ]ικ[ῆ]ς εἰώθαμεν ποιεῖν ἐπιθυμίας, τότε [δὴ] πᾶ[ν τὸ λυποῦν
αὐ]τοὺς ἐξαριθμοῦμεν [καὶ] τὰ παρακολουθοῦντα [δυσ]χερέστα[τα κοι]νῆι
(*On Anger*, col. 7.16–26)

Thus [it is necessary] to establish by rational appraisal the pure, unmixed nature of this vice, just as we customarily do with erotic passion, then indeed we enumerate one by one everything that is distressing them as well as the extreme and wretched consequences that follow [and that they share in common].[109]

The application of frankness for the purpose of curing sexual vice is contingent upon careful observation and inferences from signs (*On Frank Criticism*, fr. 57.1–5): [κἂν μὴ] κατειλήφηι ἐρ[ῶν]τας ἢ κατασ[χ]έτους κακίαις τισίν, ἀλλὰ σημειωσάμενον, "Even if it is the case that he [the sage] has not caught them in love or possessed by some vices, but has inferred it from signs." According to Philodemus as quoted previously, these signs may be physical symptoms or the extreme and wretched consequences of vice. According to the testimony of the Christian apologist Origen, moreover, the followers of Epicurus avoided adultery solely because of its painful consequences, which usually involve death, exile, or the fear of being caught by a returning husband:

οἱ δὲ ἀπὸ Ἐπικούρου οὐ διὰ τοῦτο οὐ μοιχεύουσιν, ὅτε ἀπέχονται τοῦ
μοιχεύειν, ἀλλὰ διὰ τὸ νενομικέναι τέλος τὴν ἡδονήν, πολλὰ δ' ἀπαντᾶν
κωλυτικὰ τῆς ἡδονῆς τῷ εἴξαντι μιᾷ τῇ τοῦ μοιχεύειν ἡδονῇ καὶ ἔσθ' ὅτε
φυλακὰς ἢ φυγὰς ἢ θανάτους, πολλάκις δὲ πρὸ τούτων καὶ κινδύνους κατὰ
τὸ ἐπιτηρεῖν τὴν τοῦ ἀνδρὸς ἔξοδον ἀπὸ τῆς οἰκίας
(*Against Celsus* 7.63 = Us. 535)

---

[109] The translation is partly that of Armstrong and McOsker, who, it should be noted, reject the final reconstruction of the passage (namely, [κοι]νῆι) on account of the damaged state of the treatise.

But it is not because of this [nature and the law] that the followers of Epicurus avoid adultery when they do so, but because of their conviction that pleasure is the final end, and many hindrances to pleasure attend upon one who only pursues the pleasure of adultery, such as prison, exile, or death; even before these, often there are the risks involved in observing the husband depart from the house . . . [110]

There are numerous similarities between the moral stance of this group identified as the "followers of Epicurus" and the Horatian persona: neither condemns adultery per se but rather the risks involved, which corrupt the enjoyment of pure pleasure (cf. S. 1.2.39), and both identify these risks as involving flight or exile (42: *fugiens*) and even death (43: *ad mortem caesus*).[111] In a passage from Philodemus' fragmentary treatise *On Love* (PHerc. 1384) the victims of sexual passion are described as being "manifestly in danger" (8–9: ἐν τοῖς κινδύνοις ἐπιφανές), which may allude to the observable symptoms of this particular vice, and in a related fragment (PHerc. 1167) he seems to note the "perceptible clarity" (5: [ἐ]ναργές) of the consequences of "painful desire" (1–2: λύπην [τὴν ἐπι]θυμίαν).[112] Among the observable consequences Horace mentions in connection with risky affairs is the loss of both money and reputation (S. 1.2.61: *famam*; 62: *rem patris*; 43: *nummos*),[113] which resembles Lucretius' identification of ignominy as a consequence of sexual obsession (4.1124: *aegrotat fama*) as well as Philodemus' description of salaciousness as a primary destroyer of wealth in *On Property Management* (coll. 23.42–24.2): οὐ[δ]ὲν γὰρ ἐκχεῖν [κ]α[ὶ ἀ]νατρέπειν εἴ[θιστ]αι λαμπροτάτα[ς καὶ πλ]ουσι[ωτάτας οἰκίας ὡ]ς πολυτέλι[αί τε] δι[αίτ]ης κα[ὶ] λαγνε[ῖαι], "for nothing is wont to destroy the most illustrious and wealthiest households than a profligate life, lust . . . "[114] Later in *Satires* 1.2 Horace adds to this list of the complications and problems associated with adultery by vividly listing other "hindrances" to true pleasure (S. 1.2.97: *multae . . . officient*

[110] For the significance of this passage for *Satires* 1.2, see Lejay (1966) 36 and especially Armstrong (2014a) 119–21.

[111] Pasquali (1920) 325, who refers to this poem as "una diatriba epicurea" ("an Epicurean diatribe"), observed these connections early on, as did Kiessling–Heinze (1910) 26. See also Cataudella (1950) 22–5.

[112] See Sbordone (1965) 310–12 for the evidence.

[113] Cf. S. 1.2.133: *ne nummi pereant aut puga aut denique fama*, "dreading disaster in purse or person or at least repute."

[114] Cataudella (1950) 20 n. 7 makes a similar connection.

res; cf. πολλὰ κωλυτικὰ in the above passage from Origen)[115] before contrasting them with what Philodemus describes as preferable circumstances for enjoying the fruits of love.

Toward the end of *Satires* 1.2 Horace artistically underscores the importance of observing the hedonic calculus with regard to love affairs by juxtaposing two very different poems dealing with amatory expectations. In response to the quasi-elegiac *miser amator* who expresses his preference for elusive "prey" by quoting Callimachus (105–6: *leporem venator ut alta* | *in nive* sectetur; cf. Callim. *Epigrams* 33: Ὠγρευτής . . . ἐν οὔρεσι πάντα λαγωὸν | διφᾷ),[116] he alludes to certain epigrams of Philodemus in which the pleasurable convenience of an easy love is contrasted with the "grave cares" (*S.* 1.2.110: *curasque gravis*) of a riskier and more demanding amour:

> illam "post paulo" "sed pluris" "si exierit vir"
> Gallis, hanc Philodemus ait sibi, quae neque magno
> stet pretio neque cunctetur cum est iussa venire.   (*S.* 1.2.120–3)

"By and by," "Nay more," "If my husband goes out"—a woman who speaks thus is for the Galli, says Philodemus; for himself he asks for one who is neither high-priced nor slow to come when bidden.

> πέντε δίδωσιν ἑνὸς τῇ δεῖνα ὁ δεῖνα τάλαντα
> καὶ βινεῖ φρίσσων καί, μὰ τόν, οὐδὲ καλήν·
> πέντε δ᾽ ἐγὼ δραχμὰς τῶν δώδεκα Λυσιανάσσῃ,
> καὶ βινῶ πρὸς τῷ κρείσσονα καὶ φανερῶς.
> πάντως ἤτοι ἐγὼ φρένας οὐκ ἔχω ἢ τό γε λοιπὸν
> τοὺς κείνου πελέκει δεῖ διδύμους ἀφελεῖν.   (*Epigr.* 22)

Mr. X gives Mrs. Y five talents for one favor, and he screws, shivering with fear, one who is, what's more, God knows, no beauty. I give five—drachmas—to Lysianassa for the twelve favors, and what's more I screw a finer woman, and openly. Assuredly, either I'm crazy or, after all this, he should have his balls cut off with a knife.[117]

---

[115] In addition to being a parody of epic, the asyndeton and rapid-fire description of Horace's catalogue of the wealthy matron's attendants in this passage has, as Gowers (2012) 111 notes, a comic feel (cf. Plaut. *Aul.* 501–2).

[116] For a discussion of the language of literary theory in the following passages, see Freudenburg (1993) 195–8. Dessen (1968) 207 also offers interesting observations. According to Cody (1976) 108–19, Horace not only imitates but transforms his original model in order to achieve a "moralistic reinterpretation of Callimachus' amoral epigram."

[117] I use the edition and translations of Sider (1997) 138. Cf. Horace's earlier, direct quotation of a Philodemean epigram (*S.* 1.2.92: *o crus, o bracchia!*) as discussed by Fiske (1971) 255 and especially Sider (1997) 103–10. See also Welch (2008) 66–67.

Horace's presentation of Philodemus' views in the above passage
from *Satires* 1.2 has no exact parallel in the surviving collection,
although the poem quoted immediately after makes the same moral
point and employs the same kind of language as Horace does, as
F. A. Wright demonstrated almost a century ago.[118] There also appear
to be references connected to Philodemus' *Epigrams* 38, in which the
author, applying the hedonic calculus, declares his preference for a
Corinthian *scortum* over a Roman *matrona* (3–5: ἡ μὲν ματρώνας τε
τρόπους καὶ ἤθεα στέργειν οἶδ᾽ ... ἡ δὲ χύδην παρέχει πάσῃ φιλότητι,
"The one knows how to love the ways and manners of a married
woman ... the other promiscuously lends herself to every manner of
love") and even mentions a Gallus (8: Γάλλος).[119] It is significant that
in the midst of his allusions to Greek amatory poetry Horace chooses
to correct Callimachus, as Edward Courtney has recently noted, by
subsequently quoting or referring to Philodemean epigrams.[120] Furthermore, despite the important influence of Callimachean standards
on neoteric poetry, especially that of Horace, in this satire one detects
the even greater influence of Philodemus with regard to style *and*
content: both poets refer to the financial and personal advantages of
an "easy love" (*S.* 1.2.119: *venerem facilem*), whose natural beauty, like
Horace's pithy satires and Philodemus' lean epigrams, is truthful,
unconditionally pleasurable, and not exaggerated by artificial and
unnecessary embellishments.[121] Along similar lines, some have read
Horace's subsequent emphasis on the importance of avoiding financial
strain and recognizing physical pleasure as independent of social class
(*S.* 1.2.125–6) as referring to a passage from Cercidas of Megalopolis,

[118] Wright (1921) 168–9 and, much more recently, Courtney (2013) 80. Gigante
(1993) 82 describes the language used by both Horace and Philodemus as "realismo
brutale" (cf. βινῶ above and *S.* 1.2.127: *futuo*).

[119] As Sider (1997) 200–1 explains, this epigram is probably not the original
version composed by Philodemus but rather was produced "by an *eruditus* ... with
no intention to defraud, but to provide for the amusement of himself and for his
friends a simulacrum of the lost original alluded to by Horace."

[120] Courtney (2013). Cf. Kiessling–Heinze (1910) 36: "Daß H. hier eines seiner
Epigramme dem oben zitierten Epigramm des Kallimachus gegenüberstellt, ist eine
Artigkeit gegen ihn [Philodemus]," "The fact that here Horace contrasts one of Philodemus' epigrams with the previously quoted poem from Callimachus is a compliment
to the philosopher." Freudenburg (1993) 196, however, reads Philodemus as "the perfect
foil for Callimachus."

[121] Freudenburg (1993) 196–7. For Philodemean poetry as "philosophically
correct," Sider (1997) 42–57. See also Hicks (2013) 141.

who, like Philodemus, also mentions the benefits of a cheap love free from worry:

> ἁ δ' ἐξ ἀγορᾶς Ἀφροδίτα,
> καὶ τὸ μη[δε]νὸς μέλειν, ὁπ[α]νίκα λῆς, ὅκα χρήζης,
> οὐ φόβος οὐ ταραχά. τα[ύ]ταν ὀβλῷ κατακλίνας
> Τ[υν]δαρέοιο δόκει γαμβρ[ὸς τό]τ' ἦμεν.   (fr. 2)

But Venus that paces the market—in preparation of desire demanding no thought or attention—here is no fear and no care: lie down with her for one obol and then consider yourself to be the son-in-law of Tyndareus.[122]

As Liana Lomiento indicates in her commentary of these fragments, this sentiment was "a *topos* common to the popular philosophy of Epicureans and Cynics," and it also occurs in a few fragments of Greek comic playwrights and Lucilius.[123] On the other hand, given the fact that this satire clearly invokes Philodemus (*S.* 1.2.121: *Philodemus ait*), whose application of the hedonic calculus within the context of love is identical to that of Horace, and that it alludes to his poems more than once, it is more reasonable to view his approach as an imitation of the Epicurean's philosophically correct yet entertaining epigrams.

Horace's consideration of the ideal lover as described by Philodemus provides contrast for the concluding scene, which, paralleling the end of *Satires* 1.1, involves the application of frankness through pictorial imagery. The poet's emphasis on emotional and financial stability regarding love affairs throughout *Satires* 1.2 prepares his audience for an action-packed visualization of the terrible risks involved in adultery:

> nec vereor, ne, dum futuo, vir rure recurrat,
> ianua frangatur, latret canis, undique magno
> pulsa domus strepitu resonet, vepallida lecto
> desiliat mulier, miseram se conscia clamet,
> cruribus haec metuat, doti deprensa, egomet mi.   (*S.* 1.2.127–31)

---

[122] Lomiento (1993) 9–26 provides a detailed introduction to this Cynic poet's life and works, as well as copious bibliographical references and testimonia. I give the text as it appears in her critical edition. To ἁ δ' ἐξ ἀγορᾶς Ἀφροδίτα as quoted above cf. Lucretius' *vulgivagaque vagus Venere* (4.1071).

[123] Lomiento (1993) 229. See also Rudd (1966) 25. Cataudella (1950) 28–31 argues for the possibility, which Gigante (1983) 242 seconds, that Horace had been exposed to Cercidas through Philodemus' poetry.

No fears have I while I screw that a husband may rush back from the country, the door burst open, the dog bark, the house ring through and through with the din and clatter of his knocking; that the woman, white as a sheet, will leap away, the maid in league with her cry out in terror, she fearing for her limbs, her guilty mistress for her dowry, and I for myself.

Through this unambiguously comic yet startlingly frank exemplum, in which Horace playfully dissociates himself from the typical elegiac *amator*, the audience reflects, this time in a more direct and forceful manner, on the fears and anxieties which accompany illegitimate and therefore dangerous love affairs. As others have noted, there are clear parallels between this portrayal and Plautus' *The Merchant* and *The Braggart Soldier*, both of which include scenes involving an adulterer caught in the act.[124] One may also compare Horace's use of comedy within the context of administering frankness to the following recommendation of Philodemus in *On Frank Criticism* (fr. 29.1–5): καταρχώμεθα σή[με]ρόν που καὶ α[ὐ]τὰς τ[ιθῶμ]εν εἰς ἐκε[ί]νου τὴν [αἴσθ]ησιν· ὃ κα[ὶ] τῶν κω[μωιδ]ογρ[άφων] ἐμιμή[σ]αντό τινες, "Let us begin, even today, and put these (. . .) before his (perception?), a thing which some of the comic writers imitated . . ." Despite the fragmentary state of this passage and the consequent uncertainty regarding its context, a better example of the connection between comedy and frankness may be found in Philodemus' observation (similar to that of Horace at S. 1.1.24: *ridentem dicere verum*) that, unless a "patient" is obstinate, the sage should apply frankness in a lighthearted and cheerful manner (fr. 85.5–10): δ[ια]τ[ι]θέσθω δ' ὅτι καὶ τ[ῆι δια]θέσει π[λ]ε[ί]στον ἑαυτοῦ τ[ού]των ὁ [κ]αθηγούμενος ε[ὐη]μέρωι καὶ φιλοφίλωι [καὶ ἠ]πίωι, "And let it be stated that the teacher of these people, in his disposition, at its most gentle and friend-loving and mild . . ." This is reflected by Alexander Olivieri, who summarizes the philosopher's approach to frankness in the introduction of his 1914 edition of the treatise: *qui contra non iracunde nec magna vocis contentione sed leniter et benigne, hilariter et clementer discipulos castigent, magnae eisdem esse utilitati*, "On the contrary, the ones who are of great use to their students are those who rebuke them without anger or raising their voices, but rather in a

[124] See McKeown (1979), 71–84, Fantham (1989) 158, Freudenburg (1993) 45–6, and Gowers (2012) 116.

manner that is mild, gentle, cheerful, and kind."¹²⁵ Horace's introduction of an entertaining scenario intended for admonition and moral guidance, which is also the ultimate goal of pictorial imagery as employed by Philodemus, recalls the ending of *Satires* 1.1 (80–7), which likewise incorporates colorful language and literary devices for the sake of vividness.

By "placing before the eyes" of his audience the formidable consequences of sexual excess, moreover, the poet draws a fitting conclusion to his riotously candid, though simultaneously therapeutic, criticism of Roman intemperance.

In *Satires* 1.3 Horace delivers his final, blatantly moral treatment of vice, which, aside from being a playful lesson in tolerance and mutual forbearance at the Stoics' expense,¹²⁶ is also an example of more subdued and therefore more effective frankness. In relation to their conviction that the sage is perfect in every way, traditional Stoics maintain an impossibly high standard of excellence (cf. Sen. *Ep.* 116.7: *nimis dura praecipitis*) and consequently deny any intermediate stage between virtue and vice: as Cicero puts it, for them all faults were equally reprehensible (*On Ends* 4.55: *omnia peccata paria*). Horace, probably drawing from Cicero's translation, points to Stoics "whose creed is that faults are much on par" (*S.* 1.3.96: *quis paria esse fere placuit peccata*), which is a doctrine Diogenes explains in his biography of Zeno of Citium:

ἀρέσκει δ' αὐτοῖς μηδὲν μεταξὺ εἶναι ἀρετῆς καὶ κακίας, τῶν Περιπατητικῶν μεταξὺ ἀρετῆς καὶ κακίας εἶναι λεγόντων τὴν προκοπήν· ὡς γὰρ δεῖν φασιν ἢ ὀρθὸν εἶναι ξύλον ἢ στρεβλόν, οὕτως ἢ δίκαιον ἢ ἄδικον, οὔτε δὲ δικαιότερον οὔτε ἀδικώτερον, καὶ ἐπὶ τῶν ἄλλων ὁμοίως.

(7.127)

For them, there is no mean between virtue and vice, whereas the Peripatetics say that in between virtue and vice there is progress. Thus the Stoics say that just as a stick is either straight or bent, so also something is either just or unjust and not "rather just" or "rather unjust," and similarly with the other virtues.

Although Panaetius famously attempted to soften this view among Romans by emphasizing what Diogenes calls the Peripatetic notion of "making progress" or προκοπή (cf. Sen. *Ep.* 89.1: *ad sapientiam*

¹²⁵ Olivieri (1914) vii. Cf. Philodemus' mention of "good cheer" in the same treatise (fr. 43.7: εὐφροσύνη[s]).
¹²⁶ Lejay (1966) 61: "So Horace will be in favor of Epicurus and against Zeno," "il sera donc pour Épicure contre Zénon."

120   *Epicurean Ethics in Horace*

properanti),[127] Horace makes his Epicurean persona here attack the traditional assertion, as stated by Chrisyppus according to Plutarch's account:

ὥσπερ ὁ πῆχυν ἀπέχων ἐν θαλάττῃ τῆς ἐπιφανείας οὐδὲν ἧττον πνίγεται τοῦ καταδεδυκότος ὀργυιὰς πεντακοσίας, οὕτως οὐδὲ οἱ πελάζοντες ἀρετῇ τῶν μακρὰν ὄντων ἧττόν εἰσιν ἐν κακίᾳ... οὕτως οἱ προκόπτοντες ἄχρι οὗ τὴν ἀρετὴν ἀναλάβωσιν, ἀνόητοι καὶ μοχθηροὶ διαμένουσιν.

(*On Common Notions against the Stoics* 1063a = SVF 3.539)

[They say that] just as in the sea the man a cubit from the surface is drowning no less than the one who has sunk 500 fathoms, so neither are they who apporach virtue any less in vice than those who are a long way from it...so those who are making progress remain stupid and depraved until they have attained virtue.

Such an extreme conviction, according to the poet, naturally results in arrogance and the ill-treatment of "inferiors," who, by means of a hilariously satirical inversion, become the innocent victims of the "perfect" Stoic's irrational anger (*S.* 1.3.76–95). Jerome Kemp has identified this attack on such inconsistency as criticism of the Stoic doctrine of *aequabilitas* as Cicero explains it in *On Duties* (1.111): *Omnino si quicquam est decorum, nihil est profecto magis quam aequabilitas cum universae vitae, tum singularum actionum*, "If there is such a thing as propriety at all, then it is nothing more than consistency in life as a whole as well as in individual actions."[128] From the poet's point of view, however, the average Stoic sage is grossly inconsistent in that, being blind to the fact that he is human and therefore fallible (cf. *S.* 1.3.68: *vitiis nemo sine nascitur*), he ignores his own faults while denouncing those of his friends. For his own part, Horace sides with the more moderate Epicurean view of friendship, which, in the spirit of therapeutic frankness, recognizes but attempts to correct the faults

---

[127] Also Cic. *On Duties* 1.46: *Quoniam autem vivitur non cum perfectis hominibus planeque sapientibus, sed cum iis in quibus praeclare agitur si sunt simulacra virtutis, etiam hoc intellegendum puto, neminem omnino esse neglegendum in quo aliqua significatio virtutis appareat*, "Since one lives not in the midst of perfect and wise men, but rather among those who act well if they but resemble virtue, and I think that no one who shows some sign of virtue should be utterly neglected."

[128] Kemp (2009) 2–4. See also Fraenkel (1957) 86 and Grilli (1983b) 269.

of others.[129] Such tolerance, according to Philodemus, is primarily the result of the Epicurean sage's recognition of his own imperfections, which occasionally lead him astray and require gentle correction:

[εἰ τὰ ὑπ]οπτευόμενα π[ε]ρὶ το[ῦ σ]οφοῦ, καὶ κοινῶς τ[ο]ῦ
κ[α]θηγουμένου, καθάρσεως δεῖται. Πῶς γὰρ μισεῖν τὸν ἁμαρτάνοντα
μὴ ἀπογνώ[σ]ιμα μέλλει, γινώσκω[ν] αὐτὸν οὐκ ὄντα τέλε[ι]ον καὶ
μιμνήι[σκων, ὅτι πάντες ἁμαρτάνειν εἰώθασιν;]

(*On Frank Criticism*, fr. 46.1–11)

. . . if what is suspected about the wise man, or the teacher in general, needs clarification. For how can he shun the one who has erred, but not unforgivably, knowing that he himself is not perfect and remembering that we all habitually err?

Unlike the Stoic sage, the Epicurean wise man understands his limitations and therefore "sympathizes" with patients (fr. 79.9–11: συνπαθῶ[ς] τ[ὰς ἁμαρ]τίας ὑπολαμβάνειν) rather than ridiculing them,[130] which encourages openness within the community with respect to the admission of faults and eventually leads to treatment.

Philodemus' emphasis in *On Frank Criticism* on the importance of public confession or self-revelation (cf. fr. 42.7–8: μηνύσουσιν) as a prerequisite for therapeutic frankness may relate to Horace's admission of his own imperfections. As Philodemus states, those who are suffering from vice ought to entrust themselves willingly (cf. fr. 42.8: ἐθελονταί) to the sage as if he were a physician:

[χρὴ γὰρ αὐτῶι δεικνύειν ἀνυ]ποστόλως τὰς διαμαρ[τί]ας καὶ κοινῶς
εἰπ[εῖ]ν [ἐ]λαττώσεις. εἰ γὰρ . . . παρέδωκεν [ἑαυ]τὸν θεραπε[ύ]ειν, πῶς
οὐχὶ μέλλει ταῦτ', ἐν [οἷ]ς δεῖται θεραπεύσε[ως, δει]κνύειν αὐτῶι κα[ὶ
νουθέτησιν προσδέχεσθαι;] (*On Frank Criticism*, fr. 40)

. . . one should reveal to him without reserve one's errors, and share with him in talking about one's failings. For if the student . . . has given himself over to him for therapy, how can he not show him the matter in which he needs the therapy?

---

[129] Kemp (2009) 4–10 offers an excellent consideration of Horace's adoption of Epicurean views in order to criticize Stoic extremism, although his focus does not encompass the Epicurean practice of frank criticism.

[130] See Michels (1944) 174 and Glad (1996) 38–9 for the importance of sympathy in Epicurean frankness. Schlegel (2005) alludes to this attitude by reading *Satires* 1.3 in terms of "the self among others."

The perfect example of a gentle and attentive teacher is, unsurprisingly, Epicurus himself, who listened while Heraclides "confessed his faults" to him (fr. 49.6–7: ἐμήνυεν Ἐπικούρωι τὰς ἁμαρτίας). Furthermore, Philodemus recommends that students be healed by disclosing their faults to each other (fr. 36.1–2: τὸ δ[ι᾽ ἀλ]λήλων σώ<ι>ζεσθαι),[131] even "presenting their concerns about themselves in front of the students" (fr. 55.1–4: κα[ὶ διδ]όναι παρρησίαι τὰ περὶ αὑτοὺς ἐπὶ τῶν κατασκευαζομένων). Perhaps more interesting, given the Stoic definition of the sage discussed already, the Epicurean teacher will similarly communicate his own affairs (fr. 81.2: τὰ περ[ὶ] αὑτὸν) and reveal his shortcomings to other sages (col. 9a.1–6): ἢ [μεγάλη]ν ἀσθένειαν ἢ πόν[ων ἀηδίαν] αὑτῶ[ι] παραπεπτω[κυῖα]ν καὶ τὰς αἰτίας αἶ[ς παρε]λογίσθη συνόψεται κἀκείνωι δείξει καὶ πεί[σ]ει, "[the wise man] will see either [serious] error or the [unpleasantness of troubles] that has befallen the other [wise] man, and the causes by which his reasoning was made to fail, and will demonstrate these to him and persuade him."[132] Such a communal view of frankness is an expression of what Clarence Glad calls an "ideal of non-concealment" and "participatory psychagogy," both of which are necessary for building trust and making a successful diagnosis.[133] This realistic attitude toward moral imperfection, which obviously contrasts with the idealistic view of the Stoics, and the application of therapeutic and reciprocal criticism sheds light on Horace's acknowledgement of certain faults and his rejection of shameless and, one might add, unjustified self-love:

> nunc aliquis dicat mihi "quid tu?
> nullane habes vitia?" immo alia et fortasse minora.
> Maenius absentem Novium cum carperet, "heus tu"
> quidam ait "ignoras te an ut ignotum dare nobis
> verba putas?" "egomet mi ignosco" Maenius inquit.
> stultus et inprobus hic amor est dignusque notari.   (*S.* 1.3.19–24)

Now someone may say to me: "What about yourself? Have you no faults?" Why yes, but not the same, and perhaps lesser ones. When Maenius once was carping at Novius behind his back, "Look out, sir," said someone, "do you not know yourself? Or do you think you impose

---

[131] Gigante (1975) 57 and Nussbaum (1986) 49 discuss the medical analogies involved in this practise.
[132] Cf. *On Frank Criticism* col. 8b.6–13 for a similar observation.
[133] Glad (1996) 48.

on us, as one we do not know?" "I take no note of myself," said Maenius. Such self-love is foolish and shameless, and deserves to be censured.

This important recognition of his own faults is, as Emily Gowers observes, a "defining moment in *Satires* I," since it is the first unambiguous example of Horace's fondness for disarming self-deprecation.[134] The logic behind the passage above may be that a satirist like Horace, although himself imperfect, at least acknowledges his faults and even puts them under the moral microscope for therapeutic examination (cf. *Satires* 2.3 and 2.7), which increases his self-awareness and consequently makes him better prepared to apply frankness to others. Perhaps of further significance is the fact that Horace's observation concerning Maenius occurs within the context of a poem that, in embracing the Epicurean view of friendship and forbearance, simultaneously rejects Stoic ethics as being conducive to overly harsh criticism.[135] Additionally, the ability to overlook others' faults connects this satire on friendship to the previous one, especially through the mention of lovers (*S.* 1.3. 38: *amatorem*), who, in a playful twist on a well-known passage from Lucretius (4.1157–70), Horace describes as models of mutual forbearance since they easily overlook their sweethearts' imperfections.[136]

Horace's awareness of his own failings and relative gentleness in applying therapeutic frankness not only provides a corrective model for the Stoics, but it also introduces the perfect contrast for his satirical portrayal of the latter as irascible and therefore utterly ineffective moralizers. In his following criticism of the Stoics' lack of tolerance for "fools" (*S.* 1.3.77: *stultis*) and description of their disproportionate response to perceived offenses, Horace incorporates ethical concepts and language that likewise appear in Epicurean frank treatments of vices like anger. Laying down his principal rule concerning the proper way to punish offenses, for example, he employs Lucretian rhetoric and invokes philosophical language to communicate the importance of calculations made in accordance with reason:

---

[134] Gowers (2012) 125. Cf. *S.* 1.4.130–1 and 1.6.65–6 for Horace's mention of his "moderate faults" (*vitiis mediocribus*).

[135] According to Porphyrio (*ad* 21), this Maenius was "quite infamous in Rome for his scurrility and extravagance" (*et scurrilitate et nepotatu notissimus Romae fuit*), for which reason he was probably ridiculed by Luclilius, as Fraenkel (1957) 89 notes (cf. 1203 M). See Schlegel (2005) 31–2 for the difference between Lucilius' comic branding of others by name and Horace's more constructive branding of Maenius.

[136] See Rudd (1966) 26 and Shearin (2014) 133–6.

124 *Epicurean Ethics in Horace*

denique, quatenus excidi penitus vitium irae,
cetera item nequeunt stultis haerentia, cur non
ponderibus modulisque suis ratio utitur ac res
ut quaeque est, ita suppliciis delicta coercet?   (*S.* 1.3.76–9)

In fine, since the fault of anger, and all the other faults that cleave to "fools" cannot be wholly cut away, why does not Reason use her own weights and measures, and visit offenses with punishments suited to each?

Aside from the Lucretian use of *denique* for the purpose of introducing a new argument and the emphasis on *ratio*,[137] Horace's inclusion of medical terminology in this passage in referring to the "excision" (*excidi*) of vice recalls similar references to scalpels and operations in Philodemus (cf. *On Frank Criticism*, col. 17a.4–8) and again Lucretius (3.310): *nec radicitus evelli mala posse putandumst*, "Nor should one think that evils can be torn out by the roots."[138] As both poets and Philodemus suggest, the reason anger cannot be removed completely from the human psyche is that, as mortal creatures, we are all naturally subject to pain and hence to emotional reactions (cf. *On Anger*, col. 39.29–30: ἀνέφευκτον καὶ διὰ τοῦτο φυσικόν, "natural and because of this unavoidable").[139] Horace's own description of anger as unable to be removed suggests that it is deeply ingrained in our nature (cf. *On Anger*, col. 40. 21–2: ἀνθρώπων φύσει) but that it can and should be controlled by reason. The Stoics, in contrast, view emotions, especially anger, as unqualifiedly vicious (see also Stobaeus 2.88.8–90.6 = *SVF* 3.378, 389 and Cicero, *Tusc.* 4.77–9): Seneca, for example, in his own treatise entitled *On Anger* calls it "the most hideous and frenzied of all emotions" (1.1.1: *maxime ex omnibus taetrum ac rabidum*) and asserts that it should be completely

---

[137] Obviously one of the standard uses of *denique*, but the Epicurean tone of this poem and the specifically Lucretian explanation of evolution (99–124) leave little doubt as to the allusion, as the commentators as well as Fraenkel (1957) 87 notes. See Kemp (2009) 4 for a similar observation and for the mention of *ratio* as "another ironic jibe against the Stoics."

[138] The intertext is discussed by Grilli (1983b) 270–1 and Gowers (2012) 135, who interpret Horace' mention of weights and measures within the context of Epicurus' κανών. Cf. also Cicero's *Tusculan Disputations* (3.13): *nos autem audeamus non solum ramos amputare miseriarum sed omnis radicum fibras evellere. tamen aliquid relinquetur fortasse; ita sunt altae stirpes stultitiae*, "We, however, must dare to sever not only the branches of wretchedness but even to tear out every fiber of its roots. Even then, some of it will perhaps remain, for such is the depth of folly's roots."

[139] See Asmis (2011) 160–2. Only the gods are not subject to such emotions (cf. KD 1).

eradicated, not controlled (1.8.4).[140] What is missing from the Stoics' appraisal of anger, however, and what Horace and other Epicurean authors supply, is the understanding that anger is not always "opposed to reason" (Cic. *Tusc.* 4.79: *repugnante ratione*). In fact, when it arises in someone who has a good disposition and is thus able to respond to circumstances in a rational and calculated manner (*S.* 1.3.78: *ratio*; cf. *On Anger*, col. 40.17: ἐνλόγιστον), it can even be considered to be a good thing:

> κατὰ δὲ τὴν συνπλοκὴν τῆι διαθέσει κἂν ἀγαθὸν ῥηθήσεσθαι νομίζομεν.
>
> συνίσταται γὰρ ἀπὸ το[ῦ] βλέπειν, ὡς ἡ φύσις ἔχει τῶν πραγμάτων, καὶ μηδὲν ψευδοδοξεῖν ἐν ταῖς σ[υ]μμετρήσεσι τῶν ἐλα[ττ]ωμάτων καὶ ταῖς κολάσεσι τῶν βλαπτόντων. (*On Anger*, col. 37.29–39)

In making a distinction we demonstrate that a feeling is evil in itself, since it is painful or analogous to what is painful, but in connection with one's disposition we think that it can even be called good. For this results from a consideration of the nature of things and not allowing any false opinions into the comparative calculations of the harm done and into our punishments of those who harm us.[141]

Philodemus underscores the importance of understanding the nature of the offense (φύσις) and of reacting to it with sound reason (μηδὲν ψευδοδοξεῖν) and within the context of the hedonic calculus (ἐν ταῖς σ[υ]μμετρήσεσι; cf. *S.* 1.3.78: *ponderibus modulisque*). Only by doing this will one avoid the "countless miseries" (*On Anger*, col. 38.4: μυρία δυσχερῆ) Philodemus associates with miscalculations of empty or vain anger: beheadings (fr. 12.21: τὰς κεφαλὰς ἀφαιρεῖ), beatings (fr. 13.26: τύπτειν καὶ λακτίζειν), and self-alienation in general (coll. 19–25 offer a detailed description of how the typical irascible man's

---

[140] See Tsouna (2011) 196–209 for a more detailed discussion. Seneca's main opponents are the Peripatetics, who taught that anger, when controlled by reason, could be useful, especially in the context of war (*On Anger* 1.8.9, cf. Cic. *Tusc.* 4.39–46). Although Panaetius adopted this doctrine of "moderated emotion" or μετριοπαθής (cf. DL 5.31 for the term), given Horace's intentional oversight elsewhere in *Satires* 1.3 of the Stoics' more moderate views, it seems unlikely that he is alluding to this in the above passage, as Gowers (2012) 134 suggests.

[141] See Asmis (2011) 161–2 for more on Philodemus' distinction of an emotion as (1) a "feeling" (πάθος), which is evil in itself if painful, and (2) the cognitive disposition that gives rise to the feeling, which can be good. For discussions of Philodemus' complex views on anger and their origins, see Ringeltaube (1913) 38–46, Philippson (1916) 425–60, Indelli (1988) 17–31, Annas (1989) 145–64, Indelli (2004) 103–10, Fish (2004) 111–38, and especially Tsouna (2007) 195–238, Asmis (2011) 152–82, and Tsouna (2011) 184–96.

unbearable behavior alienates him from family, friends, slaves, and society in general). This thought-process is remarkably similar to Horace's treatment of the Stoics' false opinion that all vices are equal, which inhibits calculated reasoning and correspondingly leads them to "flay with the terrible scourge what calls for the strap" (_S._ 1.3.119: _scutica dignum horribili sectere flagello_).[142] The poet criticizes this failure to respond properly to slight offenses by vividly describing, like Philodemus, the consequences of such folly: crucifixion (82: _in cruce_), hatred (86: _odisti_), and beatings with a rod (120: _ferula caedas_), all of which bring the enraged Stoic more pain, anxiety, and distress rather than genuine peace.

In response to Horace's anti-Stoic persona's call for a reasonable and proportionate response to offenses, the nameless straw man of _Satires_ 1.3, who proves to be every bit as obstinate as the poet's previous patients, arrogantly declares that he is unequivocally superior to everyone because of his complete independence and perfect virtue (_S._ 1.3.126–33). This arrogance is the result of clever manipulation on the part of Horace, who exploits the Stoic doctrine that the possession of a single virtue implies the possession of all of them (Stob. 2.63 = _SVF_ 3.280: τὸν γὰρ μίαν ἔχοντα πάσας ἔχειν) and that therefore the Stoic sage is perfect and does all things well (Stob. 2.66.14 = _SVF_ 3.560: λέγουσι δὲ καὶ πάντ᾽ εὖ ποεῖν τὸν σοφόν). Such a refusal to listen to true _ratio_, namely, the Epicurean calculus and arguments concerning the evolution of justice and the role of human convention in establishing its limits (_S._ 1.3.99–124),[143] is met by a shift from theory to reality as Horace once again introduces a final tableau that forces the interlocutor to visualize his irrational conduct:

vellunt tibi barbam
lascivi pueri, quos tu nisi fuste coerces,
urgeris turba circum te stante miserque
rumperis et latras, magnorum maxime regum. (_S._ 1.3.133–6)

---

[142] See Hicks (2013) 145.

[143] For the parodic elements of Horace's imitation of Lucretius in this passage, see Grilli (1983b) 273–4, Ferri (1993) 37–8, Freudenburg (1993) 26–7, and Turpin (2009) 133–7. For a more positive interpretation and a discussion of the distinction between Epicurean _ratio_ as calculation (mentioned at 78) and Stoic _ratio_ as inflexible, divine law (invoked ironically at 115), see Kemp (2009) 8–10. Lejay (1966) 66–7 notes that Horace "has corrected one of the blunders that are not rare in the _De rerum natura_" ("a corrigé une de ces maladresses qui ne sont pas rares dans le _De rerum natura_"), because, unlike Lucretius, he does not place the development of laws after the end of monarchical rule (during which there undoubtedly must have been at least some laws).

Mischievous boys pluck at your beard, and unless you keep them off with your staff, you are jostled by the crowd that surrounds you, while you, poor wretch, snarl and burst with rage, O mightiest of mighty kings!

This frank depiction of the irascible temperament, with its colorful, entertaining, and almost theatrical qualities and vividness, owes a great deal to, as discussed already, the florid style of Bion, which later Epicureans like Demetrius of Laconia (*c.*100 BC) employed in their philosophical treatises.[144] According to Diogenes (4.52), Eratosthenes said that Bion was "the first person who had clothed philosophy in a flowery robe" (πρῶτος Βίων φιλοσοφίαν ἀνθινὰ ἐνέδυσεν), and a similar identification occurs in one of the Herculaneum papyri (PHerc. 1055, col. 18.2–10), which has been assigned to the Demetrius mentioned immediately above.[145] The mention of Bion's style in this Epicurean treatise is significant, since he is quoted later on in order to communicate more gracefully an Epicurean philosophical point:

τοῦτον ἐχόντων τὸν τρόπον ἐπὶ τοῦ λόγου τοῦ Βιωνήου τοῦτο μὲν θήσω, διότι "γένος ἕκαστον ζώιων ἰδίαν ἔχει μορφὴν ἐν τῶι ἰδίωι γένει"

(col. 22.1–6)

Things being as they are, I shall set it down in the manner of a Bionean phrase,[146] since "each kind of living thing has its own form in accordance with its own kind . . ."

Such borrowing also occurs in the works of Philodemus, who employs Bionean language for the sake of shocking frankness in describing the symptoms of anger (cf. *On Anger*, col. 8.34–7): οἷον λέγω τὴν ὑπὸ τῆς κ[ρ]αυγῆς διάστασιν [τ]οῦ πλεύμονος σὺν αὐταῖς πλευραῖς, "For example, the swelling of the lungs along with the ribs on account of screaming."[147] For Horace and Philodemus, however, this connection

---

[144] For the evidence, see Gigante and Indelli (1978) 124–31. Conveniently placed in the same volume are studies of Demetrius' contribution to the Epicurean understanding of philology (Ferrario 2000: 53–61), the gods (Santoro 2000: 63–70), and poetry (Pace 2000: 79). For general information about Demetrius and his works, see Knoll's *RE* article in supplement 3 (1918) 329–30.

[145] See Crönert (1906) 31–3.

[146] Cf. Horace's similar adjectival use of Bion's name (*Ep.* 2.2.60: *Bioneis sermonibus*), which appears to be a *hapax legomenon*. See also Gigante and Indelli (1978) 124–5. In the fragments of *On Flattery*, Philodemus states that "we prefer to speak in the manner of Bion" (PHerc. 223, fr. 7.81–82: τὰ τοῦ Βίωνος [αἱρούμεν]οι λέγειν).

[147] Indelli (1988) 158 includes commentary on the influence of Bion's treatise *On Apathy* in this passage, evidence for which may be found in Hense (1969) 55–62. As

128   *Epicurean Ethics in Horace*

is stylistic rather than ethical, since the intention of both is to "release ourselves from [harmful emotions] by observing the magnitude and number of evils they contain and bring along with them" (*On Anger*, col. 6.18–22: [τὸ] συν[έ]χον [ἔ]χει τῆς ἀπ[ολύ]σεως ἐν [τ]ῶι θεωρῆσ[αι τ]ὸ μέγεθος καὶ τὸ πλ[ῆθ]ος ὧν ἔχει καὶ συνεπι[σπ]ᾶται κακῶν).[148]

Reflecting on these introductory satires and on Horace's concern with money, love, and friendship, a pattern or hierarchy seems to appear. Indeed, in *On Property Management* Philodemus, most likely inspired by Metrodorus' views, lists three things in descending order of importance: personal health, friendship, and money (col. 13.11–29). This resembles the poet's approach in *Satires* 1.1–3, except that the topics appear in ascending order of importance, with friendship, which was of major concern to the Epicureans, being at the top and setting the tone for the rest of the collection. For all of the entertainment and colorful language packed into Horace's portraits in the introductory satires, then, the underlying message is not only useful but also philosophically sound and consistent with Epicurean ethics. After delivering three hard-hitting diatribes on vicious behavior, however, the poet's audience—whether Maecenas or other readers within his circle of friends—must have wondered exactly how the poet planned to justify his persona's moral superiority. The full answer, part of which he gives in *Satires* 1.3 by mentioning in passing his "lesser faults" (20: *vitia...minora*), emerges in the following poem in the collection. Indeed, it is in *Satires* 1.4 where Horace reveals, in a rather idealized and convenient way, his ethical credentials by describing his positive upbringing at the hands of an attentive and suspiciously wise father.

Tsouna (2003) 243 n. 3 comments, the idea that Philodemus parodies the Stoic doctrine of ἀπάθεια in his vivid descriptions of the consequences of anger is suggested by David Armstrong and Michael McOsker in their forthcoming edition. If they are correct, this may serve to establish a stronger link with Horace's obviously parodic treatment in *Satires* 1.3 of the Stoic paradox that all faults are equal. For a similar description of the symptoms of anger (which is heavily influenced by that of Philodemus), see Sen. *On Anger* 1.1.3–4 and Tsouna (2011) 198–9.

[148] Annas (1989) 156 provides a helpful explanation of this passage within the larger context of Epicurean emotions.

3

Horace's Epicurean Moral Credentials in *Satires* 1.4 and 1.6

EPICUREAN UPBRINGING IN *SATIRES* 1.4

Horace's description of his upbringing in *Satires* 1.4 is an extremely important scene in Book 1, because it establishes his persona's ethical credentials and justifies his role as a professional critic in the introductory satires. It is also one of the most complex and multifaceted passages in the entire collection, for in the process of constructing his ethical persona Horace synthesizes various literary and philosophical influences in a sophisticated yet entertaining manner. Scholars have repeatedly shown the significant role of Roman comedy, especially Terence's *Brothers*, in what is considered to be Horace's serio-comic portrayal of his father's training.[1] Perhaps one of the least-explored facets of Horace's father's pedagogical method, however, is the more serious role of Epicurean ethics and epistemology, which, in conjunction with other traditions, has much to offer a satiric poet who is concerned with practical ethics and offers moral correction through the close observation of morally flawed individuals' defects. Aside from contributing to the ethical content of the *Satires*, Epicurean philosophy adds depth to the poet's presentation and analysis of the many foibles of contemporary Roman society. The reliance on sensation, for example, grants the audience full access to the colorful (and often disturbing) details of Roman life, but its importance for Epicurean epistemology suggests a more profound engagement with certain doctrines. Also worth consideration is the conventionality of the language Horace typically employs in the

---

[1] Leach (1971) 616–32, Hunter (1985a) 490, and Freudenburg (1993) 33–9.

Satires, which is certainly fitting for the genre but also compatible with the semantic concerns of Epicurean language theory, and his practical advice concerning choices and avoidances as motivated by a calculation of pains and foreseeable pleasures.

Horace pays tribute to his father by identifying him not only as the source (*S.* 1.4.129: *ex hoc*) of his being *purus et insons*,[2] but also as the "cause" (*S.* 1.6.71: *causa*) of his successful encounter with Maecenas. A proper understanding of his significance, therefore, is essential for an appreciation of the poet's own literary persona and an accurate interpretation of the role of Epicurean ethics in the *Satires*. His portrayal in 1.4 as the paternal source of Horace's poetry and generic origin of his subdued, morally conscious style at once distinguishes the poet from his literary predecessor Lucilius and defines the principles informing Horatian satire:

> liberius si
> dixero quid, si forte iocosius, hoc mihi iuris
> cum venia dabis: insuevit pater optimus hoc me   (*S.* 1.4.103–5)

> If in my words I am too free, perchance too light, this bit of liberty you will indulgently grant me. It is a habit the best of fathers taught me ...

This description is carefully designed to emphasize the benign tone of Horatian satire, which, as seen already in the introductory poems, criticizes "rather freely" and "jokingly," while ostensibly severing the connection to Old Comedy and hence the *modus Lucilianus* (cf. *S.* 1.4.1–5), which criticizes publicly, caustically and by name.[3] Catherine Schlegel expresses this view clearly in stating that "[t]he satire will demonstrate that ultimately Horace and Lucilius have separate genealogies" and that although Horace "writes in Lucilius' genre, they have no common ancestors," both of which are sentiments frequently reflected in the scholarship tradition.[4] This reconfiguration

---

[2] Particularly important for a boy still wearing the *toga praetexta* and *bulla*, since more license was allowed afterward (until marriage, of course). Cf. Ter. *Brothers* 101–10.

[3] See Fraenkel (1957) 126–7, Rudd (1966) 88–92, Brink (1963) 157, and Courtney (2013) 88 for the role ὀνομαστὶ κωμῳδεῖν in this satire.

[4] Schlegel (2000) 95. It was Hendrickson (1900) 124 who argued early on that in *Satires* 1.4 Horace completely severs the connection to traditional satire. Anderson (1982) 29 views Horace as a Socratic figure who is exclusively concerned with ethics, while Fiske (1971) 277–80 considers Horace's brand of humor as thoroughly influenced by Aristotle's portrayal of the εὐτράπελος ("gentleman"), for which see *Nic. Eth.* 1127b34–1128a33. For the various philosophical influences related to Horace's partial

of his literary parentage, however, is by no means absolute. Horace's description of his own satire as directed toward those who are "worthy of being blamed" (*S.* 1.4.25: *culpari dignos*; cf. *S.* 1.3.24: *dignusque notari*), as well as his criticisms of individuals by name (which has apparently caused a public reaction; cf. *S.* 1.4.70 and 78–9), plainly indicates that his works retain something of the Lucilian spirit.[5] As Eleanor Winsor Leach explains, "Horace follows Lucilius in his verisimilitude, but rejects the Aristophanic spirit, thus casting off the last vestige of old comedy."[6] Nevertheless, the major differences between Horace and Lucilius, especially with regard to their distinct approaches to style and ethics, are widely recognized. These differences are primarily communicated by the poet's shift from public criticism to the more private concerns and stock characters reminiscent of New Comedy (cf. *S.* 1.4.25–32 and 48–52), which suggests that Horatian satire will engage moral deficiency in a lighthearted manner but simultaneously at a more sophisticated and personal level. Horace's portrayal of his father within the context of this tradition is worthy of further consideration, since it has significant implications for the origin and character of Horatian satire itself.

The tradition of Roman comedy plays an important role in Horace's creation of his father's literary persona, but the complexity of this role and its programmatic significance have not been wholly appreciated. Horace recognized Terence's well-deserved reputation in antiquity for purity of diction and skill (cf. *Ep.* 2.1.59: *arte*),[7] and his willingness to employ specifically Terentian stock characters and scenes likely reflects his own concern for refinement and stylistic rigor.[8] The exploration of intimate and familial affairs typical of Terentian drama is closely paralleled by the domestic origin of Horatian satire and its concern with privacy (cf. *S.* 1.4.22–3, 1.10.74–91, and *Ep.* 1.19.35–49), although one may note that the poet's proclaimed

---

rejection of Aristophanic invective and preference for a more gentle tone, see Rudd (1966) 96–7. Freudenburg (1993) 55–108 argues for a "hybrid theory" of satiric humor that embraces both Aristophanic and Peripatetic elements.

[5] Rudd (1966) 91–2, Hunter (1985a) 486, and Freudenburg (1993) 100.

[6] Leach (1971) 622. See also Hicks (2013) 113–14.

[7] Müller (2013) 366–70 discusses Terence's language and style, and Barsby (1999) 19–27 includes a useful introduction to its general characteristics.

[8] Fairclough (1913) 188–93. Aside from the "bumpkin father" of *S.* 1.4.109–26, Horace incorporates other Terentian stock characters into the *Satires*, like the "self-tormentor" (1.2.20–2) and the "raging father" (1.4.48–52).

confidentiality regarding poetic recitation in these passages contradicts his earlier claim to have offended a wider public.[9] But Horace's allusions to his father's Terentian qualities do more than communicate the importance of stylistic refinement and poetic confidentiality. The comparison with Demea,[10] who may be a comic embodiment of the traditional Roman *paterfamilias*,[11] suggests that Horace's father (and therefore Horatian satire itself) censures vice by promoting ancestral virtue within a funny, harmlessly conservative context:

> fit sedulo,
> nil praetermitto, consuefacio. denique
> inspicere tamquam in speculum in vitas omnium
> iubeo atque ex aliis sumere exemplum sibi.
> hoc facito... hoc fugito.   (Terence, *Brothers* 414–17)

One must be careful. I don't overlook anything, I teach him good habits. Most of all I urge him to peer into the lives of all people as if into a mirror, and to take from those others an example for himself: Do this... avoid that.

Although Kiessling–Heinze had made this connection early on, it is Leach who provides the first extended consideration of the similarities between Horace's father at *S.* 1.4.109–26 and Demea in the *Brothers*. Drawing partly from this study, Kirk Freudenburg reads Horace's father as the *doctor ineptus* of Roman comedy, whose portrayal in this poem serves the programmatic function of characterizing Horace's persona in *Satires* 1.1–3 as comically inept.[12] The notion that Horace's portrayal of his father is a purely fictional creation and therefore devoid of any serious ethical content, however, is rightly challenged by some scholars.[13] Perhaps this is because the comparison rests on textual parallels that may overlook the broader context in which both Demea and Horace's father are portrayed. Poets like Menander and his Roman successors, who stage plays

---

[9] Courtney (2013) 92 n. 87 compares Horace's reluctance to recite in public to Epicurus' statement that the wise man will read in public, but only under compulsion (DL 10.121). Cf. Lucilius' consideration of his intended audience (588–96 M) and Persius' admission of a lack thereof (1.1–3).

[10] Leach (1971) 616–32, who is followed by Hunter (1985a) 490.

[11] See Traill (2013) 318–39 and Barsby (2001) 245. Hunter (1985b) is more cautious about associating the *Brothers* with "a very specific social and historical context" (109).

[12] Freudenburg (1993) 33–9.

[13] e.g. Schrijvers (1993) 50–2 and Schlegel (2000).

that center on the dynamics of the typical father–son relationship and its ethical implications and consequences, are likely engaging with Aristotle's teaching concerning the important role of education in forming a virtuous disposition (*Nic. Eth.* 1103b20–5). Of course, the connection between παιδεία and a healthy disposition goes back further to the sophist Protagoras (cf. DK B3), who, like Demea and Horace's father, employs the "example method" for moral training as discussed in the first chapter. The education of children is also encompassed by Epicurus' universal invitation to philosophy (*Men.* 122), which reappears in Philodemus' *On Choices and Avoidances* (col. 21.12–13) and in Horace (*Ep.* 1.1.24–6: *id* [sc. *philosophia*] *quod... aeque neglectum pueris senibusque nocebit*, "That task which... if neglected, will be harmful alike to young and to old").[14] The portrayals of this relationship in Terence's plays (especially the *Brothers*), however, are notoriously problematic on account of their overwhelming negativity: indeed, all of them revolve around a disobedient son's *amor turpis* (to use the Horatian description), while the fathers are typically described as unstable and overly emotional authoritarian figures who, unlike Horace's father, give barking commands that ultimately provoke their children's hatred (cf. *Brothers* 870–1).[15] Perhaps a better parallel for Horace's father can be found in a touching scene from Plautus' *Three Coins*, in which the virtuous Lysiteles fondly attributes his moral strength to his father's training:

> semper ego usque ad hanc aetatem ab ineunte adulescentia
> tuis servivi servitutem imperiis [et] praeceptis, pater.
> pro ingenio ego me liberum esse ratu' sum, pro imperio tuo
> meum animum tibi servitutem servire aequom censui.
>
> . . . .
>
> istaec ego mi semper habui aetati integumentum meae;
> ne penetrarem me usquam ubi esset damni conciliabulum
> neu noctu irem obambulatum neu suom adimerem alteri
> neu tibi aegritudinem, pater, parerem, parsi sedulo:
> sarta tecta tua praecepta usque habui mea modestia. (301–4, 313–17)

I have always obeyed your commands and precepts, father, from my youth to the present day. I consider myself free with regard to my nature, and I deemed it proper that my mind should faithfully heed

---

[14] For Epicurean education, see especially Asmis (2001) 206–39.
[15] See Hunter (1985b) 99–109 and Traill (2013) 328–9 for father–son relationships and the importance of recognition scenes in Terentian drama.

your precepts. These teachings of yours I have always considered a
protection in my youth, and I have taken careful precautions, father,
lest I should ever enter into any place where pernicious vice was
intended, or go about strolling at night, or steal from another, or
cause you grief: I have always maintained your precepts, which are a
well-made protection, by means of my temperance.

In this scene, which is an extremely rare one in New Comedy, the
mention of age (*aetas*), intellect (*animus*), precepts (*praecepta*), and the
abstinence from vicious behavior bears a significant resemblance to
Horace's description of his own upbringing (cf. *S.* 1.4.119: *aetas*, 120:
animum, 121: *dictis*). It is therefore possible that Horace's healthy
relationship with his father is intended as a success story that defies
comic tradition and "corrects" the behavior of the typical *adulescens*.[16]

Either way, Horace's portrayal of his father within the context of
the traditional *paterfamilias* from Roman comedy is deliberate, and
its significance is partly expressed by Donatus in his commentary
on Demea's pedagogical method. He observes the following (*ad*
418): *non philosophice, sed civiliter monet . . . ergo ut idioticus et
comicus pater, non ut sapiens et praeceptor,* "He does not advise
as a philosopher but as a layman . . . therefore [he advises] as a
comic and unskilled father, not as a sage and a teacher."[17] The
advantage of this portrayal for Horace's persona is twofold: first, it
creates the illusion that Horatian satire is the pedestrian ranting of
an ordinary, home-grown local rather than the educated expression
of a mind imbued with foreign doctrines. In this sense our poet is
completely in line with Lucilius' famous criticism of Albucius
(88–94 M), Juvenal's tirade against Greek philosophers
(3.114–25), and Cicero's denigration of the Greeks as liars and
flatterers in *Orator* (1.11.47), *Letters to Quintus* (1.5.16), and, in
connection with Philodemus, in his speech *Against Piso* (70). The
second advantage to this portrayal is that it advertises the *Satires* as
an unabashedly Roman creation that is committed to preserving
"ancient tradition" (*S.* 1.4.117: *traditum ab antiquis morem*), which

---

[16] For the challenge of withstanding the temptations associated with sexual license
(cf. *S.* 1.4.113–14: *concessa cum venere uti | possem*), see Persius' account of how he
entrusted himself to the philosopher Cornutus at an early age precisely for this reason
(5.30–40).

[17] Freudenburg (1993) 36, like Hunter (1985a) 490, applies Donatus' evaluation to
Horace's father, whose modest deferral to the sage (*sapiens*) at *S.* 1.4.115–16 allegedly
implies the same distinction.

recalls a similar passage from Plautus' *Three Coins* (295–6): *meo modo et moribu' vivito antiquis, quae ego tibi praecipio, | ea facito*, "Live according to my example and the ancient custom, and do whatever I enjoin upon you."[18] Regardless of whether or not Horace publicly recited his verses or promoted this traditional persona, its creation not only complements the thoroughly Roman nature of satire as revealed in *Satires* 1.10 (31–5), where Quirinus appears in a dream vision and urges the poet to compose in pure, unadulterated Latin,[19] but it also provides ample opportunity for the contradictory distinctions so typical of Horace's style. Like his poetry, the father's humble exterior may conceal a more sophisticated core shaped by contemporary ethical doctrines. Uncovering this is by no means an easy task (especially with regard to Horace's origin, which the poet himself playfully describes as *anceps* at *S.* 2.1.34), since the apparent multiplicity of Horace's persona makes it more difficult to find the significance underlying what James Zetzel calls the "surface meaning" of his satires.[20]

In some ways, Horace's potentially self-effacing description of his father's training resembles his disingenuousness regarding the literary pretensions of the *Satires*. According to his own admission (*S.* 1.4.38–65), another generic similarity between satire and comedy is that neither ranks as true poetry. Employing the standard *pater ardens* scene from comedy (48–52), which is consistent with Horace's portrayal of Chremes in the *Art of Poetry* (93–4: *interdum tamen et vocem comoedia tollit | iratusque Chremes tumido delitigat ore*, "Yet at times even Comedy raises her voice, and an angry Chremes storms in swelling tones"),[21] the poet tells us that satire's conversational tone likewise lacks the syntactical complexity and indissolubility of poetry. It is nothing more than versified, "informal conversation" (*S.* 1.4.48:

[18] Leach (1971) 619 cites Terence's *Brothers* (411–12) and notes that "the fathers are similar, both in their moral and educational convictions and in their reliance on ancestral virtue as a standard of perfection."

[19] Rudd (1986) 172–4 considers Horace's Romanization of Greek words an expression of literary "purism," although see also Ferriss-Hill (2015) 231–2. Gowers (2012) 307 discusses relevant literary parallels to the Quirinus passage.

[20] Zetzel (2009) 21. See also Martindale (1993) 1, Oliensis (1998) 2, and Gowers (2003) 55–7.

[21] Leach (1971) 62 suggests that Horace's reference to the *pater ardens* in *S.* 1.4.48–52 is consistent with his later allusion to Demea, and that both comic figures describe his father. Schlegel (2000) 105 n. 15, who suggests that the *pater ardens* is a foil to the "real" father in the satire, challenges this view.

sermo merus). In order to illustrate "real" poetry's unity, Horace introduces a passage from Ennius and declares that, unlike the *Satires*, any transposition of these epic verses would result in dismemberment and utter destruction (62: *disiecti membra poetae*). Our poet, how-ever, is not to be trusted: the insincerity of his modest claim is betrayed by the fact that he has carefully structured his *Satires* in accordance with Philodemean compositional theory, and his descrip-tion of the impossibility of transposition actually illustrates the appli-cation of this theory to his own work. Steven Oberhelman and David Armstrong provide some insight:

> To summarize what Horace is doing here. The text seems to state that Horace's satire is poetry only because of meter and word-order. But we must beware of this surface reading in an author like Horace, where texts may at any one moment be undercut by humorous undertones and ironic slippage. In fact, Horace's subtext (if we so choose to call it) may well assert that Ennius, at least in the lines quoted, lives up no better than Lucilius to Horace's poetic ideal. If we transpose Ennius' text, what have we left? Nothing more than the same pedestrian sen-tence with a different word-order... But the delicious humor is that Horace's metathesized lines... are *poetic*—Ennius' lines are not.[22]

This modesty regarding literary sophistication, therefore, which extends to Horace's deceptively simple description of his upbringing later on, is merely topical, whereas a more profound examination reveals the confidence of a skilled *vates*. Given Horace's subtle yet stimulating disingenuousness regarding the literary merits of the *Satires*, one wonders whether he plays a similar game with respect to its moral content. Catherine Schlegel suggests as much in her examination of the poet's father in this satire:

> Horace's suggestion that in writing satire, he was not writing poetry, was not entirely serious... but the playful suggestion receives a lengthy treatment and has, I think, a true meaning in preparing the reader for the redefinition of satire and what to expect of the genre, which Horace accomplishes in the second half of the poem when he makes his father's ethical training the basis, the equivalent, of his own satirical poetic activity.[23]

---

[22] Oberhelman and Armstrong (1995) 243–5. Also Freudenburg (1993) 139–45 and Kemp (2010a) 68–74.

[23] Schlegel (2000) 104. Kemp (2010a) 61 and Cucchiarelli (2001) 109 similarly take Horace's portrayal of his father in this poem as containing serious undertones and therefore not entirely comic.

Of course, such an inquiry will require a consideration of Horace's ethical training that extends beyond the function of humor (τὸ γελοῖον) and into the realm of philosophical thought (τὸ σπουδαῖον).[24] The simplicity of his father's educational method, which emphasizes his portrayal as a conservative Roman freedman interested in practical ethics, forecasts Horace's concern with offering moral correction through useful advice elsewhere in the *Satires*. This is communicated primarily by examples from everyday life and the abundance of purpose clauses, which underscore the importance of practicality:

> cum me hortaretur, parce frugaliter atque
> viverem uti contentus eo quod mi ipse parasset:
> "nonne vides, Albi ut male vivat filius utque
> Baius inops? magnum documentum, ne patriam rem   110
> perdere quis velit." a turpi meretricis amore
> cum deterreret: "Scetani dissimilis sis."
> ne sequerer moechas, concessa cum venere uti
> possem: "deprensi non bella est fama Treboni"
> aiebat. "sapiens, vitatu quidque petitu   115
> sit melius, causas reddet tibi; mi satis est, si
> traditum ab antiquis morem servare tuamque,
> dum custodis eges, vitam famamque tueri
> incolumem possum; simul ac duraverit aetas
> membra animumque tuum, nabis sine cortice."   120
> (S. 1.4.107–20)

When he encouraged me to live thriftily, frugally, and content with what he had saved, "Do you not see," he would say, "how badly fares young Albius, and how poor is Baius? A striking lesson not to waste one's patrimony!" When he deterred me from a vulgar amour, "Don't be like Scetanus." And to prevent me from courting another's wife when I might enjoy love not forbidden, "Not pretty," he would say, "is the repute of Trebonius, caught in the act. Your philosopher will give you theories for choosing or avoiding this or that: enough for me if I can uphold the rule our fathers handed down, and if, so long as you need a guardian, I can keep your health and name safe. When years have brought strength to body and mind, you will swim without the cork."

[24] Fiske (1971) 298: "[I]n lines 102–142 Horace lets us see τὸ σπουδαῖον, the earnest features of the satirist beneath the comic mask."

This method closely reflects Horace's own approach to criticism in the *Satires*, which likewise involves negative purpose clauses and advice intended either to produce or prevent certain outcomes: *denique sit finis quaerendi... ne facias* (1.1.92–4: "In short, set bounds to the quest of wealth... lest you fare like..."); *quare, ne paeniteat te,* | *desine matronas sectarier* (1.2.77–8: "Wherefore, that you may have no reason to repent, cease to court matrons"). The poet also tends to emphasize the practical reasons for his observations of everyday life: *ne te morer, audi,* | *quo rem deducam* (1.1.14–15: "Lest I should delay you any further: listen, here's where I'm going with this"); *siquis nunc quaerat "quo res haec pertinet?" illuc* (1.2.23: "If anyone should now ask 'what's this got to do with anything,' here's the answer..."); *ne longum faciam* (1.3.137: "lest I should drag this on..."); *nescis, quo valeat nummus, quem praebeat usum?* | *panis ematur, holus, vini sextarius* (1.1.73: "Don't you know what money is for, what it can provide? You may buy bread, veggies, a pint of wine"). Indeed, one of the major characteristics of the *Satires* is the concern with offering real-life criticism for the sake of correction rather than engaging in theoretical speculation. This, however, was apparently instilled in young Horace by his father, who promotes his own ignorance by casually depreciating the complicated theories behind his son's ethical decisions: *sapiens, vitatu quidque petitu* | *sit melius, causas reddet tibi,* "Your philosopher will give you theories for choosing or avoiding this or that." In his commentary Paul Lejay describes Horace's father's method as "practical education that is not concerned with the lofty speculations of philosophers but rather preserves the robust tradition of Rome" ("éducation practique qui néglige les belles spéculations des philosophes, mais qui maintient le forte tradition nationale").[25] It is possible that this approach is an intentional reversal of the Stoic method, which emphatically prescribes theory before practice (cf. Arrian, *Discourses of Epictetus* 1.26.3 and Musonius Rufus, *Discourses* 5), and, although the concept of choices and avoidances was already a philosophical conventionality by the time of Seneca (cf. *Epistles* 95.13), it was always very much

---

[25] Lejay and Plessis (1915) 305. Kiessling–Heinze (1910) 72 offers a similar evaluation. Although the mention of a *sapiens* (to say nothing of the fact that Horace studied in Rome with the sons of senators) surely suggests that his father intended for his son to pursue "higher education" among Greek thinkers.

at the heart of Epicurean ethics.[26] Epicurus, for instance, wrote a lost treatise entitled *On Choices and Avoidances* (DL 10.27), and it is likely that a treatise of the same name, recovered from the Herculaneum papyri and formerly known as the "Comparetti Ethics," belongs to Philodemus. Given the Epicurean emphasis on practicality in choice-making and daily life, Horace's father's alleged "unrefined" approach to ethical training would appear to merit some further investigation.

One must avoid taking Horace's *Satires* at face value and thus risk overlooking the possibility of more serious, underlying themes. His incorporation of an exclusively practical method, for example, has been linked to the Cynics' preference for λόγοι χρηστοί ("useful advice") and their rejection of the theoretical pursuits associated with formal education.[27] But Epicurus also rejected what he considered to be the uselessness of theoretical speculation (cf. U 117 and DL 6), which in his day included Platonic and Aristotelian elements (cf. Cicero, *On Ends* 1.42 for an explanation of Epicurean practicality and 1.72 for a criticism of the Platonic curriculum and poetry as having *nulla solida utilitas*[28]) and instead stressed the importance of efficacy with regard to his own philosophical teachings (U 221): κενὸς ἐκείνου φιλοσόφου λόγος, ὑφ᾽ οὗ μηδὲν πάθος ἀνθρώπου θεραπεύεται, "Empty is the argument of that philosopher by which no passion of humans is therapeutically treated."[29] He also especially appreciated the pedagogical role of χρήσιμα διαλογίσματα (*Pyth.* 85), and his willingness to provide followers with useful summaries of his doctrines (cf. *Hdt.* 35) likewise reveals his concern for practicality and the preservation of moral virtue, which is compatible with Horace's father's understanding of philosophy as ancillary to the preservation

---

[26] Philippson (1911) 127–34 argued that "the concepts of choice and avoidance are foundational to this philosophical sect". "vitare und petere . . . sind Grundbegriffe dieser Schule" See also DeWitt (1939) 127–34 for the prevalence of this doctrine in Horace.

[27] Fiske (1971) 298–9. For an overview of the characteristics of Cynic παιδεία, for which there is little evidence, see Dudley (1974) 87–9 and Desmond (2008) 128–9. Oltramare (1926) 44–5 provides a collection of fragments detailing the Cynics' rejection of formal education, from dialectic to music. See also Gerhard's 1909 edition and commentary of the poet Phoenix of Colophon, which considers the role of λόγοι χρηστοί in the Cynic and comic traditions.

[28] DeWitt (1954) 44–9 and Rist (1972) 2 discuss Epicurus' reaction to Platonism; Nussbaum (1994) 121 distinguishes between Epicurean and Aristotelian practicality. For Epicurean παιδεία see Chandler (2006) 1–5.

[29] As Chandler (2006) 4 and Erler (2011) 23–4 note, however, later Epicureans like Philodemus were not as critical as Epicurus regarding the potential educational value of outside (i.e. non-Epicurean) sources.

of ancient *mores* (S. 1.4.115–19). And while it is true that both the
Cynics and the Epicureans employ maxims for pedagogical purposes,[30]
it was the latter who placed more emphasis on the importance of brevity
for the sake of memorization and usefulness, to which one may compare
Horace's advice regarding useful verses in *Art of Poetry*:

> aut prodesse volunt aut delectare poetae
> aut simul et iucunda et idonea dicere vitae.
> quiquid praecipies, esto brevis, ut cito dicta
> percipiant animi dociles teneantque fideles. (333–6)

Poets aim either to benefit, or to amuse, or to utter words at once both
pleasing and helpful to life. Whenever you instruct, be brief, so that
what is quickly said the mind may readily grasp and faithfully hold.[31]

The language in this passage strongly suggests that Horace, like
Epicurus, understands the importance of practically communicating
philosophical wisdom (*idonea vitae, praecepta*) in order that it may be
quickly memorized (*animi teneant*). True, for his part Epicurus
appears to have rejected poetry as a suitable means of imparting
moral truth or even philosophical instruction in general (cf. DL
10.121b: ποιήματά τε ἐνεργείᾳ οὐκ ἂν ποιῆσαι, "[And he said that
the sage] does not spend his life composing poetry"), although this
may have more to do with polemical descriptions of his ignorance
and boorishness than with anything else. One may easily point
to such biased accounts as those found in Cicero's *On Ends* (1.25–6
and 71–2) or Plutarchs' treatises *How it is Impossible to Live*

---

[30] Hadot (1969) 347–54 discusses the importance of usefulness and memorization
in relation to Epicurean pedagogy. For the Cynics' use of maxims (χρείαι), see Dudley
(1974) 112.

[31] Cf. *Art of Poetry* 343–4. Jensen (1923) 109, Tate (1928) 67–8, Brink (1963)
128–9, and Tsakiropoulou-Summers (1995) 237–42 attribute Horace's view that
poetry should be both delightful and useful to Neoptolemus of Parium, whom
Porphyrio identifies as one of the poet's sources in his commentary on the *Art of
Poetry* (ad 1–2). This is the same grammarian Philodemus opposes in his treatise *On
Poems* (coll. 10.32–13.28 in Jensen's 1923 edition). Armstrong (1993) 223–4, on the
other hand, considers Horace's poetic theory more in line with that of Philodemus,
who views good poetry as necessarily delightful and only potentially useful (much like
his philosophically correct epigrams). Cf. especially *On Poems* col. 29.17–19: κἂν
ὠφελῇ, κα[θὸ πο]ήματ᾽ οὐκ ὠφελεῖ, "And if they [sc. poems] are beneficial, this is
not by virtue of the fact that they are poems." A similar view is put forth by Wigodsky
(2009) 7–27, who additionally considers how Horace differs from Philodemus with
regard to poetic theory.

Pleasantly According to Epicurus (1092c–1094e) and *How to Tell a Flatterer from a Friend* (58d).[32] Epicurus' later followers seem to have been more receptive to the possibilities of poetic expression. Philodemus, for example, admits to the dangers of poetry but recognizes its potential usefulness for moral instruction,[33] while Lucretius (not to mention other Roman Epicureans, such as Titus Albucius and Horace's friend Varius) wholeheartedly embraces the poetic medium in *On the Nature of Things*.[34] In addition to being practical, moreover, Epicurean doctrine is especially accessible because it transfers the source of knowledge from theoretical speculation to the familiar sense perceptions of everyday life.

Horace's father's concern for practicality, as the poet describes it, is further emphasized by his empirical method and reliance on sense perception, which involves exposure to the nitty-gritty details of life on the streets of Rome. This is communicated through the importance of observation (*S.* 1.4.106: *notando*), vision (109: *vides*), exposure (123: *obiciebat*), and hearsay (114: *fama*) in relation to the various moral and social troubles of life in Rome: abject poverty (110: *inopia*), adulterous affairs (111: *amor turpis*), and the latest gossip (125: *rumor malus*).[35] Indeed, it is obvious that the reliance on perception as a springboard for moral correction is a common feature of Horace's approach. In *Satires* 1.6, for example, he communicates the burdens and many disturbances of political ambition by means of sense impressions: the glitter of Glory's chariot (23), the color and constricting feel of the trappings of senatorial office (27–8), the sounds of envious gossip (29), the blaring of trumpets in the forum (43–4), and the sight of poor Tillius loaded down with more paraphernalia and

---

[32] See especially Asmis (1995) 15–34. It should be noted that, despite the claims cited above, Epicurus appears to have critiqued the poetry of Menander on the topic of poverty, for which see Armstrong and Ponczoch (2011) 132–7. It would not be unreasonable to suggest that, if he made the effort to engage in such criticism, then he must have appreciated poetry to some degree.

[33] Philodemus imparts politico-ethical advice to his friend Piso in his treatise *On the Good King According to Homer*, for which see Dorandi (1982) 15–21 and Asmis (1991) 1–45. Cf. also *On Anger* (col. 8.31–2 and col. 19.20–5, both quotations from Homer's *Iliad* illustrating Achilles' destructive anger). Horace also uses Homer in order to impart ethical advice in *Epistles* 1.2.

[34] Asmis (1995) 34 and Sider (1995) 35–41.

[35] Juvenal, in *Satires* 14, includes similar observations of vice in Rome and the importance of a proper upbringing.

responsibilities that he can calmly manage (107–9).[36] Other vivid examples of sensation related to vice abound in the *Satires*, especially in the introductory poems: sight (1.2.80: *niveos viridesque lapillos*); sound (1.1.66: *sibilat, plaudo*; 1.2.18: *exclamat*, 128–30: *latret canis, strepitu resonet, clamet*; 1.3.7–8: *summa | voce . . . resonat*, 18: *stertebat*, 136: *rumperis et latras*; 1.5.15: *cantat*; 1.8.46: *displosa sonat quantum vesica*); smell (1.2.27–30: *olet, olenti*); touch (1.1.38: *aestus*, 39: *hiems*, 80: *frigore*; 1.2.6: *frigus*). At the same time, however, such descriptions are also one of the satirical characteristics of Old Comedy, and Horace's father's finger-pointing and identification of specific individuals like Baius (1.4.110) and Scetanus (112)[37] owe much to the comic tradition rejected by the poet in *Satires* 1.4 (1–5), and which thrived on the public criticism of perceptible behavior through the branding of individuals by name. As G. C. Fiske notes, this method also resembles the Cynics' "empirical morality," which often involves denouncing perceptible behavior in a public setting through the character portrait or χαρακτηρισμός.[38] One may also point to the work entitled *Rhetoric for Herennius* (4.65), where, as mentioned in Chapter 1, the author refers to the positive moral function of *notationes*, which are descriptions of another's inner "nature" (*natura*) by means of "clear and perceptible signs" (*certis signis*). All of these influences are certainly important, but they also relate to the tradition of formal epistemology and its close connection to ethics. That is, the emphasis on the primacy of empirical observation as necessary for Horace's education (cf. *S.* 1.4.110: *magnum documentum*) resembles the epistemological doctrines of Hellenistic philosophers, who likewise attached great importance to sensation. Aristotle's lengthy treatment of this topic in *On the Soul* (413b2–429a9), for instance influenced the Stoic and Epicurean identification of sensation as a criterion of truth and starting-point of knowledge. Furthermore, it is worth noting that Aristotle regarded perceptions as false only "very seldom" (428b2: ὅτι ὀλίγιστον), whereas the Stoics only accepted the sense data from

---

[36] Although, as Horace suggests in *Satires* 1.4 (123), his father wanted him to imitate the *iudices selecti*, who included equestrian jurors selected to serve on the standing criminal courts. See Armstrong (1986) 255.

[37] See Bandiera (1996) in *Enc. Or.* 1.658–9 for Baius; virtually nothing is known of Scetanus. The identification of individuals by the demonstrative *hic . . . ille* combination (used by Horace's father at *S.* 1.4.126 to introduce practical examples) occurs frequently in *Satires* 1: 1.11, 29; 2.4, 7, 4; 3.57–8; 6.41–2; 9.6–7, 13–16, 41–4. Cf. also 2.3.50.

[38] Fiske (1971) 299.

"cognitive impressions" (cf. DL 7.54 = *SVF* 2.105: καταληπτικὴ φαντασία),[39] both of which are views that differ significantly from that of the Epicureans.

It was Epicurus alone who maintained that all sense impressions are true and therefore absolutely foundational for the formation of knowledge and ethical decisions. The primacy of sensation is expressed in his *Letter to Herodotus* (38), in Diogenes' biography (10.32), and in the *Principal Doctrines* (22–4), to which one may compare Lucretius' arguments (4.469–521).[40] According to Diogenes' account of Epicurean epistemology (DL 10.31), "sensation" (αἴσθησις) was one of the three "interpretive tools" (κριτήρια) for engaging with and reacting to the visible world, along with "anticipations" (προλήψεις) and "affections" (πάθη), which closely resembles Epicurus' own description of anticipations as well as sensation and affections (*Men.* 37–8).[41] In the *Satires*, as the starting-point of knowledge sense perception would have supplied young Horace with the information necessary to interpret his surroundings, as suggested by the Lucretian phrase *nonne vides* that introduces his father's empirical method. Lucretius employs this phrase to emphasize the epistemological value of sensation, and the verb *videre* occurs quite often in Book 1 (e.g., 175, 197, 208, 210, 224, 255, 262, 319, 358, 407, 450, and 465).[42] In fact, Alessandro Schiesaro examines Lucretius' use of *nonne vides* as a carefully chosen phrase that indicates to the reader that the passage entails an illustration for the sake of example, which he connects to Horace's father's use of the same expression as introducing a didactic digression into examples of moral faults.[43] This use of *nonne vides*

[39] For evidence for the role of sensation in Stoic epistemology, see the text, translation, and commentary of Long and Sedley (1987) 238–59.
[40] See also Striker (1977) 125–42 and Taylor (1980) 105–24. For the relationship between the Aristotelian and Epicurean understanding of sensation, see Bourgey (1969) 252–5 and De Lacy and De Lacy (1978) 171–3.
[41] Useful introductions to Epicurean epistemology include Bailey (1964) 232–74, Long (1986) 21–30, Rist (1972) 114–40, Mitsis (1988) 19–45 (less accessible but contains useful observations), and Asmis (1984), which is an extended study of Epicurus' "scientific method."
[42] For a more detailed study of this particular verb and its significance in other passages of *On the Nature of Things*, see Reinhardt (2016) 72–8.
[43] Schiesaro (1984) 145: "un preciso segnale che indica al lettore il passaggio ad una illustrazione esemplificativa." Horace also quotes from Lucretius within the context of his Epicurean education at *S.* 1.5.101: *namque deos didici securum agere aevom* ("I have learned that the gods lead a care-free life"), to which cf. Lucr. 5.82. It is interesting to note that whenever gods appear in the *Satires* their intervention is rife with parody: they are

similarly appears at the beginning of the *Georgics* (1.56), where Vergil employs it in order to introduce examples of the natural products peculiar to certain regions, as well as in Book 3, where it is used to describe the unseen ambition of charioteers through vivid observation of their efforts on the race-track (103) and the behavior of stallions and humans who are physically overcome by the pleasurable smell of the opposite sex (250–63). Another possible connection to the Epicurean didactic tradition lies in the pervasive use of the imperfect tense throughout Horace's description in *Satires* 1.4, which strongly implies that such sensory experiences occurred habitually and over an extended period of time: *hortaretur* (107); *deterreret* (112); *aiebat* (115); *formabat, iubebat* (121); *vetabat* (124). This raises the question: in what manner did Horace's persona's exposure to everyday life inform his understanding of the world around him and, perhaps more importantly, how did this effect the way in which he communicated this knowledge?

His philosophical persona would not have forgotten easily the multiple and repeated sensory experiences of moral corruption and virtue to which his father had exposed him at such an impressionable age.[44] On the contrary, they would have been stored away in his memory and categorized as universal concepts,[45] eventually forming a kind of database for future reference and investigation. The Epicureans identify these categorized memories as "anticipations" (προλήψεις), which, in addition to being a reference point for scientific investigation, are also a prerequisite for successful communication (cf. Lucr. 4.478–9 = DL 10.32: *invenies primis ab sensibus esse creatam | notitiem veri neque sensus posse refelli*, "You will find that it is from the senses in the first instance that the concept [i.e. πρόληψις] of truth has come, and that the senses cannot be refuted").[46] Diogenes offers the following definition:

either puffing out their cheeks (1.1.20–1), passing wind (1.8.46–7), standing in for a human (2.6.4–5), or serving the purpose of establishing an intertext (1.9.78).

[44] It is important to note that Horace's father's training also includes examples of positive behavior, which is consistent with the Epicurean view that good people can be made more secure in their goodness by philosophy (as opposed to the Stoics, who rejected any such gradations of goodness).

[45] For the meaning of "universal" (καθολική) within the context of Epicurean epistemology as distinct from the Aristotelian tradition, see Asmis (1984) 63.

[46] The most useful modern treatments of πρόληψις are Kleve (1963), Long (1971) 119–22, Manuwald (1972), Asmis (1984) 61–80, Glidden (1985) 175–217, and more

τὴν δὲ πρόληψιν λέγουσιν οἱονεὶ κατάληψιν ἢ δόξαν ὀρθὴν ἢ ἔννοιαν ἢ
καθολικὴν νόησιν ἐναποκειμένην, τουτέστι μνήμην τοῦ πολλάκις ἔξωθεν
φανέντος (DL 10.33)
And they say that an anticipation is either an apprehension, or a correct
opinion, or thought, or stored, general idea; that is to say, a memory of
that which has often appeared from outside...

Horace's empirical training would have provided him with an acute,
cognitive awareness of the vices, challenges, and temptations associated with living in contemporary Rome, of which his compatriots
certainly would have been aware. These include political corruption
(*S.* 1.6.51–2: *prava | ambitione*), sexual promiscuity (68: *mala lustra*),
and insatiable greed (68: *avaritiam*), in addition to the economic and
sexual vices mentioned in *Satires* 1.4 and the introductory poems.
Perhaps more importantly, according to Horace's description in this
same poem it was his father's verbal cues that allowed him to identify
and communicate these realities with others by associating them with
the corresponding Latin words early on (*S.* 1.4.120–1): *sic me |
formabat puerum dictis*, "Thus he would form me with his words."
His father, therefore, may be regarded as the origin not only of his
moral integrity, but also of the moral vocabulary he so often employs
elsewhere in his satiric portraits: *turpis* (1.2.85, 102; 1.3.39, 100; 1.6.63,
84; 1.9.75; 2.1.65; 2.7.55, 59, 91); *honestus* (1.2.42); *inhonestus* (1.6.36);
inutilis (2.8.12); *rectus* (1.1.107; 1.2.37, 74, 82, 90; 2.1.21; 2.2.100;
2.3.88, 162, 201; 2.6.75; 2.7.25).[47] This is the language of traditional
Roman ethics, and its presence in the *Satires* is partly a conscious
imitation of the conversational diction and plain style advocated by
the Stoic philosopher Panaetius and put into practice by Lucilius, as
revealed by his definition of virtue (1329–30 M): *virtus, scire, homini
rectum, utile quid sit, honestum, | quae bona, quae mala item, quid
inutile, turpe, inhonestum*, "Virtue is for a man to know what is right,
what is useful and honorable, what is good, bad, useless, base,

recently, Verde (2013) 64–71 and Tsouna (2016) 160–221. For a discussion of the
scholarly debate regarding whether προλήψεις are acquired through multiple sensory
experiences or inborn, the origin of which is an apparent discrepancy between the
accounts of Diogenes (10.33) and Cicero (*On the Nature of the Gods* 1.44 and *On Ends*
1.31), see Manuwald (1972) 3–39, Asmis (1984) 66–72, as well as Sedley (2011) 28–52
and Konstan (2011) 53–71.

[47] Schrijvers (1993) 58–9 connects this language to the conventionally accepted
"éthique populaire" ("popular morality") of ancient Rome, which reflects Horace's
father's persona as a traditional *paterfamilias* concerned with morality.

146 Epicurean Ethics in Horace

dishonorable." It was also employed by the Roman comic playwrights
and later satirists like Persius (cf. 5.14: *verba togae*), and for Cicero it is
a hallmark of Epicurean conversation or *sermo* as he describes it in *On
Ends* 3.3. Specifically, he makes a distinction regarding Torquatus'
conversational style (*sermone*), which has allowed for a clear discussion (*dilucida oratio*), and the Stoics' more complex and dialectical
approach to philosophy, which is a "very subtle or rather thorny style
of argument" (*subtile vel spinosum potius disserendi genus*).[48] To this
description one may add Cicero's criticism of Epicurean *sermo* in his
Academics (1.5): *didicisti enim non posse nos Amafinii aut Rabirii
similes esse, qui nulla arte adhibita de rebus ante oculos positis vulgari
sermone disputant*, "You have learned that we cannot be similar to
Amafinius or Rabirius, who discuss things that lie open to the view in
ordinary language."

What makes the language people like Horace and Amafinius use
traditional is precisely the fact that it is the conventional, universally
accepted means of communicating the moral and cultural values
shared by all Romans. In some ways this connection between concepts and words reflects Epicurus' assertion that the use of everyday
language, the utterance of which immediately evokes a shared concept in a given society, is essential for proper communication and
philosophical investigation, since one can only express common
features of reality in conjunction with linguistic convention:

πρῶτον μὲν οὖν τὰ ὑποτεταγμένα τοῖς φθόγγοις, ὦ Ἡρόδοτε, δεῖ εἰληφέ-
ναι, ὅπως ἂν τὰ δοξαζόμενα ἢ ζητούμενα ἢ ἀπορούμενα ἔχωμεν εἰς ταῦτα
ἀναγαγόντες ἐπικρίνειν, καὶ μὴ ἄκριτα πάντα ἡμῖν <ᾖ> εἰς ἄπειρον
ἀποδεικνύουσιν ἢ κενοὺς φθόγγους ἔχωμεν· ἀνάγκη γὰρ τὸ πρῶτον
ἐννόημα καθ' ἕκαστον φθόγγον βλέπεσθαι καὶ μηθὲν ἀποδείξεως
προσδεῖσθαι, εἴπερ ἔξομεν τὸ ζητούμενον ἢ ἀπορούμενον καὶ δοξαζόμενον
ἐφ' ὃ ἀνάξομεν. (*Hdt.* 37–8)

First of all, Herodotus, we must grasp the ideas attached to words, in
order that we may be able to make judgments about opinion or problems of investigation or reflection by referring them to these, and so that
we may not either leave everything uncertain and go on explaining to
infinity or use words devoid of meaning. For this purpose it is essential
that the first mental image associated with each word should be

---

[48] Cf. also Cic. *On Duties* 1.134–37 for a discussion of *sermo* as "easy and not at all
dogmatic" (*lenis minimeque pertinax*).

regarded, and that there should be no need of explanation, if we are really to have a standard to which to refer a problem of investigation or reflection or mental inference.[49]

Diogenes notes that some of Epicurus' critics viewed his style or diction as being "too pedestrian" (DL 10.13: ἰδιωτάτη), which is an opinion Cicero seconds in his acknowledgement of the Master's concern for communicating clearly (*On Ends* 2.15): *Epicurus autem... plane et aperte loqui, nec de re obscura... sed de... iam in vulgus pervagata loquitur,* "But Epicurus... speaks plainly and clearly ... not about obscure things but about what is generally familiar already." This is also one of the hallmarks of Lucretius' style (cf. 1.136–45), whereas Cicero himself apologizes for inventing new words in order to express philosophical ideas in the introduction to his exposition of Stoic ethics (*On Ends* 3.1–5), which includes the following statement: *verba parienda sunt imponendaque nova rebus novis nomina,* "Words must be created and new terms invented for new concepts."[50] This conservative approach of Epicurus and Lucretius is consistent with that of Horatian satire, which, on account of having been informed by the teachings of a *pater idioticus,* is presented as nothing more than "pure conversation" (*sermo merus*) that employs unadorned, everyday speech in order to communicate moral truth. One thinks of Horace's rejection of hybrid and unusual words (*S.* 1.10.23–30) and Quirinus' aforementioned injunction to compose in pure Latin (31–5), but also of his description of Satyr plays in *Art of Poetry,* which implies that trivial poetry (231: *levis... versus*), that is, satire (cf. *S.* 1.4.53: *leviora*), employs the "usual and conventional words" (234: *inornata et dominantia nomina*).[51] Even more intriguing is Horace's concern for the use of conventional language as explicitly stated earlier in the same work:

---

[49] Cf. *Hdt.* 75–6 and Lucr. 5.1028–90 for the Epicurean doctrine of the evolution of language. Also Verde (2010) 80–7. Other discussions are in Long (1971) 114–33, Atherton (2009) 198–203, and De Sanctis (2015) 59–70. Not all scholars agree on the precise relationship of anticipations to the words that signify them. See, e.g., the conflicting views of Manuwald (1972) 111–14 and Glidden (1983) 221–4.

[50] Bailey (1947) 623 notes: "[W]hereas Cicero invented Latin words to correspond to the Greek... Lucr. preferred to express the ideas in words for the most part already in circulation... Lucr. no doubt had in mind here Epicurus' precepts as regards the use of words in their obvious meaning." For Cicero as a pioneer in developing the philosophical vocabulary of Latin, see Powell (1995b) 288–97.

[51] Fairclough (1991) 470 and Rudd (1989) 189 equate *dominantia* with κυρία, which recalls Epicurus' writing style as described above.

> multa renascentur quae iam cecidere, cadentque
> quae nunc sunt in honore vocabula, si volet usus,
> quem penes arbitrium est et ius et norma loquendi.   (70–2)

Many terms that have fallen out of use shall be born again, and those shall fall that are now in repute, if Usage so will it, in whose hands lies the judgment, the right and the rule of speech.

Furthermore, the ostensibly prosaic, down-to-earth nature of the *Satires* is perfectly consistent with Horace's concern in the *Art of Poetry* for avoiding obscurity of expression (cf. 26: *obscurus*) and preserving syntactical clarity (41: *lucidus ordo*).[52] Lucretius similarly attempts to justify his decision to communicate Epicurean doctrine through poetry by appealing to his clarity of expression (1.933–4: *lucida...| carmina*) and charm (1.28: *leporem*), and Cicero also puts general emphasis on clarity of expression (*Orator* 1.94: *acute...dilucide*). The fact, moreover, that the obscurity traditionally associated with poetry is one of Philodemus' major objections to viewing it as an ideal medium for communicating philosophical truth may be significant for Horace. Perhaps in response to Epicurus' views on language and Philodemus' poetic theory, he composed the *Satires* as friendly chats, which after all are "closer to conversations" (*S.* 1.4.42: *sermoni propriora*) than to poetry and therefore suitably communicate moral wisdom through everyday sensations and conventional language, expressed in an ostensibly prosaic manner.[53]

The primacy of sensation and the ability to express accurately concepts that develop from sense experiences are prerequisites for knowledge and communication. As Aristotle points out in the *Nicomachean Ethics*, however, the ultimate purpose of moral virtue is correct action (1103b30: πῶς πρακτέον). Plato is perhaps the first philosopher to examine seriously the philosophical significance of pleasure or ἡδονή with regard to action (cf. *Protag.* 351b4–358d5),[54] and both Aristotle and Epicurus recognize the role of pleasure and pain in motivating ethical decisions (cf. *Nic. Eth.* 1104b4–1105a17

---

[52] See Asmis (1995) 33.

[53] Philodemus mentions the superiority of prose for communicating philosophical truth at *On Poems*, col. 28.26–32. See also Asmis (1995) 28.

[54] For a detailed examination of Plato's understanding of pleasure and the evidence from other dialogues, see Gosling and Taylor (1982) 45–192.

and DL 10.34).[55] Epicurus' position, however, was controversial because it identified all pleasure as "inherently good and natural" (*Men.* 129: ἀγαθὸν πρῶτον καὶ συγγενικόν), although he makes an important distinction regarding choices and avoidances in a passage quoted earlier but worth considering again at this point:

καὶ ἐπεὶ πρῶτον ἀγαθὸν τοῦτο καὶ σύμφυτον, διὰ τοῦτο καὶ οὐ πᾶσαν
ἡδονὴν αἱρούμεθα, ἀλλ' ἔστιν ὅτε πολλὰς ἡδονὰς ὑπερβαίνομεν, ὅταν
πλεῖον ἡμῖν τὸ δυσχερὲς ἐκ τούτων ἔπηται· καὶ πολλὰς ἀλγηδόνας ἡδονῶν
κρείττους νομίζομεν, ἐπειδὰν μείζων ἡμῖν ἡδονὴ παρακολουθῇ πολὺν
χρόνον ὑπομείνασι τὰς ἀλγηδόνας.   (*Men.* 129)

But although [pleasure] is the first good and natural, we do not on account of this choose every pleasure; rather, there are times when we pass over many pleasures if more misery will follow as a consequence. And we reckon that there are many pains better than pleasures, whenever a greater pleasure will come to us after some time as a result of enduring those pains.

The notion that pleasure is naturally ingrained in all humans, which is known as the "cradle argument," is also expressed by Aristotle (*Nic. Eth.* 1105a2–4) and corresponds to the Stoic doctrine of self-preservation or οἰκείωσις. It was, in other words, quite popular among philosophers in antiquity, as evidenced by Cicero's discussion in *On Ends* 5.55 (the same author grossly misrepresents the Epicurean view at *Tusc.* 3.36–51). Epicurus himself does not refer to this doctrine explicitly in his surviving works, but Cicero's presentation of the testimony of Torquatus in *On Ends* 1.30 proves that later Epicureans employed it (cf. also Cic. *On Duties* 1.11).[56] For Epicurus and his followers, however, ethical decisions are sound if they ultimately result in more pleasure than pain, which will only be possible if such decisions are made in accordance with desires that observe the requirements of nature (cf. *Men.* 127 and KD 29 for the division of desires).[57] Otherwise, the result will be overwhelmingly detrimental, as Philodemus explains in *On Choices and Avoidances*, col. 5.11–14:

ἕνεκα γὰρ τῶ[ν] ξενοτάτων ὡς ἀναγκαιοτάτων τὰ χαλεπώτατ'

---

[55] See Mitsis (1988) 11–58, Rist (1974) 167–79, and Gosling and Taylor (1982) for the ancient tradition regarding Aristotle (285–344) and Epicurus (345–414).

[56] Brunschwig (1986) 113–44 discusses both the Epicurean and Stoic versions.

[57] See Annas (1989) 147–52 for an explanation of the necessity of such a division and Pl. *Rep.* 558d–559c and Arist. *Nic. Eth.* 1148b15–1149a24 for discussions of necessary/unnecessary and natural/unnatural pleasures.

ἀναδέχ[ο]νται κακά, "Men suffer the worst evils because of the most
alien desires which they regard as most necessary." The reason for
this suffering is that their pleasures will be outweighed by the pains
that follow, whereas those who have grown accustomed (cf. *S.* 1.4.105:
insuevit) to calculate pleasures responsibly and whose dispositions are
morally sound (129: *sanus*) will likely escape this predicament.

Horace, for example, will choose to avoid making unnecessary
expenditures and indulging in illicit sexual affairs on account of the
terrible consequences that often accompany such behavior. This reaction is described as the practical result (*S.* 1.4.129: *ex hoc*) of his father's
training, which deterred him from social and economic failure:

> avidos vicinum funus ut aegros
> exanimat mortisque metu sibi parcere cogit,
> sic teneros animos aliena opprobria saepe
> absterrent vitiis.   (*S.* 1.4.126–8)

As a neighbor's funeral scares gluttons when sick, and makes them,
through fear of death, careful of themselves, so the tender mind is often
deterred from vice by another's shame.

As Horace implies, it is the dreaded prospect of suffering similar fates
as individuals like Baius and Scetanus that motivates his decision to
flee (*absterrent*). More likely than not, this abstinence from the
transitory pleasures offered by material possessions and sexual gratification was a source of pain for young Horace, as the verbs "wish"
(111: *velit*) and "enjoy" (113: *uti*) suggest. The poet essentially
deprives himself of what is called "kinetic" pleasure, which, according
to Epicurus, is caused by the active motion of agreeable atoms in the
sense organs (e.g. sexual gratification), in order to obtain eventually
"katastematic" pleasure, which refers to the state of physical and
mental freedom from all atomic disturbances (e.g. not being plagued
by poverty and scandal).[58] His choice to avoid kinetic pleasure, then,
is proportionately beneficial: it will ultimately contribute to the preservation of his patrimony and reputation (118: *vitam famamque*),
which is indeed a far greater good. It is worth noting that, unlike

[58] See DL 10.136. More detailed examinations of this division are in Rist (1972)
102–11, Gosling and Taylor (1982) 365–96, Giannantoni (1984) 25–44, Long (1986)
64–6, and Mitsis (1988) 45–51. It should be noted that Horace's father does not deter
his son from sexual pleasure itself, which is inherently good, but from the pursuit of
illicit pleasure, which will result in greater pain through the destruction of his
reputation.

Cynics such as Bion who were ambivalent to the concept of a good reputation (see Fiske 1971: 317, πρὸς δόξαν καὶ ἀδοξίαν ἴσως ἔχοντα, "[He said that] he was equally disposed towards a good reputation or a bad one"), Epicureans living in Italy understood its importance, as Philodemus reveals in *On Flattery* (PHerc. 222, col. 4.4–8): [ἡ] δόξα τοίνυν χάριν ἀσφαλείας ἐδιώχθη κατὰ φύσιν, ἣν ἔξεστιν ἔχειν καὶ ἰδιώτηι καὶ φιλοσόφωι, κακία[ς δ' ο]ὐ πάσης, "A good reputation, which both the philosopher and the layman can have, is found to be pursued for the sake of security in accordance with nature, but not by means of any of the vices."[59] Having a good reputation is largely the result of calculating the potential outcomes of ethical decisions in terms of foreseeable pleasure, which is an expression of the hedonic calculus clearly incorporated by Horace into his moral deliberations:

> neque enim, cum lectulus aut me
> porticus excepit, desum mihi: "rectius hoc est;
> hoc faciens vivam melius; sic dulcis amicis
> occurram; hoc quidam non belle: numquid ego illi
> imprudens olim faciam simile?" (*S.* 1.4.133–6)

For when my couch welcomes me or I stroll in the colonnade, I do not fail myself: "This is the better course: if I do that, I shall fare more happily; thus I shall delight the friends I meet: that was ugly conduct of so and so. Is it possible that I may ever thoughtlessly do something like that?"

The inclusion of the comparative adverbs *rectius* and *melius* effectively implies moral deliberation in terms of comparison or calculation, while the future tense communicates forethought.[60] Epicurus gives similar advice:

Πρὸς πάσας τὰς ἐπιθυμίας προσακτέον τὸ ἐπερώτημα τοῦτο· τί μοι γενήσεται ἂν τελεσθῇ τὸ κατὰ ἐπιθυμίαν ἐπιζητούμενον; καὶ τί ἐὰν μὴ τελεσθῇ; (SV 71)

---

[59] Cf. Cic. *On Friendship* 61: *nec vero neglegenda est fama nec mediocre telum ad res gerendas existimare oportet benevolentiam civium; quam blanditiis et adsentando colligere turpe est*, "Nor should one ignore one's reputation or regard the goodwill of fellow citizens as an insignificant weapon with regard to life; but to acquire these by means of fawning and flattery is a disgraceful thing."

[60] Kiessling–Heinze (1910) 30 recognize the "fundamental themes of Epicurean ethics" in this passage. Gowers (2012) 180, on the other hand, refers to Horace's deliberations as "hypercritical calculation," which overlooks the philosophical undertones presently under discussion.

Let the following question be posed regarding all desires: what will happen to me if this desire is fulfilled? What will happen if it is not fulfilled?

Once again, the programmatic element of this passage alludes not only to the language Horace will employ throughout the *Satires*, but also to the way in which his persona will evaluate his contemporaries' ethical decisions with respect to the pleasure calculus. In *Satires* 1.1, for instance, he illustrates the detrimental effects of unnecessary desires (57: *plenior... iusto*) by employing a weather metaphor involving drowning in "turbulent waters" (60: *turbatam aquam*), which, echoing a similar expression of Lucretius (2.1) and his father's words "you will swim without the cork" (*S.* 1.4.120: *nabis sine cortice*), probably alludes to the Epicurean predilection for such metaphors as discussed previously.[61] Horace again contextualizes decisions by the calculation of pleasures and pains in *Satires* 1.6, in which he states that he would "avoid" (99: *nollem*) carrying the distressful burden of political office (99: *onus... molestum*) because it would result in comparatively more financial (100: *maior... res*) and social (101: *salutandi plures*) responsibilities. Rather, he intends to "live more pleasurably" (130: *victurum suavius*) by being content with his meager fare and life of leisure.[62] All of this is expressed by means of comparatives, which, as in the passage from *Satires* 1.4 quoted above, suggests a calculation. It is important to note, moreover, that in *Satires* 1.6 Horace identifies the "cause" of his ability to make such decisions as his father's moral training (71: *causa fuit pater his*), indicating that the underlying foundation of this evaluative method was laid by none other than the father who had earlier disavowed any knowledge of such philosophical "causes" (*S.* 1.4.116: *causas*).

According to Horace's description, this pedagogical method provided him with a sound disposition, which the poet describes in terms of contentment (*S.* 1.4.108: *contentus*). This positive outcome may be contrasted with Demea's utter failure to educate Ctesipho in the *Brothers*, as communicated by the former's lamentation speech (870–1): *nunc exacta aetate hoc fructi pro labore ab eis fero,* | *odium*, "Now at the end of my life I get the following reward from

---

[61] The concept of ἀταραξία showcases language associated early on with weather (cf. *Od.* 5.291: σύναγεν νεφέλας, ἐτάραξε δὲ πόντον, "[Poseidon] gathered the clouds and stirred up the sea").

[62] Hicks (2013) 149.

them as thanks for my work: hatred."[63] With regard to Horace, his sense of contentment was strengthened through exposure to his father's examples of economic failure, which were intended to emphasize the benefits of living frugally and being satisfied with one's possessions (*S.* 1.4.107–8): *parce frugaliter atque | viverem uti contentus eo quod mi ipse parasset*, "he would encourage me to live thriftily, frugally, and content with what he had saved for me." Here, as in *Satires* 1.1, Horace's decision to use *contentus* is noteworthy since its literal meaning suggests that his desires will rarely exceed the limits of nature, as Cicero's Epicurean spokesman Torquatus explains in a passage from *On Ends* quoted earlier (1.44: *ut sapiens solum... naturae finibus contentus...*, "Hence, only the wise man... [can live] content within the bounds that nature has set"). That is, he will not mistake the most unnecessary things (i.e., luxury goods) for the most necessary (i.e. a secure livelihood), as Philodemus warns in *On Choices and Avoidances*:

μετὰ δ[ὲ τ]αῦτ[α καὶ] τὰς τῶν ἐπιθυμ[ιῶ]ν π[ερί] τε τὰ[ς] ἡδονὰ[ς] καὶ
τὰ ποι[ητ]ικὰ διαφορὰς ἀναλογισ[τέ]ον· ἐπ[ειδὴ] καὶ παρὰ τὴν
[ἀδι]αληψ[ία]ν [δι'] αὐτῶν μεγάλα γίνεται δ[ι]απτώματα κατὰ τὰς
αἱρέσ[εις] καὶ φυγάς.   (col. 5.4–11)

Having looked into these matters, one should also consider the differences among desires, both with regard to the pleasures and with regard to their causes. For it is on account of the failure to distinguish between them that important errors occur through them with respect to choices and avoidances.

The importance of being content with the requirements of nature and the understanding that these are "easily satisfied" (*Men.* 130, 133, and KD 15; cf. *On Property Management*, col. 16.1–12 for Philodemus' discussion of the importance of being content and satisfied with τὰ πρὸς αὐτὸν ἱκανά), which Horace owes to his father's training, forms the backdrop to many of his evaluations of vicious behavior in the *Satires*.[64] The idea of observing limits has obvious connections to

---

[63] Courtney (2013) 94 ignores this and focuses on the "minor flaws" shared by Horace and Ctesipho.

[64] The concept of being "content" occurs often in the collection: *S.* 1.1.3, 118; 1.3.16; 1.6.96; 1.10.60, 74; 2.2.110; 2.7.20, 97. For passages involving the "limits of nature," see the following: *S.* 1.1.74–5 (cf. SV 34), 1.2.111–13 and 1.6.127–8 (cf. *Men.* 130–1). On the relationship between εὐπόριστον and οὐ δυσπόριστον vis-à-vis Epicurean wealth management, see Armstrong and Ponczoch (2011) 116–17.

Aristotle's doctrine of the mean, and the "limits of nature" doctrine was also of particular importance for the Cynic understanding of αὐτάρκεια.[65] Horatian frugality, however, coincides much more closely with Epicurus' qualification of αὐτάρκεια as the willingness to subsist with few possessions rather than the actual intention to do so, which was the infamous practice of the Cynics (see *Men.* 130).

Aside from growing accustomed to living frugally, Horace also indicates that the ultimate result of calculating pleasure in accordance with correct desires is "health" (*S.* 1.4.129: *ego sanus ab illis*).[66] This allusion to the familiar medical analogy, which was enormously popular at almost every stage of Greek philosophy beginning with the sophists (if not earlier) and extending into the Hellenistic period and beyond,[67] also reflects Epicurus' description of frugality and contentment as prerequisites of health and the bulwarks of a virtuous disposition (*Men.* 131). Furthermore, Lucretius equates philosophy with medicine (cf. 3.510–11: *et quoniam mentem sanari, corpus ut aegrum,* | *cernimus et flecti medicina posse videmus*, "And since we see that the mind, like a sick body, can be healed and changed by medicine") and Epicurean doctrine was commonly described in terms of medicine, especially in reference to the first four *Principal Doctrines*, which were also known as the τετραφάρμακος or "fourfold drug." Additionally, this analogy can be detected in the twofold Epicurean *summum bonum*, which is described in terms of health (*Men.* 128: ὑγιεία) and includes the "katastematic" pleasures of freedom from physical toil as well as from mental disturbances, which Juvenal famously expresses in his conscious imitation of Epicurean ethics in *Satires* 10 (356): *mens sana in corpore sano*, "a healthy mind in a healthy body."[68] It is perhaps not a coincidence, therefore, that Horace's description of his persona's virtuous upbringing and overall health is centered on the avoidance of prodigality and lust, both of which are clearly described as resulting in physical (*S.* 1.4.110: *inopia*)

---

[65] See Oltramare (1926) 49–54 for the evidence as well as Desmond (2008) 150–61.

[66] Philodemus also describes the sage as "pure from" vice in *On Gratitude* (col. 11.18: καθαρούς).

[67] Useful treatments of this rich subject include Wehrli (1951) 177–84, Jaeger (1957) 54–61, and Nussbaum (1994). For medical imagery among the Epicureans, see Gigante (1975) 53–61, Kilpatrick (1996) 69–100, and Konstan et al. (1998) 20–3.

[68] Gowers (2012) 179 translates *sanus ab* as "free from," which resembles Epicurus' description of the greatest goods in terms of the privation or lack of evil as defined by Horace at *Ep.* 1.1.41: *virtus est vitium fugere* "To flee vice is the beginning of virtue".

and mental (114: *fama*) disturbances respectively. According to
Epicurus' explanation, the attainment of pleasures such as tranquility
of body and mind originates in the ability to exercise "prudence"
(φρόνησις),[69] which indicates a connection to practical intent as
opposed to theoretical wisdom:

τούτων δὲ πάντων ἀρχὴ καὶ τὸ μέγιστον ἀγαθὸν φρόνησις. διὸ καὶ
φιλοσοφίας τιμιώτερον ὑπάρχει φρόνησις, ἐξ ἧς αἱ λοιπαὶ πᾶσαι πεφύκα-
σιν ἀρεταί, διδάσκουσα ὡς οὐκ ἔστιν ἡδέως ζῆν ἄνευ τοῦ φρονίμως καὶ
καλῶς καὶ δικαίως. (*Men.* 132)

Of all this the beginning and the greatest good is prudence. Wherefore
prudence is a more precious thing even than philosophy: for from
prudence are sprung all the other virtues, and it teaches us that it is
not possible to live pleasantly without living prudently and honorably
and justly.

Horace suggests that such considerations motivate his ethical deliberations when he depicts them as concerned with prudent fore-
thought (*S.* 1.4.136–7): *numquid ego illi | imprudens olim faciam
simile?*, "Is it possible that someday I may thoughtlessly do anything
like that?"[70] If these self-conscious deliberations are read closely, the
implication appears to be that for Horace, as for Epicurus, the life that
is sweet (135: *dulcis*), beautiful (136: *belle*), and just (134: *rectius*)
requires a practical sense of moral uprightness or *prudentia*.

HORACE'S FATHER AND FRANK CRITICISM

As satire, Horace's poetry endeavors to provide a critical but honest
appraisal of contemporary society with regard to morality, the justification for which he owes to his virtuous upbringing as described in
Satires 1.4. Another one of the major aspects of Horace's moral

[69] Bailey (1926) 338–9 translates φρόνησις as "prudence" in contrast to the loftier
and more detached σοφία. LSJ s.v. φρόνησις offers "purpose, intention" (1) and
"practical wisdom" (2) as meanings. Stob. 2.59.4 (= *SVF* 3.262) gives the Stoic
understanding of this term: φρόνησιν δ' εἶναι ἐπιστήμην ὧν ποιητέον καὶ οὐ ποιητέον,
"[They say that] prudence is the knowledge of what ought to be done and what ought
not to be done."
[70] The connection between φρόνησις and practical intent is suggested by Gowers
(2012) 180, who translates *imprudens* as "unintentionally."

training that reflects Epicurean tradition is his father's pedagogical use of frankness, which applies many of the methods described by Philodemus in *On Frank Criticism*. As mentioned earlier, Horace's brand of satire resembles that of Lucilius, although it has been suggested that he tempers his predecessor's harsh *libertas* by employing Aristotle's doctrine of the gentlemanly and liberal jest (*Nic. Eth.* 1127b33–1128a33). This virtue is opposed to "buffoonery" (βωμολοχία) as defined by the excessive desire to ridicule others (*Nic. Eth.* 1128a33–1128b2), which is a vice Horace associates with the Cynics in *Epistles* 1.17 and 1.18, as discussed previously. Additionally, Cicero gives a definition of this vice and uses similar terms in his *Orator* (2.17), which is followed by a description that fits the Cynics in general:

> Omnium autem ineptiarum, quae sunt innumerabiles, haud scio, an nulla sit maior quam, ut illi solent, quocumque in loco, quoscumque inter homines visum est, de rebus aut difficillimis aut non necessariis argutissime disputare.   (18)

> Of all the social improprieties, moreover, which are beyond number, I doubt that any is greater than what those [Greeks] are accustomed to do: I mean engaging in strenuous arguments over the most inappropriate or trivial matters in all places and among anyone who seems suitable.

Philodemus of course responds to the Cynic tradition of moral invective in *On Frank Criticism* by frequently condemning harsh criticism for its own sake and emphasizing its importance as a therapeutic tool, which is intended to correct moral deficiency and ought to be employed with much discretion (fr. 79).[71] This is comparable to *Satires* 1.4, in which Horace attributes his "rather free speech" (103–4: *liberius si | dixero quid*), which is intended to provide moral correction and to which he contrasts the backbiting and dishonest

---

[71] Similar advice occurs at frs. 37.4–8, 38.1–6, and 60.3–10. For discussions of this tradition in Horace, largely with respect to the *Odes* and *Epistles*, see Dewitt (1935) 312–19, Michels (1944) 173–7, Hunter (1985a) 480–90, and Kemp (2010b) 65–76. Cf. also Cic. *On Friendship* 88–9: *Nam et monendi amici saepe sunt et obiurgandi, et haec accipienda amice, cum benevole fiunt* "For friends frequently must be not only advised, but also rebuked, and both advice and rebuke should be kindly received when given in a spirit of goodwill".

speech of false friends (81–5), to his father's training (105: *insuevit pater*). Furthermore, the passage which follows quickly reveals that his father's frankness is the opposite of the typical Cynic *asperitas* or *ineptia*, since it is motivated by goodwill and chiefly exercised as a preventative measure intended for the preservation of his son's physical and moral wellbeing (118: *vitam famamque*). This concern reflects the Epicurean tradition of frankness as essentially pedagogical, as confirmed by Philodemus' corresponding inclusion of young men among the largest group of recipients of frankness (*On Frank Criticism*, frs. 18.1: παῖ, 31.2: νέων, and 36.5: νεωτέροις),[72] which, in addition to being employed for corrective purposes, may also be exercised to forestall or prevent vicious behavior (although Philodemus makes it clear at col. 13b 3–4 that the main goal of frankness is to correct vice rather than to offer training in connection with deliberative rhetoric or the giving of counsel).[73] The critical and preventative aspects of frankness appear alongside one another in the introductory satires, where Horace's audience, that is, the nameless interlocutors, receives rebuke and correction while his broader circle of intimate friends, including Maecenas, may view these conversations as admonitory reflections. In fact, Philodemus' description of frankness as an ongoing treatment that regularly involves the communication of advice within a private and intimate setting suggests that, rather than a mere tool for correction, Epicurean frankness is an ἦθος or way of living that thrives within relationships in small communities,[74] a detail which may

[72] Glad (1996) 34 n. 56 discusses the theme of ἐπιμέλεια τῶν νέων with regard to this treatise.

[73] See DeWitt (1935) 313 for frankness as a paideutic method that involves "admonition (νουθέτησις) for future behavior," as well as Michels (1944) 174. The point here is that Horace portrays himself as receiving an education as a boy that reflects in many ways the methods Philodemus describes in *On Frank Criticism*. Of course, any formal training associated with a philosophical sect would have occurred later in life, when Horace was a young man and ready for travel and an office (or "ready to swim without the cork," as his father says in *S.* 1.4.120). The poet is in effect applying the methods he might have become familiar with at a later age retroactively, for the purpose of establishing the credentials of his persona.

[74] The identification of frankness as a way of life among friends is communicated by the title of the collection to which this treatise belongs, which includes mention of "characters" (ἠθῶν) and "ways of living" (βίων). See Gigante (1983) 60–1 and Gargiulo (1981) 103–4.

be reflected by Horace's portrayal of his father's private training as well as his own limited correspondence within a closely knit circle of friends.

The privacy that Horace and his father enjoy and the application of frankness for the sake of moral improvement may reflect certain developments in contemporary Epicureanism regarding the nature of friendship. The first observation regarding philosophical relationships among Epicureans is that they thrive within communities that, although not officially exclusive, are generally described in terms of privacy and intimacy.[75] In his treatises, for example, Philodemus repeatedly mentions "intimate fellows" (οἱ συνήθεις) and "the members of the household" (οἱ οἰκεῖοι), who engage in fruitful conversations and forge bonds which are not experienced by "the outsiders" (οἱ ἔξωθεν).[76] For Horace a similar intimacy is communicated by his exclusive encounter with Maecenas in *Satires* 1.6 (45–64), but foreshadowed by his private education in 1.4, which is founded upon an impressionable boy's trustful surrender to a loving parent's frank admonition concerning the outside world. Sandra Citroni Marchetti conveys this relationship beautifully: "When as children we walk alongside an adult who teaches us aspects of life, we begin to trust in him; but the adult also begins to place his trust in us: he agrees to enter into the most intimate and private part of our feelings, thoughts and memories, all of which later in life we will overlay with our own experiences."[77] His father's constructive criticism eventually enables Horace, or rather his satiric persona, to engage in private and reflective deliberations within himself (cf. *S*. 1.4.133), which are similarly frank and motivate correct behavior. Of course, Horace is willing to share these *consilia* with others, but he makes it clear that they are intended for a restricted and familiar audience (73: *amicis*), which he describes in terms of intimate friendship (*S*. 1.5.42: *devinctior*; cf. *Odes* 1.3.8 to

[75] Clay (1983) 255–79 explores the details of community life among Epicureans. For the Epicurean concept of "fellowship" (συνδιαγωγή, *convictus*), see DeWitt (1936) 55–63.

[76] See Glad (1996) 28.

[77] Citroni Marchetti (2004) 17: "Quando da bambini camminiamo al lato di un adulto che ci indica aspetti del mondo, ci affidiamo a lui; ma anche'egli, l'adulto, si affida a noi: accetta di entrare nel nucleo intimo, originario, dei nostri affetti, pensieri e memorie, che poi rivestiremo delle nostre esperienze."

Vergil: *animae dimidium meae* and 2.17.5, addressed to Maecenas: *meae . . . partem animae*) and, when necessary, constructive criticism reciprocally directed toward himself (*S.* 1.10.78–91; cf. *Odes* 1.24.7: *nudaque Veritas*). Agnes Michels reflects on this level of intimacy between Horace and his addressees by noting: "One point which Horace emphasizes in *Satires* 1.4 and elsewhere is that he is not writing for the general public, which he either despises or affects to despise, but for his own limited circle of friends."[78]

These passages reveal Horace's understanding of frank criticism as occurring within the context of private conversations among close friends who, beyond the sense of security their friendship brings, appear to be cherished in a most intimate manner. Given the evidence from Philodemus' treatises, one may say that the philosopher shares a similar point of view:

κἂν π[ε]ριδεικνύωμεν ἐπιλογιστικῶς, ὅτι πολλῶν καὶ καλῶν ἐκ φιλίας περιγινομένων οὐδέν ἐστι τηλικοῦτον ὡς τὸ ἔχει<ν>, ὧι τὰ[γ]κάρδ[ι]ά τις ἐρεῖ καὶ λ[έγ]οντος ἀκούσεται. σφόδ[ρ]α γὰρ ἡ φύσις ὀρέγεται πρ[ό]ς τινας ἐκκαλύπτειν ἃ [ν]οεῖ. (*On Frank Criticism*, fr. 28.3–10)

Even if we demonstrate logically that though many and fine things come about through friendship, none is of such magnitude as having a person to whom one can say what is in one's heart and hear replying to us. For our nature intensely longs to reveal to others what it is thinking.[79]

This description of the friendship between members of an Epicurean community as originating in a desire to share one's innermost thoughts is significant since, as David Armstrong has noted, it suggests that "for Philodemus, friendship in its ideal form transcends its beginnings as a response to our human needs and frailties."[80] The exercise of frankness within the context of friendly conversation, therefore, is motivated not

---

[78] Michels (1944) 173.

[79] Cf. *On the Gods* col. 13.36–14.6 and Armstrong (2016) 191. Asmis (1990) 2395 n. 60 says that Philodemus, in his understanding of the ideal communication quoted above, possibly "values the intimacy of friendship more than the security that results from it."

[80] Armstrong (2011) 126–7. See also Armstrong (2016) 182–4, and Chapter 1 for the distinction between friendship of utility ("F1"), a more intimate friendship that is capable of great affection ("F2"), and friendship that is completely separate from utility ("F3"), which is only available "to the gods and to us in relation to dead friends."

by self-interest but by the desire for expressing one's innermost convictions and for moral improvement, as is obvious in the case of Horace's father. The significance of Philodemus' statement is that it appears to modify or at least expand Epicurus' original conception of friendship as utilitarian and existing mainly for the sake of potential benefits (SV 23): Πᾶσα φιλία δι' ἑαυτὴν αἱρετή· ἀρχὴν δὲ εἴληφεν ἀπὸ τῆς ὠφελείας, "All friendship is chosen for its own sake, but its origin is the need for help."[81] This is not to say that Philodemus did not recognize friendship as beneficial or useful, especially within the context of patronage as an initial means to financial security (in accordance with Epicurus' teaching at DL 10.121b), but he appears to indicate that, over time and through frequent fellowship within a private community, friendship can potentially become a much stronger expression of goodwill toward another. This may be communicated in part of the damaged ending of a passage partially quoted in Chapter 1:

[κ]αὶ τοῖς φιλοφρονησαμένοις εὐχα[ρ]ιστεῖ καὶ δι' ἐλπίδας τιν[ῶ]ν αὐτοῖς μεταλήψεσθαι καὶ πάλιν ὑπὸ αὐτῶν εὖ τι π[εί]σεσθαι, καίπερ [οὐ] ταύ[τ]ηι μάλ[ισ]τα προ[. . . .]ε[- - -]τ[- - -]

(On Choices and Avoidances, col. 22.17–22)

...and he [the sage] will also consider how former decisions will benefit him in the near future. In addition to this, he will treat with much care as many people as possible and show gratitude to those who are kind to him, with the hope that he will share some things with them and receive something good from them in return, although it isn't for that most of all [sc. for any practical return] [that he makes these friendships].[82]

---

[81] Usener's above emendation of the MSS reading ἀρετή, which would give Epicurus' maxim an Aristotelian quality (cf. *Nic. Eth.* 1155a4), has been accepted by most editors and translators. O'Keefe (2001) 269–305 and Brown (2002) 68–80, however, argue extensively against it. Armstrong (2011) 126–8 and (2016) 192, with more evidence, defends Usener's emendation. See also Konstan (1997) 110 for this maxim and for the distinction between φίλοι, who are concrete and useful individuals, and φιλία, which is the more abstract concept of reciprocity as essential for survival and thus considered to be useful in itself.

[82] This translation is that of Armstrong (2011) 125, whose interpretation of the missing lines seems plausible and would suggest that Philodemus endorses the view that utility is not always the ultimate motive for friendship.

According to Cicero, certain Epicureans were concerned that the utilitarian view of friendship was too "crippling," and so endorsed a view that is similar to what seems to be the conviction of Philodemus:

> sunt autem quidam Epicurei timidiores . . . qui verentur ne, si amicitiam propter nostram voluptatem expetendam putemus, tota amicitia quasi claudicare videatur. itaque primos congressus copulationesque et consuetudinum instituendarum voluntates fieri propter voluptatem, cum autem usus progrediens familiaritatem effecerit, tum amorem efflorescere tantum ut, etiamsi nulla sit utilitas ex amicitia, tamen ipsi amici propter se ipsos amentur. (*On Ends* 1.69)

> Other less courageous Epicureans . . . fear that if we think friendship to be desirable only on account of the pleasure it brings us it will be thought to be crippled entirely. They therefore say that the first advances and overtures, and the original inclination to form an attachment, happen because of the desire for pleasure, but that when the time spent with them leads to intimacy, the relationship blossoms into an affection strong enough to make us love our friends for their own sake, even if there is no practical advantage.[83]

Horace appears to express this sentiment in his genuine concern for Vergil's safety in *Odes* 1.3 (8) as well as in his impassioned declaration: "There is nothing I would compare to a delightful friend so long as I am sound!" (*S.* 1.5.44: *nil ego contulerim iucundo sanus amico*).[84] The high value he places on friendship is likewise reflected by his interest in sharing moral advice with others through frankness, which, as his father demonstrates in *Satires* 1.4, is an expression of goodwill that cannot exist outside the context of intimate friendship.[85]

Along with being one of the signs of true friendship and a private expression of moral concern within a small community, the Epicurean practice of frankness is also a stochastic or conjectural method

[83] Tsouna (2007) 28–30 identifies the *Epicurei timidiores* as "Philodemus and his disciples." This passage is also discussed by O'Keefe (2001) 287–9, Brown (2002) 78–9, and O'Connor (1989) 165–86. For a different view, see Armstrong (2016) 188.

[84] Gowers (2012) 198 draws textual parallels between Horace's declaration and Torquatus' translation of Epicurus' famous definition of friendship (*On Ends* 1.65 = KD 27). See also Gowers (2009b) 39–60 and Welch (2008) 64.

[85] Unlike the Cynics, who valued frankness above everything and associated it with the complete freedom enjoyed by the sage, who needs no friends. See Rich (1956) 23: "The Cynic, then, had no desire for wealth, knowledge, pleasure or friendship." Scarpat (1964) 62 quotes Diogenes of Sinope's identification of frankness as "the most beautiful thing" (DL 6.69: κάλλιστον), which is preferred to everything else (71).

that relies on appropriate timing and sign inference.[86] The τέχναι στοχαστικαί itself can be traced back at least to Aristotle's *Nicomachean Ethics*,[87] although Philodemus clearly links it to the Epicurean tradition in *On Frank Criticism* (fr. 1.8): καθόλου τ' ἐπιπαρρησιάζεται σοφὸς καὶ φιλόσοφος ἀνήρ, ὅτι μὲν στοχαζόμενος εὐ[λ]ογίαις ἔδε[ιξ]ε, "And in general the wise philosopher speaks frankly because, conjecturing by reasonable arguments, he has shown reliably . . ." One may recall that for Epicurean contemporaries of Horace, the success of frankness as a conjectural method depends on arguments based on the observance of visible signs (σημεῖα) and advice given at the opportune moment (καιρός). For this reason, according to Philodemus frankness is less effective when applied to elderly pupils (*On Frank Criticism*, col. 24a.8: οἱ πρεσβύτεροι), whereas young men, on account of their lack of experience and impressionable nature, are more receptive to admonition or correction (fr. 18.1: παῖ). In particular, the successful practice of criticism depends on "appropriate timing" or καιρός, which fosters the pupil's affection and therefore leads to a heightened sense of goodwill and gratitude:

τότε μὲν δια]λαμβάνουσ[ι], καὶ μόνοις καὶ κατὰ καιρὸν καὶ ἀπ' εὐνοίας
καὶ πάντα προσφερομένους ὅσα παρη<ι>ν[ο]ῦμεν.

(*On Frank Criticism*, col. 17b1–6)

. . . at one time they (the students) grasp [words?] offered to them alone, and at the right time and from goodwill, all of it, as many things as we advise.

The careful application of frankness at the correct time, which, once again, is a conjectural rather than a scientific approach, may be imputed similarly to Horace's *pater rusticus*, who, as a parent concerned for his son's disposition and willing to expose him to examples of vice at a young age, is anything but an inept curmudgeon. On the contrary, his well-intentioned admonitions are based on observations of perceptible behavior and his advice is delivered at the critical moment, namely, while Horace's mind is still "tender" (*S.* 1.4.128: *teneros animos*) and able to be "formed" (121: *formabat*).[88]

---

[86] See Glad (1995) 142 n. 160 and Asmis (2001) 227–8: "Just like any purge, frank speech is a potentially dangerous drug. Its administration must therefore be carefully controlled. As in all practical skills, the watch-word is κατὰ καιρόν, 'at the right time.'"

[87] Isnardi (1966) 167–77. See also Gigante (1983) 62–72 and Tsouna (2007) 92–3.

[88] Michels (1944) 175. Again, Philodemus would have applied such methods of frankness to pupils significantly older than Horace. In *Satires* 1.4, however, the

As a conjectural method that is understood as the appropriate response to particular moral defects as inferred through the careful "observation of signs" (*On Frank Criticism*, fr. 57.4–5: σημειωσάμενον), frankness also has the ultimate purpose of therapeutically treating vice. It is interesting to note, however, that Horace, in the interest of serving his own agenda and affirming his virtuous disposition from early childhood, appears to interpret selectively certain observations of Philodemus. For instance, despite the philosopher's remark that a father should not use the kind of criticism available for sages (*On Frank Criticism*, col. 7a 3–6), in *Satires* 1.4 Horace portrays his father as a competent and successful moralist who relies on Epicurean doctrine for the purpose of education. Furthermore, in response to Philodemus' definition of frankness as corrective rather than "deliberative" (*On Frank Criticism*, col. 13b 3–4: συμβου[λε]υτικόν), one may point to the importance for Horace of demonstrating that his satirical persona is virtuous from an early age and that, although his father "corrects" the vice of others, the poet himself benefits from these frank observations. In other words, Horace's father uses sign inference (cf. *S.* 1.4.106: *notabat . . . exemplis*) in connection with victims of vice, but also in order to admonish his son by providing him with vivid examples of the consequences of each vice (106: *quaeque vitiorum*).[89] But one notes that his use of examples is not merely epideictic but psychological, since it invites Horace to reflect more deeply on the consequences of vice and, presumably, on the terrifying prospect that he himself is not immune from such disaster. This use of frank criticism for the purpose of both identifying and preventing vice resembles Philodemus' statement that the sage, on account of his frankness, will "point out how many have died miserably, stripped of . . . all possibility of conversing with someone frankly" (*On Frank Criticism*, fr. 72: 4–7: καὶ παραδείξει πόσοι κακῶς ἀ[π]ώλοντο παντὸς στερόμενοι τοῦ μετὰ παρρησία[ς] ὁμιλῇ [σ]αί τισι). In a similar manner, Horace's father goes beyond the perfunctory dispensation of prohibitions and mandates: he encourages his son to process visually and psychologically the horrible consequences

concept of "correct timing" in reference to the poet as a boy serves to highlight his early exposure to quasi-philosophical methods and, consequently, the early development of his virtuous disposition.

[89] Citroni Marchetti (2004) 25–35, who contrasts Horace's father with the more emotional and less effective Demea in the *Brothers* (see Traill 2013: 332–9), considers the role of the poet's empirical training in the light of Plato's *Protagoras*, *Republic*, and *Laws*.

of vice, with the ultimate intention of deterring him from such ruin (*S.* 1.4.112: *deterreret*, 129: *absterrent*) and allowing him to avoid it more easily (106: *ut fugerem*). As mentioned already, in his ethical treatises Philodemus often recommends that teachers admonish their pupils by "placing before the eyes" (*On Frank Criticism*, frs. 26.4–5, 42.1, 77.3: τιθέναι πρὸ ὀμμάτων) examples of their faults or the consequences thereof, which, when accomplished effectively and at the right time, inspires a sense of terror and motivates correct action (cf. especially *On Anger*, col. 3.13–18). The ultimate purpose of such pictorial imagery, which is corrective, must be considered preventative in the case of young Horace, especially given that the "autobiographical" scene in *Satires* 1.4 is intended to explain his virtuous disposition and justify his persona's role as moralizing satirist. As will be shown presently, his careful description in this poem is literally and figuratively central in the collection in terms of its importance for his ethical persona, especially since it provides the necessary background for understanding his encounter and relationship with Maecenas in *Satires* 1.6 and beyond.

EPICUREAN PATRONAGE IN *SATIRES* 1.6

Horace's portrayal of his relationship with Maecenas in the *Satires* owes something to the Epicurean identification of patronage as based on the exchange of philosophical advice for economic benefits, which occurs within the context of intimate friendship. Horace's correspondence with Maecenas throughout the corpus highlights the intimacy of their relationship, which is most explicitly conveyed through introductory addresses and terms of endearment. Like Epicurus and Philodemus, many of Horace's literary dedications to his patron are introduced by affectionate titles that communicate their friendship in Epicurean terms. David Konstan acknowledges this aspect of Horatian poetry, saying that the poet "was disposed to prefer private friendships to public life, and his poetry is rich in tender expressions of affection."[90] In *Odes* 1.1, for example, he invokes Maecenas as his "bulwark and sweet glory" (2: *praesidium et dulce decus meum*; cf. Verg. *G.* 2.40: *o decus*), recalling Epicurus' description of friendship as the strongest safeguard against evil (Cic. *On Ends* 1.69: *praesidium* . . .

[90] Konstan (1997) 143.

firmissimum; cf. *On Property Management*, col. 25.4: ἀσφαλέστατοι θησαυροί) and perhaps implying Philodemus' declaration that one cannot live sweetly without friends (*On Choices and Avoidances*, col. 14.1: ἡδέως). One may also observe, as R. G. M. Nisbet and Margaret Hubbard do, that *praesidium* is normally used of patrons whereas *dulcis* is "naturally used of family and friends" (cf. *S.* 1.4.135: *dulcis amicis*).[91] A similar level of intimacy is communicated when Horace addresses Maecenas as "my dear" in *Odes* 1.20 (5: *care*; cf. *S.* 1.6.70: *carus amicis*), which is a reading that follows the consensus of the ancient manuscripts (represented by 𝔈 and 𝔜) and seems more appropriate than the "correction" offered by the *codices recentiores* and Richard Bentley (i.e. *clare*).[92] This reading is also fitting for an invitation poem that undoubtedly imitates Philodemus' epigrammatic invocation to his own friend Piso in *Epigrams* 27 (1: φίλτατε). The sweetness of friendship is invoked again in *Epistles* 1.7 (12: *dulcis amice*), which recalls Philodemus' advice concerning the role of terms of endearment among members of the Epicurean community (*On Frank Criticism*, fr. 14.8–10): οὐκ ἐπιλήσεται τοῦ φιλτάτου λέγω<ν> καὶ γλυκυ[τ]ά[του] καὶ τῶν ὁμοίων, "he [sc. the sage] will not forget to say 'my dearest' and 'sweetest' and such similar things." The poet's desire to celebrate festivities with his patron is similarly expressed in the *Epodes*, in which he calls him "blessed" (9.4: *beate*; cf. DL 10.6: μακάριε) and again in *Odes* 4, in which he affectionately expresses joy at the thought of celebrating the birthday of "my Maecenas" (11.19: *Maecenas meus*; cf. Suet. *Life of Horace*, where Augustus requests from Maecenas the presence of *Horatium nostrum*). According to another passage from Suetonius, Maecenas expresses "how much he loved Horace" (*quantopere eum dilexerit*) by dedicating an epigram to him:

> ni te visceribus meis, Horati,
> plus iam diligo, tu tuum sodalem
> †nimio videas strigosiorem.[93]

If I do not love you now more than my own innermost self, Horace, may you see your friend quite emaciated indeed.

---

[91] Nisbet and Hubbard (1970) 4.

[92] Sider (1997) 153 and Nisbet and Hubbard (1970) 243–5 add that here the "poet writes with affection to a more important friend." Cf. *Odes* 3.8, in which Horace again invites his patron, this time addressed by name alone (13: *Maecenas*), to his Sabine estate in order to celebrate the anniversary of his escape from death.

[93] Some alternate readings of *nimio* include *hinnulo* (Oudendorp) and *simio* (Sudhaus).

Regardless of the poor quality of this specimen, which Fraenkel rightly calls "an exceedingly lame parody of one of the most beautiful poems of Catullus,"[94] the possibility that Maecenas dedicated and shared poetry with Horace (according to Suetonius) indicates that their relationship eventually evolved beyond the level of utility and mutual exchange (cf. especially Horace's touching words to his patron in *Odes* 2.17). In other words, even if the original motivation for both was a sense of security or utility, the frank and intimate nature of their correspondence may reveal, as will be discussed shortly, a much more profound and affectionate bond.

In the *Satires*, Horace's addresses to his patron are characterized by a sense of intimacy and exclusivity reminiscent of Epicurean tradition, which helps to contextualize their informal tone and status as friendly conversations (they are, after all, nothing more than *sermones meri*). *Satires* 1.1, for instance, opens with an intentionally blunt and personal address (1: *Qui fit, Maecenas*), thereby emphasizing the patron's prominence as financial supporter but also the client's attachment to a friend who is receptive to moral lessons (cf. *On Property Management*, col. 23.25–6: ἀνδράσιν δεκτικοῖς) and who can be addressed, as a friend, in a very direct manner.[95] Horace also apparently valued his patron's literary opinion and probably shared ideas and values with him, as revealed in the list of intimate friends in *Satires* 1.10 (81–90),[96] which involves a description that recalls Cicero's quasi-Aristotelian definition of true friendship as "the complete consensus of wants, enthusiasms, and of thoughts" (*On Friendship* 15: *voluntatum studiorum sententiarum summa consensio*) and Philodemus' beautiful description of intimate friendship in *On Frank Criticism* (fr. 28.1–12, quoted already). Despite this attachment, however, Horace does not overlook or attempt to obscure the disparity between himself and his patron: the extended opening address to Maecenas in *Satires* 1.6 is clearly intended to highlight his patron's royal Etruscan ancestry,[97] which also features prominently in *Odes* 1.1 (1: *Maecenas atavis edite regibus*) and 3.29 (1: *Tyrrhena regum progenies*). Like Horace, Epicurus did not conceal the powerful

---

[94] Fraenkel (1957) 17, referring of course to Catullus' opening address to Calvus in poem 14 (1: *Ni te plus oculis meis amarem, iucundissime Calve*, "If I did not love you more than my own eyes, dearest Calvus...").

[95] See Freudenburg (2001) 21 and Gold (1992) 164 for both views.

[96] See DuQuesnay (2009) 52.

[97] For Maecenas' Lydian origins, see Scullard (1967) 34–57.

influence of his benefactor Mithres, proudly addressing him with the titles "my savior and king" (DL 10.5: Παιᾶνα καὶ ἄνακτα), which led to accusations of shameless flattery (cf. DL 10.4). To Cicero's similar accusation in connection with Philodemus' intimate relationship with his powerful friends in the speech *Against Piso* one may compare Suetonius' description in his biography of Horace: *ac primo Maecenati, mox Augusto insinuatus non mediocrem in amborum amicitia locum tenuit*, "And having insinuated himself first with Maecenas and soon afterwards with Augustus, he held an exceptional place in the friendship of both men."[98] Nevertheless, the overall effect of Horace's correspondence underscores his patron's noble pedigree while conveying, almost paradoxically, a sense of intimacy that is perfectly consistent with Epicurean patterns of patronage. This is demonstrated by Epicurus' playful correspondence with members and associates of the Garden as well as Philodemus' promise to "drag" (*Epigrams* 27.2: ἕλκει) Piso to a house party where there will be no fancy Roman food (3–4), both of which are in line with Horace's many informal and humorous exchanges with Maecenas. For instance, in *Satires* 2.8 the poet has Nasidienus ("Mr Nose"), the host of a dinner party, offer Maecenas local Italian wine in case a Greek vintage is not to his taste (16–17), and in *Odes* 1.20 Horace himself invites his patron to a modest soirée with the warning "you'll drink the cheap Sabine stuff here" (*vile potabis . . . Sabinum*). One also thinks of his surprisingly frank declaration of independence from Maecenas' protection in *Epistles* 1.1 and especially 1.7. As Emily Gowers observes, Horace more than once uses Lyde as a slave-name in the *Odes*, and by invoking Maecenas' Lydian origin in *Satires* 1.6 (1–5), which is a poem about social status, he may be leveling the playing-field by playfully branding his patron with "potentially servile descent."[99] This kind of lightheartedness on the part of both poet and patron seems to challenge Roman social norms as revealed by certain authors: the view of *amicitia* as merely a euphemism for *clientela* or *patrocinium*, which Cicero indicates in

---

[98] Similar views of Horace are in Nisbet and Rudd (2004) 348 ("flattery") and Gowers (2012) 218 ("flattering publicity"). Of the opposite opinion, at least with regard to Suetonius' account, is Fraenkel (1957) 16.

[99] Gowers (2012) 220. MacKay (1942) 79–81 has suggested that Maecenas' father was nothing more than a *scriba* (like Horace), and it should be remembered that both Horace and Maecenas belonged to the rank of *eques*.

On Duties (2.69) are terms the social elite avoided,[100] and Seneca's assertion in *On Benefits* (6.34) that clients were only nominally friends, appears to be refuted at some level by the nature of the correspondence between Horace and Maecenas, at least as the poet depicts it in verse. In light of this, it seems possible that there may in fact be room for "true affection," as some have argued,[101] within the context of Roman patronage.

In the process of acknowledging Maecenas' superiority in *Satires* 1.6 Horace also emphasizes his own persona's social and economic disadvantages, which, conveniently in harmony with Epicurus' teaching on wealth acquisition according to Diogenes (10.121), ultimately motivated his decision to seek literary patronage. To the extended four-line description of Maecenas' greatness at the beginning of *Satires* 1.6, for example, Horace juxtaposes a measly four-word reference to his own humble status as "son of an ex-slave" (6: *me libertino patre natum*), apparently widening further the already recognizable social rift between patron and client as far as ancestry is concerned. Of course this claim, which Horace emphasizes repeatedly in the satire, is strategically designed to highlight his personal merit and inherent worth (cf. 51: *dignos*). It is, therefore, a poetic construct shaped by the author's own agenda and has no solid basis in historical fact.[102] In keeping with this agenda, Horace confirms the obvious disparity between himself and his millionaire patron by means of a pathetic description of his "poor father's little farm" (71: *macro pauper agello*; cf. Lucretius' description of primitive plots of land at 5.1367–8: *inde aliam atque aliam culturam dulcis agelli | temptabant*, "and from there early peoples began to make attempts to cultivate their small, cherished fields"), which, in conjunction with his self-proclaimed low status, re-emphasizes the poet's modest means as a child.[103] As scholars have noted, this description is rendered suspect by the fact that Horace's father managed to afford his son's high-quality education in Rome among social superiors, as described later on (76–80).[104] David Armstrong observes that his ability to abandon the small farm and accompany his son to Rome

---

[100] See Allen (1938) 167 and Syme (1939) 157.

[101] Konstan (1997) 122–4, following Brunt (1988) 360.

[102] Williams (1995) 296–313.

[103] Of course, in comparison to the landholdings of someone as wealthy as Maecenas any plot of land would have been *macer*. For modest dwellings as a "hallmark of Epicurean living" see Welch (2008) 51.

[104] See Lyne (1995) 1–8.

"implied, on Horace's father's part, all the leisure in the world, and therefore a made fortune."[105] Horace's emphasis on the "poor farm" may be intended to establish a connection to the Epicurean concept of poverty (SV 25: πενία) as the possession of few things that satisfy the requirements of nature (*Ep.* 1.2.46: *quod satis est*; cf. *On Property Management*, col. 16.6–8). Regarding the passage involving his father's farm, which echoes a similar description in *Catalepta* 8 of the Epicurean Siro's house (8: *Villula, quae Sironis eras, et pauper agelle*), the poet's language appears to give more information about the paternal inheritance mentioned earlier in *Satires* 1.4 (110: *patriam rem*), which his father had striven so eagerly to preserve. According to Horace's later account in the *Epistles*, however, these efforts were made in vain. The political chaos following the Battle of Philippi, at which, as Horace reveals in *Satires* 1.6(48), he had fought on the losing side as a *tribunus militum* (implying that he was already an *eques*, a rank valued at 400,000 sesterces[106]), seems to have resulted in the confiscation of his father's tiny property. The poet's encounter with economic disaster is dramatically, and perhaps rather humorously, related in his later correspondence with Julius Florus:

> unde simul primum me dimisere Philippi,
> decisis humilem pinnis inopemque paterni
> et laris et fundi paupertas inpulit audax
> ut versus facerem: sed quod non desit habentem   (*Ep.* 2.2.49–52)

Soon as Philippi gave me discharge therefrom, brought low with wings clipped and beggared of paternal home and estate, barefaced poverty drove me to writing verses. But now that I have sufficient store...

According to this description, Horace claims that his decision to seek employment as a professional poet was essentially forced upon him by the barefaced poverty and destitution his father had earlier sought to prevent,[107] which is at odds with his acquisition of the post of *scriba quaestorius* immediately following the battle (Suet. *Life of Horace*): *victisque partibus venia inpetrata scriptum quaestorium conparavit,*

---

[105] Armstrong (1986) 275.

[106] Cf. *Satires* 2.7 for Davus' mention of Horace's insignia, which men of his rank typically wore (53–4): *tu cum proiectis insignibus, anulo equestri | Romanoque habitu*, "You, when you have cast aside your badges, the ring of knighthood, and your Roman dress."

[107] Cf. *Odes* 1.12.43–44, in which Camillus' "cruel poverty" (*saeva paupertas*) refers to his "ancestral estate and suitable home" (*avitus apto | cum lare fundus*). See also Bandiera (1996) in *Enc. Or.* 1.658. Of course, the "poverty of poets" is a well-known motif in literature, especially in the works of Catullus (cf. poems 13, 23, and 28).

"After his faction had been defeated and he had obtained pardon, he purchased the post of treasury official."[108] The office was quite popular among individuals with literary aspirations, since it combined the possibility of *otium* with an impressive salary.[109] And although Horace had already reached the status of *eques*, his new income would have allowed him not only to continue to meet the property qualifications for this rank, but also to be able to afford a house in Rome.[110] It is intriguing that the circumstances surrounding Horace's motives for seeking financial assistance, although inconsistent with what other evidence suggests and communicated in a playfully ironic manner, perfectly satisfy Epicurus' requirement concerning obtaining wealth only when in "dire straits" (DL 10.121: ἀπορήσαντα). The identification of patronage as the poet's only source of income additionally reflects Philodemus' description of the ideal economic state, according to which financial security results from ethical conversations directed toward a receptive and grateful friend:

πρῶτον δὲ καὶ κάλλιστον ἀπὸ λόγων φιλο[σό]φων ἀνδράσιν δεκτικοῖς
μεταδιδομέν[ων] ἀντιμεταλαμβάνειν εὐχάριστο[ν ἅμ]α μετὰ σεβασμοῦ
παντ[ός], ὡς ἐγένετ᾽ Ἐπικο[ύ]ρωι

(On Property Management, col. 23.23–30)

It is superior and better by far to receive gratitude and respect in return for wise discussions shared with receptive men, which is what happened to Epicurus.

It is also interesting that, although he emphasizes his poverty and low status, Horace does not mention financial difficulty in *Satires* 1.6 as his motive for seeking literary patronage. This omission is likely intended to deflect charges of ambition, which may also explain why he overlooks his acquisition of the lucrative post of *scriba*. Besides, the many obligations associated with this supposedly sinecure position, which for Horace's persona is inextricably tied to the manifold annoyances that come with civic duty (cf. *S.* 2.6.32-39: *negotia centum*), conflict with his self-portrayal as a detached

---

[108] For the duties associated with this post, see Fraenkel (1957) 14–15, Armstrong (1986) 263-4, and Purcell (1983) 154–61. Armstrong (1986) 263 dates this event to "as soon as possible after Philippi, probably in 41."

[109] DuQuesnay (2009) 50.

[110] See DuQuesnay (2009) 50 and Mommsen (1887) 335, the latter of whom is the main source for the different salaries of the *apparitores*, among which the office of *scriba* is listed as the most lucrative (n. 1).

observer of the masses (cf. *S.* 1.6.18), which happens to coincide nicely with Philodemus' description in *On Property Management* of the advantages of a withdrawal with friends (col. 23.15–16).[111] As Emily Gowers notes, in *Satires* 1.6 Horace "lives out an escapist fantasy, a dream of independence and unassailable integrity" that is "remote from notions of bureaucratic routine."[112] Based on Horace's description, his acceptance into Maecenas' literary circle was not the direct result of political influence or wealth but rather of his moral strength as one who is *purus et insons*—a claim that is rendered all the more impressive by the fact that, notwithstanding the initial acknowledgement of Maecenas' glorious ancestry, it transcends the obvious social and economic barriers separating him from his patron. According to the poet, it is Maecenas himself who says: "it matters not who a man's parent is, if he be himself free-born" (7–8: *cum referre negas, quali sit quisque parente | natus, dum ingenuus*), which, as Oliensis observes, is a view cleverly placed in the mouth of his patron, thereby allowing the poet to avoid "making the self-promoting argument himself."[113] Overall, Horace subtly presents his readers with a relationship marked by a difference in ancestry but strengthened by the bond of friendship. It is also a relationship that involves many of the characteristics of Epicurean patronage, including the peaceful withdrawal from politics, an intimate bond between client and receptive patron, and, as Epicurus stipulates, the exchange of benefits for advice from an ethical expert or sage.

It is clear that Horace attributes this successful encounter with Maecenas to his persona's freedom from "base ambition" (*S.* 1.6.51–2: *prava | ambitione*) and his integrity (69: *purus et insons*), and that in an effort to avoid charges of ambition he does not portray himself as actively seeking patronage. On the contrary, his poet-friends vouched for his personal merit and secured an interview on his behalf (54–5: *optimus olim | Vergilius, post hunc Varius*). Horace's passing mention of Vergil and Varius undoubtedly implies his poetic capabilities but, as with wealth and status, nowhere does he explicitly

---

[111] See Armstrong (2016) 204 for similar expressions of withdrawal into the countryside in connection with Horace's friends.

[112] Gowers (2009a) 305.

[113] Oliensis (1998) 30. For *ingenuus* as "freeborn" or "gentlemanly," see Gowers (2012) 222–3.

identify this as the reason for his initial meeting with Maecenas.[114] Instead, he declares his personal worth and subordinates the relationship entirely to his virtuous disposition (55: *quid essem*; 60: *quod eram*).[115] Many scholars have pointed out that this passage involves a conscious imitation of Bion's audience with Antigonus Gonatas,[116] in which the Cynic declares: "consider me for what I am" (σκόπει δέ με ἐξ ἐμαυτοῦ), and by means of which Horace firmly situates his literary persona within the context of philosophical patronage. Immediately following the encounter scene, the poet discusses his ethical credentials and identifies his father's training as the direct cause of this virtuous nature, the description of which is fittingly introduced by the inclusion of the same philosophical terminology employed earlier in *Satires* 1.4:

> atque si vitiis mediocribus ac mea paucis
> mendosa est natura, alioqui recta, velut si
> egregio inspersos reprendas corpore naevos,
> si neque avaritiam neque sordes nec mala lustra
> obiciet vere quisquam mihi, purus et insons,
> ut me collaudem, si et vivo carus amicis,
> causa fuit pater his   (*S.* 1.6.65–71)

And yet, if the flaws of my otherwise sound nature are but trifling and few in number, even as you might find fault with moles spotted over a comely person—if no one will justly lay to my charge avarice or meanness or lewdness; if, to venture on self-praise, my life is free from stain and guilt and I am loved by friends—I owe this to my father . . .

The word *natura* expresses the result of his father's pedagogical influence, which over time made him predisposed toward virtue and consequently able to resist the temptations associated with political power and success. As common usage of the verb *nascor* reveals, especially in Roman comedy,[117] Horace's disposition is the gradual product of a continuous and repeated "formation" (*S.* 1.4.120: *formabat*), which eventually encouraged the development of good habits

[114] Rudd (1966) 41, Oliensis (1998) 32, Bowditch (2010) 59.
[115] Schlegel (2000) 111.
[116] See Kindstrand (1976) F1A–C and F2 for the biographical account. This connection was noted early on by Rudd (1966) 49, Fiske (1971) 316, and Freudenburg (1993) 14–16. Moles (2007) 166 presents the many parallels and similarities between Horace and Bion in this passage.
[117] Konstan (2011) 67–8 gives many examples.

(cf. 105: *insuevit*). His "moderate imperfections" (130–1: *mediocribus vitiis*, as in the passage quoted above) reflect this temperate disposition, which is "straight" (134: *rectius*) and neither overlooks nor transgresses the requirements of nature. By living frugally, sparingly and content with his father's modest wealth (cf. 107), he has become content with his own status (*S.* 1.6.96; cf. 1.4.108: *contentus*) and unaccustomed to bearing "distressful burdens" (*S.* 1.6.99: *onus molestum*).[118] For these reasons, Horace is not plagued by desires for unnecessary things like limitless wealth (*avaritia*), or by meanness (*sordes*), or lewdness (*mala lustra*), which coincides to a certain degree with Philodemus' identification of financial vice as involving lust and envy (*On Property Management*, col. 23.42–6) and Lucretius' vivid description of the economic effects of lust (4.1123–4): *labitur interea res et Babylonica fiunt, | languent officia atque aegrotat fama vacillans*, "Meanwhile, wealth vanishes, and turns into Babylonian perfumes; duties are neglected, good name totters and sickens." As in *Satires* 1.4, here Horace once again identifies his persona's distaste for such disturbances in philosophical terms as a reflection of his physical and mental "health" (*S.* 1.6.98; cf. 1.4.129: *sanus*), just as Lucretius asserts (4.1073–6) that only "healthy" individuals (*sanis*) enjoy "pure pleasure" (*pura voluptas*) unmixed with pain and refers to freedom from all anxiety.[119] It is likely that Horace intends a similar meaning by referring to himself as *purus* in *Satires* 1.6 (64 and 69), and in his treatise *On Gratitude* Philodemus mentions the appreciation of those who receive moral advice from sages, who are "pure" (col. 11.18: καθ[αρούς]) and "free from toil" (7–8: ἐλε[υθέ]ραν ἀναπν[ο]ήν). With regard to Maecenas, therefore, it is neither Horace's family history, political status, nor poetic talent but rather his healthy nature and freedom from ambition, avarice and other vices that form the foundation of their relationship and also the source of his wisdom, which, like the Epicurean sage, he shares with his patron in the form of moral advice communicated through the *Satires*.

It is significant that Horace viewed conversational poetry as a suitable medium for educating and transmitting moral advice, the

---

[118] DuQuesnay (2009) 50: "It should be stressed that Horace's underlying assumption is that *cura rei publici* is an *onus* which requires considerable expenditure and is not simply an *honos*." Gowers (2012) 241 connects this passage to Horace's description of Tillius (107–11).

[119] See Konstan (1973) 32.

ultimate source of which, as revealed in the *Art of Poetry*, is philosophical wisdom (309): *scribendi recte sapere est et principium et fons,*
"Of good writing the source and font is wisdom."[120] This is also
evident in Horace's epistolary correspondence with Augustus, in
which he identifies the ideal poet as one who is "useful to the city"
(*Ep.* 2.1.124: *utilis urbi*) and "nurtures the mind by friendly precepts"
(128: *pectus praeceptis format amicis*).[121] The power and authority of
Horatian verse to communicate public *consilia* is again prominently featured in the "Roman Odes," where the poet, invoking the
philosophical patronage of his Hellenistic predecessors, refers to
his lyrics as "soothing advice" (3.4.41: *lene consilium*) while
emphasizing their indispensability and tempering effect (cf. 65–6:
vis consili expers . . . vim temperatam).[122] In contrast to this, in the
Satires Horace dispenses private *consilia* directly to his patron
through informal conversations that, despite their allusions to
contemporary politics and concern with popular issues,[123] generally take place in an intimate setting (cf. *S.* 1.4.23: *volgo recitare
timentis*) and are more akin to simple conversations. Philodemus'
preference in *On Poems* for the linguistic and syntactical clarity of
prose (col. 28.27) and its potential influence on Horace, whose friendly
chats communicate moral wisdom through conventional language,
has already been discussed.[124] Like Lucretius, moreover, who
attempted to challenge the Epicurean view of poetry as obscure
and unsuitable for communicating wisdom, Horace is concerned
above all with clarity (*Art of Poetry* 25–6): *brevis esse laboro,* |
obscurus fio, "striving to be brief, I become obscure" (cf. 40–1: *cui
lecta potenter erit res,* | *nec facundia deseret hunc nec lucidus ordo,*
"Whoever shall choose a theme within his range, neither speech

---

[120] For the moral sense of this passage, see Rudd (1989) 202. As Tate (1928) 68
notes, the identification of the ideal poet as sage owes more to the Stoics than to any
other Hellenistic tradition.

[121] For the influence of the Augustan program on Horace, see Newman (1967),
especially the section on Horace (270–364), as well as White (1993) 123–33 and
Lowrie (2007) 80–5.

[122] See Nisbet and Rudd (2004) 69 for the political significance of these lines.

[123] DuQuesnay (2009) 19–58.

[124] Horace's claim that writing verse does not necessarily make one a poet in
S. 1.4.56–63 resembles that of Aristotle in *Poet.* 1447b17–20: οὐδὲν δὲ κοινόν ἐστιν
Ὁμήρῳ καὶ Ἐμπεδοκλεῖ πλὴν τὸ μέτρον, διὸ τὸν μὲν ποιητὴν δίκαιον καλεῖν, τὸν δὲ
φυσιολόγον μᾶλλον ἢ ποιητήν, "Homer and Empedocles have nothing in common
except their meter; so one should call the former poet, the other a natural scientist."

will fail him, nor clearness of order").[125] Horace's satiric exchanges with Maecenas, therefore, may be read in the light of Philodemus' description of "philosophical discussions" (*On Property Management*, col. 23.24–5), which are clear, beneficial, and ideally take place with friends in isolation (cf. 15–16). Perhaps with an additional nod to the *otium* and ambience of a Ciceronian villa, this is likely the very setting the poet has in mind when he identifies the philosophical conversation which takes place at the Sabine estate as *sermo* (*S.* 2.6.71). By a similar token, his concern with brevity reflects the influence of Callimachean standards and engages with the traditional Roman view of philosophers as long-winded (cf. Plaut. *Ps.* 687: *sed iam satis est philosophatum. nimi'diu et longum loquor*, "But that's enough philosophizing! I've been talking forever, saying too much"),[126] but his bluntness similarly conforms to Philodemus' description in *On Property Management* of his own approach as rather succinct and to the point (cf. col. 27.35–9). The poet's self-portrayal as a pithy advisor who shares moral advice with his friend, however, is one-sided: it remains to consider in what manner Maecenas is presented as the ideal Epicurean patron.

Horace's depiction of his patron as withdrawn from society, unaffected by political ambition and involved in intimate friendships is in many ways consistent with Epicurean tradition.[127] This is not to say that Maecenas was actually an Epicurean, but that Horace creates a persona for him (as he does for his father) that in many ways seems to put into action Philodemus' economic theory and is convenient within the ethical framework the poet creates for himself in the *Satires*. Some scholars have indeed advanced the view that Maecenas was truly an Epicurean, whereas others, like Pierre Boyancé, declare that "Maecenas was not the kind of man to attach himself to a particular school of philosophy, least of all one as demanding as Epicureanism."[128] In any event, the ethical considerations Horace

---

[125] Tsakiropoulou-Summers (1995) 254–6 discusses *luciditas* within the context of Roman aesthetics.

[126] Gowers (2012) 84. For Callimachus and Horace, see Cody (1976), esp. 103–19, Thomas (2007) 50–62, Freudenburg (1993) 185–235, and also Cucchiarelli (2001) 168–79.

[127] See La Penna (1996) *Enc. Or.* 1.792–803 for general observations concerning Maecenas.

[128] Boyancé (1959) 334: "Mécène n'était pas homme à adhérer à une école, surtout à une école exigeante comme l'était l'épicurienne." But cf. Avallone (1962) 111, André (1967) 15–61, and Mazzoli (1968) 300–26. Cicero probably would not have agreed with Boyancé's description of Epicureanism as rigorous and demanding (cf. *On Ends* 3.1–3). Ferguson (1990) 2263–5 discusses the "Epicureanism of Maecenas" and quotes

shares with Maecenas in *Satires* 1.6 suggests that, like the poet and in
harmony with Epicurean tradition, the millionaire patron was likewise free from political ambition, which is apparently corroborated by
the ancient testimony regarding his contentment with equestrian
status.[129] Velleius Paterculus gives the following description (*History
of Rome* 2.88): *C. Maecenas . . . non minus Agrippa Caesari carus, sed
minus honoratus—quippe vixit angusti clavi plene contentus—nec
minora consequi potuit, sed non tam concupivit*, "Gaius Maecenas . . .
was not less dear to Caesar than Agrippa, but he was honored less,
since he lived fully content with the narrow stripe of the equestrian
order. He could have achieved a position not less high than Agrippa,
but he did not have the same desire for it." This observation appears
to agree with Horace's description in *Satires* 1.6 of both himself and
Maecenas as "very far withdrawn from the vulgar masses" (18: *nos . . . a
volgo longe longeque remotos*), which, aside from being consistent
with Epicureanism, also reflects the standards of Callimachean
poetry. Both individuals, like the Hellenistic poet, remove themselves
from the rabble and prefer to adhere to their current rank, which in a
way represents a political golden mean not unlike the literary *genus
tenue*.[130] Elsewhere Horace mentions how Maecenas provides his
friends with a secluded place within the city (*S.* 1.9.49: *domus*) and
a salubrious paradise (*S.* 1.8.14: *Esquiliis . . . salubribus*) in which
social gatherings and friendly discussions take place. The fact that
Maecenas' safe haven is a garden—the famous *horti Maecenatis*—
provides yet another connection to Epicureanism, since, as Pliny
explains in his *Natural History*, such havens were clearly associated
with this sect (19.19): *iam quidem hortorum nomine in ipsa urbe
delicias agros villasque possident. primus hoc instituit Athenis Epicurus otii magister*, "Now in fact they possess delightful land and
villas within the city, which they call 'gardens.' Epicurus, the teacher
of leisure, was the first to establish this tradition in Athens." In

passages from Seneca's *Epistles* (92 and 101) that seem to confirm the patron's affinity
for this philosophical tradition.

[129] Lyne (1995) 135, however, argues that Maecenas' decision to remain a knight
was motivated by a desire to exercise "real power, interesting power, inside power"
without the bureaucratic obstacles of senatorial office. See also Talbert (1984) 78.

[130] See Hicks (2013) 147. It is worth noting that it is not only Maecenas who could
have risen to the rank of senator, but as Talbert (1984) 75-6 argues, Horace as well,
although both (as the poet decribes it) refused to do so on account of the many
responsibilities and cares such status implied.

keeping with his self-promoting agenda, Horace passes over the possibility that Maecenas' wealth was the result of profits from proscriptions and evictions following the civil war, events which Horace later identifies as the cause of his own poverty, and that his patron seems to have played an active role in the battles of Philippi and Actium (cf. *Epodes* 1).[131] Instead, the poet selectively underscores his patron's concern for privacy and the importance of camaraderie and friendship that is far removed from the public sphere.

Perhaps it is no coincidence, then, that in his *On Property Management* Philodemus also describes the ideal friend as a landowner who offers his dwelling to friends as a tranquil getaway. His opinion regarding the importance of such a place in the midst of political chaos is as follows:

ἥκιστα γὰρ ἐπιπλοκὰς ἔχει πρὸς ἀνθρώπους, ἐξ ὧν ἀηδίαι πολλαὶ παρακολουθοῦσι, καὶ μετὰ φίλων ἀναχώρησιν εὔσχολον καὶ παρὰ τοῖς [σώφροσι]ν εὐσχημονεστάτην πρόσοδον.   (col. 23.11–18)

For this [i.e. being a gentleman landowner] least of all brings involvements with men from whom many difficulties follow, since it offers a leisurely withdrawal with friends and the most fitting profit for those who are prudent.

It is clear that the ideal landowner and host offers a suitable retreat from the turmoil of politics and a safe haven for philosophical discourse among friends,[132] which recalls Horace's identification in the *Satires* of a private community of poets who "abandon political ambition" (1.10.84: *ambitione relegata*) and gather with Maecenas in a venue that is pure and virtuous (cf. 1.9.49–50: *domus hac nec purior ulla est*). Further on in his economic treatise, Philodemus emphasizes

---

[131] For the origin of Maecenas' wealth, see Griffin (1984) 192–3 and Lyne (1995) 133–5. For a challenge to Lyne, see the review of Armstrong (1997) 394–400. Evenpole (1990) 104–5 discusses Maecenas' involvement in the battles.

[132] As Fish (2011a) 72–104 explains, however, this negative view does not entail the complete rejection of political life, which, depending on the circumstances, could actually be the best option in terms of the pleasure calculus. For the most part, however, Epicureans like Philodemus tended to advise against engaging in politics because of the many risks and dangers involved. See Roskam (2007) 104–15. Also of importance is the Epicurean understanding of "security coming from people" (ἀσφάλεια ἐξ ἀνθρώπων), which can involve political connections, and "security coming from tranquility" (ἀσφάλεια ἐξ ἡσυχίας), which is "focused on a confined circle of neighbours, and far away from the multidude and political life," as Roskam (2007) 37–41 explains.

the dangers of friendlessness and misanthropy regarding relationships based on economic exchanges (*On Property Management*, col. 24.19–33: ἀφιλία ... ἀφιλανθ[ρω]πία). He also notes that in times of financial hardship property-managers should be harder on themselves than on their friends (col. 26.1–9), and even recommends that they make provisions for them "as for children" (col. 27.9: οἷα τ[έ]κνα).

In comparing patronage to fatherhood, Philodemus probably has in mind the traditional Roman designation *patronus*, which is etymologically related to *pater* and effectively communicates the similarities between the patron–client and father–son relationships (cf. *Ep.* 1.7.37: *rexque paterque*, "O my king and my father").[133] Horace likewise expresses this in *Satires* 1.6, in which he underscores his dependency on Maecenas by saying that he virtually adopted the poet and thus became his father and, by implication, a source of protection and financial stability (Horace does this without rejecting or trivializing the important role of his biological father, of whom he was obviously quite proud).[134] This relationship is underscored by references to the poet's "speechless modesty" (*S.* 1.6.57: *pudor infans*), "innocence" (64: *pectore puro*; cf. Lucil. 296–7 M: *quod pectore puro, | quod puero similis*, "with a pure heart, like a child") as well as the patron's nine-month gestation period (61: *nono post mense*).[135] Philodemus also notes that, like a good father, the ideal patron ensures that his friends are "economically provided for after his death" (*On Property Management*, col. 27.7–8): ἵν᾽ ἔχωσιν καὶ τελευτήσαντος ἐ[φ]ό[διον], which, according to Suetonius' *Life of Horace*, is exactly what Maecenas did for the poet: *Maecenas quantopere eum* [sc. *Horatium*] *dilexerit ... testatur ... multo magis extremis iudiciis tali ad Augustum elogio: "Horati Flacci ut mei esto memor,"* "And the degree to which Maecenas loved Horace is witnessed ... even more by the following plea made to Augustus in his last will: 'Remember Horatius Flaccus as you have remembered me.'"[136] Of course, the most fundamental provision an ideal patron can make in response to a friend's useful advice is the bestowal of various benefits during his

[133] Schlegel (2000) 112.   [134] See Harrison (1965) 111–14.
[135] See Schlegel (2000) 110 and Henderson (1999) 184. For *pudor* as an expression of virtue, cf. *S.* 1.6 (82–3): *pudicum, | qui primus virtutis honos*, "He kept me chaste—and that is virtue's first grace." Gowers (2012) 234 discusses the social undertones of *pudor*, which suggests an "unservile nature." DuQuesnay (2009) 46 notes that this nine-month period coincided with Maecenas' diplomatic mission to Antony on behalf of Octavian.
[136] Ferguson (1990) 2264 briefly discusses this passage.

lifetime, particularly financial rewards, just as Philodemus observes in *On Gratitude* that the mark of "genuine friendship" (col. 5.9–10: [φι]λίας ... νομίμης) is a patron's eagerness "to anticipate his friends' needs" (col. 10.10–11: περὶ φίλων [προνοεῖ]ν). In accordance with the Roman custom of calling patronage *amicitia*, the philosopher euphem-istically refers to these benefits as gratitude and honor (*On Property Management*, col. 23.27–9)[137] and, if it can be assumed that the quantity and quality of such goods indicates something about a client's worth, then one may safely conclude that Horace was especially "hon-ored" by Maecenas (cf. *Ep.* 1.7.15: *tu me fecisti locupletem*, "you made me rich").[138]

The management strategy Philodemus recommends in his eco-nomic treatises also appears in Horace's charming account of his so-called "Epicurean day" in *Satires* 1.6 (110–28), which reveals something about the philosophical convictions underlying his perso-na's economic choices. The poet's description of Maecenas and himself as far removed from the masses is complemented by his quasi-psychological retreat into a safe haven within the heart of Rome, a scene Emily Gowers describes in terms of "Epicurean contentment" involving "perfect Epicurean *otium*" but without offering further details.[139] This is clearly an application of the famous Epicurean maxim "live unknown" (λάθε βιώσας),[140] which Lucretius expresses in similar language when he pleads with Memmius to have a mind "removed from cares" (1.51: *semotum a curis*) and when he describes the divine nature as "separated and far removed from the affairs of humans" (2.648: *semota ab nostris rebus seiunctaque longe*). Like the pure house of Maecenas on the Esquiline in *Satires* 1.9, moreover, Horace's own "townhouse" (*S.* 1.6.114: *domum*) is a place of mental health and refreshment, which, though situated in the midst of urban chaos, offers freedom from (cf. *On Property Management*, col. 23.15–16) the distressful "interactions" (11: ἐπιπλοκάς) and "many

---

[137] Saller (1982) 28: "the traditional rewards for poets were *pecunia* and *honores*."

[138] For Horace's mention of his patron's "generosity" (*benignitas tua*) and his own "wealth" (*me ditavit*), which is probably a reference to the Sabine estate given to him around 33 BC, see *Epodes* 1 (31–2).

[139] Gowers (2012) 219, 245 respectively. Armstrong (1986) 277–80 refers to this passage as "pure convention," but adds further observations concerning Horace's "luxury" which will be discussed below.

[140] See Roskam (2007) 33–44, who also considers this saying with regard to Horace's *Epistles* (166–79).

pains" (13: ἀηδίαι πολλαί) associated with political ambition and avarice. It is true that, as David Armstrong observes, "owning one's house in Rome was as unusual as in modern New York city," and that such ownership indicates substantial wealth,[141] but this did not result (at least according to Horace's account) from the ambitious effort to build a fortune, which would involve painful toil and anxiety (cf. *On Property Management*, col. 15.37–43). In order to emphasize his own freedom from ambition and the negative consequences of "success," especially in connection with the senatorial office, Horace introduces Tillius[142] as the perfect counter-example. The phrase "I go about alone" (*S.* 1.6.112: *incedo solus*), for instance answers to "[one must] drag about all sorts of companions" (101–2: *ducendus et unus | et comes alter*); the declaration "I don't worry about having to wake up early tomorrow" (119–20: *non sollicitus, mihi quod cras | surgendum sit mane*) counters "[one must] greet many clients with the morning *salutatio*" (101: *salutandi plures*), which also recalls Philodemus' description of waking early in order to attend to household business as "wretched and unseemly for the sage" (*On Property Management*, col. 11.30: ταλαίπωρον δὲ καὶ ἀνοί [κε]ιον φιλοσόφου).[143] Furthermore, the fact that Horace's restful withdrawal is largely the result of freedom from physical labor, which is performed by servants (*S.* 1.6.116: *pueris tribus*), may draw from Philodemus' recommendation that managers transfer such mundane chores to their servants (*On Property Management*, col. 23.7–11). As David Armstrong rightly notes, however, this modest description certainly

---

[141] Armstrong (2010) 17.

[142] See Kiessling–Heinze (1910) 108. There is much disagreement among scholars regarding the identity of Tillius. The scholiasts identify him as L. Tillius Cimber, one of Caesar's assassins; Bellandi (1996) *Enc. Or.* 1.917–918 conjectures that he was his brother; Armstrong (1986) 272–3 and DuQuesnay (2009) 47 interpret lines 38–41 as referring to Tillius, and therefore conclude that he was the overly ambitious son of a freeman father (a tempting theory, since it would provide the perfect contrast with Horace). Toher (2005) 183–9, who provides a more detailed summary of the debate, agrees that he was L. Tillius Cimber. According to Toher, the phrase *sumere depositum clavum* at line 25 refers to Tillius' decision to withdraw from politics at some point, only to return later on because of his overwhelming ambition. Cf. Lucr. 3.60–1 for political ambition and greed as causing men to "transcend the limits of justice" (*transcendere fines | iuris*) and engage in "crimes" (*scelerum*).

[143] Lejay (1966) 173: "La vie tranquille et sûre d'Horace opposée aux ennuis de Tillius et de ses pareils est la condamnation de toute ambition," "Horace's tranquil and safe life, contrasted with the troubles of Tillius and his peers, is a condemnation of all ambition."

does not imply that Horace only had three servants, but that he required three at suppertime:

> [T]he "Epicurean day" in Horace is more of a luxury item than it looks. We need hardly believe … that Horace could afford no more than three slaves to serve his table at his Roman house. The *topos* of Epicurean "simplicity," rather, is plainly one for the luxurious and gentlemanly, who can afford better but consider this much tasteful.[144]

Although perfectly willing to live with what suffices and able to endure humble circumstances (cf. *Odes* 1.1.18: *pauperiem pati*), like the Epicurean sage Horace "inclines in his wishes toward a more affluent way of life" (*On Property Management*, col. 16.4–6: ῥέπει δὲ τῆι βουλήσει μᾶλλον ἐπὶ τὴν ἀφθονωτέραν) and "accepts more whenever it comes easily and without harm" (44–6: τὸ [δὲ π]λεῖον, ἃ[ν ἀ]βλ[α]βῶς καὶ [εὐ]πόρως γίνηται, δεκτέ[ον]; cf. *Ep.* 1.15.43–4: *cum res deficient, satis inter vilia fortis;* | *verum ubi quid melius contingit et unctius*, "when means fail, I cry up a safe and lowly lot, but when something better and richer comes my way…"). In general, the language Horace uses to characterize his pleasurable existence at home is informed by Philodemus' description of the ideal ἀναχώρησις εὔσχολος: he lives "more pleasantly" than Tillius (*S.* 1.6.110: *commodius*), his "pleasure" dictates his destination (111: *quacumque libido est*), he "lies abed until late morning" (122: *ad quartam iaceo*), and wanders about (122: *vagor*), he is "not troubled" by business (119: *non sollicitus*[145]) and, taking into account the positive results of his calculated choices and avoidances, he lives "more sweetly" (130: *victurum suavius*[146]) than the general population. According to Horace, his pleasurable existence is largely the result of choices made in accordance with the requirements of nature, some of which are economic in the modern sense: his food purchases, which consist of "greens and wheat" (112: *holus ac far*) as well as "leeks and chickpeas" (115: *porri et ciceris*), reflect actual physical needs rather than the over-indulgent choices of a glutton (cf. 127: *pransus non avide* and *Odes* 1.31.15–16: *me pascunt olivae,* | *me cichorea levesque malvae*, "My fare is the olive,

---

[144] Armstrong (1986) 278–9.
[145] Gowers (2012) 247: "another defensive denial, Romanizing Epicurean *ataraxia.*"
[146] For *suavis* as an allusion to Epicurean ἡδονή, cf. Lucr. 2.1 (*suave*) and Gowers (2012) 249.

the endive, and the wholesome mallow").[147] In many ways, therefore, Horace's description of his secluded and otiose life, which is
made possible by income that made him more affluent (as his
ownership of an urban *domus* and at least three servants shows)
but not insensitive to the requirements of nature, agrees with the
principles of Philodemean economic theory.[148]

EPICUREAN FRANKNESS IN *SATIRES* 1.6

It has been suggested that the poet's charming recollection in *Satires*
1.6 of the initial meeting with his future benefactor portrays Horace
as an honest and virtuous candidate for Maecenas' favor. Aside from
this, it is also designed to combat the traditional identification of the
sage-client as a subservient flatterer.[149] In this sense, Philodemus'
own concern with defending his reputation as a moral expert and
close associate of the wealthy Piso in light of Cicero's criticisms might
have influenced Horace's depiction of his persona's relationship with
Maecenas. Horace begins by immediately disassociating himself from
the overly ambitious and headstrong toady, who characteristically
propels himself towards his unsuspecting prey like a hunter. This
aggressiveness is clear in Eupolis' portrayal of the flatterer as tracking
down his prey in the agora (*PCG* 5.172),[150] which ultimately inspired
the poets of New Comedy, as Plautus' characterization of Artotrogus
in the *Braggart Soldier* (31–45) and especially Terence's portrayal of
Gnatho in the *Eunuch* suggests:

hoc novomst aucipium; ego adeo primus inveni viam.
est genus hominum qui esse primos se omnium rerum volunt
nec sunt. hos consector; hisce ego non paro me ut rideant,
sed eis ultro arrideo et eorum ingenia admiror simul.

---

[147] Oltramare (1926) 141 interprets Horace's meager fare as "végétarianisme
cynique." For the notion of *mensa tenuis* in Horace and its connection to Callimachean aesthetics, see Mette (1961) 136–9. Cf. also Juv. 11.64–76.
[148] This will be discussed further in connection with *Satires* 2.6 in Chapter 4.
[149] In contrast to the thesis of Turpin (2009) 129–37. Kemp (2009) 5 defends
Horatian satire against the charge of moral incompetence.
[150] For the fragments, see Storey (2003) 190.

quiquid dicunt laudo; id rursum si negant, laudo id quoque.
negat quis, nego; ait, aio. postremo imperavi egomet mihi
omnia assentari. is quaestus nunc est multo uberrimus.   (248–53)
This is a new way to catch prey, and I'm the first one to discover
it. There are some men who want to be the first in everything but
aren't. I follow these closely. I don't set out to make them laugh at me;
instead, I laugh at them while at the same time expressing admiration
for their cleverness. It doesn't matter what they say—I praise it. But if
they say the opposite, then I praise that, too. If they say "no," I say "no."
If they say "yes," I do the same. In a word, I've commanded myself to
agree to everything. That's the most profitable way to make a living
nowadays.[151]

In order to drive a wedge between himself and the typical flatterer
who ensnares his quarry like a hunter, Horace prefaces the carefully
constructed scene in *Satires* 1.6 by declaring that Maecenas rejects
shameless ambition (51–2), which, as Philodemus notes in *On Flattery*, motivates obsequious people to seek glory through relationships
with millionaires:

[ἡ] δόξα τοίνυν χάριν ἀσφαλείας ἐδιώχθη κατὰ φύσιν, ἣν ἔξεστιν ἔχειν
καὶ ἰδιώτηι καὶ φιλοσόφωι, κακία[ς δ᾽ ο]ὐ πάσης, ἐν αἷς ἡ κολακεία
[πρ]ωτα[γ]ωνι[στ]εῖ καὶ μεί[ζον]ά [γ᾽] ἀδοξ[ί]αν αἰ[κ]ῆ π[ε]ριτίθ[ησιν
ὅταν ε]ὐδοξίαν ἀποτελ[εῖν προσδοκᾶται. χάριν περιου]σίας ἢ δόξης
ἢ καί τινος ἀ[ρ]χῆς ἀρέσαντες ἀνθρώπ[οις] μεγαλοπλούτοις καὶ
δυν[α]στευτικοῖς ἢ καὶ δημοκό[ποις].   (PHerc. 222, coll. 4.4–5.4)

A good reputation, which both the philosopher and the layman can
have,[152] is found to be pursued for the sake of security in accordance
with nature, but not by means of any of the vices, in which flattery plays
the foremost role, and brings only greater shame when it is expected to
produce fame. [Flatterers] aim to please magnates, potentates, or even
demagogues for the sake of possessions or glory or even some public
office.

Philodemus' understanding of the dangers of flattery as producing
more infamy than fame reflects the principles of the hedonic calculus,

---

[151] Cf. Cic. *On Friendship* 93. Juvenal makes a similar observation in *Satires*
3 (100–3).
[152] See Fiske (1971) 317, quoted above, on Bion's ambivalence regarding a
good reputation. This is obviously not Horace's father's view when he expresses
concern for "preserving your livelihood and reputation" (S. 1.4.118–19: *vitam
famamque . . . incolumem*).

but it also underpins Horace's warning concerning placing oneself in "Glory's chariot" (*S.* 1.6.23: *Gloria curru*), which ultimately results in slavery to political responsibilities and possible infamy, as Tillius quickly discovered (107). This passage may likewise be read within the context of Philodemus' discussion of the similarities between politicians and flatterers, both of whom must please their subjects in order to achieve fame or notoriety:

πονοῦσιν οὖ<ν οἱ> πολι[τ]ευόμενοι· προσεπιφέρε[ι] τοιγαροῦν· ʽπαραιτο[ῦ]
ντα[ι] διὰ μὲν τὸ περὶ πολλοῖς δυσαρεστεῖν στυγοῦντες αὐτούς, διὰ δὲ τὸ περὶ
πλείστου ποιε[ῖ]σθα[ι] τὰς παρ᾽ αὐτῶν δό[σεις] καὶ [τ]ειμάς, πάλιν ἀν[τι]
ποι[ού]μενοι δουλεύειν· [τοιοῦτό]ν τι [γ]ίνεται, φησί, καὶ [π]ερὶ τοὺς
κόλ[α]κας (PHerc. 1675, col. 11.15–25)

Thus do politicians work hard, and he [Hermarchus] adds accordingly "They ask for favors because, on the one hand, they suffer annoyances on account of the mob and they hate them, but, on the other hand, because they put great value in gifts and honors from them they exert themselves in return by serving them like slaves." And this sort of thing happens, he says, to flatterers as well . . .

The connection between politicians and flatterers is clearly relevant to Horace's self-portrayal in *Satires* 1.6 as unambitious and uninterested in politics, which, according to his own description (100–4), is a life that violates the pleasure calculus since it involves more pain than pleasure.

Horace emphasizes his passive immunity to ambition by employing the verb *obferre* to explain his encounter with Maecenas, which has important implications for his own persona. At line 54 he states *nulla etenim mihi te fors obtulit* ("For it was no case of luck thrusting you in my way"). This expression communicates that it was not Horace who "thrust himself" into the millionaire's path like an ambitious flatterer; rather, their initial meeting was owed to the intervention of the poet's close friends, who thrust Maecenas into the poet's path (cf. Lucilius' encounter with Scipio at 1009 M: *producunt me ad te, tibi me haec ostendere cogunt*, "They brought me to you and forced me to show you these verses").[153] His mention of high-quality and prominent friends like Vergil and Varius, who freely

---

[153] Gowers (2012) 233 notes that the verb *obferre* "suggests thrusting something in someone's path." Cf. *S.* 1.4.123, where Horace's father similarly "throws" (*obiciebat*) examples into his son's line of vision.

vouch for his ethical credentials (cf. *S.* 1.6.55: *quid essem*), is also significant: it would seem that from its very inception Horace's relationship with Maecenas is attributed to, as well as contextualized and defined by, honesty and genuine friendship, which, as Philodemus notes, is "the adversary of flattery" (PHerc. 1082, col. 2.1–3: φιλία . . . ῆς ἀντ[ί]παλός ἐστιν ἡ κολακεία).[154] By choosing to overlook completely his literary talents, then, Horace attempts to emphasize further his personal worth and thereby deflect any possible charges of flattery (cf. *S.* 1.6.46–8). Niall Rudd interprets *rodunt* at line 46 as resentment and Emily Gowers comments that this verb is "part of the traditional vocabulary of satirical *invidia*," although Jerome Kemp adds to this the implied charge of flattery.[155] Indeed, one wonders whether Horace was deterred from explicitly mentioning such charges by Cicero's critical portrayal of Philodemus as a flattering poet in his denunciation of Piso (70: *ut Graeculum, ut adsentatorem, ut poetam*, "a Greekling, a flatterer, and a poet"). Regardless of Horace's reason, his overwhelmingly positive self-portrait assures the Maecenas of *Satires* 1.6 that he has nothing to fear from this potential client, who, in accordance with Philodemus' description of the sage in *On Gratitude* (PHerc. 1414), is "pure" (col. 11.18: καθαρούς; cf. *S.* 1.6.64: *pectore puro* and 69: *purus*) and does not snatch away his friends' wealth the way flatterers often do (col. 9.2–6). There is a strong literary tradition of depicting flatterers as thieves (cf. Eupolis, *PCG* 5.162: φοροῦσιν, ἁρπάζουσιν ἐκ τῆς οἰκίας | τὸ χρυσίον, τἀργύρια πορθεῖται, "They carry off and snatch away the gold from one's house, and the silver is hauled away"[156]), especially in later satire such as Lucian's *Fisherman*, which portrays them as conmen in the guise of philosophers and concerned solely with making money (42–5). In the case of Horace, such a connection is rendered almost impossible not only by his as well as Maecenas' outright rejection of ambition in general, but also by his emphasis on being content with meagre fare and simple living at the end of *Satires* 1.6.

---

[154] Kemp (2010b) 67. Cf. Arist. *Nic. Eth.* 1126b20–1, in which "friendship" (φιλία) is regarded as the most suitable mean between "flattery/obsequiousness" (κολακεία/ἀρεσκεία) and "surliness/quarrelsomeness" (δυσεριστία/δυσκολία).

[155] Rudd (1966) 41, Gowers (2012) 232, and Kemp (2010b) 65. Cf. Schlegel (2005) 54 for a different interpretation.

[156] This passage is discussed by Storey (2003) 183, who attributes it to Callias or a slave.

Another aspect of Horace's self-portrayal in this poem that further highlights his distance from self-seeking ambition is the combined role of frankness and pithiness, both of which are antithetical to the flatterer but characteristic of the sage. In contrast to the expressed criticisms of nameless aristocrats (*S.* 1.6.29 and 38–9), the sound of trumpets in the forum (43–4), and the jeers of envious poetasters (45–8), Horace's encounter with Maecenas occurs within the context of remarkable silence and tranquility:

> ut veni coram, singultim pauca locutus—
> infans namque pudor prohibebat plura profari—
> non ego me claro natum patre, non ego circum
> me Satureiano vectari rura caballo,
> sed quod eram narro.   (*S.* 1.6.56–60)

On coming into your presence I said a few faltering words, for speech-less shame stopped me from more. My tale was not that I was a famous father's son, not that I rode about my estate on a Saturian steed: I told you what I was.[157]

The language Horace employs in this passage, which contains an astonishing array of monosyllabic and disyllabic words surrounding the jarring presence of the five-syllable *Satureiano* (which represents the boaster's inflated arrogance), has rightly been identified as an expression of Callimachean brevity (cf. *Aet.* 1.23–4),[158] although the anaphoric repetition of negatives and the denial of wealth also occurs in Lucilius (132 M: *ostrea nulla fuit, non purpura, nulla peloris*, "I had no crimson clothes, no purple trappings, and no large mussels"). Without any explicit reference to the nature of his poetry, therefore, Horace subtly communicates that the mark of his satire will be a terse frankness directed toward a discerning patron, who is more of a genuine father-figure or parent than a king (cf. *S.* 1.6.61). Nevertheless, the entire scene is an expression of a traditional *topos* involving the truthful sage's exchange with a powerful ruler, which recalls Herodotus' account of Solon before Croesus (*Histories* 1.30–3) and was apparently of great interest to Philodemus. In the doxogra-phical treatise *History of the Stoics*, for instance, he examines

---

[157] As Armstrong (1986) 260 notes, in the *Art of Poetry* the poet himself defines an *eques* as "one who has a horse and a father and land" (248: *quibus est equus et pater et res*).

[158] Freudenburg (1993) 206 and Oliensis (1998) 32 discuss the programmatic nature of this Callimachean passage. For the significance of *Satureiano*, which may contain a pun with *satur*, see Gowers (2012) 234.

the philosophical nature of frankness as employed by Zeno of Citium
before Antigonus Gonatas (coll.

8–9), whose relationship with his
patron, according to Philodemus, was similar to that of Horace and
Maecenas: the column cited immediately above contains a friendly
insult of Antigonus directed toward the Stoic, whose response has not
survived (col. 8.1–13). In the following column, however, Philodemus
reports that Zeno communicated with Antigonus as his "equal" (9.2:
ἴσον τε καὶ ὅμοιον) and that he enjoyed "sweet competitions" (3:
φιλονικίαν ἡδεῖαν) with the Macedonian king, who "marveled at the
man and honored him exceedingly" (5–7: τὸν [δ'] ἄνδρα θαυμάζειν καὶ
τιμ[ᾶ]ν καθ᾽ ὑπερβολήν).[159] Philodemus offers a different consideration of Plato before Dionysius I of Syracuse in the counterpart treatise
History of the Academics (2X.12–15): καὶ τ[ο]ύτου σκαιότερ[ον] αὐτοῦ
τὴν παρρησία[ν] ἐνέγκα[ντ]ος, ὅτι ἐρωτηθεὶς τίς αὐτῶι [δο]κ[εῖ] φα[ν]
ἦναι εὐδαιμονέστερος, οὐ[κ] εἶπεν αὐτ[όν], "and this one [Dionysius]
showed himself to be ill at ease with his [Plato's] frankness, because
when he [Plato] was asked who he thought was more blessed than
others, he [Plato] did not say him [Dionysius]."[160] As mentioned
already, the most popular precedent cited among scholars and commentators for Horace is that of Bion before Antigonus, although one
immediately observes that the exchange between him and Maecenas is
much pithier than Bion's eleven lines of autobiographical details,
complete with allusions to Homer.[161] The poet's simplicity and
straightforwardness in this scene are carefully complemented by the
silence that characterizes Horace's demeanor before the wealthy Maecenas, and which may reflect the principles of Philodemean homiletics
as expressed in his treatise On Conversation.

According to Philodemus' fragmentary explanation, virtuous "conversation" (ὁμιλία) between true friends employs frankness whenever
necessary but also observes the "power of silence" (col. 6.2: [σ]ιωπῆς . . .
δύναμίς) and the "limits of speech" (col. 5.2: ὁμιλίας . . . τὸ πέ[ρας]),

---

[159] Clay (2004) 62–4 offers a concise but enlightening summary of its contents.
Cf. Diogenes' account of Zeno's correspondence with Antigonus (7.6–9).

[160] According to Olivieri (1914) 54 and, more recently, Clay (2004) 69, a similar
reference to Plato's frankness can be found at On Frank Criticism col. 15b5–6, which
contains a quotation of Socrates' "second sailing" (δεύτερον πλοῦν) from Phd. 99d1–2
(cf. also Plut. How to Tell a Flatterer from a Friend 52d and 67c–e).

[161] Moles (2007) 166–7 discusses the parallels between Bion's frank but rather
prolix explanation and Horace's much more condensed version. See also Rudd (1966)
49 and Freudenburg (1993) 205–6.

188 Epicurean Ethics in Horace

which is an expression of the sage's tranquility and underscores his disdain for dishonest or "evil talk" (col. 7.17: κ[ακ]ῆς ὁ[μιλίας]).[162] That is to say, unlike the flatterer or ambitious politician, who will say anything to his targeted audience, a true friend's conversations are motivated by goodwill and therefore communicate only what is relevant or helpful, as emphasized in *On Frank Criticism*:

πᾶς [τίς] ποτε εὐνοῶν καὶ συνετ[ῶς] κα[ὶ συν]εχῶς φιλοσοφῶν καὶ μέγας
ἐν ἔξει καὶ ἀφιλόδοξος καὶ [δη]μαγωγὸς ἥκιστα καὶ φθόνου καθαρὸς καὶ
τὰ προσόντα μόνον λέγων καὶ μὴ συνεκφερόμενος, ὥστε λοιδορεῖν ἢ
πομπε[ύ]ε[ιν] ἢ [κ]αταβάλλε[ιν ἢ] βλάπτ[ειν], μηδ᾽ ἀσ[ε]λγε[ί]αις κα[ὶ
κολ]ακευτ[ι]καῖς χρώ[μενος τέχναις]. (col. 1b.2–14)

... [and from a good disposition] everyone who is well disposed and intelligently disposed, and continually talking philosophically, and lofty in character, and careless of his own glory, and not at all a crowd-pleaser [politician?], and free of spite, and says only what is relevant and is not carried away into reviling, and strutting, or into casting people down, and doing harm, nor using the arts of insolence and flattery.

In a similar fashion, Horace does not portray himself as an obsequious flatterer whose rhetoric tickles the ear with "honeyed words" (PHerc. 222, col. 7.9–10: μει[λίττει] δὲ τὸν κολα[κε]υόμεν[ον])[163] and whose physical appearance is similarly designed to please the eyes (PHerc. 1457, col. 6.27–31 [fr. 7]): καὶ πλεῖστο[υ δὲ ἀποκείρα]σθαι καὶ τοὺς [ὀδόντας λευ]κοὺς ἔχειν κ[αὶ τὰ ἱμάτια δὲ χρη]στὰ μεταβά[λλεσθαι καὶ χρίσ]ματι ἀλείφε[σθαι], "For the most part the obsequious man keeps his hair nicely trimmed, his teeth are whitened, he wears fashionable clothes and stays well-oiled with chrism."[164] In contrast to this, the poet shows and tells Maecenas exactly "what he was" (*S.* 1.6.60: *quod eram*), without the cosmetic trappings of rhetoric or fashion, which is something he highlights once again in his later, rather frank correspondence in the *Epistles*:

si curatus inaequali tonsore capillos
occurri, rides; si forte subucula pexae
trita subest tunicae vel si toga dissidet inpar,
rides. (*Ep.* 1.1.94–7)

---

[162] Tsouna (2007) 122–3 briefly discusses its contents. Cf. Arist. *Nic. Eth.* 1126b11–21 for a consideration of the different kinds of ὁμιλία.

[163] Cf. Bion's statement that those who love flattery are "like amphorae, being easily lead about by their ears" (Kindstrand 1976: F51): ἀμφορεῦσιν ἀπὸ τῶν ὤτων ῥᾳδίως μεταφερομένοις.

[164] In this passage Philodemus quotes extensively from Theophrastus' character portrait of the "obsequious man" or ἄρεσκος in *Characters* 5.

If, when some uneven barber has cropped my hair, I come your way, you laugh; if haply I have a tattered shirt under a new tunic, or if my gown sits badly and askew, you laugh.[165]

The same candor appears in *Satires* 1.6, when Horace's few words are identified as originating in a pure heart, which, as mentioned, implies freedom from envy and ambition. Unlike the flatterer, whose greatest enemies are his competitors (cf. PHerc. 222, col. 2.13–14), Horace does not envy Varius or Vergil, whom he considers "the best of friends" (*S.* 1.6.54: *optimus*) rather than rivals for Maecenas' favor (cf. *S.* 1.9.50–2). Overall, Horace's self-description in this scene is, as in *Satires* 1.4, programmatic for the rest of the collection: his poems will be neither obsequious nor slanderous and overly critical, but truthful and terse for the sake of his audience's moral benefit.

The poet's self-promoting "autobiography" in *Satires* 1.4 establishes his moral authority and justifies his criticisms in the introductory poems. At the same time, it provides the key to understanding the portrayal of his relationship with Maecenas in *Satires* 1.6 and his status as an unambitious and virtuous client-friend who, in accordance with Philodemus' description of patronage, offers private *consilia* to a receptive patron in exchange for gratitude. As will be seen presently, an important part of the development of this Epicurean persona is the emphasis on friendship as different from flattery, which, in Horace's day, was a distinction that was anything but easy to make. Horace's approach involves satirical contrasts in both books of the collection between himself and contemporary as well as traditional—even mythological—flatterers, all of which is ultimately relevant to his famous account of the "divine" gift of the Sabine estate in *Satires* 2.6.

---

[165] Cf. the possible intertext in Ovid's description of the flattering *amator* in *Art of Love* 1 (513–22).

4

Flattery, Patronage, Wealth, and Epicurean Ethics

Satires 1.9, 2.5, and 2.6

PHILODEMUS AND THE TOADY IN *SATIRES* 1.9

One of the most colorful and extended portraits of vicious or other-wise reprehensible behavior in the *Satires* begins when Horace intro-duces the popular character sketch of a garrulous and self-seeking chatterbox in 1.9. Originally referred to in English as "the coxcomb" and "the bore," Niall Rudd renamed him "the pest," although, for reasons that will soon become obvious, for the present he will be called "the toady."[1] The setting of this poem in the Roman forum (1: *Ibam forte via sacra*), and its abrupt, almost annoying conversational form originate partly in Catullus (cf. 10.2: *foro*) and perhaps also in Vergil's *Eclogues* 9,[2] which involves a conversation between Moeris and the aspiring and inquisitive poet Lycidas en route to the city (1: *in urbem*). The beginning of the sketch itself also appears to point to Lucilius, who uses the very same expression "[Scipio] was on his way home by chance" in one of his fragments (1142 M: *ibat forte domum*).[3] The existence of a Lucilian prototype for this satire is contested among

---

[1] Rudd (1966) 74, followed by Courtney (1994) 1–8 and Gowers (2012) 280–3, although Diggle (2004) 181 refers to him as "the toady."

[2] See Fraenkel (1957) 114–16 and Freudenburg (1993) 209–11 for the literary significance of Horace's imitation of Catullan "compositional variation." For Courtney (1994) 2, the poem's brief clauses reflect "spasmodic actions seeking escape." See also Van Rooy (1973) 69–88.

[3] Fraenkel (1957) 112, Rudd (1966) 76–7, and Fiske (1971) 330–6, who gives more parallels. The precise nature and extent of Lucilius' influence is unclear, as demon-strated by the conflicting views of Rudd (1966) 284 n. 38 and Anderson (1982) 84–5.

scholars like Niall Rudd, although Jennifer Ferriss-Hill has recently argued that the nameless interlocutor should in fact be identified with Lucilius himself.[4] It should also be noted that there are important connections between Horace's portrayal of the toady and the *character dramaticus*, as Herbert Musurillo, taking his cue from Porphyrio (*ad* 1: *dramatico charactere*) and perhaps Plutarch (*How to Tell a Flatterer from a Friend* 50e: τραγικός ἐστιν), has demonstrated.[5] Other aspects of this sketch recall earlier comic treatments of the flatterer, particularly with regard to the grand entrance Horace gives his subject at *S.* 1.9.3–4: *accurrit quidam notus mihi nomine tantum | arreptaque manu "quid agis, dulcissime rerum?,"* "when up there runs a man I knew only by name and seizes my hand: 'How are you, sweetest of all things?'" This headstrong manner of accosting a victim in the open and catching him completely unawares resembles Eupolis' description of the flatterer's technique (*PCG* 5.172.7–8): . . . εἰς ἀγοράν. ἐκεῖ δ' ἐπειδὰν κατίδω τιν' ἄνδρα | ἠλίθιον, πλουτοῦντα δ', εὐθὺς περὶ τοῦτόν εἰμι, "[I run] into the marketplace, and there, when I catch sight of some fool—but a rich one!—I am immediately at his side."[6] For W. S. Anderson, the tension between Horace and the toady relates to the context of an epic battle, as suggested by the poet's use of battle terms (*S.* 1.9.16: *persequar* and 29: *confice*) and citation of a line from the *Iliad* (78: *sic me servavit Apollo* = *Il.* 20.443: τὸν δ' ἐξήρπαξεν Ἀπόλλων).[7] As is clear, the importance of the epic and comic traditions as possible sources for Horace's portrait in *Satires* 1.9 is well established; also possible, however, is a more profound consideration of contemporary,

---

[4] Rudd (1966) 90–6, Ferriss-Hill (2011) 429–55.

[5] Musurillo (1964) 65–8. Cf. also Rudd (1966) 75–6 and Cairns (2005) 49–55. Plutarch goes on to say that the flatterer's act is akin to a tragedy in that it is serious and not meant as a joke (καὶ κολακείαν ἡγητέον χαλεπήν . . . οὐδὲ τὴν παίζουσαν ἀλλὰ τὴν σπουδάζουσαν). See also Montiglio (2011) 119.

[6] Cf. Theophr. *Char.* 5.1–2: ὁ δὲ ἄρεσκος ἀμέλει τοιοῦτός τις, οἷος πόρρωθεν προσαγορεῦσαι καὶ ἄνδρα κράτιστον εἴπας καὶ θαυμάσας ἱκανῶς, ἀμφοτέραις ταῖς χερσὶν ἁψάμενος μὴ ἀφιέναι καὶ μικρὸν προπέμψας καὶ ἐρωτήσας, πότε αὐτὸν ὄψεται, ἐπαινῶν ἀπαλλάττεσθαι, "To be sure, the obsequious man is the kind who addresses his target from a distance and calls him 'most excellent' and expresses great reverence. He holds on to him with both hands lest he should escape and walks alongside him for a little while, asking when he will see him again and praising him as he departs." See also Storey (2003) 190 for the fragment and Damon (1997) 122 for parallels in Roman comedy.

[7] Anderson (1982) 84–102. Of course, epic parodies are a commonplace in satire (cf. e.g. Juv. 12.18–24). For the view that Apollo fails to save Horace at the end of *Satires* 1.9, see Mazurek (1997) 1–17.

namely Epicurean, observations regarding the disposition of a typical flatterer and its significance for Horace's persona as it relates to patronage.

The inclusion of a nameless interlocutor, which is already familiar from Horace's three introductory satires, establishes connections not only to comedy but also to the moral portraits of character types written by philosophers like Theophrastus (especially *Characters* 2, 3, 5, and 7) and, as will be argued presently, to Philodemus. In the case of Philodemus, Cicero's misrepresentation of Epicurus' infamous doctrine of pleasure and his understanding of utilitarian friendship, not to mention the fact that he had accused the Syrian philosopher living in Italy of flattering his companion Piso, was more than enough to compel him to provide an outline of the differences between flatterers and philosophers. It is also probable that Horace himself was interested in making a similar distinction in the *Satires*, as suggested by the significant differences between his self-portrayal as quiet and unambitious in 1.6 and his portrait of the loquacious and opportunistic toady in 1.9. Both "characters" anticipate or hope for the approval of the wealthy Maecenas, although the poet's calculated descriptions reveal enormous discrepancies in their respective dispositions regarding honesty and candor. The flatterer's ambition and desire for fame is suggested by the proactive "snatching" of Horace's hand in *Satires* 1.9 and the overly charming address "O sweetest of all things" (4: *dulcissime rerum*), which is consistent with Philodemus' observation that the flatterer "speaks honeyed words to his victim" (PHerc. 222, col. 7.9–10: μει[λίττει] δὲ τὸν κολα[κε]νόμεν[ον]).[8] More importantly, this abrupt entrance and perverted hijacking of one of Horace's favorite terms of endearment (cf. *Ep.* 1.7.12: *dulcis*) underscores the toady's status as a charlatan and an "actor" (PHerc. 1675, col. 13.35–6: ὑποκριτάς), which is only further confirmed by his tactless self-appropriation of the title "learned poet" (*S.* 1.9.7: *docti sumus*; cf. *Ep.* 1.19.1: *Maecenas docte*). The use of such terms is one of the characteristics of Epicurean conversation, as Philodemus suggests in *On Frank Criticism* (cf. fr. 14.5–10). Horace's "friend" in *Satires* 1.9, however, attempts to win favor by mimicking his victim's language and peremptorily insinuating himself into Maecenas' circle by

---

[8] Gowers (2012) 284 observes that *arripio* "signifies his opportunistic attitude to life."

claiming poetic excellence, which apparently includes the ability to compose quickly (23–4: *quis me scribere pluris | aut citius possit versus?*) and dance effeminately (23–5: *membra movere | mollius;* cf. Lucr. 4.980: *cernere saltantis et mollia membra moventis,* "see them dancing and softly moving their limbs").[9] The notion that the opportunistic flatterer imitates others for the purpose of self-gain appears in Philodemus' *On Flattery,* in which such behavior is described as resembling that of a "little dog or a small monkey" (PHerc. 222, col. 9.14–15: κυνίδιον . . . ἢ [π]ιθή[κ]ιον), which he condemns by saying "it is one thing to mimic someone, and another to emulate him" (col. 10.8–10: [ἅ]λ[λο μὲν γὰρ] τὸ μιμεῖσθαί τ[ιν', ἕτερον δὲ] τὸ ζηλοῦν). Perhaps Philodemus' description influenced to some degree Plutarch's similar assessment in *How to Tell a Flatterer from a Friend* (51c): ὁ κόλαξ αὐτὸν ὥσπερ ὕλην τινὰ ῥυθμίζει καὶ σχηματίζει, περιαρμόσαι καὶ περιπλάσαι ζητῶν οἷς ἂν ἐπιχειρῇ διὰ μιμήσεως, ". . . the flatterer bends and shapes himself like some material for molding, seeking to adapt and mold himself to his victims through imitation." Plutarch also mentions the "ape" (πίθηκος), "cuttlefish" (πολύποδος), and "chameleon" (χαμαιλέοντος) in connection with the flatterer as imitator (52b–53b),[10] which connects with Horace's condemnation in *Epistles* 1.18 of clients who flatter their patrons and mimic their every action:

> alter in obsequium plus aequo pronus et imi
> derisor lecti sic nutum divitis horret,
> sic iterat voces et verba cadentia tollit,
> ut puerum saevo credas dictata magistro
> reddere vel partis mimum tractare secundas   (*Ep.* 1.18.10–14)

The one man, over-prone to servility, a jester of the lowest couch, so reveres the rich man's nod, so echoes his speeches and picks up his words as they fall that you would think a schoolboy was repeating his lessons to a stern master or a mime-player acting a second part.

---

[9] Edwards (1996) 63–97 discusses *mollitia* and dancing as an effeminate activity to be avoided by men. Cf. also Priam's emotional rebuke (immediately after Hector's death) directed toward his other sons, who are not manly because they are "lying dancers and only good at choral dancing" (*Il.* 24.261: ψεῦσταί τ' ὀρχησταί τε, χοροιτυπίῃσιν ἄριστοι). Herodotus makes a similar connection in his tale in the *Histories* of how Hippoclides ruined his chances of marrying Agariste when her father saw him dancing like a woman (6.128–131).

[10] See Longo Auricchio (1986) 88.

Of course, the irony of the toady's clumsy assimilation of the poet's talents is that he is, as Herbert Musurillo puts it, "Horace by inversion, embodying as he does all the qualities that Horace most feared and disliked in a man."[11] All of this strongly contrasts with Horace's rejection in *Satires* 1.4 of verbose, anti-Callimachean poems and compositions, like those of Lucilius (9–10: *in hora saepe ducentos,* | *ut magnum, versus dictabat stans pede in uno,* "often in an hour, as though a great exploit, he would dictate two hundred lines while standing, as they say, on one foot"), and his declaration in *Satires* 1.6 that he "told Maecenas what he really was" (60: *quod eram narro*) rather than trying to be someone else (89–98). This obviously contrasts with the toady, who is far from pithy, honest, and content with his own status, but rather says anything out of ambition and the desire to achieve "success."

Closely related to shameless imitation and the false association of poetic skill with shoddy overproduction, which is emphatically condemned in *Satires* 1.4, is the important antithesis in *Satires* 1.9 between garrulity and silence. Horace highlights the contrast between his persona and the toady in this regard early on (*S.* 1.9.12–13): *aiebam tacitus, cum quidlibet ille* | *garriret, vicos, urbem laudaret,* " . . . I kept saying to myself quietly while the fellow rattled on about everything, praising the streets and the city." Scholars have read the poet's description of his interlocutor's chattiness and productiveness in different ways. Jennifer Ferriss-Hill, as mentioned above, views it as an indication that he is none other than Lucilius, who receives a similar description in *Satires* 1.4 (12): *garrulus atque piger scribendi ferre laborem,* | *scribendi recte,* "[he was] garrulous and too lazy to bear the task of writing properly."[12] Others, like Emily Gowers, have made connections to Theophrastus' *Characters*, which offer similar portraits of garrulity (3: ἀδολεσχία) and loquacity (7: λαλιά).[13] Also worth considering is Philodemus' description of the flatterer as one who "speaks in order to please" (PHerc. 1457, col. 1.9: [ὁ λέγων πρὸ]ς χάριν) and its potential influence on Horace's qualification of the speaker's loquacity as an "act specifically aimed at praising

---

[11] Musurillo (1964) 6. See also Rudd (1966) 83: "Part of the fun in this satire comes from the pest's failure to recognize his own absurdity." Hicks (2013) 121–2 refers to the toady as "an outsider par excellence in Horace's satiric corpus, in particular as a poet who fails to understand the Callimachean literary aesthetics that animates Horace's reading circle."

[12] Ferriss-Hill (2011) 431–3.   [13] Gowers (2012) 286.

everything" (PHerc. 1457, col. 2.6–8: πάν[τ]ων [τ]ὴν ἐπιμέλει[α]ν
π[ρ]οσποι[εῖσ] θαι... καὶ λαλεῖν; cf. S. 1.9.12: garriret, vicos, urbem
lauderet). The toady's insincere and opportunistic chat with the poet
is therefore completely opposed to wholesome conversation, which is a
contrast Philodemus also makes in On Flattery (PHerc. 222, col. 12.8:
ὁμιλίαν ἀντὶ τοῦ [λ]a[λ]ε[ῖν]) and in On Conversation with regard to his
views on the importance of silence and the observation of certain limits
when speaking. Also important is Philodemus' statement in On Property Management that the sage engages in "conversations that are
truthful and devoid of spite" (col. 23.30–1) rather than imitating the
flatterer's garrulity and rhetorical charm. Instead, he is trustworthy
because his conversation is not only "frank" (PHerc. 222, col. 3.27–8:
παρρη[σιαζό]μενον) but also concise and beneficial, since he observes
the previously mentioned limits of speech. The recipient's response to
the sage's companionship, which is pleasing without being obsequious,
is described as profound and genuine gratitude (On Property Management, col. 23.27–8). This has potential significance for the Satires, since
Horace identifies his critical observations as informal exchanges or
conversations that are concise, frank, truthful (cf. S. 1.1.24: dicere
verum), and directed toward a patron who shows interest in and an
appreciation of such advice. Philodemus' views regarding conversation,
which likely inform the poet's self-portrayal as a humble taciturn in his
encounter with Maecenas (S. 1.6.56–62), similarly sheds light on his
description of himself in Satires 1.9. Ellen Oliensis refers to Horace's
attitude toward the toady in this poem as "unresponsive silence," which
reflects his inability "to be anything but civil."[14] In contrast to the
benefits of truthful conversation, which, like Horatian satire, is characterized above all by frankness, Philodemus describes the flatterer as
engaging in shameful conversation (PHerc. 222, col. 12.2: αἰσχρὰν
ὁμιλία[ν]), including begging and lying (PHerc. 1089, col. 7.5–6: κολα-
κικῶς ὁμιλήσε[ι καὶ πτω]χεύσει καὶ ψεύσεται, "he will converse in a
flattering manner as well as beg and lie") and as an actor who praises
one moment and slanders his rivals the next (PHerc. 1457, col. 12.21–2:
φθονοῦσι καὶ διαβάλλουσι). As Horace's persona soon discovers,

---

[14] Oliensis (1998) 37. Cf. Schlegel (2005) 108, who argues that the poet's irritating
portrait "invites the reader to practice the very invective against the interlocutor that
Horace's own character in the poem refuses to practice," and Gowers (2012) 281, who
views the poet as "taking the part of a satirist to suite the times, inoffensive, reticent
and passive aggressive."

moreover, his pesky companion's jabbering is ultimately motivated by envy of potential rivals and personal ambition, both of which are intended to secure his prospect of self-gain.

In the course of this carefully designed portrait, Horace exposes the interlocutor's true disposition by juxtaposing his flattering conversation to his brazen competitiveness and desperate desire to win Maecenas' favor. Early on in the dialogue the toady betrays his selfish ambition by predicting that, rather than accept him as just another friend, Horace will be so impressed by the flatterer's skill that he will view him as an equal and possibly prefer his company even to that of Varius and Viscus (*S*. 1.9.22–3): "*si bene me novi, non Viscum pluris amicum, | non Varium facies,*" "If I do not deceive myself, you will not think more of Viscus or Varius as a friend than of me" (for the expression, cf. *Ep*. 1.18.1–2: *Si bene te novi, metues, liberrime Lolli, | scurrantis speciem praebere, professus amicum*, "If I know you well, my Lollius, most outspoken [frank?] of men, you will shrink from appearing in the guise of a parasite when you have professed the friend"). Such a comparison is of course ridiculous, especially given the tremendous amount of respect Horace has for Varius as a poet (cf. *S*. 1.10.81) as well as a friend (cf. *S*. 1.5.40–4). It is perhaps Vergil, however, who in the *Eclogues* gives the best indication of the impressive caliber of Varius' poetic talent:

> et me fecere poetam
> Pierides, sunt et mihi carmina, me quoque dicunt
> vatem pastores; sed non ego credulus illis.
> nam neque adhuc Vario videor nec dicere Cinna
> digna   (*E*. 9.32–6)

The Muses have also made me a poet: I make poetry as well and shepherds call me *vates*—but I don't believe them, for I don't think that the verses I speak are yet worthy of a Varius or a Cinna . . .

With respect to *Satires* 1.9, it is the flatterer's vicious disposition and false beliefs about self-worth that cloud his reason, thus precluding any possibility for self-awareness. Plutarch makes this connection clearly in *How to Tell a Flatterer from a Friend* (49b): ἀντιτάττεται γὰρ ἀεὶ πρὸς τὸ γνῶθι σαυτόν, ἀπάτην ἑκάστῳ πρὸς ἑαυτὸν ἐμποιῶν καὶ ἄγνοιαν ἑαυτοῦ καὶ τῶν περὶ αὐτὸν ἀγαθῶν καὶ κακῶν, "For [the flatterer] always sets himself up against the maxim 'know thyself,' creating in each person deception concerning himself and also ignorance of both himself and the good and evil that concern him." Philodemus had already stated the irrationality connected to this particular vice, saying that flatterers are motivated by ambition and "the love of glory" (PHerc. 1089, col. 4.13: [φιλο]δοξ[ία]ν) and "out of the compelling desire to insinuate themselves men falsely think that they will be valued more than many" (PHerc. 1675, col. 13.17–20: καὶ δ' ἐπιθυμίαν ἠναγκ[α]σμένην ὑποτρέχειν δοκοῦσι καὶ π[ρ]ὸ πολλῶν παραλογίζεσθαι... [ψευδῶς]). As mentioned already, the view that vice is irrational is consistent with Hellenistic thought in general, but especially with that of Philodemus in his ethical treatises, as Voula Tsouna explains: "The failures of understanding of vicious persons involve, importantly, understanding of themselves. They do not recognize the falsehood of their beliefs, the inappropriateness of their attitudes, and the wrongness of their actions."[15] An overwhelming desire for success is what drives the toady's ludicrous comparison of himself to Varius, the chief significance of which lies in the latter's important connection with Maecenas as mentioned in *Satires* 1.6 and elsewhere. The implication is that if the flatterer replaces Varius as *amicus optimus* or "best friend," Horace will not only become better acquainted with Maecenas, but he will also eliminate the competition and emerge as sole beneficiary of the wealthy patron's gifts:

> "haberes
> magnum adiutorem, posset qui ferre secundas,
> hunc hominem velles si tradere: dispeream, ni
> summosses omnis." (*S.* 1.9.45–8)

"You might have a strong backer, who could be your understudy, if you would introduce your humble servant. Hang me, if you wouldn't find that you had cleared the field!"[16]

---

[15] Tsouna (2007) 34. See also Nussbaum (1994) 37–40 for more on the concept of irrationality in Hellenistic philosophy.

[16] Anderson (1982) 97 notes the military implication of *summosses* as "treacherously seizes power from within." Cf. the military context of PHerc. 222, col. 12.13–14, in which Philodemus quotes Homer (*Il.* 18.535) in order to characterize the nature and effects of flattering conversation: ἐν δ' Ἔρις, ἐν δὲ Κυδοιμὸς ὁμίλεον, ἐν δ' ὀλοὴ Κήρ, "There were present together Strife and Confusion and destructive Death." The verb *consisto*, however, may indicate that the toady intends to serve as Horace's lictor, since these attendants were in charge of "clearing the streets" for their magistrates. Cf. Ferriss-Hill (2011) 443–4, who argues that these lines as well as the interlocutor's (i.e. Lucilius') apparent interest in Maecenas in general are to be understood ironically: "Lucilius professes to desire an introduction to Maecenas, offering himself as a useful sidekick to Horace, but he can easily be understood to mean quite the opposite: as the *inventor* of Roman Satire, Lucilius is confident that it is Horace who would play second fiddle to him, were Maecenas presented with both at once."

198   *Epicurean Ethics in Horace*

In this passage, the appeal to Horace's desire for recognition further underscores the toady's complete misunderstanding of the poet, whose initial audience with his patron was not the result of intrigue but rather of the willingness to cooperate peacefully with others. The suggestion that success within Maecenas' circle is achieved by internal strife and treachery, moreover, marks the apex of the flatterer's ineptitude as indicated by the poet's subsequent reaction.

For Horace, who is the self-proclaimed modest and virtuous client-friend of Maecenas, his interlocutor's perverted understanding of friendship and contentment in the company of talented poets is more than reprehensible. In fact, it is intolerable and provokes his persona finally to address the nature of his dealings with Maecenas:

> "non isto vivimus illic,
> quo tu rere, modo; domus hac nec purior ulla est
> nec magis his aliena malis; nil mi officit, inquam,
> ditior hic aut est quia doctior; est locus uni
> cuique suus." (*S.* 1.9.48–52)

"We don't live there on such terms as you think. No house is cleaner or more free from such intrigues than that. It never hurts me," I say, "that one is richer or more learned than I. Each has his own place."

This impassioned and spontaneous response is intended as a frank defense of Maecenas' circle on the part of a loyal and trustworthy friend, and Niall Rudd observes that the poet puts even grammatical distance between himself and the toady, using the second person plural to exclude him throughout (cf. 48: *vivimus* and 62: *consistimus*).[17] It is also the first time in this satire that he has taken an assertive stance and voiced his opinion directly, thereby breaking the awkward silence as well as the passive-aggressive tone of earlier reactions, as Ellen Oliensis observes:

Horace immediately rushes to the defense of his friends and thereby also of himself. The spontaneity of this defense, which is represented as an outburst forced out of an otherwise reticent poet by his companion's intolerably offensive insinuations, is underwritten by the dislocated word order characteristic of authentic excitement.[18]

[17] Rudd (1961) 83. See also Fraenkel (1957) 116.
[18] Oliensis (1998) 38. Cf. Zetzel (2009) 38: "[Horace] is smug, elitist and rude, with no sympathy for the man who is in the position in which he himself once was." This evaluation overlooks the fact that his portrayal of the flatterer, who is obnoxious,

Philodemus also hints at this contrast between the flatterer, whose conversation is full of strife, and the Epicurean sage, who observes certain "limits in speaking" (*On Conversation*, col. 5.2: [τῆ]ς ὁμιλίας . . . τὸ πέ[ρας]) but is not afraid to voice the truth when necessary (cf. col. 8.2–5). As a man who "knows both how to keep his mouth shut and when to open it,"[19] Horace likewise refuses to engage in shameful conversation with the toady and observes silence until it becomes necessary to express the true nature of his dealings with Maecenas by means of a straightforward description. With regard to winning the favor of his patron, Horace's final advice to the flatterer implies that this will inevitably be impossible: Maecenas is impressed by virtue and integrity (*S.* 1.9.49: *purior*, 54: *virtus*; cf. *S.* 1.6.64: *puro*), while the flatterer's strategy involves corrupting his servants (*S.* 1.9.57: *corrumpam*); Maecenas holds audience with those who are worthy (56: *difficilis aditus*; cf. *S.* 1.6.54: *obtulit*), while the flatterer, in his usual way, intends to force a meeting by accosting him abruptly in the streets (*S.* 1.9.59: *occurram*, cf. 3: *accurrit*). Cynthia Damon underscores the toady's behavior in these passages and reveals an important distinction between him and the traditional parasite:

> There are other touches in *Satire* 1.9 that show that the pest is not simply a comic parasite transplanted: no comic parasite has his own legal business to attend to, and parasites do not bribe slaves for admittance. In fact, in this *Satire* the figure of the parasite has been adapted to serve as a caricature for the ambitious *cliens* in first-century B.C. Rome.[20]

Notwithstanding the toady's clever strategy for joining the circle of Maecenas, Horace's obviously positive description of his patron both here and in *Satires* 1.6 implies that he is not one of the many "lovers of flattery" mentioned by Philodemus in PHerc. 1457 (fr. 15.6: φιλοκόλακες), who enjoy such praise even when they realize that it is false and unwarranted.[21] The flatterer's use of *occurrere*, moreover, which is usually positive and often refers to the appearance of true friends (cf. *S.* 1.4.135–6: *dulcis amicis* | *occurram*, 1.5.40–1: *Plotius et*

---

chatty, ambitious, and relentlessly self-interested, is *intended* to be annoying, as Schlegel (2005) 108–26 observes. In other words, the poet's manipulation of a popular character portrait for his own purposes has made sympathy an impossible (or at least an unwarranted and inappropriate) reaction.

[19] Oliensis (1998) 39.   [20] Damon (1997) 123.

[21] See Tsouna (2007) 133–4.

Varius Sinuessae Vergiliusque | occurrunt, and 1.9.61: *Fuscus Aristius occurrit*), may be yet another example of the toady's self-deception and misunderstanding of true friendship. Overall, Horace's entertaining portrayal of the flatterer provides his audience with social commentary on corrupt relationships between patrons and clients in contemporary Rome, but it also creates space between himself and his interlocutor by emphasizing the "purity" of his own friendship with Maecenas and the other members of his literary circle. Indeed, Horace concludes Book 1 with a description of the honesty and goodwill that characterizes his group of friends and that reveals the true nature of the *domus pura* of Maecenas:

> Plotius et Varius, Maecenas Vergiliusque,
> Valgius et probet haec Octavius optimus atque
> Fuscus et haec utinam Viscorum laudet uterque
> ambitione relegata. te dicere possum,
> Pollio, te, Messalla, tuo cum fratre, simulque   85
> vos, Bibule et Servi, simul his te, candide Furni,
> conpluris alios, doctos ego quos et amicos
> prudens praetereo, quibus haec, sint qualiacumque,
> adridere velim, doliturus, si placeant spe
> deterius nostra.   (S. 1.10.81–90)

Let but Plotius and Varius approve of these verses; let Maecenas, Vergil, and Valgus; let Octavius and Fuscus, best of men; and let but the Viscus brothers give their praise! With no desire to flatter, I may name you, Pollio; you, Messalla, and your brother; also you, Bibulus and Servius; also you, honest Furnius, and many another scholar and friend, whom I purposely pass over. In their eyes I should like these verses, such as they are, to find favor, and I should be grieved if their pleasure were to fall short of my hopes.[22]

Certainly by design, various words in this passage emphasize Horace's honesty and humility, in that his recognition of his colleagues' literary prowess—he calls them, not himself, "the best" and "learned"—is not motivated by any ambition or desire for gain. In this sense it appears to serve as a corrective model for someone like the toady, who, it turns out, does not understand the healthy nature of this relationship and thus could never be included in such a list of friends.[23] This tactic of

---

[22] See Gowers (2012) 336 for the identities of these individuals.
[23] See Hicks (2013) 116–17 for the identification of these men as the "true insiders" of Horace's reading circle.

underscoring who Horace is in the *Satires* by emphasizing, through entertaining examples, who he is not is one the poet will employ again in Book 2, in which, taking a step back and relying on various representative mouthpieces, he continues to promote an ethical persona that engages closely with Epicurean doctrines.

CONSULTANTS, CLIENTS, AND *CAPTATORES* IN *SATIRES* 2.1 AND 2.5

The satires of Book 2 have received much less attention from scholars than those of the first collection, partly because many of them are sometimes regarded as an enfeebled poet's detached or Platonic observations of various issues, which seems quite different from his initial approach to the genre.[24] Older scholars have duly noted that in Book 2 Horatian satire's already subdued *libertas* becomes further restrained, in accordance with Trebatius' legal advice in *Satires* 2.1 (5: *quiescas*), by the withdrawal into what Niall Rudd has described as a "walled garden."[25] This personal withdrawal, according to W. S. Anderson's widely accepted interpretation, is made obvious by Horace's delegation of the satiric role to other speakers described as *doctores inepti*,[26] who are generally portrayed as dispossessed or bankrupt sages (Ofellus, Tiresias) and loquacious diatribists (Damasippus, Davus). Of course, there is much truth to this particular reading of the *Satires*, but at the same time it may overlook the fact that Horatian satire tends to employ ethical doctrines and truths in a reflexive manner and, as discussed previously, for the purpose of self-justification in response to literary or social challenges. In other words, no matter how foolish or detached the dunces of *Satires* 2 appear to be, every word they speak has some bearing on the poet's self-representation and reflects in some way, to some degree, his persona's moral convictions. In order to elucidate this representation one may briefly consider his self-portrayal in *Satires* 2.1, which will

[24] But Ferriss-Hill (2014), Freudenburg (2001) 71–124, McNeill (2001), and Oliensis (1998) 41–63, to name a few, have made more or less recent contributions.
[25] Rudd (1966) 131. See also Freudenburg (2001) 71–5.
[26] Anderson (1982) 42. For a useful introduction to *Satires* 2 in general, see Muecke (2007) 109–20.

provide the necessary background for another consideration of the evidence from Philodemus' treatise *On Flattery*. This time it will be examined not in connection with a conversation between Horace and a flatterer as in *Satires* 1.9, but with the perverted advice of Tiresias to Ulysses in *Satires* 2.5, which, although cast in a mythical setting, is neither detached nor irrelevant to Horace or his contemporaries. One may recall that while some have called into question the overall seriousness and integrity of Horace's persona in the *Satires*,[27] others have detected a certain unity to his self-presentation.[28] The idea that Horace as a satirist is unified has been the focus of previous chapters, but it is particularly essential to his self-portrayal in the second book of poems, which, like the first, focuses on the moral aspect of his persona and his concern with self-promotion as a virtuous, honest, and unambitious client-friend of Maecenas. As in the poems of Book 1, in *Satires* 2.5 and in Book 2 in general one can detect a degree of coherence throughout the portraits based on the poet's consistent attention to ethical problems such as the proper administration of wealth, the value of friendship, the dangers of flattery, and the importance of frank criticism. These issues admittedly preoccupied all who were interested in moral philosophy, but it is worth keeping in mind that Philodemus was a contemporary neighbor of Horace and someone who promoted himself as a frank client rather than a flatterer, which increases the likelihood that he was a source, even years after the publication of the first book, for a poet with similar concerns.

Following closely on the heels of Octavian's victory over Marc Antony at Actium in 30 BC, *Satires* 2.1 deals largely with the dangers of frankly criticizing contemporaries through satire, as Lucilius once did (cf. *S.* 1.10.3–4), which seemingly provides a smooth transition between the two books.[29] The fact that Horace needs legal advice from Trebatius, however, implies that times have certainly changed and that the dangers of writing satire or anything like it are more real than ever (5–6): *"quid faciam? praescribe" "quiescas." "ne faciam, inquis, omnino versus?" "aio"* "'Give me advice, Trebatius. What am I to do?' 'Take a rest.' 'Not write verses at all, you mean?' 'Yes'".[30]

---

[27] Freudenburg (1993) 3–46.   [28] Sharland (2009b) 63.

[29] Lejay (1966) 285.

[30] As Cicero reveals (*Letters to Friends* 7.6–22), Trebatius Testa was his intimate friend and on very good terms with Julius Caesar, with whom he spent some time in Gaul and Britain, and he also advised Maecenas as well as Octavian. For the connections between Trebatius and Epicureanism, see Hicks (2013) 170–4.

Horace responds to the prospect of abandoning satire by saying "But I cannot sleep" (7: *verum nequeo dormire*),[31] and the lawyer's subsequent concern for Horace's safety,[32] expressed bluntly at verses 60–1, initially takes the form of a calculation of the greater pleasures to be derived from praising Caesar relative to the labor required (11–12): *multa laborum | praemia laturus*, "many a reward for your pains will you gain" (cf. *S.* 1.2.78–9). Trebatius recommends that Horace compose a different kind of poetry, epic praise of Octavian, the most powerful man in Rome, to which Horace responds with a clever *recusatio* in miniature that in effect signals his reluctance to become like Ennius, who wrote an epic panegyric for the elder Scipio Africanus (12–15).[33] At this point the poet's advisor offers another, more appealing option that follows the example of Lucilius, who wrote about the younger Scipio:

> "attamen et iustum poteras et scribere fortem,
> Scipiadam ut sapiens Lucilius." "haud mihi dero,
> cum res ipsa feret: nisi dextro tempore Flacci
> verba per attentam non ibunt Caesaris aurem:
> cui male si palpere, recalcitrat undique tutus." (*S.* 2.1.16–20)

TREBATIUS: "But you might write of himself, at once just and valiant, as wise Lucilius did of Scipio."

HORACE: "I will not fail myself, when the occasion itself prompts. Only at an auspicious moment will the words of Flaccus find with Caesar entrance to an attentive ear. Stroke the steed clumsily and back he kicks, at every point on his guard."

A number of important observations are necessary here, the first of which is the insistence on the part of Trebatius that Horace write

---

[31] Lejay (1966) 296 explains by saying that, unless Horace writes satire, he will not be able to rest at night. Cf. Juv. 1.77: *quem patitur dormire nurus corruptor avarae*, "Who can sleep at night thinking about the seducer of a greedy daughter-in-law?"

[32] For the Epicurean concern with preserving safety by establishing positive relationships with others, see Roskam (2007) 37–41, Hicks (2013) 169, and Armstrong (2014a) 124.

[33] See Freudenburg (2001) 87–92 for Lucilius' criticism of Ennius, whose "precious efforts at glorifying his patron were credited to him not as groundbreaking and ennobling, but as laughable, and a permanent blot on his otherwise stellar record." Cf. *S.* 1.10.54: *non ridet versus Enni gravitate minores*, "Does he [Lucilius] not laugh at the verses of Ennius lacking in dignity..." In light of this tradition of literary criticism, it is likely that Horace's apprehension is motivated by his own calculation: the negative repercussions of writing such poetry would far outweigh any possible rewards.

poetry of some kind for Octavian—if not epic, then perhaps something could be inserted into the *Satires*, as Lucilius did for Scipio. For Horace, however, who was the son of a freedman rather than an aristocrat like his predecessor, the informal tone of satire would not be the proper venue; rather, as Kirk Freudenburg suggests, with the expression *dextro tempore* the poet is likely indicating that his praise of Caesar will have to wait for the meters of a more suitable genre as represented by the *Odes*.[34] Furthermore, the abysmal distance in status between Horace and Octavian is underscored by the contrast between the poet, who is a donkey with floppy ears (*Flacci*), and Octavian, who is a steed with pricked up ears (*attentam ... aurem*) and a powerful kick (*recalcitrat*).[35] With the words "I will not fail myself" Horace appears to allude playfully to the toady from *Satires* 1.9 (56), although the two contexts in which this expression occurs are quite different. Whereas the toady aggressively and willingly searches for a way to gain Maecenas' favor, Horace, as Kirk Freudenburg puts it, is feeling the "post-Actian squeeze" and realizes that, due to his connections and success by the end of the decade, it was only a matter of time before he would be required to address Octavian in verse.[36] It is perhaps this difference, then, that contributes to the humor of the situation: the toady must win over Maecenas through flattery and bribing his slaves, whereas Horace has already gained the favor of both Maecenas and Octavian and will keep it by continuing to publish works of poetry.[37] For the moment, however, he declines to switch genres and declares his intention to exercise frankness in writing satire without regrets and, using his stylus as a sword (39–41), to defend himself from the attacks of others.[38] In this way

[34] Freudenburg (2001) 97–8.

[35] Of course, the immediate sense of *nisi dextro tempore, Flacci verba per attentam non ibunt Caesaris aurem* is that Octavian is too busy at the moment to enjoy such poetry (cf. Lucr. 1.40–3). See also McNeill (2001) 115–16 on this passage.

[36] As *Caesaris invicti* at verse 11 suggests, Horace composed *Satires* 2.1 shortly before Book 2 was published in 30 BC and therefore seven years before the first book of the *Odes*.

[37] Hicks (2013) 167 mentions the "inherent satiric effect" of this passage and the poet's awareness that his detractors "may have been altogether too ready to entertain the implications of such unflattering allusions."

[38] Of course, Horace, unlike Lucilius, is reduced to attacking "quintessential nobodies," as Freudenburg (2001) 101 notes, but these lesser individuals embody the vices that are the real targets of his criticisms. See also Lejay (1966) 285: "Lucilius wrote political satire above all, whereas Horace wrote especially moral satire". "Lucilius faisait surtout de la satire politique; Horace, surtout de la satire morale""Lucilius

the poet remains faithful to his earlier commitment to "speak the truth while laughing" (*S.* 1.1.24–5) and to continue boldly denouncing vice in all its forms, thereby preserving his literary persona's moral assertiveness and philosophical consistency.[39] The nature of these attacks from others becomes more apparent toward the end of *Satires* 2.1, when Horace reintroduces the notion that people were envious of his successful career and connections with the likes of Maecenas:

> quidquid sum ego, quamvis
> infra Lucili censum ingeniumque, tamen me
> cum magnis vixisse invita fatebitur usque
> invidia et fragili quaerens inlidere dentem
> offendet solido (*S.* 2.1.74–8)

Such as I am, however far beneath Lucilius in rank and native gifts, yet Envy, in spite of herself, will ever admit that I have lived with the great, and while trying to strike her tooth on something soft, will dash upon what is solid . . .

In this passage Horace refocuses the attention on himself and on the complaints and grumbling of those who are jealous of his success as a poet and friend of a wealthy patron.[40] For this reason it may serve as a useful transition to his portrayal of Tiresias (another expert advisor[41])

faisait surtout de la satire politique; Horace, surtout de la satire morale" Despite the fact that Horace is in a difficult situation, he still finds a way to express himself frankly: rather than attacking powerful individuals by name, his criticisms are most often linked to himself in the *Satires*. Of course, this does not mean that they did not resonate with the powerful individuals in his audience, but, as the poet indicates at the end of this satire, the fact that he is on good terms with Octavian means that he can continue to make such criticisms without being anxious about potential repercussions (2.1.83–6). As Hicks (2013) 173 notes: "[H]is connections to Maecenas and Octavian offer him the genuine security that he needs to fulfill his basic Epicurean desires."

[39] Hicks (2013) 174: "Horace will continue to write the seemingly tame kind of satire (in comparison with Lucilius), but could always at a moment's notice deploy it more aggressively to confront the enemies of Octavian and Maecenas."

[40] Kiessling–Heinze (1961) 190, who connect Horace's mention of *invidia* to *Satires* 1.6 (45–8), 2.6 (47–8) and *Epistles* 1.14 (37–8), say the following: "This passage indicates that attempts had been made to push Horace out of this relationship, and one suspects that his *Satires* were intended to serve as a firm grip in that respect" ("unsere Stelle lehrt, daß auch Versuche gemacht worden sind, ihn aus diesem Verhältnis zu verdrängen, und läßt vermuten, daß seine Satiren dabei als Handhabe dienen sollten"). See also McNeill (2001) 48–52.

[41] Keane (2006) 116 similarly views 2.1 and 2.5 as a pair united by the theme of "legal consultation." Also Hicks (2013) 162.

and Ulysses in *Satires* 2.5, which is concerned with the potential
problems that arise when great wealth is involved in a relationship.

Although Horace does not explicitly mention accusations of flattery made by his detractors in the *Satires*, one senses the poet's
concern regarding this in various satiric and epistolary treatments.
In the description of his first encounter with Maecenas in *Satires* 1.6,
for instance, the reader is made privy to the envious and apparently
incessant gossip of his peers (46: *quem rodunt omnes*), who grumble
at Horace's swift progress in status from the son of a freedman to the
beneficiary and wealthy friend of a millionaire.[42] The encounter itself,
which is significant on account of its indirectness (55) as well as the
speaker's own candor, reticence, and patience (56–62), stands in stark
contrast to his portrait of the toady, who, as examined above, is
characterized as a headstrong opportunist and an impatient chatterbox.
Despite the obvious differences between Horace and this loquacious
individual, however, in *Satires* 2.7 Horace engages in self-deprecation
through his servant Davus, who openly accuses his master of being an
opportunistic parasite (32–5),[43] and his reluctance to name Maecenas
as the source of the Sabine estate in *Satires* 2.6 is probably intended
to deflect similar charges of flattery from his enemies. The concern
with avoiding such charges is further underscored in *Epistles* 1.17 and
1.18, in which the poet gives advice to the prospective client of wealthy
patrons on how to avoid flattery while remaining agreeable. This
point is clearly acknowledged by R. G. Mayer:

> The poem is, then, in effect an apologia for Horace's own way of life.
> The autobiographical strain in his poetry is not only exemplary but at
> times also defensive. This is perhaps more apparent in his earlier poetry,
> published at a time when Horace was first coming into notice and
> needed to answer his personal critics. The sixth satire of the first book

---

[42] See Glad (1996) 24–5 and Damon (1997) 128–9, who also note the connection to
Horace's problem with detractors who were envious of his relationship with Maecenas. McNeill (2001) 49 notes that, in response to the reactions of people as Horace
moves through the streets in *Satires* 2.6 (28–31), the poet "immediately tries to deflect
any sneers or allegations of toadyism that might come from his outside readers by
suggesting that only with great reluctance does he admit it means this much to him to
be Maecenas' friend ('non mentiar')." According to McNeill (2001) 36–8, these
detractors and social climbers belong to the fourth of five "rings of audience," as
discussed in the Introduction.
[43] See Turpin (2009) 127–40.

is a case in point... A defensive note is less prominent in the *Epistles*, perhaps because the poet's own position is more secure, but it is still there, especially in the seventeenth letter. We should recall that in its origins ancient autobiography often was apologetic.[44]

Although some of his advice in these epistles is centered on securing generous food offerings, which is clearly the realm of the parasite, the overall content of the letters is philosophically sound and quite different from the advice of Tiresias in *Satires* 2.5.[45] In addition to all of this, one may also observe that Horace's reception of benefits from Maecenas, which depends on the poet's production of ethical and quasi-philosophical conversations as literary satire, is fully consistent with the Epicurean understanding of patronage as the exchange of gratitude from a receptive patron for the chance to engage in informal, philosophical chats, which certain individuals like Cicero depict as flattery. It is also important to remember that both Epicurus (DL 10.4–5) and Philodemus had been branded as flatterers, and that both ancient and modern scholars have interpreted Horace's affectionate invocations to his own patron as synonymous with flattery. Clearly there must have been some concern on the part of Horace with these and similar accusations (whether real or exaggerated by his Epicurean persona), which would have threatened to ruin the reputation his father had worked hard to preserve, and, like Philodemus, a defense through satire and the character portrait likely would have furnished the poet with an effective rebuttal. Nor does the fact that *Satire* 2.5 is pure dialogue make it irrelevant to Horace's self-portrayal as an honest client: no scholar would deny that his portrayal of Ofellus as a rustic farmer who enjoys meager fare, for example, has important implications for Horace's literary persona. The same is true of Ulysses, except that the comparison is negative and, as a result of the mythological setting, it creates the distance necessary to make a provocative assertion delicately and in a manner consistent with the poet's artistic license.[46] A few points need clarification before moving on: although

---

[44] Mayer (1995) 289.

[45] As Hunter (1985a) 484–6 observes, the poet's advice to Lollius, although based for the most part on philosophical doctrines, playfully draws "a very thin line" between the flatterer and the successful client.

[46] Keane (2006) 117: "The satirist comes out of this comparison looking far more respectable than his heroic counterpart."

captatio and *amicitia* are certainly not identical, (the former is a perversion of the latter, with *captatio* as the embodiment of a particular kind of base ambition and opportunism for the sake of personal gain), flattery is a vice that characterizes both the legacy-hunter and the client.[47] It is interesting that in this poem Horace has chosen to satirize legacy-hunters, and, it seems, for two reasons: the character of Ulysses, whose deceptive and eloquent ways were instrumental for the reacquisition of his former wealth and status, was an obvious candidate for the poet's treatment of a social ill that was particularly common in his day. At the same time, both Ulysses and Horace's persona share certain characteristics involving the loss of wealth and its restoration by means of finding favor with a wealthy patron, as will be discussed further below. The connection is not perfect, of course, but it is one the poet himself likely intended to be made and as such bears some credibility. As far as the intended audience of this comic dialogue is concerned, it would have been Maecenas first and foremost, but Horace's criticisms and observations also would have been of interest to his friends and fellow clients as well as to other readers among the social elite. It goes without saying that the poet's detractors, sycophants, and those outside his social circle would not have been his main audience (after all, this satire is intended to defend the poet's persona against the accusations and envy of these very individuals).

Before attempting to establish a connection between Horace's portrayal of Ulysses and Tiresias in *Satires* 2.5 and Philodemus' treatment of flattery, it may be useful to give a brief overview of the genres and authors traditionally regarded as having shaped or influenced these satiric portraits. The poet's decision to deliver an invective through Ulysses' conversation with the blind sage in the Underworld obviously owes a great deal to Homer (cf. *Od.* 11.100–37),[48] but it is also influenced by subsequent comic treatments of καταβασις adventures, such as that of Dionysus in Aristophanes' *Frogs*. Another probable source for Horace is the tradition of dramatic and often burlesque criticisms motivated by philosophical debates in the Hellenistic period, especially the *Lampoons* of Timon of Phlius, which included two books

[47] Hicks (2013) 196–7: "[T]he practice of *captatio* depends upon a notion of abusing friendship for personal gain linking the poem here to the abusive bore in 1.9 who attempts to overpower Horace and act as his assistant for self-promotion within Maecenas' circle. The one engaged in *captatio* is a flatterer, one of the extremes with respect to friendship." See also Montiglio (2011) 120.

[48] For Homeric parody in satire, see Plaza (2006) 72.

of dialogues out of three with dead sages (DL 9.111).[49] Within this category also falls Menippus of Gadara's lampoon entitled *The Underworld* (DL 6.101), which, judging by Lucian of Samosata's later imitation in *Menippus*, portrayed the philosopher as interrogating Tiresias concerning "the best life" (6: ὁ ἄριστος βίος).[50] For G. C. Fiske, this last source's apparent polemical underpinnings, namely, Cynic criticism of the Stoics' idealization of Ulysses as the perfect sage, provides a suitable background for reading *Satires* 2.5 as a "sarcastic attack[s] on the teaching of Chrysippus and the earlier Stoa that the sage is a χρηματιστικός."[51] On the other hand, despite the enormous popularity of Ulysses among Stoic philosophers,[52] it also appears as though Antisthenes, traditionally regarded as the founder of Cynicism,[53] also had a devotion to Ulysses and might even have written at least three treatises dealing with the hero (DL 6.15–18). Additionally, a similar attraction might have been felt by none other than Bion,[54] and Horace's eulogy of Ulysses in *Epistles* 1.2 (17–31) reveals some affinity for the hero on the part of the poet. Given the rather inconsistent nature of the philosophical tradition surrounding this "man of many turns," instead of reading Horace's satire within the context of debates between Cynics and Stoics it may be more helpful to regard it as involving clever manipulation of a traditional scene that is transported from Greece to Rome and used as a vehicle for social commentary on contemporary problems.

Horace's use of mythological tradition, and in particular of a popular figure's character traits for ethical reasons, closely resembles Philodemus' utilization of Homeric rulers for a similar purpose. Of course, this approach becomes the vehicle for political commentary in his treatise *On the Good King According to Homer*, which examines the nature of good kingship through the examples and characteristics of certain rulers: Ulysses, for example, is extolled for his ability to provide council and prevent civil strife (coll. 15.32–7 and 29.22–4). In

[49] Diogenes describes the second and third books of this poem as dialogues, whereas the first is written in the first person. This source is also discussed by Rudd (1966) 237–338 and Coffey (1976) 86.
[50] See Kiessling–Heinze (1910) 241–2, Oltramare (1926) 139, and Rudd (1966) 237–8.
[51] Fiske (1971) 401. For objections to Fiske's interpretation of this satire, see Rudd (1966) 238.
[52] See Stanford (1954) 118–27.
[53] Stanford (1954) 99–100, although cf. Dudley (1974) 1–15.
[54] Desmond (2008) 33.

one of his fragments of *On Flattery*, however, which endeavors to distinguish the Epicurean client-sage from the flatterer, Philodemus describes Ulysses as a parasite among the tables of wealthy old men as well as a banqueter among the dead in the Underworld. This, of course, is a much more likely philosophical and satirical model for Horace:

> — — — τὰ] μὲν ἐπὶ τῆς τ[ρα]πέζης, τὰ δ᾽ ἐπὶ κλίνης τοῦ Αἰόλου, †καὶ τοὺς
> ἐμούς† παρεσίτει· παρ᾽ Ἀλκινό[ωι δ᾽ ἀρί]στωι τὴν γαστέρ᾽ ἐμπλή[σας, τ]ὴν
> πήραν ἠξίου μεστὴν [λαβεῖν·] εἰς Ἅιδου δὲ καταβὰς [τραπέζ]ας κατέλαβε
> νε[κ]ρῶν [αἵματη]ρούς
>
> (PHerc. 223, fr. 3.1–8)

... some things on the table and the couch of Aeolus, and he was acting like a parasite [to my men]. And having filled his belly at the house of noble Alcinous he thought it fit to take the full wallet. Then, having descended into Hades, he occupied the bloody tables of the dead ... [55]

It is unclear just how popular this view of Ulysses was before the Hellenistic period,[56] but it became increasingly common among Hellenistic and later authors. In Lucian's *Parasite*, for example, the spokesman Simon identifies the hero as a full-fledged parasite on account of his infamously high regard for "tables laden with bread and meat" (10: τράπεζαι σίτου καὶ κρειῶν = *Od.* 9.8–9) as well as his "Epicurean way of life" (10: καὶ ἐν τῷ τῶν Ἐπικουρείων βίῳ γενόμενος), and Plutarch similarly associates "wily Ulysses" with the changeable flatterer in *How to Tell a Flatterer from a Friend* (52c: πολύμητις Ὀδυσσεύς = *Od.* 22.1). For Horace, whose depiction of Ulysses is described by Paul Lejay as being completely Roman,[57] this connection becomes a useful medium for addressing the Roman issue of *captatio*, which as a technical term meaning "legacy-hunting" is not attested before this satire.[58] With regard to

---

[55] Gigante and Indelli (1978) 124–31 discuss the Bionean flavor of this passage. See also Montiglio (2011) 100.

[56] For ancient criticism of Ulysses regarding food, see Stanford (1954) 66–71 and Montiglio (2011) 96. The most recent evidence for the popularity of Ulysses, mostly in the fragments of Middle Comedy, is Casolari (2003) 197–225. Heracles is also often the butt of jokes involving gluttony and parasitism, for which see, e.g., Ar. *Frogs* 503–18.

[57] Lejay and Plessis (1915) 416.

[58] For background on Roman legacy-hunting, including the social, financial, and legal contexts leading up to the prevalence of this practise, see Frank (1933) 295–9, Rudd (1966) 224–7, Crook (1967) 119–21, Saller (1982) 124–5, Mansbach (1982), and Hopkins (1983) 99–103 and 238–41. Sallmann (1970) 182 n. 2 points out that the poet's technical use of *captator* and *captare* is unprecedented and may be a

the practise itself, Cicero had already described it as a scam aimed primarily at wealthy but childless seniors (*orbi*) and employing flattery as a primary tactic (*Parad.* 5.39): *hereditatis spes quid iniquitatis in serviendo non suscipit? quem nutum locupletis orbi senis non observat?*, "What iniquity does the hope for inheritance not undertake, what call of a rich but childless old man does it fail to heed?"[59] Horace, of course, provides satirical commentary on this observation in *Satires* 2.5, although, like Philodemus in *On Flattery* and *On the Good King According to Homer*, he communicates an ethical point to his Roman audience somewhat indirectly and through a Homeric medium.

At the same time, his exaggerated portrayal of Ulysses as a social climber endeavoring to recover his wealth conveniently reflects the financial and social circumstances of his persona's encounter with Maecenas,[60] but with notable differences. In *Satires* 1.6 Horace depicts the dangers and anxieties associated with ambition, and in *Epistles* 2.2 he playfully admits that "barefaced poverty drove me to writing verses" (49–52: *paupertas inpulit audax | ut versus facerem*). The circumstances surrounding his motives for seeking financial assistance have already been connected to Epicurus' requirement concerning making money as a consequence of "dire straits" (DL 10.121b), as well as to Philodemus' description of the ideal economic state, according to which financial security results from the honest patronage of a grateful friend in exchange for concise and always truthful advice. The obvious contrast with Ulysses, then, may be read as an effective if playful exercise that promotes the poet's honesty and genuineness with regard to patronage and the recuperation of wealth. Furthermore, rather than providing general criticism of obsequious individuals or even of specific philosophical sects, in this poem Horace, for personal reasons, draws from a rich tradition of invective of which Philodemus was an important and immediately accessible part. The incorporation of mythology into his satire also allows

---

"Horace's own satirical coinage" "satirische Wortprägung des Horaz". Mansbach (1982) 15, Roberts (1984) 428, and Damon (1997) 121 make the same observation. As Muecke (1993) 177 notes, however, the Romans were certainly already aware of the phenomenon itself (cf. Cic. *On Duties* 3.74).

[59] See Palmer (1893) 328 and Muecke (1993) 177–8.
[60] Keane (2006) 117.

Horace to create between himself and contemporary society a safe distance from which to play his comparison game. At the same time, he succeeds in furnishing his wealthy benefactor with a detailed manual outlining the flatterer's dirty secrets and thus promotes himself as a champion of candor and "proves" that he has absolutely nothing to hide.[61] The moral content of this satire may be compared to the poet's quasi-satiric correspondence with Scaeva in *Epistles* 1.17 and Lollius Maximus in *Epistles* 1.18. Both letters treat patronage in a seemingly lighthearted manner and offer advice to potential clients on how to avoid parasitism while maximizing rewards through proper conduct toward a "king" (*Ep.* 1.17.43: *rege*) or "powerful friend" (*Ep.* 1.18.44: *potentis amici*). Despite the unserious tone of Horace's advice,[62] certain scholars have interpreted these letters as proof of his corruption, self-interest, and materialism,[63] which appears to ignore the fact that these poems were dedicated to Maecenas after all and obviously would have been read by him very closely. On the other hand, if one considers the presence of Horace's "telling the truth while laughing" motif and frankness (*S.* 1.4.103–4: *liberius si | dixero quid*; cf. *Ep.* 1.18.1: *liberrime Lolli*) in these very sarcastic poems, then the underlying themes of virtue (*Ep.* 1.17.41: *virtus*) and its positive influence on proper conduct emerge. The relationship between being virtuous, morally responsible, and providing for one's welfare in the context of patronage is one Cicero emphasizes in works like *On Duties* (1.12): ... *ad cultum et ad victum, nec sibi soli sed coniugi liberis ceterisque quos caros habeat tuerique debeat: quae cura exsuscitat etiam animos et maiores ad rem gerendam facit*, "[Nature drives one] to look to the care and livelihood not only of oneself but also of one's spouse, children and any others in his care and whom he ought to protect, which is something that rouses his courage and makes him better at managing his affairs." Ross Kilpatrick explains its relevance for Horace's epistolary works:

> [I]n the light of Cicero's discussions, the related value terms show the pursuit of *amicitia* with great men as a test of virtue and modesty; material advantage flows naturally from such relationships and ought to

---

[61] On this topic with reference to Lucretius, see also Allen (1938) 172–3.

[62] Fairclough (1991) 367 and Mayer (1994) 241.

[63] See Fraenkel (1957) 321, Morris (1931), 103, Perret (1964) 120–1, and Damon (1997) 136–8. This is discussed by Kilpatrick (1986) 43–55 and Mayer (1995) 285–6, both of whom offer much more positive readings of these letters.

be accepted in the same spirit. *Decus* and *pretium* do not conflict. *Decus* brings *pretium*, without being sacrificed to it.[64]

This statement closely connects with the advice in Philodemus' treatise *On Gratitude* as well as *On Property Management*, in both of which he states that a sense of genuine gratitude on the part of a patron is the normal and appropriate response to the helpful advice of a friend. The friend, in turn, is highly encouraged to accept *pretium* from his grateful benefactor but only when it comes freely and without much toil (col. 16.44–6): τὸ [δὲ π]λεῖον, ἄ[ν ἀ]βλ[α]βῶς καὶ [εὐ]πόρως γίνηται, δεκτέ[ον], "... but with regard to more wealth, the wise man should accept it whenever it comes easily and without harm ..." Taking all of this into consideration, one may view the nature of Horace's advice on patronage as generally positive and sound, even if communicated at times in a humorous or openly sarcastic way. As will be seen below, this is not at all true of Tiresias' advice in *Satires* 2.5, which reflects the pure corruption, self-interest, and utter desperation of the legacy-hunter.

Intriguing connections emerge when Horace's exploitation of character traits in which Ulysses traditionally abounds are interpreted in the light of Philodemus' treatment of flattery and patronage. Through Ulysses' initial exchange with the Underworld prophet the poet immediately highlights these traits, which include eloquence, craftiness, and, within the context of his desire for reacquiring lost property, greed:

> "Hoc quoque, Tiresia, praeter narrata petenti
> responde, quibus amissas reparare queam res
> artibus atque modis. quid rides?" "iamne doloso
> non satis est Ithacam revehi patriosque penatis
> adspicere?" (*S.* 2.5.1–5)

ULYSSES: "One more question pray answer me, Tiresias, besides what you have told me. By what way and means can I recover my lost fortune? Why laugh?"
TIRESIAS: "What! not enough for the man of wiles to sail back to Ithaca and gaze upon his household gods?"

From his very first words, Ulysses is already portrayed as ambitious, restlessly curious, and acquisitive (*hoc quoque ... petenti*), which are merely symptoms of an avaricious disposition as revealed by his impatient demand (*responde*) that Tiresias show him how to recover his lost property (*amissas... res*). The notion of "searching for" (*petenti*) one's lost property and receiving a response appears in Vergil's *Eclogues* 1, which is spoken by the shepherd Tityrus who had recently reacquired property from Caesar (44): *hic mihi responsum primus dedit ille petenti*, "He was the first to give a response to me here in my search." The mention of *res* also reflects the emphasis in *Satires* 1 on preserving one's "inherited property" (*S.* 1.2.62: *rem patris*; cf. 1.4.110–11: *patriam rem*), which is obviously foremost in Ulysses' mind in *Satires* 2.5 and central to Horace's description of Maecenas' gift of the Sabine estate in the next poem. Contrary to the poet's frequent claim to be "content" with his current situation, however, Ulysses' response to the prophet, borrowing a typically Horatian expression loaded with moral undertones, identifies the underlying reason for the hero's greed as discontentment (*non satis est*). This combination of ambition and greed is at the center of Horace's criticisms in his first collection of the *Satires*, in which the theme of "never enough" (1.1.62: *nil satis est*) is repeatedly communicated to Maecenas through friendly chats as part of his private advice. The content of these chats, both for Philodemus as well as for Horace's persona, involves the importance of accepting greater wealth when it comes easily but also of being truly content with what nature provides (cf. *On Property Management*, coll. 15.45–16.4 and Cic. *On Ends* 1.44), and, above all, not fearing the loss of ones' property or the prospect of living a life of little means (cf. *On Wealth*, col. 12.14). As a consequence of this state of contentment and willingness to accept losses with confidence, Epicureans were perfectly satisfied with their current circumstances, which is something Horace constantly emphasizes through his self-portrayal as content with regard to his economic (*S.* 1.1.108: *contentus*) and social status (1.6.96: *contentus*).

Discontentment and avarice, which provide the moral foundation for Horace's character portrait of Ulysses, are also identified by Philodemus as the main passions afflicting flatterers and motivating their behavior. They suffer, for example, from "desire for wealth" (PHerc. 1457, col. 12.22: φιλαργυροῦσι; cf. fr. 12.5: πλοῦ[τ]ον) as well as "love of fame" (PHerc. 1089, col. 4.13: [φιλο]δοξ[ία]), both of which drive them to praise for the sake of gain. Horace plays with the Homeric warrior's typical lack of self-modesty by having Ulysses, when faced with the prospect of serving an old man, declare: "Not

so did I bear myself at Troy, but ever was I matched with my betters"
(*S.* 2.5.18–19: *haud ita Troiae | me gessi, certans semper melioribus*),
which to some degree echoes Homer's line at the beginning of *Odyssey*
9 (19–20): *Εἴμ' Ὀδυσεὺς Λαερτιάδης, ὃς πᾶσι δόλοισιν | ἀνθρώποισι
μέλω, καί μευ κλέος οὐρανὸν ἵκει*, "I am Ulysses, son of Laertes, who am
known among men for all sorts of wiles, and my fame reaches to
heaven." In the case of Horace's version of Ulysses, who reluctantly
expresses his willingness to become a "nobody" (*S.* 2.5.20: *fortem hoc
animum tolerare iubebo*, "I'll bid my valiant soul endure this"), the
demotion is clearly subordinate to the ultimate desire to recover his
wealth and former status as a glorious king. This is consistent with
earlier portrayals of Ulysses as unwilling to follow what would become
the Epicurean tradition of "living unnoticed," as his words in the
prologue to Euripides' fragmentary play *Philoctetes* show:

πῶς δ' ἂν φρονοίην, ᾧ παρῆν ἀπραγμόνως
ἐν τοῖς πολλοῖσι ἠριθμημένῳ στρατοῦ
ἴσον μετασχεῖν τῷ σοφωτάτῳ τύχης;   (*TrGF* 5.2, fr. 787)

How could I be a wise man? It was possible for me to live quietly among
the Achaean ranks as a cipher and share an equal fortune with the
wisest of men.

As Geert Roskam observes, his words in this passage imply a
subordination of philosophical tranquility to personal ambition,
since the hero "wonders if his reputation for wisdom is justified
after all."[65] Ulysses' refusal to "live unnoticed" and his ambition are
also comparable to that of Tillius in *Satires* 1.6, who is likewise
hungry for fame and glory, although in this case the Roman desires
to relinquish his original status as a nobody in order to join the
ranks of the wealthy and senatorial elite. Either way, both individuals are overly ambitious and end up suffering the consequences: for
Ulysses, this involves becoming a shameless flatterer continuously
tending to the needs of his wealthy victim with the hope of someday recovering lost wealth; for Tillius, it involves being ensnared by
the constricting responsibilities and cares of political office, as communicated by the metaphor of Glory's chariot. In a sense, Horace
prefaces the portraits of both individuals by highlighting early

---

[65] Roskam (2007) 8–9, who discusses this passage in more detail.

on the dangers of "shameless ambition" (*S.* 1.6.51–2: *prava | ambitione*), which, according to Philodemus, motivates flatterers to seek glory through relationships with millionaires:

[χάριν περιου]σίας ἢ δόξης ἢ καί τινος ἀ[ρ]χῆς ἀρέσαντες ἀνθρώπ[οις]
μεγαλοπλούτοις καὶ δυν[α]στευτικοῖς ἢ καὶ δημοκό[ποις].

(PHerc. 222, col. 5.1–4)

[Flatterers] aim to please millionaires, potentates and demagogues for the sake of possessions or glory or out of some other motive.

In both *Satires* 1.6 and 2.5 the poet is deeply concerned with social tact, which is opposed to the folly of unbridled ambition and the obsession with fame. Tillius and Ulysses are clearly discontented with their current lots and immediately prepare an aggressive plan for acquiring wealth. Contrasted to this is Horace's contentment, lack of ambition and willingness to wait patiently for nine months while Maecenas decides on whether to accept him into his literary circle or not (cf. *S.* 1.6.61–2). Horace also emphatically states that it was his virtue that impressed Maecenas rather than anything else, and that, unlike Ulysses, he is not ambitious but rather more than satisfied with his modest way of life (cf. *S.* 1.6.111–28).

Ulysses' fear of poverty (*S.* 2.5.9: *pauperiem...horres*) and refusal to endure a life of little means (6: *nudus inopsque*) conflicts not only with the poet's advice elsewhere in the *Satires* (cf. 1.1.93: *pauperiem metuas minus*), but also with Ofellus' philosophical equanimity and Epicurean understanding of the requirements of nature as easily fulfilled in *Satires* 2.2. Similar to the Stoics, Philodemus teaches that the fall from wealth into poverty is indifferent (*On Wealth*, col. 53.2–5) since nature's requirements are easily fulfilled:

Τίνος ἂν οὖν ἕνεκα τηλικαῦτ' ἔχων ἐφόδια πρὸς τὸ ζῆν καλῶς ἐν πολλῆι
ῥαισ[τώ]νηι, κἂν πλοῦτον ἀποβάληι, πέραι τοῦ μετρίου κακοπαθήσει
σωτηρίας ἕνεκ[α χ]ρ[η]μάτων;   (*On Property Management*, col. 16.12–18)

For what reason, therefore, would one who can acquire such means for the good life with such easiness undergo extreme suffering on account of financial loss, even if he should lose his wealth?

Like Ulysses and Ofellus, Horace declares that he had lost his property and wealth (*Ep.* 2.2.50: *inopemque paterni | et laris et fundi*) to forceful confiscations during a war and had become poor, although, unlike Ulysses—and this is a crucial point of comparison—he regained wealth by means of a virtuous disposition and frankness (*S.* 1.6.83: *virtutis*; 60: *quod eram narro*), by which he had managed to gain the favor of Maecenas (63: *placui tibi*). Oliensis highlights the tension between the two:

> The irony is blatant, but the alternative perspective of true friendship goes unexpressed. Is Horace an honest Ofellus, content with his lot, whose farm has been miraculously restored, or a Ulysses who has worked hard and deviously to accomplish such a restoration? While Horace might like to fancy himself an Ofellus, he knows that others may accuse him of being a Ulysses. By making the implicit comparison first himself, Horace precludes their attack and shows himself to be nobody's fool.[66]

Far from Horace's calculated self-portrayal as an honest and hard-working client is Ulysses' casual subordination of his noble pedigree and virtue to money, as he declares most colloquially, "birth and virtue without riches aren't worth a damn!" (*S.* 2.5.8: *et genus et virtus, nisi cum re, vilior alga est*). The proverbial worthlessness of seaweed also appears in Horace's *Odes* 3.17 (10: *alga... inutili*) and in Vergil's *Eclogues* 7 (42: *vilior alga*), and a similar expression involving the connection between money and personal worth is voiced by the Horatian miser at *Satires* 1.1 (62: *tanti quantum habeas sis*, "you are worth only as much as you have"). With regard to the colloquial language in *Satires* 2.5, Frances Muecke describes it as an "ironic counterplay between the heroic status of the characters and the perversion of values implied in *captatio*, mirrored in shifts between epic style and the informal style of conversation."[67] Perhaps more to the point is the fact that Ulysses' lowbrow expressions reveal something about his interior disposition as shaped by what Epicureans called empty fears and desires. In fact, these fears and desires are what drive him to seek advice concerning what to do and, in a manner perfectly consistent with the "man of many turns" (*Od.* 1.1: πολύτροπος; cf. *Odes* 1.6.7: *duplicis... Ulixei*), to inquire about the necessary "skills and methods" (*S.* 2.5.3: *artibus atque modis*) required in order to accomplish his purpose.

---

[66] Oliensis (1998) 57. Freudenburg (2001) 99 has similar considerations.
[67] Muecke (1993) 178. This antithetical juxtaposition between the high and low styles is also discussed by Sallmann (1970) 180. Klein (2012) 97–119 reads this poem as a dramatization of the typical client's "social performance" in contemporary Rome.

The hero's understanding of legacy-hunting as a learnable skill and source of income also appears in Philodemus, who identifies the need to satisfy false desires as the underlying cause of flattering behavior, which manifests itself through the conscious manipulation of rich people by various tactics of deception collectively identified as "the flatterer's art" (*On Frank Criticism*, col. 1b.13–14: [κολ]ακευτ[ι]καῖς ... [τέχναις]). Descriptions of flattery as a skill appear already in Plato's discussion of rhetoric (*Soph.* 222e7–223a1: κολακικὴν ... τέχνην), in Terence's humorous parody of its teachability (*Eu.* 260–4),[68] and in Seneca's description of legacy-hunting in *On Benefits* (6.38: *qui captandorum testamentorum artem professi sunt*, "those who are professionals in the art of legacy-hunting"). Apart from Theophrastus' character portrait of the flatterer in *Characters* 2 as well as later treatments like Plutarch's *How to Tell a Flatterer from a Friend* and Lucian's *Parasite*, however, it is Philodemus alone who provides an extended treatment of flatterers' deceptive strategies, concerns, and motives,[69] some of which have been discussed already in connection with *Satires* 1.9. Many of these same details emerge in Tiresias' exposition of the flatterer's techniques with regard to legacy-hunting, which, according to Horace in *Epistles* 1.1, is an utterly shameless way to grow rich (65–6): *isne tibi melius suadet, qui*, "*rem facias, rem,* | *si possis, recte, si non, quocumque modo, rem,*" "Does that man better convince you who says 'make money honestly, if you can, otherwise make it any way you can—but make money'?" (cf. Juv. 14.207 and also Lucil. 717 M: *sic amici quaerunt animum, rem parasiti ac ditias*, "Thus also do friends seek to know the person (lit. "the mind") but parasites wealth and riches"). The antithesis between legacy-hunting and genuine *amicitia* in the technical sense is discussed by Edward Champlin (legacies were, after all, one of the *beneficia* attached to patronage) and succinctly captured by Richard Saller, who states that, "Paradoxically, to hunt legacies

---

[68] For other references to flattery as a skill, see the still useful study of Ribbeck (1884) 63–4. The passage from Terence is discussed in more detail by Starks (2013) 277–8; for parasites in Terence and Plautus, see Barsby (1999) 126–7 with references, and especially Damon (1997) 23–101.

[69] For lost treatises on flattery and their authors, see Trapp (1997) 125, who translates Maximus of Tyre's philosophical orations, in which Ulysses is held as a model of virtue rather than as a flatterer.

was base, yet to receive legacies was an honor, an expression of esteem from friends and kin."[70] Despite being a shameless practice that is diametrically opposed to friendship, legacy-hunting and flattery in general have their own procedure and therefore require a certain level of expertise, as Tiresias indicates in his response to Ulysses' demand for skills and methods (*S.* 2.5.10): *accipe qua ratione queas ditescere*, "learn, then, the strategy for recovering your wealth." It is clear that the verb *accipere* in this context has a didactic tone, implying that what follows is, as Klaus Sallmann describes it, "a learnable skill and therefore one that is worthy of being taken seriously and capable of being taught in a didactic poem."[71]

The first important lesson, according to Tiresias, is to select a victim with specific qualifications and thereby ensure that one's flattering is properly received and quickly rewarded. His opening instructions include a clear description of the preferred *testator* and his potential weaknesses, such as advanced age and financial prosperity, which additionally hint at his susceptibility to exaggerated praise:

> turdus
> sive aliud privum dabitur tibi, devolet illuc,
> res ubi magna nitet domino sene; dulcia poma
> et quoscumque feret cultus tibi fundus honores
> ante Larem gustet venerabilior Lare dives.   (*S.* 2.5.10–14)

Suppose a thrush or other dainty be given you for your own, let it wing its way to where grandeur reigns and the owner is old. Your choice apples or whatever glories your trim farm bears you, let the rich man taste before your Lar; more to be reverenced than the Lar is he.

Horace humorously communicates the seer's instructions in mock-epic fashion through a parodic reference to augury and the prophetic power of birds, which in this case is a delicious thrush. The poet himself attests to the extravagant quality of such fare in *Epistles* 1.15, stating that "there is nothing better than a fat thrush" (40: *cum sit*

[70] Champlin (1989) 212 and Saller (1982) 125. As Tracy (1980) 400 shows, however, a significant number of legacy-hunters, such as lawyers and praetors, were from "the highest orders of society" (*splendidissimi*, quoting from Tacit. *Dial.* 6).

[71] Sallmann (1970) 181: "... die Erbschleicherei sei eine erlernbare Kunst, und dazu eine ernsthafte und würdige, nämlich lehrgedichtsfähige." Also Muecke (1993) 181 and Courtney (2013) 145.

obeso | nil melius turdo), which Kiessling–Heinze similarly describe as "a favorite delicacy."[72] In fact, Horace, distinguishing himself from legacy-hunters who use food as the primary bait for attracting wealthy old men, observes in his correspondence with Maecenas in *Epistles* 1.1 that "they hunt greedy widows and catch old men with tidbits and fruits" (78–9: *frustis et pomis viduas venentur avaras | excipiantque senes*).[73] In the case of *Satires* 2.5, the bird will in a sense lead Ulysses (11: *devolet illuc*) to the proverbial "golden bough," which recalls Vergil's description in *Aeneid* 6 of Venus' doves (190–204), which, according to Servius, relates to the fact that the use of such birds in augury was closely associated with royalty (*ad* 190): *nam ad reges pertinet columbarum augurium*, "for augury by doves pertains to kings." Of course, with regard to Ulysses, who was a king in his own right, Horace's inclusion of a game bird provides additional, although subtle, parody, especially since Juvenal speaks of legacy-hunters as offering "large turtledoves" (6.39: *turture magno*). Tiresias' advice concerning the detection and discovery of a suitable victim is again at odds with the poet's self-portrayal in *Satires* 1.6, according to which Maecenas is brought to him at the instigation of a third party (cf. 54: *nulla etenim mihi te fors obtulit*). In contrast to Horace's apparent lack of ambition and Maecenas' sober deliberation, Tiresias' emphasis on the proprietor's ownership of great quantities of shining wealth (*S*. 2.5.12: *res ubi magna nitet*) not only indicates a suitable source of money but also points to an acquisitive disposition that will likely be receptive to all manner of gifts, whether physical objects or exaggerated praise (cf. *On Frank Criticism*, coll. 24a9–11, 24b.1–9, quoted below). Like the *orbus* in *Satires* 2.5, moreover, Maecenas himself is also loaded in a financial sense, but unlike the flatterer's ideal quarry he as well as his entire household are, as Horace announces to the opportunistic toady in *Satires* 1.9, free of ambition (a point already made in 1.6) and morally pure beyond compare, which is precisely why Maecenas can be won over but never corrupted (55: *est qui vinci possit*; cf. the toady's words at 57: *muneribus servos corrumpam*).

According to Tiresias, the ideal victim is also advanced in age (*S*. 2.5.12: *domino sene*), not only because this expedites the transfer of

---

[72] Kiessling–Heinze (1910) 244: "*turdus*, als beliebte Delikatesse."
[73] Cf. Plaut. *Casket* 93: *in amicitiam insinuavit... blanditiis, muneribus, donis*, "He insinuated himself into friendship through flattery, favors, and gifts."

the inheritance, but because such individuals feel self-entitled and
worthy to receive high honors (13–14: *honores... venerabilior Lare*),
while they reject honest criticism. Philodemus explains this disposition in more detail in *On Frank Criticism*:

ὅτι συνετωτέρους οἴοντ[α]ι διὰ τὸν χρόνο[ν] ἑαυτούς...καὶ
θ[αυ]μαζ[ό] μενοι καὶ τιμώμενοι παρὰ τοῖς πλ[ε]ίοσι παράδοξον ἡγοῦν-
ται τὸ πρός τινων ἐπι[τιμ]η[θῆναι], καὶ καταξ[ιού]μενόν τ[ι]νων τὸ
γῆρας θ[ε]ωροῦντε[ς] εὐλαβοῦνται μὴ τούτων ἀποστερῶνται φανέντες
ἀνάξιοι.

(coll. 24a9–11, 24b.1–9)

...they [old men] believe themselves to be more intelligent because of
their age... and because they are admired and held in honor by most
people, they think it is untoward to have been reproached by some folk,
and as they know old age is considered worthy of certain honors, they are
afraid of being denied these if they look as if they didn't deserve them.

It would seem that a rich old man is the legacy-hunter's perfect
target not only for practical reasons, but because his acquisitiveness
and inflated sense of self-worth make him predisposed to become a
"lover of flattery" (PHerc. 1457, fr. 15.6: φιλοκόλακες). In some cases
these are people who, "although they realize they do not possess the
qualities which they are said to possess and that they have imperfections, rejoice at the ones praising them" (fr. 14.5–9: τινες καίπερ
εἰδότες ὅ[τι] οὐκ ἔχουσιν ἃ λέγον[τ]αί τινα δ᾽ὡς ἐστ[ι]ν ἁμαρτήματα
χαίρουσιν ἐπὶ τοῖς ἐγκωμιαζομένοις).[74] With regard to Ulysses' target,
however, whose age suggests a susceptibility to flattery and who
appears to suffer from avarice and self-love, Tiresias' advice relates
more closely to "lovers of flattery" who cannot understand their
imperfections and therefore truly believe that they have virtues (cf.
S. 2.5.33: *virtus tua*) and actually deserve praise.[75] This keen observation also appears in Plutarch's *How to Tell a Flatterer from a Friend*,
in which he states the following:

δι᾽ ἣν [φιλαυτίαν] αὐτὸς αὑτοῦ κόλαξ ἕκαστος ὢν πρῶτος καὶ μέγιστος οὐ
χαλεπῶς προσίεται τὸν ἔξωθεν ὢν οἴεται καὶ βούλεται μάρτυν ἅμ᾽ αὑτῷ
καὶ βεβαιωτὴν προσγιγνόμενον.   (49a)

---

[74] See Kondo (1974) 48–9 and Tsouna (2007) 133–4 for a discussion of this
passage.
[75] See Tsouna (2007) 133 for this category of "lovers of flattery." Roberts (1984)
428 describes the ideal *senex* in terms of "self-deception" and "blind self-esteem."

It is because of this self-love that everybody is himself his own foremost
and greatest flatterer, and hence finds no difficulty in admitting the
outsider to witness with him and to confirm his own conceits and
desires.

As Philodemus notes, such individuals are likely to take advantage
of or even maltreat flatterers (cf. PHerc. 222, col. 7.12–17), especially
if they eventually discover that their praise is insincere. As will be
explained in more detail below, Tiresias makes similar observations,
warning his pupil about vengeful and manipulative *captandi* through
the examples of Coranus (64–9) and the old Theban woman (84–8),
both of whom finally realized their respective flatterers' intentions
and, after having taken advantage of their services, ultimately cheated
them of their inheritance.[76]

The intended victim's complete lack of self-knowledge and consequent debasement are further emphasized in this satire by the various
dehumanizing metaphors Tiresias employs, which underscore the
corrupt and materialistic nature of the relationship. As Michael
Roberts has keenly observed,[77] the old man is transformed into an
"inflated bladder" (98: *crescentem . . . utrem*), a set of "soft ears"
(32–3: *molles | auriculae*), a "head" (94: *caput*), "skin" (38: *pelliculam*),
and, perhaps most fitting given the hunting metaphor suggested by
captare, a "greasy hide" (83: *corio . . . uncto*). Such metaphors recur in
striking fashion in the expressions of the satirist Persius, who
describes flattering poetry that tickles the senses as providing "feasts
for other people's ears" (1.22: *auriculis alienis colligis escas*), which are
"tender" and cannot stand to be "bitten by the truth" (107–8: *teneras
mordaci radere vero | auriculas*). Better by far, according to this
satirist, it is to have a reader whose ears are "steamed clean" (126:
vaporata . . . aure) and thus prepared to receive something pure and
true. Aside from the bodily metaphors that foreshadow Persius'
satires, there is also a hint of Juvenalian invective in Horace's seemingly gratuitous criticism of the greedy victim in *Satires* 2.5. Nevertheless, Roberts additionally states that, despite the Juvenalian tone of
his negative portrayal of this relationship, its main purpose is not to

---

[76] For the theme of "hunted as hunter," see Tracy (1980) 399–402, Hopkins (1983)
240–1, and Champlin (1989) 212. Sallmann (1970) 200 describes the symbiosis
between these two as "the dishonest relationship of exchange between *captator* and
testator" ("die unlauteren Wechselbeziehungen zwischen Captator und Testator").

[77] Roberts (1984) 428–31.

blame without reason like the Cynics but rather to connect with an audience, namely Maecenas, who is already predisposed to recognize and reject its moral defects: "[I]t is an *indignatio* that is not directed by the persona of the satirist, but must emerge from our own reaction to the message presented. The indignation is implicit in the content of the satire. It presupposes a like-minded audience, not one that needs to be persuaded."[78] In this sense, it seems that Horace's persona exploits a character portrait that, for all its humor, implies something that will undoubtedly be perceived by his like-minded patron as unacceptable. This point is further emphasized if one takes into consideration Philodemus' observations in his treatise *On Property Management* concerning gratitude and friendship between client and patron, whose conversations, as discussed in connection with *Satires* 1.9, are truthful (col. 23.30–1), beneficial to both (col. 27.37–9), and frank (cf. PHerc. 222, col. 3.27–8: παρρη[σιαζόμενον]). The wealthy old man in *Satires* 2.5, on the other hand, will reward Ulysses only because his "soft ears" have been tickled by empty praise. Given the victim's vulnerable disposition and consequent attraction to the hunter's bait, which make him the ideal quarry for a clever speaker like Ulysses, Tiresias next explains the manner in which he may successfully apply the skill of flattery.

It is perhaps unsurprising that the bulk of Tiresias' advice on successful legacy-hunting involves adulatory speech. The specifically Roman context in which it is given, however, interestingly emphasizes the flatterer's competitive spirit and perversion of the role of "advocate" (*S.* 2.5.30: *defensor*). Ulysses' skill as a persuasive speaker, which in Homer is either frank and aimed at preventing stasis within the Achaean ranks (*Il.* 2.182–206) or gentle like falling snow (*Il.* 3.216–24), was easily portrayed by later authors in terms of guile and deception.[79] In Horace's satire it forms the backdrop for his characterization as a flatterer, who, to borrow expressions from Philodemus, "speaks with honeyed words" (PHerc. 222, col. 7.9: μει[λίττει]) and is "crafty" (PHerc. 1457, col. 4.27: [τοῖς] αἱμύλοις) in showing "favor and charm in every way with regard to the commonest things" (fr. 5.31–3: χάριν ... δὲ καὶ γοητεία παντελῶς ἐπὶ

---

[78] Roberts (1984) 428–31. His point also applies to Horace's portrayal of the toady in *Satires* 1.9.
[79] See Stanford (1954) 90–117 for the references, which point to Ulysses' popularity among the sophists and tragedians, especially Euripides.

κοινότερα). Theophrastus similarly highlights the flatterer's tendency to praise everything in sight: (*Char.* 2.12): καὶ τὴν οἰκίαν φῆσαι εὖ ἠρχιτεκτονῆσθαι καὶ τὸν ἀγρὸν εὖ πεφυτεῦσθαι καὶ τὴν εἰκόνα ὁμοίαν εἶναι, "He [the flatterer] will remark how tasteful is the style of his patron's house, how excellent the planting of his farm, how like him the portrait he has had made." To these descriptions one may easily add that of the toady in *Satires* 1.9, who, according to Horace, "rattled on about everything, praising the streets and the city" (12–13: *cum quidlibet ille | garriret, vicos, urbem laudaret*). Part of this barrage of praise, as Tiresias reveals to Ulysses in *Satires* 2.5, is addressing a victim intimately by employing the first name, since this is pleasing and more likely to win favor as it coddles the "gentle ears" (32–3): *gaudent praenomine molles | auriculae* (cf. *S.* 2.6.36–7: *de re communi scribae magna atque nova te | orabant hodie meminisses, Quinte, reverti*, "The clerks beg you, Quintus, to be sure to return today on some fresh and important business of common interest"). Another way to curry favor apparently involves the use of affectionate language in general, as when Ulysses is encouraged to send his victim home so that he can "pamper his precious little hide" (38: *pelliculam curare*).[80] This is certainly not how Horace portrays his initial interaction with Maecenas, which, according to the poet, was imbued with a spirit of candor, honesty, and—perhaps most important—very few words (cf. *S.* 1.6.56: *singultim pauca locutus*). There is an obvious Callimachean element at play here, although in Horace's *Satires* the concern with refinement and brevity is also connected to the need for communicating useful advice to Maecenas, which falls into the realm of moral philosophy and Epicurean patronage specifically. This is quite different from the flatterer, who in many ways is a skilled actor (cf. *S.* 2.5.91: *Davus sis comicus*; cf. PHerc. 1675, col. 13.35–6: ὑποκριτὰς εἶναι) who feigns concern for everything (36–8: *mea cura est... curare*; cf. PHerc. 1457, col. 2.6–8: πάν[τ]ων [τ]ὴν ἐπιμέλει[α]ν π[ρ]οσποι[εῖσ]θαι), from ensuring his target's health (cf. *S.* 2.5.94: *velet carum caput* and Theophr. *Char.* 2.10: καὶ ἐρωτῆσαι μὴ ῥιγοῖ, καὶ εἰ ἐπιβάλλεσθαι βούλεται, καὶ εἴ τι περιστείλῃ αὐτόν, "[He will] ask him whether he is not cold, and whether he wants a blanket

---

[80] Muecke (1993) 184 notes that the use of *pellis* instead of *cutis* may underscore the victim's dehumanization and foreshadow the metaphor of the greasy hide. Kiessling-Heinze (1910) 246 associate this expression with the "informal tone" ("zwanglose Ton") of the poem in general.

tossed around him and whether he would like to draw his cloak a little closer about him...") to extolling his "bad poetry" (*S.* 2.5.74: *mala carmina*). This last bit of advice is particularly funny, since Horace's persona cannot refrain from criticizing bad poetry, even that of his great predecessor Lucilius (cf. *S.* 1.4.6–13 and 1.10.1–3).[81] He is, therefore, quite unlike Ulysses in the sense that his own advice is frank and truthful, whether this involves moral issues or critical observations concerning literary style.

In Horace's blatantly Romanized depiction of flattery such feigned concern of the *defensor* extends into the Forum and the realm of legal support. Philodemus observes that flatterers "very quickly pretend to pity their victims when they encounter bad fortune and at the same time provide assistance" (PHerc. 1457, fr. 2.36–9: ἂν ταχύτα[τα] ἐλεεῖν προσπο[ι]εῖσθαι εὖ ἀτ[υ]χοῦντας καὶ βο[ηθ]εῖν ἅμ[α]).[82] Of course, in this poem such assistance occurs within the context of legal disputes involving the victim's quarry, whose shady past and immorality (cf. *S.* 2.5.15–17) would be quite conducive to such public encounters:

> magna minorve foro si res certabitur olim,
> vivet uter locuples sine gnatis, inprobus, ultro
> qui meliorem audax vocet in ius, illius esto
> defensor   (*S.* 2.5.27–30)

If someday a case, great or small, be contested in the Forum, whichever of the parties is rich and childless, villain though he be, the kind of man who would with wanton impudence call the better man into court, do you become his advocate.

The flatterer's unconditional support of his "client," which is a perversion of justice (34: *ius anceps*) as well as of friendship (33: *amicum*), quickly becomes an overprotective obsession fueled by insatiable avarice (cf. 4: *non satis est*). Beyond being instructed to spurn all others (31: *sperne*), for instance, Ulysses is encouraged to insinuate himself into a favorable position by maintaining a constant

---

[81] Courtney (2013) 148 strangely suggests that Horace mentions praising bad poetry because "out of tactfulness he sometimes had to do the same," although this contradicts the frank criticism Horace describes as characteristic of his circle of friends (cf. *S.* 1.10.36–91 and *Odes* 1.24.5–8).

[82] This passage reflects the reconstruction of Kondo (1974) 50. See Kiessling–Heinze (1910) 246 and Muecke (1993) 183 for Horace's extended development of the topic of legal services.

presence and becoming the old man's personal bodyguard (35–6), health consultant (37–8), and attorney (38). These are just some of the many tactics by which flatterers promote themselves on various occasions, as Cicero explains in *On Friendship*, saying that "one must beware lest that clever and subtle fellow carefully insinuate himself" (99: *callidus ille et occultus ne se insinuet studiose cavendum est*).[83] Jerome Kemp, who very briefly discusses the influence of Philodemus' *On Flattery* in this satire, makes a clearer connection by citing this very passage from Cicero alongside Tiresias' words (47–8): *leniter in spem | adrepe officiosus,* "by your attentions worm your way into the hope that . . . "[84] Interestingly enough, Philodemus uses a Greek equivalent of the verb *adrepere* in PHerc. 1457 (fr. 5.36: εἰσδύωνται) in order to describe the flatterer's clever deception (cf. *LSJ* s.v., which translates this verb as "to worm oneself into something" and cites Demosthenes 11.4: εἰς τὴν Ἀμφικτυονίαν εἰσδεδυκώς, "and having wormed himself [Philip] into the Amphictyonic League"). All of these observations highlight the flatterer's concern with making himself absolutely indispensable to his quarry on every level (cf. again PHerc. 1457, fr. 2.36–9), which consequently involves spurning others and eliminating any competition.

The closeness and exclusivity of this kind of personal attachment leaves little room for potential rivals, who, as Philodemus describes them, are generally on the receiving end of a suspicious flatterer's persecutions. He notes that obsequious individuals are generally overprotective of their patrons, but feel particular animosity toward other flatterers (cf. PHerc. 222, col. 7.1–12). As Voula Tsouna further explains, according to Philodemus, "The flatterer makes deliberate efforts to isolate his victims, chasing away everyone who loves them and also every other flatterer who competes for their favors."[85] One may recall that in *Satires* 1.9, which, among other things, is about social tact and proper etiquette within literary circles, the toady employs a similar tactic. With regard to the immediate context of that poem, however, Horace himself is in some ways the victim of an ambitious flatterer, who, as the self-proclaimed *defensor* (cf. S. 2.5.30) of the poet, characteristically pretends to offer help and protection to

[83] Cf. Suetonius' description of Horace as having "insinuated himself" (*insinuatus*) into friendship with Maecenas and Augustus, which is an opinion the poet obviously challenges throughout the *Satires*.
[84] Kemp (2010b) 71.   [85] Tsouna (2007) 128.

his quarry, specifically by promising to destroy any of the poet's competition for Maecenas' favor (cf. *S*. 1.9.47–8). The assertion in *Satires* 1.9 that rivalry and jealousy do not exist within Maecenas' circle (48–9) is bolstered by Horace's description of his initial encounter with him in 1.6, which was made possible by the peaceful and even enthusiastic collaboration between Varius and Vergil in presenting him freely to their patron (54–5). In *Satires* 2.5 the notion of rivalry and competition alluded to above recurs, only this time with regard to the victim's family members and relatives, toward whom the flatterer is even more aggressively disposed and hostile (cf. PHerc. 222, col. 7.1–4): [μισεῖ δ᾽ ὁ κόλαξ] πάντας ἁπλῶς τοὺς [ἐπιτη]δείους τῶν κολακευ[ομένων,] μάλιστα δὲ γονεῖς κ[αὶ τοὺς] ἄλλους συγγενεῖς, "And the flatterer generally hates those who are intimate with their victims, especially their children and other relatives." This hostility is especially understandable in the case of *captatio*, since family members as favorable heirs would most likely present the biggest threat to legacy-hunters (*S*. 2.5.45–6: *filius . . . sublatus*), who would be in competition with them and constantly anxious about their status in the will (54–5): *solus multisne coheres,* | *veloci percurre oculo*, "swiftly run your eye across to see whether you are sole heir or share with others."[86] As Tiresias explains next, however, at times legacy-hunters willingly cooperate with others (cf. 70–1), but only in order to gain their favor and ensure that they themselves are praised when absent (71–2): *illis* | *accedas socius: laudes, lauderis ut absens*, " . . . make common cause with them. Praise them, that they may praise you behind your back." Tiresias seems to present this option as a necessary evil, since is it far better to work alone and be the sole victor (73–4): *sed vincit longe prius ipsum* | *expugnare caput*, "but far better is it to storm the citadel itself."[87] The flatterer's false congeniality toward his rivals, then, is merely a tactic of self-promotion designed to win the victim's trust, as Philodemus notes (PHerc. 1675, col. 12.37–41): καὶ σπεύδοντες α[ὐ]τοῖς ὑποττάτειν αὐτούς, ἵνα καὶ στέγωσι καὶ συνεργῶσι καὶ πίστιν ἐμποιῶσι[ν] τοῦ [ἔ]ξωθεν, " . . . taking care to subordinate them [sc. other servants] to themselves, so that they may protect them, collaborate with them and gain the

---

[86] See Kemp (2010b) 70.
[87] Kiessling–Heinze (1910) 251 likewise read this passage as implying strong rivalry among the victim's servants.

outsider's trust." Despite all of this, knowing how to select an ideal
victim, successfully apply various methods of flattery and rule out
potential rivals is not enough: Tiresias' final lesson emphasizes the
care which Ulysses must exercise in order to conceal his true intentions and avoid being suspected of betraying this trust.

An important purpose of Tiresias' advice is to warn his pupil regarding the prospective victim's rather inconsistent temperament,
which, upon recognition of the flatterer's true intentions, may be
drawn to irascible outbursts or vengeful plots. In his observation of
flattery Philodemus describes victims who are completely unaware of
their flatterers' insincerity and therefore believe the praise rather
than playing along with it (PHerc. 1457, fr. 14.2–5): [ἀπι]θανότητος οὐ
[σ]υναισθανόμενοι κατὰ λό[γ]ον οὐδὲ παράγονταί, "since they do not
think rationally and are not aware of the insincerity, they are
not willingly led astray..." Unsurprisingly, having realized the
truth of their flatterers' intentions some victims react violently and
express their frustration in the form of abusive outbursts (cf.
PHerc. 222, col. 7.12–17, where the abuse is the result of drinking:
[πρόθυμ]ος ὑβρίζεται καὶ πάνυ [πολλὰς] ἀναδ[έ]χεται παροινί[ας καὶ]
προ[π]ηλακισμοὺς ἄχ[ρι ἅ]μα [τ]ρ[ώσε]ων καὶ πληγῶ[ν] πολ]λῶ[ν], "the
flatterer is willingly mistreated and receives very great abuses caused by
drunkenness, even maltreatment that results in many wounds and blows").
Ulysses must prevent this, as Tiresias explains, by means of artfulness
(*S.* 2.5.23: *astutus*) and opportunistic propriety (43: *aptus*), which partly
involves ensuring that his obsequious praise is carefully regulated:

> cautus adito
> neu desis operae neve immoderatus abundes.
> difficilem et morosum offendet garrulus: ultra
> non etiam sileas. (*S.* 2.5.88–91)

Be cautious in your approach; neither fail in zeal, nor show zeal beyond
measure. A chatterbox will offend the peevish and morose; yet you must
not also be silent beyond bounds.[88]

---

[88] Samuelsson (1900) 1–10, citing Cicero's *Prior Academics* 2.104 as a parallel,
suggests the following punctuation: *ultra "non" "etiam" sileas*, "Beyond 'yes' and 'no'
be silent." Although Kiessling–Heinze (1910) 253 and Muecke (1993) 191, not to
mention Klingner and Shackleton Bailey in their editions, follow him, yet I prefer the
punctuation and translation of Fairclough: *ultra non etiam sileas*, "Yet you must not
also be silent beyond bounds." This interpretation seems to be more consistent with
Tiresias' general advice, which is elsewhere far less restrictive and encourages more

This is evidently a perversion of truthful and beneficial conversation, which Philodemus says is candid rather than obsequious or self-serving (cf. *On Conversation*, col. 9.15–16: τοὺς δηλ[οῦ]ν[τ]ας καὶ [τοὺς σ]υκοφαντοῦντας, "...those who show things clearly and those who are slanderers...") and exercises frankness even when this may cause offense (col. 10.10–12): π[ο]λλὰ καὶ κατὰ πλεῖστον οὐκ ἐπιτεύξεσθαι νομ[ίζ]οντες, οἱ φρόνιμοι λαλοῦσ[ι], "...even when they suppose that much of it will generally not be received favorably, prudent men speak." At the same time, according to Philodemus virtuous "conversation" or ὁμιλία between true friends employs frankness whenever necessary while recognizing the "power of silence" (*On Conversation*, col. 6.2). That is to say, unlike the flatterer or ambitious politician who will say anything to their listeners, a true friend's conversations are motivated by goodwill and therefore communicate only what is relevant or helpful, as Philodemus emphasizes elsewhere:

πᾶς [τίς] ποτε εὐνοῶν καὶ συνετ[ῶς] κα[ὶ συν]εχῶς φιλοσοφῶν καὶ μέγας ἐν ἕξει καὶ ἀφιλόδοξος καὶ [δη]μαγωγὸς ἥκιστα καὶ φθόνου καθαρὸς καὶ τὰ προσόντα μόνον λέγων καὶ μὴ συνεκφερόμενος, ὥστε λοιδορεῖν ἢ πομπε[ύ]ε[ιν] ἢ [κ]αταβάλλε[ιν ἢ] βλάπτ[ειν], μηδ' ἀσ[ε]λγε[ί]αις κα[ὶ κολ]ακευτ[ι]καῖς χρώ[μενος τέχναις].

(*On Frank Criticism* col. 1b.2–14)

Everyone who is well disposed, and intelligently disposed, and continually talking philosophically, and lofty in character, and careless of his own glory, and not at all crowd-pleasing, and free of spite, and saying only what is relevant, and who is not carried away into reviling, and strutting, or into casting people down, and doing harm, nor using insolence and flattering techniques.

The sage advisor also understands that speech should observe certain limits, and thus knows perfectly well when to speak and when to keep silent (*On Conversation*, col. 8.2–5): παρυπομνήσομεν ὅτι μάλιστα μελ[η]ετή[σ]ει καλῶς λαλεῖν, ποτὲ λαλῶν, οὐκ ἀε[ὶ σ]ιωπῶν, "We recall that the sage will be particularly careful to speak appropriately, voicing his opinion on certain occasions rather than always keeping silent."[89]

---

verbal deception and manipulation than Samuelsson's reading would allow (cf. 93: *obsequio grassare*).

[89] The role of silence is discussed by Tsouna (2007) 122–3.

This moral framework may be applied to Horace's short but useful and beneficial chats and contrasted with the long-winded, overwhelmingly negative diatribes of Stoics like Damasippus in *Satires* 2.3 and Davus in 2.7, which will be considered in the next and final chapter. With Ulysses the point is not only that he ignores certain limits when speaking, but that, as flatterer par excellence, he completely inverts the proper order of virtuous conversation. In conversing with his quarry, he does the exact opposite of what Philodemus recommends: his speech (*S.* 2.5.98: *sermonibus*) and silence (91: *sileas*) are neither therapeutic nor intended to be beneficial, but rather manipulative and inspired by a desire for self-gain.[90] Tiresias explains that such care is necessary to avoid suspicion, which, given the victim's demented self-love (74: *vecors*) and peevish nature (90: *difficilem et morosum*),[91] would likely result in Ulysses' expulsion from his company and utterly ruin any of his prospects of inheritance. Philodemus also emphasizes the flatterer's concern with avoiding such consequences by maintaining a semblance of friendship and thereby remaining undiscovered:

[ἔ]τι δ' οὐ διὰ φιλι[κ]ωτέρου πράγματος ἀλλὰ διὰ κολακείας ἐξαγίστου π[αρ']
ἁπ[άν]των πάσας ἐκπορίζεται τὰ[ς] ἐν τῶι βίωι χρείας, ὧν ἀτευκτήσει
μᾶλλον [ὑ]πονοηθεὶ[ς] μόνον εἶναι κό[λ]αξ, οὐχ ὅτι καὶ καταγνωσθ[εὶς]...
[βέ]βαιον μὲ[ν φίλ]ον ὃν πείθο[νται] δι' αὐτῆς ἐν[ν]οεῖσθαι φω[ράσα]ντες δ'
ἐξο[ρί]ζουσι καὶ π[ικρῶς] βλάβαις με[γ]άλαις ἁ[πωσ]άμενοι·

(PHerc. 222, col. 3.3–17)

No longer then does he acquire from all every advantage of life by means of agreeable endeavors, but by means of abominable flattery, which he would not be able to accomplish if he were even suspected of being a flatterer let alone fully recognized as one... For when they

---

[90] For Philodemean homiletics as "the sage's opportunity for pedagogy" ("momento paideutico del sapiente"), see Amoroso (1975) 63.

[91] This description not only reflects Philodemus' observations concerning old men's difficulty with accepting frank and honest criticism (*On Frank Criticism*, coll. 24a9–11, 24b.1–9, quoted above), but also with the traditional Roman characterization (Cic. *On Old Age* 65): *At sunt morosi et anxii et iracundi et difficiles senes... idque cum in vita tum in scaena intellegi potest ex eis fratribus qui in Adelphis sunt*, "and yet they are peevish, touchy, irascible and difficult... and just as this can be seen in real life, so also on the stage from those two brothers in the *Brothers*." Cf. Muecke (1993) 191 and Kiessling–Heinze (1910) 253, who call this a "general truth" ("allgemeine Wahrheit") especially prominent in comedy.

discover that a "friend" whom they believe to be reliable is plotting through flattery, they banish him and bitterly thrust him out with great blows.

Philodemus makes a similar observation in another fragment of *On Flattery*, in which he describes flatterers as "fearing that they should be kicked out as well and creating the illusion that they truly love their masters . . ." (PHerc. 1675, col. 13.4–6: καὶ φοβούμενοι μὴ παρωσθῶσι καὶ δόξαν ἐκκόπτοντες ὡς ἀληθινῶς φιλοῦσιν). Tiresias' warnings regarding the importance of maintaining this illusion and the dangers of being too obvious presuppose a similar kind of violent reaction from the disillusioned victim, although they may also address another possible danger mentioned above, namely, vengeance through disinheritance. In this sense, the prophet's earlier advice to avoid "open devotion" (*S.* 2.5.46–7: *manifestum* | . . . *obsequium*) and read the victim's will stealthily (53–5: *ut limis rapias . . . veloci percurre oculo*) fitfully precede his example of Nasica, the *captator* whose plan to ensnare his victim through marriage backfired when he was struck from the will (69: *nil sibi legatum*).[92] Similarly, his advice to avoid loquacity is followed by the story of the Theban crone, who posthumously ridiculed an heir for his "overbearing manner" (88: *quod nimium institerat viventi*) by making him her pallbearer and thus reversing the roles. In light of these two examples, Tiresias ironically recommends that his pupil observe the "golden mean" (89: *neu desis operae neve immoderatus abundes*, "neither fail in zeal, nor show zeal beyond measure"),[93] which, though espoused by Horace elsewhere as a prerequisite for virtuous living (cf. *S.* 1.1.106: *est modus in rebus*), in this context will allow the selfish hero to remain undiscovered and more easily achieve his guileful purpose. Horace's exposé of the flatterer's methods of hunting for rewards is both a satiric attack on a contemporary problem as well as a means of reinforcing and reorienting the poet's own position with regard to Maecenas. His incorporation of Philodemean ethics, furthermore, not only adds depth and credibility to the portrait of the flatterer's disposition, but

[92] See Mansbach (1982) 18–19 for the difference between *hereditates*, which enjoined upon the heirs certain legal responsibilities and duties, and *legata*, which appear to have been gifts freely bestowed upon legatees and without any demands. Ulysses is mentioned twice as a potential heir (54: *coheres* and 101: *heres*).
[93] Muecke (1993) 191.

it also imparts a kind of organizational structure to Tiresias' advice regarding the ideal victim, the necessary tactics, and the pitfalls associated with legacy-hunting. By means of this portrait Horace bolsters his image as trustworthy friend at the expense of a fictitious but (in)famous interlocutor, thus securing his patron's favor at the same time. His supposed "withdrawal" from satire, therefore, is little more than a defensive tactic that, as in the case of *Satires* 2.5, allows the poet to promote himself through implied contrast and offer a robust response to any challenges from envious or less successful detractors.

WEALTH AND PHILOSOPHICAL
WITHDRAWAL IN *SATIRES* 2.6

It is probably no coincidence that Horace's highly critical portrait of a sweet-talking flatterer whose intrigue and ambition are aimed at financial rewards appears alongside the positive description of Maecenas' generosity in *Satires* 2.6. The contrast is essentially twofold in that it implies something about both patron and client and their relationship toward one another, all of which has its origins in *Satires* 1.[94] In the first book the poet promoted the virtuous nature of his persona through "autobiographical" descriptions of his philosophical upbringing, which apparently led to his successful encounter with a scrutinizing patron who is attentive to honesty and candor. Horace confirms his patron's favorable evaluation of his character by including the introductory diatribes in which he offers salubrious advice on wealth, sex, and anger, all in a manner that is direct, useful, and therefore in line with Philodemus' observations of Epicurean patronage in *On Property Management* and other treatises. At the same time, Horace attempts to address the challenges and criticisms of jealous rivals by introducing the character portraits of the toady and then Ulysses, which, echoing the similar concerns of Philodemus, provide necessary contrast between himself and flatterers. What is missing from his self-justifying

---

[94] Hicks (2013) 197: "*Sermo* 2.5 then contrasts with the peaceful depiction of friendship within Maecenas' circle that Horace has already portrayed elsewhere in the first book of *Sermones*, and again with the depiction that follows in his Sabine farm in 2.6."

representation is concrete proof of Maecenas' genuine gratitude for his friendship and of the fact that, rather than actively searching for such rewards, he merely accepts wealth from his grateful patron. This wealth, of course, is the famous property known as the Sabine estate, which, according to Horace's own description and in harmony with Philodemus' advice, is suitable and worthy of acceptance because it leads to philosophical conversations with true friends in a withdrawn setting in the country.

The idyllic portrayal of life in the country in *Satires* 2.6 is deceptively simple, since, in addition to addressing the important theme of leisure as a prerequisite for poetic activity, it also involves an expression of gratitude that reconnects Horace's audience to the complicated issue of patronage. This poem, which has been closely associated with *Satires* 2.2 on account of its praise of rural simplicity, may also engage further with the tension between city and country implicitly communicated at the beginning of *Satires* 2.3 (5: *huc fugisti*, 10: *villula*).[95] Indeed, it may offer a response to the criticisms of Damasippus concerning the adequacy of country life for literary productivity, which, in accordance with the characteristics of Horatian satire, requires *otium* and often draws inspiration from the poet's own life experiences (whether accurately portrayed or exaggerated to promote a literary persona). Horace's acquisition of the Sabine estate, which probably occurred in 33 BC,[96] was undoubtedly one of these experiences, the significance of which is clearly revealed at the outset by an elaborate prayer of thanksgiving:

Hoc erat in votis: modus agri non ita magnus,
hortus ubi et tecto vicinus iugis aquae fons
et paulum silvae super his foret. auctius atque
di melius fecere. bene est. nil amplius oro,
Maia nate, nisi ut propria haec mihi munera faxis.   (*S.* 2.6.1–5)

This is what I prayed for!—a piece of land not so very large, where there would be a garden, and near the house a spring of ever-flowing water,

[95] Boll (1913) 143 was the first to arrange the poems in Book 2 as intentionally paralleled to one another, a thesis which Fraenkel (1957) 137 doubts but Rudd (1966) 160–1 is more willing to accept. For the role of tension or opposition in this poem, especially that of civic duty/leisure and Stoicism/Epicureanism, see Muecke (1993) 194.

[96] Reckford (1959) 200. But cf. Bradshaw (1989) 160–86, who points out that there is no explicit evidence in the corpus to identify Maecenas as the source of the Sabine estate.

and up above these[97] a bit of woodland. More and better than this have
the gods done for me. I am content. Nothing more do I ask, O son of
Maia, save that thou make these blessings last my life long.

It is curious that the poet should choose to express his gratitude to
Maecenas in the form of a solemn invocation to Mercury, complete
with formulaic lines used in traditional prayers.[98] There are, however,
various possible reasons for this: in addition to containing the mob's
jealousy (48: *invidiae*), which was a bittersweet reality that plagued
Horace constantly (cf. *S.* 1.6.45–7), this prayer may reflect the
Romans' general distaste for explicit references to the exchange of
services between patrons and clients, which would have been especially inappropriate within the context of a sophisticated poem.[99]
Ellen Oliensis gives an explanation of Horace's indirect expression
of gratitude:

> [T]he displacement is sufficient to stave off the self-incriminating
> "thank you" (portraying Horace as a poet for hire) that we might have
> expected Horace to produce. Moreover, had Horace thanked Maecenas
> directly, the poem might be read as an enforced or ungraciously punc-
> tual pay-off of Maecenas' generous gift. As in *Satires* 1.6, the obliquity of
> Horace's "thank you" keeps the satire's value from being exhausted in
> the act of exchange.[100]

Perhaps on a more personal level, the omission of an explicit acknowledgement of Maecenas as Horace's benefactor may additionally
suggest a certain level of autonomy on the part of the poet, who, in
an earlier dedication to his patron, had boldly reserved gratitude for
his biological father (*S.* 1.6.65–71).[101] As a poet, moreover, Horace
was entirely justified in associating Maecenas, to whom he refers
elsewhere as a source of wealth (cf. *Epod.* 1.31–2 and *Ep.* 1.7.15),

---

[97] This is the translation offered by Kiessling–Heinze (1910) 257 and Muecke
(1993) 197, both of whom support it by citing Varrro's *On Agriculture* 1.21.1 (a
passage encouraging proprietors to establish their villas below a wild wood). Cf. also
Odes 3.1.17: *districtus ensis cui super inpia | cervice pendet* "for whom a drawn sword
hangs upon impious head". Of course, the alternative is to take *super his* as "moreover" or "in addition to this," as does Fraenkel (1957) 138 n. 2.

[98] See Fraenkel (1957) 138 n. 1.

[99] Rudd (1966) 253: "As Maecenas heard that magnificent opening, in which a
human name would have been quite out of place . . ."

[100] Oliensis (1998) 48. Cf. Bowditch (2001) 144–5.

[101] Cf. *Ep.* 1.7, in which Horace famously and unabashedly asserts his independence from Maecenas and his gifts, particularly the Sabine estate.

with the god of financial prosperity, thereby transforming an otherwise
perfunctory expression of gratitude into a lofty and traditional invocation to a deity.[102] This association is further confirmed by Horace's
deliberate use of the matronymic *Maia nate*, which, aside from reflecting the traditional Greek formula (cf. *Hom. Hymn Merc.* 1),[103] also
appears conveniently to echo his patron's name.[104] The allegorical
identification of a Roman benefactor as Mercury likewise appears in
Odes 1.2 (43: *filius Maiae*), although Horace's model was perhaps
Vergil's *Eclogues* 1, in which the shepherd Tityrus extols the source of
his rural property in the following manner (6–7): *O Meliboee, deus
nobis haec otia fecit. | namque erit ille mihi semper deus*, "O Meliboeus,
it is a god who wrought for us this peace—for a god he shall ever be to
me."[105] As Phoebe Bowditch explains, calling one's "human benefactor
a god is rhetorically consistent with the genre of the *eucharistikon*, a
speech of gratitude usually addressed directly to the donor in question."[106] In Horace's version, the connection to patronage is strongly
implied by means of the carefully chosen vocabulary: he is "pleased
with the favor" (13: *gratum iuvat*; cf. *Epod.* 1.24: *tuae spem gratiae*) of
Maia's son, who has granted him "gifts" (5: *munera*; cf. *Ep.* 1.7.18:
dono)[107] and who offers him protection as a "guardian" (15: *custos*; cf.
Odes 1.1.2: *praesidium*). Certainly Mercury could be regarded as
Horace's protector just as easily as Maecenas, since both offer assistance with regard to poetic activity: the former through inspiration and
the latter through his gift of a suitable venue for leisurely withdrawal.[108]

[102] According to Fraenkel (1957) 140 and Rudd (1966) 248, the religious tone of
this introductory prayer and the gravity of words such as *carmen* (22) are uncharac-
teristic of the *Satires* and look forward to his lyric odes. Courtney (2013) 151, however,
notes that he "would not press the point."
[103] Muecke (1993) 197. Cf. also Alcaeus' fragmentary hymn to Mercury, which
contains the phrase Μαῖα γέννατο (fr. 308b). Horace's imitation of this poem in *Odes*
1.10 begins with the vocative *Mercuri*, which, of course, would have been metrically
impossible in hexameter poetry.
[104] Oliensis (1998) 48, Bowditch (2001) 154, and Armstrong (2016) 205.
[105] Cf Sen. *Ben.* 3.15.4: *qui dat beneficia deos imitator*, "he who gives benefits
resembles the gods." Cf. also Lucr. 5.7–8 and see Welch (2008) 54–56 for the Epicurean
undertones of Vergil's *Eclogues*.
[106] Bowditch (2001) 125. For the genre itself, see DuQuesnay (1981) 98–103.
Philodemus' statement that the sage will receive "gratitude" (*On Property Management*, col. 23.27–8: εὐχάριστο[ν]) from a grateful patron comes to mind.
[107] The word *munus* is often associated with divine gifts (cf. Verg. *A.* 12.393 and
Cic. *Arch.* 18) as well as buildings or property.
[108] For the identification Maecenas = Mercury as parodic, see Bond (1985) 74–5.

Horace's acceptance of the Sabine estate when he was already prosperous may seem to contradict Epicurus' economic restrictions and views of natural wealth, which impose strict limits on financial success. The details related to the acquisition of his newfound estate, however, very much align with Philodemus' economic advice, which was explained in Chapter 1 but is worth revisiting briefly at this point. As mentioned already, Epicurus sanctioned moneymaking only out of dire necessity (DL 10.121b); in other words, wealth should be acquired for the purpose of satisfying the necessary desires associated with survival, such as food and drink. This is consistent with his view of natural wealth as the equivalent of having few possessions (SV 25), since such desires are easily satisfied and therefore cannot justify the acquisition of substantial resources (KD 15). Philodemus echoes this advice in his economic treatises, stating that poverty is a "good thing" (*On Wealth* 49.12: ἀγαθ[όν]), that the loss of resources is indifferent to happiness (col. 53.3–5), and that the sage will be content with the thought of living a poor and meager life, since nature is easily satisfied (*On Property Management*, col. 19.16–19). But he also cautiously suggests that responsibly acquired wealth, although contributing nothing of itself to happiness and pleasure, affords relief from difficulties and is conducive towards leisure and the contemplative life. It is, therefore, much preferable to a life of little means:

ἡ γὰρ ἐπιμέλεια καὶ τήρησις, ὅση πρέπει τῶι κατὰ τρόπον αὐτοῦ
προεστῶτι, παρέχει μὲν τιν᾽ ἐνίοτ᾽ ὄχλησιν, οὐ μὴν πλείω γε τοῦ κατὰ
τὸν ἐφήμερον [πο]ρισμόν, ἂν δὲ καὶ πλείω, τῶν ἄλ[λ]ων ὧν ἀπαλλάττει
δυσχερῶν [ο]ὐ πλεῖον᾽, ἂν μ[ὴ] δείξῃ τις ὡς οὐκ ἀποδί[δω]σιν ὁ φυσικὸς
πλοῦτος [πο]λλῶ[ι] μείζους τὰς ἐπικαρπίας ἢ τοὺς πόνους τῆς ἀπ᾽
[ὀ]λίγων ζωῆς, ὃ πολλοῦ δεήσε[ι παρ]ιστάνε[ιν.]

(*On Property Management*, col. 14. 9–23)

For the concern and vigilance fitting for one who takes proper care of his things do at times bring a certain amount of trouble, but certainly not more than the trouble that comes with the acquisition of daily needs; but even if it did, this trouble would not be greater than the other difficulties from which it frees us, unless anyone can prove that natural wealth does not in fact result in greater benefits by far than the hardships of a life of little means, a thing which he will be far from demonstrating.

The significance of Philodemus' point lies in the subtle but meaningful opposition between natural wealth and the "life of few possessions," which is different from Epicurus' equation of natural wealth with the possession of few things. This is not to say that Philodemus places the highest value on wealth; rather, like the Stoics he describes the change from wealth to poverty as indifferent with regard to happiness or virtue, and he rejects the notion that there is a great "difference" (col. 41.36–7: διαφορά . . . οὐ μεγάλη) between the two economic states, since both are able to produce "equal pleasures" (col. 56.5: ἴσ[ας] ἡδονάς; cf. *On Property Management*, col. 16.1–4). There is, however, a subtle yet important difference between the views of Philodemus and the Stoics. One may cite Stobaeus, for instance, according to whom Antipater regarded wealth as having "selective value" (2.83.10–84.2 = *SVF* 3.124: ἐκλεκτικὴ ἀξία), which means that, all things being equal, it should always be sought out or preferred to poverty. Added to this observation is that of Plutarch, who mentions how Chrysippus considered it madness not to pursue wealth in *On Common Conceptions* (1047e = *SVF* 3.138), and Cicero, who places no limit on wealth acquisition so long as "no one is harmed in the process" (*On Duties* 1.25: *amplificatio nemini nocens*).[109] In contrast to this, Philodemus never claims that wealth must be pursued as a moral obligation or that it can be amassed without limits so long as no one is harmed. Instead, he suggests that the sage accept wealth but simultaneously expresses the value of πενία, which the sage is never obligated to avoid (cf. *On Property Management*, coll. 15.45–16.4 and *On Wealth*, coll. 41.9–15 and 47.9–11). In the passage following the block quotation above, he carefully states that the Epicurean sage, though content with little and unwilling to suffer for the sake of wealth, merely "inclines in his wishes towards a more bountiful way of life" (*On Property Management*, col. 16.4–6: ῥέπει δὲ τῆι βουλήσει μᾶλλον ἐπὶ τὴν ἀφθονωτέραν).[110] Furthermore, Philodemus

---

[109] Cf. *On Duties* 2.87: *Res autem familiaris quaeri debet iis rebus a quibus abest turpitudo, conservari autem diligentia et parsimonia, eisdem etiam rebus augeri. Has res commodissime Xenophon Socraticus persecutus est in eo libro qui Oeconomicus inscribitur,* "As for property, it is a duty to seek for it (but only by means that are not dishonorable). It is also a duty to preserve one's property through diligence and thrift, and to increase it in the same way. Xenophon, the follower of Socrates, examined all of this most properly in his book entitled *Oeconomicus.*"

[110] In other words, the sage should coolly accept but not endeavor to accumulate wealth, which is "easily destroyed and easily taken away after all" (*On Wealth*, col. 54. 8–9: [εὔ]φθαρτός ἐσ[τι] καὶ [τελ]έως εὐαφαίρετος ὁ [πλ]οῦτος). This is consistent with Epicurus' teaching concerning the "independence" (SV 44: αὐτάρκεια) of living with few possessions. In this sense, Philodemus' expression "inclines in his wishes"

makes it clear that the sage freely accepts more wealth but only when it comes easily. In other words, he receives it from grateful patrons (e.g. Piso and Maecenas) rather than actively seeking it out (*On Property Management*, coll. 16.44–17.2). In this sense the Epicurean manager, who is content with little, prefers but does not *desire* to live affluently, and he receives more wealth when it does not involve much toil and, in the ideal situation, in the form of "gratitude" (*S*. 2.6.13: *gratum*; cf. *On Property Management*, col. 23.27–8: εὐχάριστο[ν]) from patrons and friends.

The preceding summary of Philodemus' defense of wealth, which differs from the more restrictive attitude of Epicurus, may help to contextualize morally Horace's acquisition of the Sabine estate. This property, far from being a "tiny farm" like that of his father (*S*. 1.6.71: *macro pauper agello*) or Ofellus (*S*. 2.2.114: *metato in agello*), was likely a rather spacious property with agricultural potential. The size of his beloved "farm" is hinted at in the introductory description of *Epistles* 1.14:

> Vilice siluarum et mihi me reddentis agelli,
> quem tu fastidis habitatum quinque focis et
> quinque bonos solitum Variam dimittere patres   (1–3)

> Bailiff of my woods and of the little farm which makes me myself again—while you disdain it, though it is the home of five households and wont to send to Varia their five honest heads . . .

Horace's description of his estate as a "little farm" may easily be read either as a playful understatement or as an allusion to the bailiff's disdain, especially since it contradicts the subsequent emphasis on the fact that it contains *five* hearths and provides shelter for *five* households. As Roland Mayer notes, "the repetition [of *quinque*] boasts of the size of his holding" and also underscores his financial success as the client of a wealthy patron.[111] In fact, archaeological evidence from the remains outside of modern Licenza (ancient Digentia, not far from Varia mentioned above), which many have identified as the site of the Sabine estate,[112] appears to contradict the poet's many descriptions of its humble nature (cf *Odes* 2.16.37: *parva rura* and 3.29.14:

---

certainly does not imply a "desire for wealth" (*On Wealth*, col. 58.8–9: τῆς [ἐ]πιθυμίας τῆς π[ρ]ὸς πλοῦτον), which is reprehensible.

[111] Mayer (1994) 206. Cf. Mayer (1995) 293.
[112] See Frischer (1995b) 214–15.

parvo sub lare).[113] The reality is that the site identified with Horace's Sabine estate measures 1,300 meters^2 in terms of area, which is only slightly smaller than that of the luxurious Villa of the Papyri in Herculaneum (1,600 meters^2) and does not include the probable existence of a second floor.[114] In fact, according to contemporary standards of land size in terms of *iugera* (approximately two-thirds of an acre) as Ernst Schmidt calculates them, Horace's Sabine estate would have been around 321 *iugera*, which places the "small farm" in the category of estates with medium-sized productivity.[115] The evidence also reveals that the outside of what may be the Sabine estate featured peristyle architecture quite similar to that of the Villa of the Papyri, and that the bases of its columns were made of pink-and-yellow marble imported from Numidia (contrary to Horace's repudiation in *Odes* 2.18.4 of *columnas ultima recisas | Africa*, "columns hewn from Africa beyond"). This material is obviously costly, but, as Varro shows in *On Agriculture*, even the colonnade style itself is associated with eastern luxury:

> ... nec putant se habere villam, si non multis vocabulis retinniat Graecis, quom vocent particulatim loca, procoetona, palaestram, apodyterion, peristylon, ornithona, peripteron, oporothecen.   (2.1)

---

[113] Frischer (1995b) 220 notes that, since Horace was writing satire rather than a traveler's guide in the style of Stabo or Pausanias, "it is not surprising that his descriptions of his villa are far from being accurate and have been crafted with a generous amount of false modesty" ("non sorprende che le descrizioni della sua villa siano lontane dall'essere accurate e siano elaborate con una buona quantità di falsa modestia").

[114] Frischer (1995b) 216. For evidence regarding the existence of a second level, which depends largely on the relative thickness of inner walls (16 to 18 inches) that "compare favorably in thickness with the walls of some of the two-story houses in Pompeii," see Price (1932) 139. Leach (1993) 272, reporting the observations of this young philologist regarding the remains of Horace's villa in Italy, states: "[H]is confrontation with the architectural actualities disturbed his literary preconceptions in one particular. The unanticipated spaciousness of the villa and its properties seemed out of keeping with Horace's own protestations of a modest lifestyle."

[115] Schmidt (1997) 21, drawing from ancient sources including Cato the Elder, Columella, and Pliny the Younger, calculates the land requirements for Horace as follows: 45 *iugera* for a family living in the country multiplied by 5 (cf. *Ep.* 1.14.2–3) equals 225 *iugera*. To this he adds 12 *iugera* per slave and multiplies that by 8 (cf. *S.* 2.7.118) to equal a total of 321 *iugera*. The three categories are: 10–80 *iugera*, small productivity; 80–500, medium-sized productivity; more than 500 *iugera*, large productivity on par with Roman *latifundia*. Like Seneca, our poet delivers philosophical criticisms of luxury and excess that are not necessarily invalidated by his personal but responsible enjoyment of what appears to be substantial wealth, as Schmidt (1997) 26 notes.

Nor do owners reckon they own a villa at all unless they can refer to each and every part of it using fancy Greek terms, like "entrance-room," "exercise-room," "dressing-room," "colonnade," "aviary," "pergola," and "fruit-room."

Based on the architecture and the nature of the remaining mosaic fragments as well as frescos and other decorations, Bernard Frischer has even entertained the possibility that Horace's estate was actually modelled on the luxurious Herculaneum villa, which of course is where Philodemus' works were preserved and where there was a thriving Epicurean community and school.[116]

Horace also hints at the superiority of this property in *Satires* 2.6 by mentioning its size and quality, both of which have exceeded his moderate hopes (1–4): *Hoc erat in votis: modus agri non ita magnus... auctius atque | di melius fecere*, "This is what I prayed for!—a piece of land not so very large... More and better than this have the gods done for me."[117] His use of *modus* is noteworthy, for in addition to being a technical term indicating a measure of land (cf. Plaut. *Pot of Gold* 13: *agri reliquit ei non magnum modum*, "He left him not a large measure of land"), this word elsewhere denotes the proper measure which corresponds to moderation and correct behavior.[118] The Sabine estate, however, clearly exceeds this important measure or limit, which is a very strange admission on the poet's part that is paralleled only by his recognition of Maecenas' generosity in *Epodes* 1 (31–2): *satis superque me benignitas tua | ditavit*, "enough has your generosity enriched me and more than enough."[119] As scholars have noted, the mention of *divitiae* is undoubtedly a reference to the Sabine estate, the overall quality of which, shockingly enough, appears to violate Horace's persona's usual demand for moderation

---

[116] Frischer (1995b) 211–29. Roskam (2007) 175 similarly states that "Horace's Sabine estate was probably not a simple farm; it could be compared to luxurious villas such as the *Villa dei papyri* at Herculaneum."

[117] Lyne (1995) 20. Kiessling–Heinze (1910) 257 interestingly translate *auctius atque melius* as "reichlicher und besser" ("richer and better").

[118] See Muecke (1993) 196 and Gowers (2012) 81 for this double meaning.

[119] Catullus famously employs this same phrase in poem 7 and equates it with the "great number of grains of sands in Libya" (3: *magnus numerus Libyssae harenae*) and of the "many stars in the night sky" (7: *sidera multa, cum tacet nox*). As mentioned already, both Catullus (cf. esp. 13 and 28) and Horace employ the conventional "poverty of the poet" motif in their works, which makes the latter's few admissions to having great wealth all the more unusual.

and contentment. Besides this if Suetonius' testimony is taken into account, it seems that Horace was the recipient of not one but possibly two or three—depending on the interpretation of *Sabini aut Tiburtini*—properties (*Life of Horace*): *vixit plurimum in secessu ruris sui Sabini aut Tiburtini, domusque ostenditur circa Tiburni luculum,* "He lived for the most part either in his Sabine or Tiburtine country retreat, and a house of his is visible near the grove of Tiburnus."[120] Indeed, the actual magnitude of what many modern commentators (undoubtedly misled by Horace) inaccurately describe as a "farm" is carefully and discreetly revealed by the poet himself.[121] Despite the bailiff's complaints regarding the Sabine estate's inability to produce wine in *Epistles* 1.14, for instance, Phoebe Bowditch notes that "the farm appears to be a place of *fructus*, producing goods for the market at Varia," and that "insofar as Horace's estate . . . returns him to himself, such spiritual commerce depends on the very real economic returns."[122] In his epistolary correspondence with Quinctius the poet again addresses the issue of the Sabine estate's agricultural productivity (*Ep.* 1.16.1–16), which consequently indicates something about its economic potential, as Eleanor Windsor Leach notes:

> The hypothetical questions he attributes to Quinctius locate his description within the discourse of agricultural self-sufficiency. All the products he has listed—crops, olives, orchards, pasturage, and vines—imply a major agricultural establishment, suggesting that the question being answered is really, "How large and how productive is the farm?" If we were to answer this question on the basis of Horace's offerings in Ode 1.17 to Tyndaris, of *copia . . . ruris honorum opulenta,* we would have to

---

[120] Lyne (1995) 9–11 also accounts for Horace's extended description of a retreat at Tarentum at *Odes* 2.6 (cf. *Ep.* 1.7.45: *sed vacuum Tibur placet aut inbelle Tarentum,* "either unpopulated Tibur pleases me or peaceful Tarentum") and of the townhouse he had acquired soon after his purchase of the post of *scriba* in *Satires* 1.6.

[121] See Oliensis (1998) 42, Leach (1993) 275–6, and Lyne (1995) 6.

[122] Bowditch (2001) 235. On the other hand, in light of Horace's mention of Sabine wine in *Odes* 1.9 (8: *quadrimum Sabina*) and 1.20 (1: *vile . . . Sabinum*), as well as his mention of "my vines" in *Epistles* 1.8 (5: *vitis*), it seems possible that he was in fact able to produce wine on the estate. See Schmidt (1997) 18–20, esp. nn. 38 and 42: "The negative catalogue in *Odes* 3.16 (33–6) of honey, wine, and sheep in that order obviously does not mean that Horace did not grow or produce any of these items at all, but that he lacked the ability to produce a significantly superior quality of them on his estate." "Der Negativkatalog in c. 3,16,33–36 der neben Bienen Wein und Schafe nennt . . . bedeutet offenbar nicht, daß Horaz dies alles nicht besitze, sondern, daß es ihm in der dort genannten superioren Qualität fehle,"

say "very productive," but in the immediate situation Horace plays down productivity.[123]

All of this, of course, begs the question: how are we to reconcile Horace's status as a successful and almost opulent proprietor of a productive estate with Epicurean frugality and the importance of *vivere parvo* expressed in *Satires* 2.2 (1)? As suggested above, the answer lies in the views expressed by Philodemus in his economic treatises, which sanction the acquisition of wealth under specific conditions. The first important observation is that, in accordance with Philodemus' teaching, Horace neither pursues wealth nor does he constantly desire more like the "foolish" manager (*S.* 2.6.8: *stultus*).[124] On the contrary, he is able to "endure Poverty" (*Odes* 1.1.18: *pauperiem pati*), whom he "courts and whose virtue is her own dowry" (*Odes* 3.29.55–6: *probamque | pauperiem sine dote quaero*) since she is easily satisfied and always provides "what is enough" (*Ep.* 1.2.46: *quod satis est*).[125] In spite of this profound respect for poverty and his overall contentment, however, Horace clearly indicates that he is not poor: as a result of his patron's generosity, not only does he "lack troublesome poverty" (*Odes* 3.16.37: *inportuna tamen pauperies abest*; cf. *Ep.* 2.2.199: *pauperies . . . absit*) but he enjoys substantial wealth, as he plainly states in a later correspondence (*Ep.* 1.7.15): *tu me fecisti locupletem* ("You have made me rich").[126] The point is that Horace, like the Epicurean manager, does not grab, he accepts[127] (cf. especially *Ep.* 1.17.44–45: *distat, sumasne pudenter | an rapias*, "it makes a difference whether you accept rewards prudently or snatch them away"), and that this prosperity is

---

[123] Leach (1993) 281. Cf. Barbieri (1976) 501, who notes that Horace "does not show interest in the output or the economic characteristics of his estate" ("non mostra interesse per la rendita e per le carateristiche economiche del fondo"). On this poem in general, see Kilpatrick (1986) 96–9. For a study of the differences between the poetic and historical Sabine property, see Frischer (1995a) 31–45.

[124] Rudd (1966) 243–4.

[125] See Vischer (1965) 147–52, whose analysis does not consider the fact that, despite Horace's respect for poverty, he was willing to accept wealth.

[126] For the meaning of this adjective, which is rarely applied to people, as denoting "abundant in land" (i.e. *locus* + *plenus*), see Cic. *Rep.* 2.9.16: *quod tunc erat res in pecore et locorum possessionibus, ex quo pecuniosi et locupletes vocabantur*, "Because in the past wealth was understood in terms of livestock and the possession of land: whence people were called *pecuniosi* or *locupletes*." Philodemus mentions the troubles and difficulties associated with poverty and wealth's ability to remove them at *On Property Management*, col. 14.9–23.

[127] Cf. Asmis (2004) 159.

the result of a generous patron's favor, which he freely receives and responsibly enjoys without toil or anxiety. As he makes perfectly clear in *Epistles* 1.7, the poet is certainly not afraid to lose his wealth or return to a state of poverty, but he presently requests that, if possible, his newfound fortune should last a lifetime (*S.* 2.6.4–5): *oro, |... ut propria haec mihi munera faxis,* "My only prayer is that you should make these gifts mine forever" (Cf. *On Property Management,* col. 13.34–9: τινὰ δὲ δεκ[τέον], ὧν καὶ τὸν πλοῦτον, τ[ὸ] βάρος ἔχοντα με[ῖ]ον ὅταν παρῇι, μᾶλλον π[ρ]ὸς ὅλον [βί]ον ἀλλὰ μὴ πρός τ[ι]να καιρό[ν], "Certain things ought to be accepted, among which is wealth, since it is less of a burden when present, especially if it lasts a lifetime rather than for a moment").[128] Far from attempting to avoid poverty and desiring limitless wealth, therefore, Horace simply "inclines in his wishes" towards affluence. And as he consciously demonstrates in the rest of *Satires* 2.6, his decision to accept such prosperity reflects Philodemus' concern for applying the pleasure calculus to every economic decision and ensuring that increased wealth does not result in increased pain.

Rather than functioning as a superficial foil to the later description of country life,[129] Horace's account of the cares associated with Rome in *Satires* 2.6 (23–57) are necessary for justifying his acceptance of the Sabine estate and his leisurely withdrawal there with friends. Following the poet's second prayer to a deity, which, despite the grandiloquent tone, is merely a "counterpoint to his own rueful groans,"[130]

---

[128] Unlike the paternal inheritance he lost in the confiscations. On the formulaic nature of this prayer, see Muecke (1993) 197. On the difference between ownership and use of the Sabine estate, Bowditch (2001) 149–50 and cf. *Satires* 2.2 (112–15). It is important to note that, despite his grateful acceptance of this gift, Horace clearly states in *Epistles* 1.7 that he would not hesitate to return it if it began to threaten his peace of mind:

> nec somnum plebis laudo satur altilium nec
> otia divitiis Arabum liberrima muto.
> saepe verecundum laudasti rexque paterque
> audisti coram nec verbo parcius absens;
> inspice, si possum donata reponere laetus.   (*Ep.* 1.7.35–49)

I neither praise the poor man's sleep, when I am fed full on capons, nor would I barter my ease and my freedom for all the wealth of Araby. Often have you praised my modesty, and have been called "king" and "father" to you face, nor do I stint my words behind your back. Try me, whether I can restore your gifts, and cheerfully too.

[129] Fraenkel (1957) 142.

[130] Rudd (1966) 249. See also Courtney (2013) 151.

he introduces a long list of duties and responsibilities, all of which violently thrust him (24: *urge*) into the bustling, crowded streets of Rome (28: *in turba*).[131] The setting is aptly conveyed by the turbulent weather that accompanies him (25: *sive aquilo radit terras seu bruma*, "whether the north-wind sweeps the earth or winter . . . ") and projects his interior, psychological disturbances (26: *interiore . . . gyro*) all the way to the "black Esquiline" (32–3: *atras | . . . Esquilias*), which used to be salubrious (cf. *S.* 1.8.14) but is now the source of infinite anxieties (33: *negotia centum*). Through his vivid description of the innumerable cares and problems of urban life, Horace intentionally obscures the real source of his wealth, which is not the pastoral god Mercury but the city-dweller Maecenas. Ellen Oliensis, perhaps unknowingly, establishes a connection between Horace and the Philodemean "acceptance of wealth" doctrine:

> Horace's country retreat is not just an alternative to but a gift from the city, a crumb, as it were, from the master's table. Unlike the country mouse, that is, Horace has chosen the path not of virtuous poverty but of (to give it its best construction) virtuous wealth—his relation with Maecenas involves *usus* as well as *rectum*.[132]

Of course, the dizzying flurry of requests and demands which buffets the audience for almost thirty lines (29–56) provides the perfect setup for Horace's contrasting description of the serenity and tranquility of country living, which, instead of reminders and early business meetings (37: *meminisses*, 34: *ante secundam*; cf. *S.* 1.6.122: *ad quartam iaceo*) offers sleep and forgetfulness (*S.* 2.6.61: *somno* and 62: *iucunda oblivia*). Catullus offers a similar description of the tranquility and peace offered by his own rural escape to Sirmio:

---

[131] Cf. Juvenal's more detailed description of life on the busy streets of Rome (3.236–59). As Hicks (2013) 231 observes in connection with this passage, "part of what it means to be an Epicurean in Rome concerns the creation of a viable middle path between politics and duty to society on the one hand, and commitment to Epicurean *ataraxia* on the other. Thus, one of the goals is to discern how to retain that sense of *ataraxia* even while engaged in city life." The Epicureans did not condemn involvement in politics outright, but they acknowledged that such involvement typically leads to cares and anxieties. See Roskam (2007) 104–15.

[132] Oliensis (1998) 50. She also states that Horace is partly attempting to establish his independence and "defend himself from charges of unmanly subservience" (51), although it should be noted that, according to Horace's own words, he has not chosen wealth but freely accepted it (cf. the passive tone of admissions like *benignitas tua me ditavit* and *tu me fecisti locupletem*). Braund (1989) 42 describes Horace's negative account of life in the city as intended to "condemn the jealousy and curiosity" of others.

> o quid solutis est beatius curis,
> cum mens onus reponit, ac peregrino
> labore fessi venimus larem ad nostrum
> desideratoque acquiescimus lecto?   (31.7–10)

What is more blessed than to have done away with cares, when the mind rests from its toil and when we, drained by our labor, come to our own home and rest upon the couch we longed for?

The identification of Catullus' rural getaway resembles that of Horace in the sense that, along with being a kind of stronghold or refuge from worldly cares (cf. *S.* 2.6.16: *in arcem ex urbe*), it appears to be an ideal venue for convivial gatherings. Catullus suggests this not so much by the plurals *venimus* and *acquiescimus*, which probably refer to the owner alone (that is, the poet), but by the fact that villas were generally places of gathering, as the mention of laughter and mirth at the end of the poem suggest (14): *ridete quidquid est domi cachinnorum*, "laugh out loud all the laughter that is in your halls" (cf. 13.5: *et vino et sale et omnibus cachinnis*, "with wine and wit and all manner of laughter," and also Lucr. 5.1397–8: *tum ioca, tum sermo, tum dulces esse cachinni | consuerant*, "then cheer, friendly conversations and sweet laughter became common"). What is not revealed is the substance of the conversation at the villa in Sirmio, which makes Catullus' description distinct from that of Horace.

More specifically, the Sabine estate offers Horace as landowner and host the opportunity to provide his friends with the kind of leisurely withdrawal into a rural stronghold that is conducive toward philosophical discussions.[133] After a convivial meal and a few rounds of relaxed and free drinking, which recalls the hospitality of Ofellus in *Satires* 2.2 (118–25), philosophical debate among equals begins:

> sermo oritur, non de villis domibusve alienis,
> nec male necne Lepos saltet; sed, quod magis ad nos
> pertinet et nescire malum est,[134] agitamus; utrumne
> divitiis homines an sint virtute beati,

---

[133] See Braund (1989) 40. Cf. also Verg. *G.* 2.458–74 for the pleasures of country life, which includes plenty of *otium* and *secura quies*.

[134] Cf. *Ep.* 1.1.24–6 (note especially the opposition of *pauperes*, i.e. people like Ofellus and Horace's father, to *locupletes*, i.e. Horace himself): *id quod | aeque pauperibus prodest, locupletibus aeque, | aeque neglectum pueris senibusque nocebit* ("[Philosophy], which shall benefit the poor and the rich alike, and which will be damaging to both children and old people if neglected").

quidve ad amicitias, usus rectumne, trahat nos
et quae sit natura boni summumque quid eius.   (*S.* 2.6.71–6)

Conversation arises, not about other people's villas or town-houses, not
whether Lepos dances badly or not, but we discuss what has more
relevance to us and not to know is an evil: whether it is wealth or virtue
that makes men happy; or what leads us to friendships, self-interest, or
rectitude; and what is the nature of goodness and what its highest form.

This scene, which identifies the contemplative life and the search for
wisdom among friends as the perfect expression of tranquility,
reflects Cicero's idealized portrait of Cato (*On Old Age* 46), but also
recalls Philodemus' description of landownership as an acceptable
source of income:

ἥκιστα γὰρ ἐπιπλοκὰς ἔχει πρὸς ἀνθρώπους, ἐξ ὧν ἀηδίαι πολλαὶ
παρακολουθοῦσι, καὶ διαγωγὴν ἐπιτερπῆ καὶ μετὰ φίλων ἀναχώρησιν
εὔσχολον   (*On Property Management*, col. 23.11–16)

For it brings the least involvement with men from whom many difficulties follow, since it offers a pleasant life and a leisurely withdrawal
among friends . . .

These "men from whom many difficulties follow" appear to correspond to individuals such as Horace's colleagues from the quaestor-
ship (cf. *S.* 2.6.36–7) as well as the other nameless individuals whose
requests "dance around my head and on all sides" (34: *per caput et
circa saliunt latus*). According to David Armstrong's threefold division of Epicurean friendship as explained in Chapter 1, the poet's
connections to these men in the city would correspond to F1 or the
utilitarian understanding of friendship as a means of security and
safety originating in the goodwill of others.[135] In contrast to the trivial
concerns related to such urban business, the poet's country villa
provides the setting for philosophical conversation, the informal
and friendly nature of which is effectively communicated by the
conviviality of the gathering as well as the mention of "chats" (118:
sermo; cf. *S.* 1.1.42: *sermoni propriora* and *On Property Management*, col. 23.30–3).[136] This description would in turn correspond

---

[135] Armstrong (2016) 182–93 and 206.
[136] For Philodemus' implied contrast between leisurely discussions and the formal
debates characteristic of forensic oratory, see Tsouna (2012) 97. Zetzel (2016) 58 is
worth quoting here: "Horace's version of street-philosophy . . . calls attention to a
different kind of philosophical discourse at Rome that shows every sign of having

to the second level of Epicurean friendship or F2, which involves a much more intimate relationship described as "undying" and characterized by "close companionship" and "wondering admiration."[137] David Armstrong even says that the above passage is "portrayed in an artificially pure form... morally and spatially and even temporally separated from the urban daytime world of F1," especially since it resembles the ideal friendship of the gods (which he calls F3; cf. *S.* 2.6.65: *o noctes cenaeque deum!*, "O nights and feasts of the gods!") in being set aside from all considerations of utility and centered on equality and the detached contemplation of the highest things.[138] Furthermore, this kind of leisure is made possible by the complete absence of labor, which Horace associates exclusively with the city (21: *operum... labores*). Whether at home in the city or on the estate, Horace portrays himself as preoccupied with philosophy and poetry, while his meals are served by personal waiters (*S.* 1.6.116: *pueris tribus*) or household slaves (*S.* 2.6.66: *vernas procacis*),[139] and elsewhere he implies that agricultural work in the Sabine fields is performed by a team of at least eight laborers (*S.* 2.7.118: *opera agro nona Sabino*).[140] Horace's mention of laborers within the context of his repeated emphasis on rural *otium* echoes the advice of Philodemus, who also emphasizes the importance of delegating manual labor to servants in order to make oneself available to one's friends and to the pursuit of wisdom (*On Property Management*, col. 23.7–11): ταλαίπωρον δὲ καὶ τὸ "γεωργο[ῦν]τ᾽ αὐτὸν οὕτως ὥστε αὐτουργεῖν"· τὸ δ᾽ "ἄλλων, ἔχοντα γῆν" κατὰ σπουδαῖον, "but 'cultivating land oneself so as to be actively involved' is wretched, whereas 'having others do the work on the land one owns' is appropriate." This freedom from manual labor allows one time for more important things such as the topics of discussion Horace mentions, which, in addition to reflecting current debates among contemporary philosophical sects, also highlights wealth (*S.* 2.6.74:

been much more vigorous than Cicero's dialogues: Horatian satire at least pretends to represent philosophy as a topic of everyday conversation and general interest."

[137] Armstrong (2016) 183.
[138] See Armstrong (2016) 206–7 for this interpretation and relevant passages from Philodemus' *On the Gods*.
[139] See Armstrong (1986) 278–9 for the luxury involved in Horace's gentlemanly way of life and his ownership of servants.
[140] As discussed already, Horace also employed the services of a bailiff when away from the country.

divitiis), friendship (75: *amicitias*), and tranquility (76: *summum bonum*) as the primary concerns of Epicurean economic theory.

The fact that *Satires* 2.5 and 2.6 appear alongside one another is no surprise if one considers the message they communicate and its relevance for Horace's satiric persona. The poet is able to strengthen his self-portrayal as a virtuous client whose frank advice results in financial rewards from a wealthy patron by contrasting it with that of Ulysses, whose riches are a result of opportunistic and ambitious flattery. Horace's description in *Satires* 2.6 is didactic in the sense that it serves as a model of how an Epicurean sympathizer should accept substantial wealth from a grateful patron when it comes easily and leads to the pleasure of philosophical enrichment. As will be seen in the next chapter, the poet augments this Philodemean lesson in wealth acquisition and administration in *Satires* 2.2, which complements 2.6 as advice on how to deal with financial crises and the loss of wealth in general. This is communicated by Ofellus, a rustic sage whose useful and pithy advice, which is largely an adaptation of Epicurean ethical doctrines, differs greatly from the much less constructive—and far less pithy—criticisms of the Stoic enthusiast Damasippus in the next poem. Overall, Horace's portrayal of the overly harsh views of both Damasippus in *Satires* 2.3 and Davus in *Satires* 2.7 reconnect the audience with his observations in *Satires* 1.3 concerning the Stoics' impossible standards and ineffectual style of offering frank criticism.

5

Deficient Wealth, Excessive Frankness

Satires 2.2, 2.3, and 2.7

UNUSUAL ECONOMISTS IN *SATIRES* 2.2 AND 2.3

Through his poetic persona Horace communicates the importance of being a virtuous client-friend and knowing when and how to accept wealth in various poems in both books of the *Satires*. He does so indirectly through characters that embody social vice and shameless ambition like the toady and Ulysses, but he also underscores his ethical message concerning economics and the reception of substantial wealth in a more direct manner in *Satires* 2.6. This portrayal of Horace accepting greater wealth than he had expected, along with his remarkable description of philosophical *noctes cenaeque* on the estate as equaling those of the gods (65), is suitably complemented by his description of Ofellus in *Satires* 2.2. One may regard these poems as illustrating the proper way to acquire and enjoy money, with the toady and Ulysses functioning as counter-examples leading up to the positive scene in *Satires* 2.6, which in turn may be read alongside *Satires* 2.2 as an observation regarding the true nature of wealth and how to respond to its acquisition as well as its loss. Taking these two complementary poems into consideration, the general message seems to be, as will be discussed in this chapter, the following: although the Epicurean manager certainly accepts wealth whenever it comes easily and provides one with more opportunities to enjoy leisure and philosophical discussion, as Philodemus explains in *On Property Management* and as Horace demonstrates through his self-portrayal as host on the Sabine estate, like Ofellus he is not anxious about losing it because he knows that the requirements of nature are easily fulfilled.[1] Furthermore, the Epicurean manager views the pleasure offered by the bonds of friendship in such a way that, even if financial disaster should strike, he would continue to live as contentedly and cheerfully as ever. All of this provides an interesting contrast with Horace's portrayal of Damasippus in *Satires* 2.3, who, unlike Ofellus, has not borne his own financial difficulties in a virtuous manner but, emboldened by the Stoic teaching that "all fools are mad," freely delivers critical advice on the proper administration of wealth.

In *Satires* 2.2 Horace's persona indirectly expounds the virtues of economic restraint by casting philosophical precepts into the mouth of a rustic sage, whose portrayal as a conservative Roman recalls *Satires* 1.4 and similarly conceals "suspicious" Greek doctrines.[2] The sage is identified as Ofellus, an Apulian local who had recently been dispossessed of his "little farm" (*S.* 2.2.114: *metato . . . agello*), which is a financial loss he has borne with equanimity and transformed into the opportunity for an Epicurean diatribe on simple living:

> Quae virtus et quanta, boni, sit vivere parvo,
> —nec meus hic sermo est, sed quae praecepit Ofellus
> rusticus, abnormis sapiens crassaque Minerva—,
> discite non inter lances mensasque nitentis   (*S.* 2.2.1–4)

What and how great, my friends, is the virtue of frugal living—now this is no talk of mine, but is the teaching of Ofellus, a peasant, a philosopher unschooled and of rough mother-wit—learn, I say, not amid the tables' shining dishes . . .

---

[1] Wealth, in other words, is not necessary for obtaining the pleasure that comes from philosophical conversation and friendship, as the life of Ofellus proves.

[2] With regard to his role as speaker, Palmer (1893) 255 says that Horace quotes Ofellus verbatim throughout the poem, although Rudd (1966) 171 and Courtney (2013) 131 think that the rustic's knowledge of Plato and other authors makes this highly unlikely. Muecke (1993) 114 notes that very little of what is said in this dialogue belongs unequivocally to Ofellus. Rather than displaying the "excessive zeal" Anderson (1982) 44 attributes to both him and Damasippus, however, Ofellus is a model of restraint and virtue. The truth regarding the speaker is most likely somewhere in between these views: Horace represents the "teachings of Ofellus" (2: *quae praecepit Ofellus*) not verbatim but in his own words and as a satirist with artistic concerns, as Hicks (2013) 214–15 notes. But since his persona claims that these "teachings" essentially belong to the rustic sage and since he even quotes from Ofellus (cf. 116: *narrantem*) in order to voice his persona's convictions (the two clearly agree on the issue at hand), for the purpose of this examination he will be regarded as Horace's spokesman.

The character of Ofellus resembles Horace's father, who was also a type of rustic sage who was not rich but once owned a "small farm" (*S.* 1.6.71: *macro pauper agello*) and whose virtuous ability to live frugally and content with few possessions is transmitted to others as precepts.[3] Ofellus also resembles the poet himself, who similarly lost his land as a result of the resettlement program and communicates philosophical advice through informal *sermones* (cf. *S.* 1.4.49, 2.2.2, and 2.6.71) with friends.[4] And while it is possible that Ofellus was a historical figure known to Horace in his youth (cf. *S.* 2.2.112–13: *puer hunc ego parvus Ofellum* | ... *novi*),[5] the parallels between this rustic sage and the poet suggest that the former functions as the latter's mouthpiece for communicating philosophical and economic advice to a contemporary Roman audience. As with his father, in *Satires* 2.2 Horace attempts to disassociate his surrogate from the Greek philosophical tradition by emphasizing his rusticity and homespun wisdom.[6] Furthermore, both his qualification of Ofellus as an unschooled sage and the use of Athena's Roman name emphasize his portrayal as a traditional local (3: *abnormis sapiens crassaque Minerva*; cf. Cicero's preference for local, Roman examples of virtue over the more rigid and extreme demands of the Stoics in *On Friendship* 19: *agamus igitur pingui ut aiunt Minerva*, "let us then have recourse to our own 'dull wits,' as they say"). This description also contrasts with the exotic luxury and overindulgence that for centuries traditional Romans had associated with the effeminate East, as implied a few lines later (*S.* 2.2.10–11): *si Romana fatigat* | *militia adsuetum graecari*, "If Roman military training is too rigorous for one accustomed to Greek culture... "[7] On the other hand, the abundance of philosophical terms (*virtus* = ἀρετή; *boni* = ἀγαθοί; *sapiens* = σοφός), the reference to

---

[3] Barbieri (1976) 486 acknowledges some of these parallels.

[4] This connection is also made by Coffey (1976) 83, Oliensis (1998) 54, and Freudenburg (2001) 99.

[5] For the rare historical and epigraphic evidence for this name, which appears to be Oscan, see Schulze (1904) 291.

[6] See also Lejay and Plessis (1915) 374, Kiessling–Heinze (1910) 168, and Courtney (2013) 131. Muecke (1993) 117 notes that, although Ofellus is a home-schooled rustic, he nevertheless transmits his values "in the terms of Hellenistic ethics." Bond (1980) 114–23 argues for "conscious inconsistency" in Horace's depiction of Ofellus, whom he views as an Italian rustic with a knack for (in Bond's view) mostly Stoic doctrines.

[7] See Rudd (1966) 161–5, who notes that *austerum* (12), *discus* (13), and *aera* (13) are Greek importations. Also Muecke (1993) 118. Juvenal offers similar criticism (11.100–2).

Socratic frugality (*vivere parvo*; cf. *Odes* 2.16.13: *vivitur parvo bene*), which, according to Cicero, was the ideal of Greek philosophers like Epicurus (*Tusc.* 5.89; cf. also the almost identical expression of Lucretius at 5.1118–19: *divitiae grandes homini sunt vivere parce | aequo animo*, "for man the greatest wealth is to live frugally and with a calm mind"), and the learned imitation of the Platonic opening "this is not my story" (*Sym.* 177a: οὐ γὰρ ἐμὸς ὁ μῦθος)[8] appear to communicate something more. Collaboratively they threaten to destroy the poet's smokescreen and reveal that what follows is a sophisticated reflection that draws partly from various philosophical traditions, especially in connection with Epicurean convictions relating to wealth.

Regarding the delivery of Ofellus' advice, it has been noted by scholars like G. C. Fiske that his portrayal as a lowly but fervent preacher borrows many elements from the Cynic tradition,[9] although his identification as an Epicurean sage may actually be a better fit. The rustic sage's rejection of the *sordidus victus* (*S.* 2.2.53–69) typically associated with Cynic ἀναίδεια is not only consistent with the views of Horace's persona in the *Satires*, but it also reflects the views of conservative Romans like Cicero (cf. *On Duties* 1.130).[10] Unlike the Stoics, moreover, whose philosophical ideal was extreme and unattainable enough to elicit playful sarcasm from the poet in *Epistles* 1.1 (106–8), Epicurus' universal invitation to philosophy (cf. *Men.* 122) effectively attracted Romans from all walks of life, including, as Cicero notes in *On Ends*, respectable but not fully educated rustics like Ofellus:

> itaque ut maiores nostri ab aratro adduxerunt Cincinnatum illum ut dictator esset, sic vos de plagis omnibus colligitis bonos illos quidem viros, sed certe non pereruditos.   (2.12)

> Just as our ancestors brought old Cincinnatus from the plough to be dictator, so you ransack the country villages for your assemblage of doubtless respectable but certainly not profoundly learned adherents.

One may note the connection between Cicero's *bonos* and Ofellus' identification of his audience as *boni* (*S.* 2.2.1), which R. P. Bond,

---

[8] Some of these philosophical parallels are also given by Kiessling–Heinze (1910) 168, Rudd (1966) 170, Muecke (1993) 116, Freudenburg (2001) 110–11, and Courtney (2013) 131. For *aequo animo* as the Latin equivalent of Epicurean tranquility of mind, see Welch (2008) 51.

[9] Fiske (1971) 379: "In this satire Ofellus is a Romanized counterpart of the popular Cynic preacher, who is used as the mouthpiece for Horace's own philosophical ideas, just as Horace's father was in satire 1.4."

[10] For the evidence, see Griffin (1996) 190–6.

briefly tracing its development from the Classical period in which it refers strictly to the landed aristocracy (cf. the Roman usage), to Aristotle, in whose writings it takes on the moral and philosophical meaning of "virtuous," identifies as the Greek equivalent of ἀγαθοί.[11] As landowners and individuals who had achieved independence and financial success to some degree, these men would have been entitled to their convictions regarding virtue and the good life (like Horace's father in *Satires* 1.4), even if they had not received formal training in philosophy. Aside from being virtuous, Epicurus also states that, like Ofellus, the sage will be "fond of the countryside" (DL 10.120a: φιλαγρήσειν) and will closely associate the practise of philosophy with economic matters (cf. SV 41). One wonders, therefore, whether this connection influenced Horace's choice to portray his sage as a country-dwelling local whose advice is economic in nature, or even whether the name Ofellus is intended to evoke the concept of ὠφελία in the context of economics (cf. *On Property Management*, col. 27.39: ὠφελή[σ]οντος).[12] One thing is certain: the nature of Horace's spokesman's economic advice in this satire rules out any substantial connection to ὠφελία among Cynics, who reject all of the conventions of modern life including, of course, money and the benefits of its proper administration.[13]

Following the introduction of Ofellus as Horace's authoritative replacement is an extended consideration of the requirements of nature as easily satisfied and affording the "highest pleasure" (*S.* 2.2.19–20: *voluptas | summa*). This is briefly prefaced by the description of luxurious delicacies as originating in "false desires" (6: *adclinis falsis*) and resulting in poor physical health (5: *insanis*), both of which corrupt the mind's ability to engage in discussions concerning the truth (7–9). Kiessling–Heinze confirm the ethical tone of these expressions by interpreting *insanis* in terms of "the unlimited" ("über das Maß des Gewöhnlichen hinausgehend") and by reading *adclinis falsis* in terms of the "implied meaning 'inclining toward what is false'" ("in übertragener Bedeutung... *inclinat ad falsa*").[14]

---

[11] Bond (1980) 114–16.
[12] Rudd (1966) 144 suggests that Ofellus' name may also communicate the frugality associated with small bits of food (*ofella*).
[13] Gerhard (1909) 32–3.
[14] Kiessling–Heinze (1910) 169. Muecke (1993) 117 considers the possibility that this metaphor communicates the "prone to" (εὐέμπτωτος) of Stoic ethics. Pseudo-Acro interprets the passage as meaning "rather prone to what is false" (*pronior ad falsa*).

Along similar lines, Epicurus identifies "physical health" (*Men*. 128: τὴν τοῦ σώματος ὑγίειαν) as essential for living happily but readily acquired through a simple diet, which gives "health to the full" (*Men*. 131: ὑγιείας ἐστὶ συμπληρωτικόν).[15] In contrast to this, he portrays a luxurious diet as a distraction and juxtaposes it to the sober reasoning and truth seeking associated with frugality:

> οὐ γὰρ πότοι καὶ κῶμοι συνείροντες οὐδ᾽ ἀπολαύσεις παίδων καὶ γυναικῶν
> οὐδ᾽ ἰχθύων καὶ τῶν ἄλλων ὅσα φέρει πολυτελὴς τράπεζα, τὸν ἡδὺν γεννᾷ
> βίον, ἀλλὰ νήφων λογισμὸς καὶ τὰς αἰτίας ἐξερευνῶν πάσης αἱρέσεως καὶ
> φυγῆς καὶ τὰς δόξας ἐξελαύνων, ἐξ ὧν πλεῖστος τὰς ψυχὰς καταλαμβάνει
> θόρυβος. (*Men*. 132)

For it is not continuous drinking and reveling, nor the satisfactions of boys and women, nor the enjoyment of fish and other luxuries of the wealthy table, which produce a pleasant life, but sober reasoning, searching out the motives for all choices and avoidances, and banishing mere opinions, to which are due the greatest disturbances of the spirit.

A blessed life, therefore, is attained not through overindulgence but through the careful observation of the limits and requirements of nature, which not only satisfy one's basic needs and produce physical health (cf. KD 29), but also eliminate distractions and are thus more conducive towards the contemplative life and the search for truth (cf. *S*. 2.2.7: *verum . . . mecum disquirite*). On this basis, Ofellus states that one should avoid the useless toil and cost involved in acquiring Athenian honey, Falernian wine, and fish (15–17), for nature only requires simple fare and, besides, the pleasant life is to be found in sober reasoning and self-control:

> cum sale panis
> latrantem stomachum bene leniet. unde putas aut
> qui partum? non in caro nidore voluptas
> summa, sed in te ipso est.[16] tu pulmentaria quaere
> sudando: pinguem vitiis albumque neque ostrea
> nec scarus aut poterit peregrina iuvare lagois.   (*S*. 2.2.17–22)

---

[15] For the role of Epicurus' advice to Menoeceus in this poem, see Lejay (1966) 314–16, Fiske (1971), Courtney (2013) 131, and Armstrong (2016) 207. Vischer (1965) 71–4 examines Epicurus' doctrine of "simple living."

[16] Cf. Persius' similarly introspective advice at 1.7: *nec te quaesiveris extra*, "and do not search outside yourself."

Bread and salt will suffice to appease your growling belly. Whence or how do you think this comes about? The highest pleasure lies, not in the costly savor, but in yourself. So earn your sauce with hard exercise. The man who is bloated and pale from excess will find no comfort in oysters or trout or foreign grouse.

As Pliny the Elder mentions, the reference to bread and salt as proverbial representatives of a meager fare had been made already by Varro (*Nat.* 31.89), and Lucilius similarly refers to the stomach's need for "a poultice such as milled barley" (813–14 M: *molito hordeo | uti cataplasma*).[17] The point in the passage quoted above, however, is not that one should avoid luxuries on principle but that such refinements should not be regarded as necessary, especially since nature only requires the bare minimum (cf. *Men.* 130–1), which is something Philodemus echoes in *On Property Management* (coll. 16.3–4 and 19.16–19). Taking this context into consideration, Ofellus' discussion of simple food is certainly not to be equated with the Cynics' wholesale rejection of luxury and complete dependence on nature, as some scholars have suggested.[18] Instead, he seems to be criticizing the view that luxury goods are of prime importance and necessary for happiness. This is expressed by means of the barking-belly metaphor, which originates with Homer (*Od.* 7.216 and 20.13) and Ennius (*Ann.* 584), but here more likely reflects a similar passage from Lucretius (2.17–18): *nil aliud sibi naturam latrare, nisi utqui | corpore seiunctus dolor absit,* "[not to see that] all nature barks for is this, that pain be removed away out of the body."[19] For this purpose simple foods easily suffice, as Epicurus' well-known identification of "bread and water" (*Men.* 131: μᾶζα καὶ ὕδωρ) as able to afford the greatest pleasure shows. Closely related to this teaching is the assertion that pleasure cannot be increased once necessary needs have been met (KD 18), which explains why delicacies such as oysters, trout, and foreign grouse will bring "no pleasure" (*S.* 2.2.22: *nec … iuvare*) to one who has gorged himself and thus exceeded the natural appetite for food (cf. SV 59: Ἄπληστον οὐ γαστήρ, ὥσπερ οἱ πολλοί φασιν, ἀλλ' ἡ δόξα ψευδὴς ὑπὲρ τοῦ <τῆς> γαστρὸς ἀορίστου πληρώματος, "It is not the belly that is insatiable, as

---

[17] See Kiessling–Heinze (1910) 170 and Courtney (2013) 131. Fiske (1971) 381–2 examines the evidence from Lucilius in more detail. Hudson (1989) 75 says that Horace's "salt" translates Epicurus' μᾶζα at *Men.* 131 (quoted below).

[18] Cf. Kiessling–Heinze (1910) 170 and Fiske (1971) 379.

[19] On this passage, see Bailey (1947) 799.

many say, but rather the false opinion concerning the belly's limitless greed").[20]

In addition to ignoring the requirements of nature and promoting useless overindulgence, which does not contribute to an increase in pleasure, such luxurious feasting is actually detrimental to good health and therefore violates the pleasure calculus. As Lucretius notes in his explanation of the sense of taste, the ultimate purpose of self-nourishment is to promote the stomach's constant health, especially since the pleasure of flavor does not extend to the belly:

> Deinde voluptas est e suco fine palati;
> cum vero deorsum per fauces praecipitavit,
> nulla voluptas est, dum diditur omnis in artus.
> nec refert quicquam quo victu corpus alatur,
> dummodo quod capias concoctum didere possis
> artubus et stomachi validum servare tenorem.[21]   (4.627–32)

Moreover, the pleasure that comes from flavor is limited by the palate; indeed, once it has gone down through the throat there is no pleasure while it is all being distributed throughout the limbs of the body. Nor does it matter at all by means of what food the body is nourished, as long as you are able to digest what you take in, distribute it through the limbs, and preserve the healthy course of your stomach.

All the culinary ostentation that goes with serving exotic peacocks (*S.* 2.2.23: *posito pavone*) and oversized fish (33–4: *trilibrem | mullum*), therefore, contributes absolutely nothing to the actual nourishing process, a view Ofellus expresses in the form of a rhetorical question (27–8): *num vesceris ista, | quam laudas, pluma?*, "Do you eat the feathers you so admire?" (the indifference regarding peacocks' tail feathers with regard to flavor is similarly expressed by Lucilius at 716 M: *cocus non curat caudam insignem esse illam, dum pinguis siet*, "The cook cares not whether those tail feathers are pretty, provided that the peacock is plump"[22]). Furthermore, the vain appearance of the bird (cf. *S.* 2.2.25: *vanis rerum*) is a reflection of the glutton's false opinion concerning the

[20] The condemnation of excessive greed and overly luxurious food (which of course recurs in *Satires* 2.4 and 2.8), as well as the concise nature of Ofellus' advice in this satire, can also be read in the light of literary criticism and as a tribute of sorts to Callimachean standards of poetry. See Mette (1961) 138 and Freudenburg (1993) 188.

[21] This version of the passage is taken from W. H. D. Rouse's 2006 Loeb edition.

[22] As mentioned above, Horace repeats Ofellus' criticisms of the obsession with sumptuous feasting in *Satires* 2.4 (the recipe for a luxurious feast) and 2.8 (the consequences of actually following such a recipe). See Muecke (1993) 227. As

purpose of food and his preference for a "big fish on a big dish" (39: *porrectum magno magnum spectare catino* | *vellem*), which echoes the miser's irrational desire in *Satires* 1.1 to "drink from a broad river rather than a tiny brook" (55–6: *magno de flumine mallem* | *quam ex hoc fonticulo tantundem sumere*)[23] as well as Epicurus' observation regarding gluttony (SV 69): Τὸ τῆς ψυχῆς ἀχάριστον λίχνον ἐποίησε τὸ ζῷον εἰς ἄπειρον τῶν ἐν διαίτῃ ποικιλμάτων, "The ungrateful greed of the soul makes the creature everlastingly desire varieties of dainty food." As Philodemus states, the natural pleasure of self-nourishment, which is easily satisfied, is one of the "necessary [desires] . . . for the health of the body" (*On Choices and Avoidances*, col. 6.2–4: [εἰσὶ]ν ἀναγ[καῖαι] . . . αἱ δ[ὲ πρὸς] τὸ ἄγ[ει]ν [ἐν ὑγι]είαι τὸ σῶ[μα]), whereas unnecessary overindulgence and desires associated with "sumptuous fare" (col. 5.17: τ[ρυ]φῶν τοιούτων) result in physical harm. Interestingly, in his treatise *On the Good King According to*

Classen (1978) 344–8 argues, the Catius in *Satires* 2.4, whom Cicero (*Letters to Friends* 15.16), Porphyrio (*ad* 1), and Quintilian (10.1.124) identify as an Epicurean author, is the victim of Horace's parody because he was one of the "incompetent translators of Epicurus' teachings" (Cic. *Letters to Friends* 15.19: *mali verborum [Epicuri] interpretes*; cf. *S.* 2.4.91: *non tamen interpres tantundem iuveris*, "yet merely as a reporter you do not give me the same pleasure"). So also Hicks (2013) 222. This connection to Epicurean philosophy is emphasized in the poem by expressions such as "you will be wise" (19: *doctus eris*), "nor is it enough" (37: *nec satis est*), and Catius' mention of the "sage" (44: *sapiens*, "immense vice" (76: *immane est vitium*), "care" (48: *curam*), "nature" (45: *natura*), and "teachings" (11: *praecepta*), along with Horace's inclusion of the Lucretian expression (cf. 1.927–8) "to drink in the precepts" (95: *haurire . . . praecepta*). Added to all of this is the fact that Catius refuses to reveal the name of his "source" (11: *celabitur auctor*), in contrast to faithful Epicureans' proud acknowledgement of the Master as *auctor*, and he refers to himself as a "first discoverer" (74: *primus et invenior*; cf. the claim of Nasidienus at *S.* 2.8.51: *ego primus*) of these teachings, which again is a decription often used in connection with Epicurus himself (examples abound in Lucretius). As Classen (1978) 345 explains, "[I]n ridiculing Catius and his anonymous teacher, Horace's target is not likely to be Epicurus or Epicurus' philosophy as such, nor Catius or his master as such, but as examples, representing those who follow Epicurus without understanding his philosophy, those who believe that Epicurus' ἡδονή may be attained to by means of bodily pleasure and are, therefore, pictured as concerning themselves with cookery books and wholesome and tasty food." One would do well to remember that Philodemus often criticizes other Epicureans for their lack of understanding of their own doctrine (cf. *On Anger*, coll. 1–6 for his rebuke of Timasagoras, a member of the sect who himself had criticized other Epicureans). For more on Catius, see Gowers (1993) 141 and Rudd (1966) 208–9.

[23] Kiessling–Heinze (1910) 173 compare the glutton's words to that of the miser at *Satires* 1.1.51: *at suave est ex magno tollere acervo*, "But it is sweet to draw from a large heap."

258   *Epicurean Ethics in Horace*

Homer Philodemus employs this same expression in reference to the Phaeacians' carefree feasting and emphasis on culture:

οὐ γὰρ μ[ό]νον νη[φό]ντων ᾄδειν "κλέα ἀνδρῶν," ἀλλὰ καὶ πινόντω[ν], οὐδὲ παρὰ μόνοις τοῖς αὐστηροτέροις, ἀλλὰ καὶ παρὰ τοῖς τρυφεροβίοις Φαίαξι. (col. 19.26–31)

For it is characteristic not only of the sober but also of those drinking to sing the "glories of men," and this is the case not only among the more severe but also among the soft-living Phaeacians.[24]

As Elizabeth Asmis argues, although Philodemus appears to praise this mythical people as showing the "correct way of spending leisure time by depicting orderliness at parties" and also by "proposing heroic poetry as a universally appropriate type of entertainment,"[25] his use of τρυφεροβίοις implies a rejection of their excessive luxury.[26] This is similar to Horace's self-deprecating descriptions as they appear in *Epistles* 1.15 (24: *pinquis ut inde domum possim Phaeaxque reverti*, "so that I may return home from there a fat Phaeacian") and 1.4 (15–16: *me pinguem et nitidum bene curata cute vises,* | *cum ridere voles, Epicuri de grege porcum*, "As for me, when you want a laugh, you will find me in fine fettle, fat and sleek, a hog from Epicurus' herd"). David Sider notes that Philodemus appears to make the same playful connection in his invitation poem to Piso (*Epigrams* 27.5–6): ἀλλ' ἐπακούσῃ | Φαιήκων γαίης πουλὺ μελιχρότερα, "you will hear things much sweeter than the land of the Phaeacians"),[27] and Horace provides similar criticism in *Epistles* 1.2 (28–9: *Alcinoique* | *in cute curanda plus aequo operata iuventus*, "young courtiers of Alcinous, unduly busy in keeping their skins sleek"), while Athenaeus in his *Scholars at Dinner* makes the same observation as both Philodemus and Horace in referring to the Phaeacians as "extremely luxurious" (1.9a): τοὺς τρυφερωτάτους ... Φαίακας (cf. 1.16c: τὴν τῶν Φαιάκων τρυφήν). This rejection of excessive luxury and, as immediately quoted above in Philodemus' *On Choices and Avoidances*, its consequences is expressed by Ofellus, who gives a vivid description of the detrimental effects of such fare on the body:

[24] Fish (2011b) 65–8, whose translation and text I have used above, provides a more detailed examination of this passage.
[25] Asmis (1991) 36. See also Gordon (2012) 54–5.
[26] Gordon (2012) 55–6.
[27] Sider (1997) 159. For the relationship between Epicureans, Phaeacians and feasting in connection with *Satires* 1.5, see Welch (2008) 49–53.

quamquam
putet aper rhombusque recens, mala copia quando
aegrum sollicitat stomachum, cum rapula plenus
atque acidas mavolt inulas.　(*S.* 2.2.41–4)

And yet they are already rank, the boar and fresh turbot, since cloying
plenty worries the jaded stomach, which, sated as it is, prefers radishes
and tart pickles the while.

As this passage indicates, the overabundance of fancy foods is transformed into an evil concoction that disturbs the poor stomach, whose
bloated sickness could have been avoided by the consumption of the
simple fare it prefers.[28] As a result of such irrational feasting, the goal of
which was identified earlier as the "highest pleasure" (19–20), the body
actually experiences severe pain. Offelus quickly notes, moreover, that
the satisfaction of necessary desires can be fully accomplished by a
meager diet of eggs and black olives (45–6), which he equates with
"poverty" (*pauperies*).[29] As discussed previously, Horatian poverty
should to be contrasted with the desire for more, which is reprehensible
(cf. *Odes* 3.29.55–6), and identified with the willingness to live content
with few possessions (cf. *Odes* 1.1.18) and to avoid the economic vices
of sumptuousness and meanness, the latter of which is the central focus
of Ofellus' subsequent consideration.

Ofellus' continuing discourse on plain living expresses the importance of avoiding meanness (*S.* 2.2.53–4: *sordidus a tenui victu distabit,
Ofello | iudice,* "a mean style of living will differ, so Ofellus thinks,
from a simple one"), which leads to the maltreatment of servants and
makes for a careless and stingy host, both of which Philodemus
addresses in his economic treatises. Horace's description of the characteristics associated with this vice is introduced by Avidienus, a
shameless miser whose unwillingness to spend money has led to his
deplorable appearance and, as a consequence, to the "appropriate
nickname of Dog" (56: *cui Canis ex vero dictum cognomen adhaeret*;
cf. Pseudo-Acro's interpretation of *canis* as *perditus avaritia*). Rather

---

[28] The theme of indigestion in connection with moral advice reappears in Persius
(3.98–106) and Juvenal (e.g. 1.142–3, 4.107, and 6.428–432), for which see Rimell
(2005) 81–9. Hudson (1989) 69–88, Ferriss-Hill (2015) 112, and especially Gowers
(1993) 109–219 discuss the role of food and food metaphors in Roman satire.

[29] See Vischer (1965) 149–50.

than suggest, as some commentators do,[30] that this individual was actually a Cynic (which would be inconsistent with his obsession for eliminating expenditures and amassing wealth like a miser), the label may simply reflect conservative Romans' association of sordidness in general with Cynic beggary.[31] In addition to being associated with Cynic poverty, sordidness was also a byproduct of meanness, as Horace shows in *Satires* 1.6 (107: *obiciet nemo sordis mihi, quas tibi, Tilli*, "No one, Tillius, will accuse me of your meanness") and especially in *Satires* 2.3 (111–28), which, as will be discussed shortly, includes a description that bears striking resemblance to the Avidienus passage. Avidienus' willingness to serve sour wine to his guests and anoint himself with rancid oil (*S.* 2.2.58–9: *mutatum . . . vinum . . . odorem olei*) also calls to mind Theophrastus' portrait of the "mean man" or αἰσχροκερδής, who similarly feeds his guests poor fare (*Char.* 30.2–3) and is overly concerned with the preservation of his oil (8–9).[32] Such extreme parsimony is condemned, along with its opposite vice, by Epicurus, who states that the wise man will prudently impose limits on frugality (SV 63): Ἔστι καὶ ἐν λιτότητι μεθόριος,[33] ἧς ὁ ἀνεπιλόγιστος παραπλήσιόν τι πάσχει τῷ δι' ἀοριστίαν ἐκπίπτοντι, "There is likewise a certain limit to frugality, which, if ignored, results in pain similar to the one who has succumbed to sumptuous living." This is precisely the reason why, as Ofellus states in the following lines, the sage will avoid both extremes (*S.* 2.2.65–6: [*sapiens*] *mundus erit, qua non offendat sordibus atque* | *in neutram partem cultus miser*, "[The sage] will be neat, so far as not to shock us by meanness, and in his mode of living will be unhappy in neither direction"), which seems to echo the words of Terence's Chremes in his *Self-Tormenter*:

> vehemens in utramque partem, Menedeme, es nimis
> aut largitate nimia aut parsimonia.
> in eandem fraudem ex hac re atque ex illa incides.   (440–2)

---

[30] Kiessling–Heinze (1910) 175 mention Avidienus' "kynishen Askese" ("Cynic asceticism") and Muecke (1993) calls him a symbol of radical Cynic poverty.

[31] Courtney (2013) 132 notes that the nickname "Dog" likely "implies a filthy life" and cites line 65 (*mundus*) in addition to *Ep.* 1.2.26 (*canis inmundus*). For Cynicism in Horace's *Epistles*, see also Moles (1985) 33–60. For the expression *hac urget lupus, hac canis* (*S.* 2.2.64) and its moral significance, see Houghton (2004) 300–4.

[32] Cf. Juv. 14.126–134.

[33] I follow here Usener's reading rather than that of the MSS (V: λεπτότητι καθάριος) or Muehll (λεπτότητι καθαριότης), the latter of which is accepted by Arr.

You are too excessive in either direction, Menedemus, being either too
generous or too stingy. You will be cheated either way, because of the
one or the other.

The importance of observing the Epicurean "measure of wealth," is
underscored by two relevant examples of economic vice: Albucius is
"cruel to his servants" (*S.* 2.2.64–8: *servis . . . saevus*) while Naevius
"serves his guests greasy water" (68–9: *unctam | convivis praebebit
aquam*). The first example resembles Philodemus' description
of the vicious economist (*On Property Management*, col. 11.3:
φιλοχρημάτου), whose decisions are motivated by greed and who
mistreats his servants and subordinates by denying them certain
staples such as wine (col. 9.32–6: σκληρῶς μέντ[οι] τ[ὴ]ν τοῦ ο[ἴ]νου
πόσιν κοιν[ῶς] ἀλλ' [οὐ τὴν] τοῦ πλείονος καὶ τοὺ[ς] ἐλευθέρους
[ὑβ]ριστὰ[ς] ποιε[ῖ]ν, "But it is harsh to say [as Theophrastus does]
that the mere drinking of wine—not just overdrinking—in general
makes even free men violent"; cf. Pseudo-Acro's interpretation of
Horace's *saevus erit* as *neglegens ad conparanda obsonia*, "Neglectful
at providing food"). The vicious economist will also force them into
cruel and dangerous work conditions (col. 23.3–5: τὸ δ' "ἀπὸ με[ταλ]-
λικῆς, δούλων ἐρ[γ]αζομέν[ων"] οὐκ εὔκληρον, "[The idea of making a
profit] from mining metals through the labor of slaves is not at all
fortunate"),[34] and even breed them like animals:

τὸ δ' ἐξομηρεύειν ταῖς τεκνοποι[ΐ]α[ις ε]ἰρηκέναι κοινῶς χεῖρο[ν ε]ἶναι
δοκεῖ τοῦ παρὰ Ξενοφῶντι {κελεύειν} τρέφειν [ἐ]κ τῶν ἀγαθῶ[ν], οὐκ ἐκ
τῶν πονηρῶν κελεύοντι· (col. 10.15–21)

But asserting that one bind slaves to one's service through the begetting
of children without distinction seems worse than what Xenophon says
about breeding children from the good slaves rather than the bad ones.

The acquisitive manager is also stingy and views guests as a burden,
since he equates convivial gatherings with financial loss and consequently imagines that "friendlessness procures relief from costs" (col.
24.19–21: καὶ μὴν ἀφιλία δοκεῖ μὲν ἀναλωμάτων κουφίζε[ιν]). The
ideal economist, on the other hand, whom Ofellus subsequently
identifies as the "sage" (*S.* 2.2.63: *sapiens*), will not only be content
with few possessions but will also know how to administer wealth
responsibly and in a spirit of kindness and generosity.

---

[34] On this last point, cf. *On Property Management*, col. 8.42–5.

Ofellus' previous descriptions provide an important contrast with his treatment of the prudent manager's administration of wealth, which includes physical health, forethought, and generosity. The importance of moderation is communicated by his emphasis on the sage's good health (*S.* 2.2.71: *valeas bene*), whereas the overindulgent glutton's distended and onerous belly prevents his mind from soaring to the lofty heights of philosophical contemplation:

> quin corpus onustum
> hersternis vitiis animum quoque praegravat una
> atque adfigit humo divinae particulam aurae.   (*S.* 2.2.77–9)

Indeed, clogged with yesterdays' excess the heavy body drags down the mind as well and fastens to earth a fragment of the divine spirit.

Like the belly stuffed full with a variety of delicacies (cf. 77: *cena...dubia*), Horace has crammed into this passage, in an undoubtedly playful and parodic manner, multiple references to and different expressions of Platonic and Stoic doctrines (Edward Courtney even states that "[T]his is a sarcastic Epicurean joke at this belief, a joke that belongs to Horace, not Ofellus"[35]). The poet seems to have in mind Plato's idea that physical pleasure "affixes" the soul to the body (*Phd.* 83d: προσήλοι), a passage Cicero also likely had in mind in his *Tusculan Disputations* when he says "what about the fact that we cannot make proper use of the mind when stuffed with food and drink?" (5.100: *quid quod ne mente quidem recte uti possumus multo cibo et potione completi?*).[36] Horace's passionate identification of the corporeal as an impediment to wisdom and the soul as connected to the divine ether, both of which threaten to transport the audience into the realm of theoretical speculation, is tempered by the following verses, in which Ofellus mentions the ancient and practical tradition of enjoying culinary pleasures moderately and sharing surplus wealth with one's friends (*S.* 2.2.89–93). The importance of friendship within the context of sharing and convivial gatherings is underscored once again in a later passage:

> ac mihi seu longum post tempus venerat hospes
> sive operum vacuo gratus conviva per imbrem

---

[35] Courtney (2013) 133. For the literary and aesthetic undertones of this passage, see Hicks (2013) 216.

[36] Horace also alludes to Stoic physics in calling the mind a "particle," which translates the Stoic ἀπόσπασμα (cf. *SVF* 1.128 and 2.633), and associating it with the "divine breath" or πνεῦμα. See Kiessling–Heinze (1910) 178 and Muecke (1993) 125.

vicinus, bene erat non piscibus urbe petitis,
sed pullo atque haedo; tum pensilis uva secundas
et nux ornabat mensas cum duplice ficu.
post hoc ludus erat culpa potare magistra
ac venerata Ceres, ita culmo surgeret alto,
explicuit vino contractae seria frontis.   (*S.* 2.2.118–25)

And if after long absence a friend came to see me, or if in rainy weather,
when I could not work, a neighbor paid me a visit—a welcome guest—
we fared well, not with fish sent from town, but with a pullet and a kid;
by and by raisins and nuts and split figs set off our dessert. Then we had
a game of drinking, with a forfeit to rule the feast, and Ceres, to whom
we made our prayer—"so might she rise on lofty stalk!"—smoothed out
with wine the worries of a wrinkled brow.

The purpose of Ofellus' emphasis on occasional indulgences with
guests is to communicate advice that is not only practical, but also
conducive towards physical health and the cultivation of friendships.
Philodemus, who places significant value on the economic benefits of
sharing wealth with friends, expresses a view that is quite similar
toward the end of *On Property Management*:

χρὴ δέ, καθάπερ πλειόνων προσπεσόντων χαρίζεσθαι ταῖς ἀβλαβέσι τῶν
ὀρέξεων αὐτοῖς καὶ φίλοις, οὕτω συμβάσης ἁδρᾶς κοιλότητος ἀναμάχεσθαι
ταῖς μὴ ἀνελευθέροις συστολαῖς, καὶ μᾶλλόν γε ταῖς εἰς αὑτοὺς ἢ ταῖς εἰς
φίλους   (col. 26.1–9)

And just as one should be generous to oneself and one's friends in
satisfying desires that are harmless when a greater quantity of goods
becomes available, so also one should compensate for losses with financial
restrictions that are liberal and directed more toward oneself rather than
one's friends when one's resources happen to be seriously depleted . . .

According to this description, friendship is a major priority for the
good manager, who, rather than indulge himself in private, would
rather save the "wild boar" (*S.* 2.2.89: *aprum*; cf. 2.4.41 and 2.8.6) for a
special occasion and in the meantime subsist on plain fare, as Ofellus
does (116–17): *non ego . . . temere edi luce profesta | quicquam praeter
holus fumosae cum pede pernae*, "I was not the man to eat on a
working day, without good reason, anything more than greens and
the shank of a smoked ham."[37]

For Philodemus, such consideration and generosity on the part
of the sage economist attracts friends, who, in the case of an economic

[37] Cf. Juv. 11.82–5.

crisis, can lend assistance by providing financial or, perhaps more importantly, emotional support. This is emphasized in an important and previously quoted passage from *On Property Management* (coll. 24.46–25.4): εἰσὶν δὲ κτήσει[ς λ]υσιτελέστεραι . . . ἥπερ ἀγρῶν καὶ πρὸς τὴν τύχην ἀσφαλέστατοι θησαυροί, "[the care bestowed on friends] is considered to be more profitable . . . than tilled land and it is a treasure that is most secure against the turns of fortune." The sharing of surplus wealth with one's friends is of course the hallmark not only of Epicurean philanthropy as described by Philodemus above, but also an expression of the Greek notion of "liberality" (ἐλευθεριότης), as Aristotle explains in his *Nicomachean Ethics* (1120a5–35). As Kiessling–Heinze note, Cicero also mentions the importance of generosity in the *Tusculan Disputations* (4.46): *misericordiam (utilem) ad opem ferendam et hominum indignorum calamitates sublevandas,* "pity is useful for affording assistance and alleviating the woes of unfortunate men" (cf. *S.* 1.2.5: *inopi dare nolit amico,* "he refuses to give to a friend who is destitute") and, according to Jan Fredrik Kindstrand, the Cynics also highly valued generosity (χρηστότης).[38] At the same time, however, the Cynic understanding of philanthropy involves "stripping oneself of wealth" (cf. Kindstrand 1976: F38A: . . . χρηστότης δὲ ἀφαιρεῖται [sc. πλοῦτον]) in order to live a completely independent life, as André Oltramare's collected maxims show.[39] This view contradicts Aristotle's teaching concerning proportionate generosity (*Nic. Eth.* 1120b5–1121a10), which is echoed by Philodemus' observations on giving to friends in accordance with one's means (*On Property Management,* col. 25.24–31). It should also be noted that Ofellus urges his wealthy interlocutor to give out of his "surplus" (*S.* 2.2.102: *quod superat*), not to do away with all his possessions. One may contrast this with the ostentatious manager, whose uncontrollable spending and lavishness have won him not only the hatred of others (96–7), but have also resulted in financial loss (cf. 96: *damno*) and "pennilessness" (98–9: *egenti | as*).[40]

---

[38] See Kiessling–Heinze (1910) 181 and Kindstrand (1976) F38A–C with commentary (247).

[39] Oltramare (1926) 51–2.

[40] See Courtney (2013) 133 for *damnum* and *dedecus* as an alliterative pair that also appears in Plautus (*Asses* 371 and *Bacch.* 67). As Kiessling–Heinze (1910) 181 note, the spendthrift's extreme poverty is underscored by his inability to afford even the "purchase of a noose" (*S.* 2.2.99: *laquei pretium*), which is a reference to the Greek comic tradition and also appears at Plaut. *Pseud.* 88 (Calidorus explains his reason for

Philodemus similarly states that financial vice engenders the hatred of others (*On Property Management*, col. 24.19–33), and he identifies, in a passage featuring a list of moral faults strung together through polysyndeton, prodigality as a primary destroyer of wealth:

οὐ[δ]ὲν γὰρ ἐκχεῖν [κ]α[ὶ ἀ]νατρέπειν εἴ[θιστ]αι λαμπροτάτα[ς καὶ πλ]ουσι[ωτάτας οἰκίας ὡ]ς πολυτέλι[αί τε] δι[αίτ]ης κα[ὶ] λαγνε[ῖαι καὶ] π[ε]ριβλέψε[ις] κα[ὶ]   (coll. 23.42–24.1)

For nothing is wont to drain and upset the most illustrious and wealthiest estates like prodigality and lustfulness and the desire for admiration and . . .

Even if one's financial resources are substantial enough to avoid serious depletion, as Ofellus' imaginary interlocutor smugly retorts (*S*. 2.2.99–101), the implication in this passage is that changes of fortune (cf. 108: *casus dubios*) may nevertheless lead to economic crises, which the friendless and myopic manager will find extremely difficult to endure.

This economic sermon concludes with a concrete example of how one should endure the changes of adverse fortune,[41] which is afforded by the life of Ofellus himself. This is introduced by a passage that resembles the ant simile in *Satires* 1.1, and likewise communicates the principal attributes of an ideal economist in terms of wisdom and forethought with regard to financial administration:

> uterne
> ad casus dubios fidet sibi certius? hic qui
> pluribus adsuerit mentem corpusque superbum,
> an qui contentus parvo metuensque futuri
> in pace, ut sapiens, aptarit idonea bello?   (*S*. 2.2.107–11)

Which of the two, in the face of changes and chances, will have more self-confidence—he who has accustomed a pampered mind and body to superfluities, or he who, content with little and fearful of the future, has in peace, like a wise man, provided for the needs of war?

Imitating the wisdom of the Horatian ant (cf. *S*. 1.1.38: *sapiens*), the sage economist rations his stores carefully and is mindful of the future (cf. *S*. 1.1.35: *non incauta futuri*), knowing that nature will easily fulfill

---

borrowing a drachma): *restim volo* | *mihi emere . . . qui me faciam pensilem*, "I want to buy a rope . . . to hang myself with."

[41] Rudd (1966) 169.

the needs of one who is content with little (cf. *Men.* 130–1 and *On Property Management*, col. 19.16–19). This involves careful preparation (cf. *S.* 2.2.111: *aptarit . . . bello*), as Horace indicates employing a military metaphor, which Frances Muecke notes[42] is paralleled in Latin only by a fragment of Publilius Syrus (465): *Prospicere in pace oportet, quod bellum iuvet,* "One ought to foresee in time of peace that which helps war" (Kiessling–Heinze cite Plato's *Laws* 8.829a–b: οὐκ ἐν πολέμῳ τὸν πόλεμον ἑκάστοις γυμναστέον, ἀλλ᾽ ἐν τῷ τῆς εἰρήνης βίῳ, "Let each man train for battle in peacetime, not wartime"[43]). One may also compare this passage, as Pseudo-Acro does, to a similar observation made by Juvenal:

> tecum prius ergo volute
> haec animo ante tubas: galeatum sero duelli
> paenitet.   (1.168–70)

Therefore, ponder these things within yourself before the trumpets sound: once you've got a helmet on it'll be too late to have second thoughts about the battle.

The emphasis on bravery or αὐτάρκεια in the face of adverse fortune, which is expressed at the end of the poem (*S.* 2.2.135–6), may likewise recall the teachings of Epicurus (*Men.* 131), whom Philodemus quotes in his treatise *On Wealth* as having said: "whenever the sage yields, having fallen into poverty, he alone is not defeated" (col. 40.11–14: κ[αθ]άπερ εἶπεν Ἐπίκουρος, [ὅτα]ν παρῆι ποτὲ πεσώ[ν . . .ὁ σο]φὸς εἰς πενίαν, μόνον οὐ τρέπεται). It may also echo the teaching of the Cynics,[44] although their underlying reasons for such courage are quite different from that of the Epicureans. For the former, it originates in the complete rejection of all conventions, so that the loss of wealth becomes literally impossible, as William Desmond explains:

> [T]he Cynic boasts that he lives in utmost simplicity, without house, furniture, cups, weapons, clothes, jewelry or money: in short, without the products of human craft and technology. Unhoused, unwashed, unshaven, unshod and almost unclothed, eating figs, lupin-beans, lentils

---

[42] Muecke (1993) 127.
[43] Kiessling–Heinze (1910) 182. Perhaps Ofellus' words contain a veiled reference to the Battle of Philippi, at which Horace himself was stripped of his inheritance (cf. *Ep.* 2.2.49–52).
[44] See Oltramare (1926) 57.

and whatever else he finds growing in the fields or hills nearby, the Cynic is an "all natural" philosopher who would . . . simplify everything. Eat when hungry, drink when thirsty. Seek shelter from the elements when you have to. Relieve sexual needs when they arrive. Use only what is immediately available. Live here, now.[45]

As this description indicates, the Cynics were unafraid of losing wealth precisely because they had none,[46] whereas the Epicurean manager is able to endure financial loss with equanimity because he is "confident with regard to the future and the possibility of a poor and meager life" (*On Property Management*, coll. 15.45–16.3: [οὔ]τε [γ]ὰρ ἀσχαλᾶι σώφρων ἀνὴρ καὶ πρὸς τὸ μέλλ[ον εὐ]θ[α]ρρὴς τῆι ταπεινῆι καὶ πενιχρᾶι διαίτηι). The reason for the sage economist's confidence, moreover, is that "he knows that the requirements of nature are satisfied even by this [i.e. the bare necessities]" (col. 16.3–4: τὸ φυσικὸν εἰδὼς καὶ ὑπὸ ταύτης διοικούμενον).

Unlike the overindulgent spendthrift, therefore, who has become accustomed to an abundance of fancy delicacies (cf. *S.* 2.2.109: *pluribus adsuerit*) and will undoubtedly be crushed by their absence when his wealth is gone, Ofellus draws "unwavering confidence" (108: *fidet sibi certius*; cf. *On Property Management*, col. 16.1–2 quoted more fully above: πρὸς τὸ μέλλ[ον εὐ]θ[α]ρρής) from the fact that he is "content with little" (*S.* 2.2.110: *contentus parvo*) and that "cheap eggs and black olives" (45–6: *vilibus ovis | nigrisque . . . oleis*), which provide the body with health and are conducive to the good life, will always be readily available. This logic is very similar to the argument made by Philodemus in *On Property Management* regarding an individual who "is good at procuring what suffices for himself" (col. 16.6–8 οὔτε κ[α]κὸς εὑρέσθαι τὰ πρὸς αὐτὸν ἱκανά) and how such a person would react to financial loss:

τίνος ἂν οὖν ἕνεκα τηλικαῦτ᾽ ἔχων ἐφόδια πρὸς τὸ ζῆν καλῶς ἐν πολλῆι ῥαις[τώ]νηι, κἂν πλοῦτον ἀποβάληι, πέραι τοῦ μετρίου κακοπαθήσει σωτηρίας ἕνεκ[α χ]ρ[η]μάτων; (col. 16.12–18)

For what reason, therefore, would one who can acquire such means [i.e. τὰ πρὸς αὐτὸν ἱκανά] for the good life with such easiness undergo extreme suffering on account of financial loss, even if he should lose his wealth?

---

[45] Desmond (2008) 151. Much of the evidence for this passage is collected by Oltramare (1926) 51–2. Cf. also Kindstrand (1976) F17.
[46] See Rich (1956) 23–4.

The realization that a *victus tenuis* is easily supported explains why Ofellus is not disturbed by the loss of his wealth, which, as Philodemus states in *On Wealth*, "is something indifferent" (col. 53.3: [ἀδιά] φορο[ν μὲ]ν εἶναι). Horace also tells us that, even after the confiscation of his property and reduction of wealth, Ofellus continued to enjoy the same degree of satisfaction as before:

> Ofellum
> integris opibus novi non latius usum
> quam nunc accisis. (*S.* 2.2.112–14)

This Ofellus, as I well know, used his full means on no larger scale than he does now, when they are cut down.

This is understandable, as Frances Muecke observes: "Because he lived frugally before he lost his farm, he has not had to change the way of life in which he is happy."[47] Additionally, the rustic sage has "prepared for war" by cultivating friendships and being generous to his friends (118–25), who are a secure treasure that fortune cannot deplete or destroy. This may provide the context for Ofellus' defiant assertion that, no matter how wildly Fortune rages, she will never diminish the bond of camaraderie (*S.* 2.2.126–7): *saeviat atque novos moveat Fortuna tumultus: | quantum hinc inminuet?*, "Let Fortune storm and stir fresh turmoils; how much will she take off from this?"[48] Horace ends this discourse on plain living by reminding his audience of the fickleness of fortune, which, as the Cynics would point out, has not "given her goods to the rich, but only lent them" (Kindstrand 1976: F39A–D: τὰ χρήματα τοῖς πλουσίοις ἡ τύχη οὐ δεδώρηται, ἀλλὰ δεδάνεικεν),[49] and of the transience of wealth, which, according to Philodemus, is "easily destroyed and perfectly subject to being taken away" (*On Wealth*, col. 54.8–10: [εὔ] φθαρτός ἐσ[τι] καὶ [τελ]έως εὐαφαίρετος ὁ [πλ]οῦτος). This concept was also popular among Roman authors in the first century BC, as evidenced by both Lucilius (701 M: *cum sciam nihil esse in vita*

---

[47] Muecke (1993) 127. See also Freudenburg (2001) 99.

[48] For the language in this line as a possible imitation of "epic grandeur," see Muecke (1993) 129, who cites relevant parallels.

[49] Cf. also Eur. *Phoen.* 555 and Men. *Grouch* 797–812. One may recall Horace's prayer to Mercury for the lifelong preservation of his Sabine estate (*S.* 2.6.4–5): *nil amplius oro,| Maia nate, nisi ut propria haec mihi munera faxis,* "Nothing more do I ask, o son of Maia, save that thou make these blessings last my life long."

proprium mortali datum, "Since I know that nothing in life has been
given to mortals as their own possession")[50] and Lucretius (3.971:
vitaque mancipio nulli datur, omnibus usu, "Life has been loaned to
everyone and freely granted to no none"). As a remedy for the
unpredictability associated with financial success both Ofellus
and Philodemus recommend that one maintain a "stout heart"
(*S.* 2.2.136: *fortiaque... pectora*) in the face of such economic uncertainty and be content with little, which nature easily procures, and that
one draw strength from friends, who are a most stable defense "against
adverse fortune" (*On Property Management,* col. 25.3: πρὸς τὴν τύχην;
cf. *S.* 2.2.108: *ad casus dubios*).

Immediately following Ofellus' advice on simple living Horace
introduces the character of Damasippus, a recent convert to Stoicism
whose tirade against moral deficiency, which is much longer and
harsher than that of Ofellus, focuses largely on economic vice. The
extreme zeal of Damasippus is the result of a conversion to Stoic
philosophy following a financial crisis and the realization that "all
fools are mad" (cf. *S.* 2.3.32: *insanis et tu stultique prope omnes*), which is
clearly a translation of the Greek πᾶς ἄφρων μαίνεται (for which, see
especially Cicero's *Tusculan Disputations* 3.7–11).[51] According to
Horace's description, Damasippus had suffered the complete loss of
his wealth (cf. *S.* 2.3.18–19), which is interesting given that Cicero
mentions a man named Damasippus who was involved in the purchase of antiquities and real estate (*Letters to his Friends* 7.23.2–3, to
which cf. *S.* 2.3.20–6) and Juvenal mentions a certain Damasippus
who had suffered "the destruction of his riches" (8.185: *consumptis
opibus*).[52] Regardless of the exact identity of this individual, this was a
misfortune that, unlike Ofellus, the Stoic was obviously unable to bear
(*S.* 2.3.37–8): *nam male re gesta cum vellem mittere operto | me capite
in flumen,* "For when, after my financial failure, I'd covered my head
and was intending to hurl myself into the river..."[53] The extreme

---

[50] Fiske (1971) 385–6 cites a handful of other interesting Lucilian parallels.

[51] Horace's interlocutor, however, does not observe the distinction Cicero draws
between moral unsoundness (*insania*) and mental illness (*furor*), for which see Rudd
(1966) 181–7. Pigeaud (1990) 9–43 examines at length the Stoic tradition of madness
as a sickness in this poem.

[52] Shackleton Bailey (1976) 29–30 identifies him as the son of Licinius Crassus
Junianus (Brutus) Damasippus.

[53] Muecke (1993) 130. Cucchiarelli (2001) 160 notes "various common experiences" ("varie esperienze in commune") between Damasippus and the Cynic

reaction to his bankruptcy is probably intended to expose Damasippus as a hypocrite, especially in light of his earlier advice to Horace concerning fulfilling promises "with equanimity" (16: *aequo animo*). Furthermore, the entire scene is conveyed in a strongly parodic manner: covering the head, which was customary near death, recalls Plato's dramatic telling of Socrates' last moments (*Phd.* 118a6–7); Damasippus' savior, whom he identifies as a Stoic sage named Stertinius (mentioned again in an unfavorable manner at *Ep.* 1.12.20: *Stertinium deliret acumen*, "clever Stertinius is crazy")[54] suddenly and auspiciously "appears on his right side" (38: *dexter stetit*) like a *deus ex machina*[55] and employs the archaic subjunctive "doeth" (38: *faxis*), which Horace uses elsewhere in his solemn prayer to Mercury (*S.* 2.6.5); the Stoic sage's teachings, which, according to Damasippus, were "rattled off" (33: *crepat*), are rehashed in the form of ὑπομνήματα (34: *descripsi . . . praecepta*) that create bathos when compared to Xenophon's record of Socrates' teachings and, later on, Arrian's preservation of those of Epictetus.[56] To make matters worse, Damasippus is identified as a "fool" not only by his own teacher (40: *insanus*) but also by Horace (326: *insane*), which is a label this "late learner" (cf. *S.* 1.10.21: *o seri studiorum*) confirms by his misapplication of Stertinius' doctrines.[57] J. P. Cèbe observes that Damasippus' "words betray the characteristic intolerance of neophytes" ("Ses paroles respirent l'intolérance des neophytes"[58]), as does his inability to use philosophy to self-medicate in accordance with Cicero's recommendation:

> est profecto animi medicina, philosophia; cuius auxilium non ut in corporis morbis petendum est foris, omnibusque opibus et viribus, ut nosmet ipsi nobis mederi possimus elaborandum est.
>
> (*Tusculan Disputations* 3.6)

The medicine of the soul is indeed philosophy, whose aid must be sought not, as in diseases of the body, outside ourselves, and we must

Menippius of Gadara, including the loss of wealth and desire to commit suicide (cf. DL 6.99–100).

[54] Regarding Stertinius, Pseudo-Acro states the following: *Stertinius philosophus, qui CCXX libros Stoicorum Latine descripsit*, "Stertinius was a philosopher who wrote 220 books on Stoicism in Latin." Very little is known about this individual, for which see Rawson (1985) 53 and Desideri (1996) in *Enc. Or.* 1.906. His name, which appears to be connected to the verb *stertere*, may conceal a pun in identifying the longwinded sage as "Mr Snore." See Sharland (2009a) 113–31.

[55] Courtney (2013) 136.   [56] Fiske (1971) 387.
[57] Rudd (1966) 175.   [58] Cèbe (1966) 263.

work hard, employing all our resources and strength, that we may have the power to be ourselves our own physicians.[59]

Cicero's observation is certainly a traditional one and resembles closely those of Stoic sympathizers such as Persius (cf. 1.7) and Epictetus:

ὡς γὰρ τέκτονος ὕλη τὰ ξύλα, ἀνδριαντοποιοῦ ὁ χαλκός, οὕτως τῆς περὶ βίον τέχνης ὕλη ὁ βίος αὐτοῦ ἑκάστου. (Arr. *Diss. Epict.* 1.15.2)

For just as the carpenter's material is wood and that of the statuary bronze, so also the life of each individual is the material of the art of living.

Despite all of this, instead of evaluating his own life in the light of his recent conversion and education, Damasippus immediately takes the opportunity to attack mercilessly everyone else's faults, including those of Horace (*S.* 2.3.307-25). In order to do so, he relates the doctrines of Stertinius, who, like a comic actor in a Plautine prologue,[60] now takes center stage and requests the audience's attention while carefully outlining the content of his "play" (78-80): base ambition (*ambitio mala*), avarice (*argenti amor*), self-indulgence (*luxuria*), and superstition (*tristis superstitio*). As is immediately clear from this list, vices associated with avarice and the mismanagement of wealth in general promise to be the main focus of his diatribe, which is indeed the case. The overemphasis on economic vice, moreover, is intriguing given the content of the previous satire, and although there are certain thematic similarities between these two as well as Horace's treatment of avarice in *Satires* 1.1, there are also important differences.

Stertinius' attack on avarice focuses largely on examples of meanness (*S.* 2.3.82-157), which establish numerous connections to the immediately preceding treatment of Ofellus as well as to that of the poet's persona in *Satires* 1.1. The first representative of avarice is the miser Staberius, an individual who is otherwise unknown[61] and whose obsession with displaying the sum total of his amassed wealth on a tombstone is explained as originating in his great fear of poverty:

> quoad vixit, credidit ingens
> pauperiem vitium et cavit nihil acrius, ut, si

---

[59] See also Courtney (2013) 135.
[60] I owe this observation to Muecke (1993) 141.
[61] See Kiessling–Heinze (1910) 199 and Muecke (1993) 142.

> forte minus locuples uno quadrante perisset,
> ipse videretur sibi nequior.   (*S.* 2.3.91–4)

As long as he lived, he believed poverty a huge fault and there was nothing he took keener precaution against, so that, if by chance he had died less rich by one farthing, he would think himself so much the more worthless.

Like the unnamed miser in *Satires* 1.1, who fears poverty (93: *pauperiem metuas*; cf. *S.* 2.3.110: *metuensque*) and equates any reduction of wealth with a corresponding reduction of self-worth (cf. *S.* 1.1.62), Staberius hoards his money and mistakenly identifies it as the *summum bonum* (Ofellus identifies a similar mistake in *S.* 2.2.19–20: *non in caro nidore voluptas | summa*, "The greatest pleasure does not lie in a costly aroma"). Of course, these convictions are the expression of a false opinion (cf. *S.* 1.1.61: *cupidine falso*): in the case of the Horatian miser, limitless wealth is associated with pleasure (*S.* 1.1.51: *suave est*; 78: *hoc iuvat?*), while for Staberius it is far better than virtue and produces all of the defining characteristics one would traditionally associate with the Stoic sage:

> "omnis enim res,
> virtus, fama, decus, divina humanaque pulchris
> divitiis parent; quas qui construxerit ille
> clarus erit, fortis, iustus." "sapiensne?" "etiam, et rex
> et quiquid volet."   (*S.* 2.3.94–8)

"For all things—worth, repute, honor, things divine and human—are slaves to the beauty of wealth, and he who has made his pile will be famous, brave and just." "And wise too?" "Yes, wise, and a king and anything else he pleases."

Kiessling–Heinze note that this identification of wealth as "beautiful" (*pulcher*) has religious connotations, implying that Staberius views wealth as "the true God" ("der wahre Gott"),[62] which is very different from, and perhaps a parody of, Cicero's description of the orthodox position (*Letters to his Friends* 9.14.4): *nihil est enim, mihi crede, virtute formosius, nihil pulchrius, nihil amabilius*, "Take it from me, nothing is more handsome, beautiful, or worthy of love than virtue." As the preceding passage clearly illustrates, Staberius' intense zeal for riches is a complete perversion of Stoic doctrine, which states that

---

[62] Kiessling–Heinze (1910) 201.

virtue alone is inherently good while external factors such as riches and health are considered to be "preferred indifferents," indicating that they should be chosen for their benefits although they contribute nothing to happiness or virtue.[63] As has been discussed already, Epicurus similarly states that great wealth cannot make one truly happy or provide the benefits associated with the *summum bonum* (SV 81), but nowhere does he come close to suggesting, like the Stoics do, that, all things being equal, one is morally obligated to "prefer" it to other things (cf. Cic. *On Ends* 3.51: *quibusdam anteponerentur*).

Philodemus, who recognizes the usefulness of wealth without describing it as morally obligatory warns against making financial acquisition an end in itself (*On Property Management*, col. 17.2–9). He also notes that one should never associate the loss of revenue in and of itself with poverty, which results in intense pain and anxiety (col. 19.4–16; cf. *On Wealth*, col. 27.6–10 (fr. 2): ποιούμενοι τὴ[ν φυ]λακὴν καὶ σὺν μερίμναις ἐ[π]ωδύνοις· καὶ περὶ τῆς ἀποβολῆς οὕτως ἀγωνιῶντες ὡς ἀνυπ[αρξίας], "Endeavoring to preserve wealth with painful anxieties and agonizing over the loss of revenue as if it were penury"). It should also be remembered that, although Philodemus does not describe wealth as a "preferred indifferent," he does borrow Stoic terminology in stating that "the fall from wealth to poverty is indifferent" (*On Wealth*, col. 53.2–5), and he considers riches beneficial or detrimental in relation to the disposition of the one using it:

οὐ φαίνεται δ᾽ ὁ πλοῦτος ἐπιφέρειν ἀλυσιτελεῖς δυσχερείας παρ᾽ αὐτὸν ἀλλὰ παρὰ τὴ[ν] τῶν χρωμένων κακίαν.

(*On Property Management*, col. 14.5–9)

Wealth does not seem to bring profitless troubles of its own accord, but rather as a result of the baseness of those who misuse it.[64]

With regard to *Satires* 2.3, the refusal to make expenditures because of the risk of poverty or a reduction of self-worth leads to wretched squalor, as the sorry life of Staberius shows. He feels compelled, for instance, to keep constant vigil over his enormous heap (111–12: *ingentem ... semper acervum | porrectus vigilet*; cf 1.1.76: *vigilare metu*), from which, unlike the wise ant in *Satires* 1.1, he refuses to

---

[63] For ancient evidence regarding the Stoic doctrine of "preferred indifferents" (ἀδιάφορα προηγμένα), see Long and Sedley (1987) 349–55.

[64] Diogenes preserves a similar Stoic version of this teaching (7.101–3).

subtract despite his intense hunger (2.3.113: *esuriens*). Instead, he chooses to subsist on bitter herbs (114: *foliis parcus vescatur amaris*) and sour wine (116–17: *acre | potet acetum*; cf. *S.* 2.2.55–62) and his tattered, moth-bitten rags are a poor excuse for clothes (117–19). In these descriptions Horace draws heavily from traditional depictions of "meanness" (ἀνελευθερία) and the "desire of base gain" (αἰσχροκερδία), especially those of Aristotle (cf. *Nic. Eth.* 1121b10–15) and Theophrastus (cf. *Char.* 30), but the notion that keeping vigil day and night is a symptom of meanness also appears in Roman comedy. As Stertinius indicates, Staberius' twisted views regarding wealth not only result in miserable living conditions, but they actually prevent him from using it properly:

> qui discrepat istis,
>   qui nummos aurumque recondit, nescius uti
>   conpositis metuensque velut contingere sacrum?   (*S.* 2.3.108–10)

How differs from these [madmen] the one who hoards up silver and gold, though he does not know how to use his store and fears to touch it as though it were hallowed?

Here again Horace is inspired by serio-comic literature, for, as discussed in an earlier chapter, the idea of hiding gold in the earth (cf. *S.* 1.1.41–2) was a traditional motif in diatribes (cf. Hippoc. [*Ep.*] 17.8) and on the comic stage (cf. Plaut. *Pot of Gold* 6–8). The underlying cause of such behavior is ignorance of the purpose of money, as Horace suggests when he chides the miser in *Satires* 1.1 for being "ignorant of money's potential, of the enjoyment it can bring" (*S.* 1.1.73: *nescis quo valeat nummus, quem praebeat usum?*). Being ignorant about money and its value was also a common theme of moral philosophy in general, but of particular importance to Epicurus, who identifies philosophical αὐτάρκεια as the ability to be satisfied with and enjoy one's possessions (*Men.* 130).[65] Philodemus communicates the same view in his economic treatises, which emphasize the sage economist's ability to acquire and use wealth beneficially (*On Property Management*, coll. 19.45–20.1): ἐπειδὴ κατὰ τὸ συμφέρ[ον] μάλιστ[α] καὶ κτᾶται καὶ χρῆται καὶ ἐπιμέ[λεται πλούτο]υ, " . . . although the sage in particular acquires, uses and cares for wealth to his own advantage" (cf. *On Wealth*, col. 23.30–1, fr. 2: πλοῦτον ὠφελ[εῖν . .] εὖ χ[ρωμένους],

---

[65] See Rudd (1966) 183 and Gowers (2012) 76.

"[They say that] wealth can be beneficial for those who use it properly").

In contrast to this, Staberius' hoarding of wealth results not only in sordidness and physical discomfort, but also in much anxiety as he fearfully keeps imagined despoilers away and worries about not having enough (cf. *S.* 2.3.123: *custodis? ne tibi desit?*, ". . . are you guarding it? Is it that you fear want?").

The other examples of economic vice Stertinius presents are associated with greed as well as self-indulgence, both of which Damasippus eventually attributes to Horace himself. Regarding the consequences of being unable to enjoy wealth, perhaps the best or at least most extreme example is afforded by the miser Opimius, whose greedy refusal to make expenditures brings about his own death (*S.* 2.3.147–57). Stertinius refers to him as "poor Opimius" (142: *pauper Opimius*), which, given the obvious connection to *opimus*, is certainly intended as a clever oxymoron (cf. *Odes* 3.16.28: *magnas inter opes inops*, "poor in the midst of great riches"),[66] but also alludes to Epicurus' famous paradox describing the desire for great wealth as spiritual poverty (SV 25): Ἡ πενία μετρουμένη τῷ τῆς φύσεως τέλει μέγας ἐστὶ πλοῦτος· πλοῦτος δὲ μὴ ὁριζόμενος μεγάλη ἐστὶ πενία, "Poverty measured by the limits of nature is great wealth, but unlimited wealth is great poverty." It is worth noting that a similar view was expressed by the Cynics: Πρὸς πλούσιον μικρολόγον, "οὐχ οὗτος," ἔφη, "τὴν οὐσίαν κέκτηται, ἀλλ' ἡ οὐσία τοῦτον," "Regarding a wealthy miser, he [Bion] said 'he does not own his possessions; rather, his possessions own him.'"[67] Unlike the hospitable Ofellus, moreover, who, in accordance with Philodemus' economic advice, knows how to enjoy good things with friends and visitors on occasion (cf. *S.* 2.2.118–25), the rich miser's inclination to "drink bad wine on holidays" (*S.* 2.3.143: *Veientanum festis potare diebus*)[68] and "vinegar on working days" (144: *vappamque profestis*) closely resembles the meanness of Avidienus (*S.* 2.2.59–62) as well as the stinginess of the inhospitable Naevius (68–9). A life of squalor and bad wine, however, is by no means the only consequence of meanness. Like the miser in *Satires* 1.1, on his deathbed Opimius is not surrounded by neighbors and family members, but by his joyfully expectant heir:

[66] See Kiessling–Heinze (1910) 205–6. Rudd (1966) 141 and Muecke (1993) 147 discuss the possible identity of this individual.
[67] Kindstrand (1976) F36.
[68] For the low quality of Veientine wine, which Kiessling–Heinze (1910) 206 call "a foul red blend" "ein abscheulicher roter Krätzer", see Pers. 5.147.

> quondam lethargo grandi est oppressus, ut heres
> iam circum loculos et clavis laetus ovansque
> curreret. (*S.* 2.3.145–7)

One day he was overcome by a tremendous lethargy, so that his heir was
already running around among the cashboxes and keys, happy and
jubilant.

Philodemus of course describes "friendlessness" (ἀφιλία) as one of
the major consequences of love of money (*On Property Management*,
col. 24.19–33), although, as Stertinius indicates, Opimius has not
been totally abandoned. The final scene of this example involves a
brief dialogue between the gravely ill Opimius and his "very quick-
witted and faithful doctor" (*S.* 2.3.147: *medicus multum celer atque
fidelis*), recalling a similar mention of a "doctor" in connection with
the Horatian miser's hypothetical illness (*S.* 1.1.82: *medicum*). In
both cases, meanness is associated with death: for the miser, it results
in universal abandonment and a complete lack of medical assistance;
for Opimius, it prevents him from accepting the nourishing "rice
pudding" (*S.* 2.3.155: *tisanarium oryzae*)[69] that will save his life by
restoring blood and raising his collapsed stomach (153–4). The
reason for his rejection is that, like Staberius, he mistakenly views
poverty as a "sickness" (157: *morbo*) and the most horrendous
"defect" (92: *vitium*), which prevents him from enjoying the many
benefits wealth can provide. All of this contrasts with Philodemus'
observations in *On Wealth*, where he describes poverty as a "good"
(col. 49.12: ἀγαθ[όν]) that is not worthy of fear, as well as in *On
Property Management*, where he discusses the many benefits that a
resource like wealth can afford (col. 14.9–23).

   In his remaining treatment of economic vice, Stertinius considers
the madness of those who suffer from the opposite extreme, namely,
self-indulgence (*S.* 2.3.224–46). It is generally acknowledged that the
general focus on *vitia contraria*, which is a commonplace of Horatian
satire (cf. *S.* 1.2.24: *dum vitant stulti vitia, in contraria currunt*, "in
avoiding a vice, fools run into its opposite"), largely reflects Aristotle's
doctrine of the mean. One will remember, however, that it may also

---

[69] André (1981) 54 discusses the medicinal uses associated with rice, which, as
Pliny notes (*Nat.* 18.71), had to be imported from India and therefore cost more than
local barley. See also Muecke (1993) 148.

express the Epicurean understanding, as Philodemus explains it, of a "measure of wealth," which holds that it is the management of one's desires and fears that results in the proper administration of wealth (*On Property Management*, col. 23.36–42). One must eliminate the fear of poverty, which inevitably leads to meanness, as well as the unnecessary desire for exotic foods and pleasure, all of which originates in a self-indulgent disposition and often results in the destruction of wealth (coll. 23.42–24.2). In Stertinius' diatribe in *Satires* 2.3, the self-indulgent type is exemplified by individuals like Nomentanus (224–38; cf. *S.* 1.1.102)[70] and the sons of Aesopus and Quintus Arrius, whose desire for extravagant commodities and dainties such as pearls and nightingales eventually stripped them of their resources:

> filius Aesopi detractam ex aure Metellae,
> scilicet ut deciens solidum absorberet, aceto
> diluit insignem bacam: qui sanior ac si
> illud idem in rapidum flumen iaceretve cloacam?
> Quinti progenies Arri, par nobile fratrum
> nequitia et nugis pravorum et amore gemellum
> luscinias soliti inpenso prandere coemptas,
> quorsum abeant? sani ut creta, an carbone notati?   (*S.* 2.3.239–46)

The son of Aesopus took from Metella's ear a wondrous pearl, and meaning to swallow a million at a gulp, steeped it in vinegar. How was he more sane than if he had flung that same thing into a running river or a sewer? The sons of Quintus Arrius, a famous pair of brothers, twins in wickedness, folly, and perverted fancies, used to breakfast on nightingales, bought up at vast cost. Into which list are they to go? Marked with chalk as sane, or with charcoal?

It is Damasippus, however, who, in response to Horace's question: "With what folly do you think I am mad?" (301–2: *qua me stultitia . . . insanire putas?*), criticizes the poet for being avaricious and overly indulgent: this is directly connected to his "mad passion" for love (325: *mille puellarum, puerorum mille furores,* "your thousand passions for boys and girls") and perhaps to his otiose life in the countryside (3: *vini somnique benignus,* "generous of wine and of sleep"), but also includes his desire to imitate Maecenas by extending his property (308: *aedificas*), which is generally understood as a reference to the Sabine estate. With reference to this verb, Frances Muecke (confirming

---

[70] See Rudd (1966) 142.

to some degree H. R. Fairclough's translation as quoted above) reckons that "Horace was probably building or extending the villa on the Sabine farm, where the conversation is imagined as taking place."[71] Horace's self-deprecating response to these accusations involves the comic portrayal of himself as irascible and frustrated with his mad interlocutor (326: *insane*), with no serious attempt to raise an objection or provide a defense of his administration of wealth. Part of his reaction to this occurs in *Satires* 2.6, in which, as seen already, Horace demonstrates the ethical benefits of owning a country estate that functions as a venue for philosophical conversation. On the other hand, another part of his answer to Damasippus' criticisms is cleverly woven into the manner in which the Stoic himself expresses his opinions: one thinks immediately of *Satires* 1.3, where Horace explicitly underscores and rejects the Stoics' harshness and complete lack of mutual forbearance. The difference, of course, is that in *Satires* 2.3 the poet provides an extended example of this insensitivity directly from the mouth of a member of the philosophical sect in question. Indeed, Damasippus' tirade against Horace—to say nothing of Davus' similar observations in *Satires* 2.7— serves the dual purpose of discrediting the former's authority as an effective moralizer and justifying the latter's humility and ability to acknowledge his own faults, as will be seen presently.

INEFFECTUAL FRANKNESS IN
SATIRES 2.3 AND 2.7

Satires 2.3 and 2.7 may be read as complementing or paralleling one another for specific reasons. To begin with, both poems involve overly harsh criticisms from Stoic supporters that recall the observation in *Satires* 1.3 concerning that particular sect's rejection of mutual forbearance. It would appear that in Book 2 the Stoics are given a chance to respond to the poet, but, far from resulting in vindication, the furious attacks of Damasippus and Davus only further highlight their inability to conform to Horace's ethical and aesthetic standards. That is to say, not only are their diatribes far too harsh and divorced from a genuine concern for helping others (like those of Horace), they

[71] Muecke (1993) 165. See also Courtney (2013) 139.

completely violate the doctrine of Callimachean brevity as practiced by Horace and his friends. The long-windedness of Stoics like Crispinus (cf. *S.* 1.1.120 and 1.4.14) and Fabius (cf. *S.* 1.1.14) in Book 1, which additionally characterizes Lucilian satire (cf. *S.* 1.4.9–11), seems to be an inseparable characteristic of this philosophical sect. Diogenes Laertius, for example, states that Chrysippus was said to have written "five hundred lines daily" (DL 7.181: πεντακοσίους γράφοι στίχους ἡμερησίους). Damasippus' sermon, which is approximately 290 lines long and therefore roughly the length of two Horatian satires,[72] seems to have prevented the poet from producing ten poems and thus perfectly complementing Book 1. Aside from both *Satires* 2.3 and 2.7 being merciless Stoic invectives that fail in terms of literary aesthetics and their usefulness for moral correction, both also involve direct and personal criticism of Horace (in the case of Damasippus, this occurs at the end), which causes the poet to lose his patience. Finally, both poems allow Horace to manipulate the diatribe tradition and engage in self-deprecation for the purpose of illustrating how not to apply frank criticism and showcasing the confidence of his literary persona.

As with most of the previous satires, the initial verses of *Satires* 2.3 provide the context in which this diatribe occurs and reveal something about the speaker's views regarding the nature of frank criticism:

> "Sic raro scribis ut toto non quater anno
> membranam poscas, scriptorum quaeque retexens,
> iratus tibi, quod vini somnique benignus
> nil dignum sermone canas. quid fiet? at ipsis
> Saturnalibus huc fugisti." (*S.* 2.3.1–5)

"So seldom do you write that not four times in all the year do you call for the parchment, while you unweave the web of all you have written, and are angry with yourself because, while so generous of wine and of sleep, you turn out no poetry worth talking about. What will be the end? Why, you say, even in the Saturnalia you fled here for refuge."

The preceding lines indicate that Damasippus has taken upon himself the task of criticizing Horace for his excessive leisure in the country,[73] which is preventing him from filling notebooks with the kind of

[72] Hicks (2013) 178.
[73] Rudd (1966) 173 imagines the setting as the Sabine estate. He is followed by Muecke (1993) 133 and Courtney (2013) 135. Hutchinson (2013) 67 briefly discusses the importance of rural seclusion for writing for authors like Cicero and Horace.

satiric invective he had "promised" (6: *promissis*; at this time Horace was also composing the *Epodes*, and it is probable that Damasippus' mention of Archilochus at verse 12 refers to these iambic poems[74]). The impetuousness of this city-dwelling street-preacher differs significantly from the appreciation of the value of convivial *otium* accorded to Ofellus, whom, as Frances Muecke states, Horace portrays as the "ideal of the frugal life in the countryside."[75] Perhaps more importantly, the rookie Stoic's failure to appreciate the philosophical and—for Horace—literary advantages of a "leisurely withdrawal with friends" (*On Property Management*, col. 23.15–16; cf. the poet's description of the literary advantages of *otium* and the withdrawal from society at *Ep.* 2.2.77: *scriptorum chorus omnis amat nemus et fugit urbem*, "The whole chorus of writers loves the grove and flees the city") reflects his misunderstanding of the poet's high standards, which call for refinement and brevity rather than the sheer productivity of an anti-Callimachean, Lucilian "flow" (*S.* 1.10.50: *fluere*). Kirk Freudenburg effectively captures this important difference between the two by noting that: "[W]hat Damasippus sees as a playboy's failure to buckle down and produce vast amounts can be taken as an allusion to the poet's Callimachean aesthetic sense," which is a reference to his "determination to produce small amounts, finely crafted."[76] Instead of appreciating Horace's love of the countryside, Damasippus blames him for his laziness and overindulgence (*S.* 2.3.3: *vini somnique benignus*; cf. 14–15: *inproba Siren | desidia*; for wine and sleep as promoters of poetic excellence and providing inspiration, see *Ep.* 1.19.1–11 and 2.2.78 respectively) and wishes to transport him back to Rome, where the "walking Muse" (*S.* 2.6.17: *musaque pedestri*) will be more productive. In fact, Damasippus is so thirsty for hardcore invective that he virtually hijacks the narrative for his own purposes, as, once again, Kirk Freudenburg explains:

> Damasippus sees no trace of "virtue" [13: *virtute*] in Horace, no satiric vigour, so he has to assume it was "left behind" [ibid.: *relicta*] like some

---

[74] See Kiessling–Heinze (1910) 186, Muecke (1993) 133, Cucchiarelli (2001) 120–5, and also Courtney (2013) 135. Damasippus as well as Davus appear to belong to the group of critics, mentioned at the outset of *Satires* 2.1, who think that Horace's satire is too soft and lacks a certain vigor (2: *sine nervis*).

[75] Muecke (1993) 114. Cf. *Ep.* 1.10.1–2, dedicated to Aristius Fuscus, in which the poet draws a distinction between Epicurean "lovers of the country" (*ruris amatores*) and Stoic "lovers of the city" (*urbis amatorem*). See also Barbieri (1976) 502.

[76] Freudenburg (2001) 113.

forgotten pair of socks that did not make it into the bag. He cannot see it because he equates it with something Horace has failed "miserably" [14: *miser*] to produce: endless reams of lectures against vice; hard-hitting Stoic diatribe. And because Horace cannot produce it, Damasippus undertakes to produce it for him, and so we have the rest of the poem, *ad nauseam*, the second longest lecture Horace (n)ever wrote.[77]

The harshness (to say nothing of the extraordinary length) that characterizes Damasippus' bitter attack is at odds with Horatian satire's usually helpful or in some way constructive criticisms. Frances Muecke marks this difference in her description of the poet's usual approach: "Horace . . . disassociates himself from the Stoics' rigid dogmatism, which swamps the listener without encouraging him to reach the balanced perspective and sense of reality which Horace himself offers elsewhere."[78] Similarly, W. S. Anderson refers to the neophyte's ravings as "impractical moral fanaticism," presumably because they rigidly apply philosophical doctrines without the slightest concern for moral correction.[79] And although in his treatise *On Anger* Philodemus appears to defend the possible usefulness of diatribes (col. 1.12–27), as David Armstrong clearly explains, at the same time he "could not make it clearer that he is keeping his distance from the rhetorical style of Bion in his *On Anger* and Chrysippus' *Remedy for Anger*."[80] In this particular satire, which is one of Horace's longest poems, he clearly parodies the prolixity and endless vitriol of such treatments, even though this humorous imitation is not itself devoid of moral truth, which, despite the poem's nominally Stoic content, is eclectic in nature

---

[77] Freudenburg (2001) 115. For the various mannerisms and *topoi* of the traditional Stoic diatribe which Horace imitates in this poem, see Lejay and Plessis (1915) 384, Cèbe (1966) 262, and Fiske (1971) 388.

[78] Muecke (1993) 131. Mader (2014) 419 calls it a "strident, over-the-top sermon." Plaza (2006) 200 offers a similar observation: "Finally, the accusation that Damasippus hurls against Horace, that he writes rarely and in small quantity, falls flat when we consider its context. The speaker, Damasippus, is a garrulous loser who has changed his profession from merchant to philosopher, and, being bankrupted in his own business has made a habit of interfering with the business of others. This ex-dealer in bric-a-brac is himself not in the least affected by poverty in words, and once he gets to speak, carries on, with very few cues from the main persona, for about 325 lines, making 2.3 the longest poem in Horace's two books of satires. The pseudo-Stoic sermon he delivers is surely meant to sound at least partly silly."

[79] Anderson (1982) 45.   [80] Armstrong (2014a) 108.

(perhaps highlighting Damasippus' lack of understanding) and therefore incorporates many of the commonplaces of Hellenistic ethics, including, as seen previously, Epicurean doctrine.[81] Although the frank criticism employed by the recent convert Damasippus in Satires 2.3 does contain some truth, its overly harsh application and ambitious handling of an extremely broad range of vices is ultimately confusing and unhelpful. Horace immediately makes it clear that the Stoic preacher takes issue with satire that is "kind" (cf. 3: benignus, strictly a reference to Horace's wine-drinking but implying a lack of work ethic regarding critical poetry) and that his predilection is for "threats" (9: minantis), whether those hurled publicly by the poets of Old Comedy or the more private invective of iambographers (cf. 12: Eupolin, Archilochum), some of whom the poet associates with Lucilius in Book 1 and from whom he attempts to distinguish his own satire (cf. 1.4.1–6 for the list of comic poets).[82] The temperament of these poets contrasts especially with the diatribe style of Horace, who, in accordance with Philodemus' observations concerning frankness, is "cheerful, friendly, and gentle" (On Frank Criticism, fr. 85.8–10: ε[ὐη]μέρωι καὶ φιλοφίλωι [και ἠ]πίωι).[83] The result of this is that the Epicurean sage is careful "not to be frank in a haughty and contentious way, nor to say any insolent and contemptuous or disparaging things..." (fr. 37.5–8: [μ]ηδὲ σοβ[αρῶ]ς καὶ [δι]ατε[ταμένως παρρησιάζε]σθαι, [μηδ᾽ ὑβριστικὰ] καὶ καταβλ[ητικά τινα μη]δὲ διασυρτικὰ [λέγειν]; cf. fr. 6.8: [ἐ]πιτιμᾶι μετρίως, "[Epicurus] reproaches in moderation"). As Plutarch observes, although rebukes are not always easy to hear, they should always be beneficial:

ἡ μὲν γὰρ ἀληθὴς καὶ φιλικὴ παρρησία τοῖς ἁμαρτανομένοις ἐπιφύεται, σωτήριον ἔχουσα καὶ κηδεμονικὸν τὸ λυποῦν, ὥσπερ τὸ μέλι τὰ ἡλκωμένα δάκνουσα καὶ καθαίρουσα, τἆλλα δ᾽ ὠφέλιμος οὖσα καὶ γλυκεῖα
(How to Tell a Flatterer from a Friend 59d)

[81] See Rudd (1966) 183 and Fiske (1971) 389. Cf. also Cèbe (1966) 262–3, who says that "Horace denigrates the Stoics' approach and word choice rather than the substance of their doctrine" ("ce sont leurs procédés et leur langage qu'il dénigre, non la substance de leur enseignement").
[82] See Muecke (1993) 133. But the appearance of names like Plato and Menander in Satires 2.3 also signals the switch from the poet's monologue approach to the lighter dialogue format of Book 2.
[83] Michels (1944) 174 makes this connection and Glad (1996) 36–8 discusses it in more detail.

For true and friendly frankness applies itself to those who are commit-
ting errors, and the pain it causes is salutary and benignant, and, just
like honey, it causes the sore places to sting and purifies them as well . . .

Horace's own moderate approach to criticism originates in a sober
realization of his imperfections (cf. *S.* 1.4.130–1: *mediocribus . . . vitiis*
as well as *S.* 1.3.20 and *S.* 1.6.65 for similar admissions), which reflects
Philodemus' description of the sage's gentle criticism and avoidance of
hypocrisy as fundamentally grounded in self-knowledge:

πῶς γὰρ μισεῖν τὸν ἁμαρτάνοντα μὴ ἀπογνώ[σ]ιμα μέλλει, γινώσκω[ν]
αὐτὸν οὐκ ὄντα τέλε[ι]ον καὶ μιμνή<ι>[σκων, ὅτι πάντες ἁμαρτάνειν
εἰώθασιν;]   (*On Frank Criticism*, fr. 46.5–11)

For how can he shun the one who has erred, but not unforgivably,
knowing that he himself is not perfect and remembering that we all
habitually err?

In contrast to this, Damasippus is haughty on account of his recent
conversion to Stoicism (cf. *S.* 2.3.33–45), which has inflamed his mind
with such philosophic zeal that he feels compelled to condemn the entire
world (32: *omnes*). One of the obvious symptoms of this newfound
"wisdom" is his extremely dogmatic and long-winded presentation of
Stoic doctrine, which, as Frances Muecke observes, "is characteristic of
an academic approach, not of Horatian satire's conversational mode."[84]
And although it is true that some of the poems in *Satires* 2 do not display
a strong conversational element, the extraordinary length and doctrin-
aire tone of this particular satire are enough to characterize it as abnor-
mal. The main purpose of Damasippus' lecture is to give a rather
emotional yet systematic condemnation, in light of the Stoic paradox
"all fools are mad," that encompasses every vice but does not offer any
real solution. The regurgitation of his master's lecture, for example,
involves prolix attacks on avarice, ambition, self-indulgence, and superstition, whereas one notes that Horace's diatribe on avarice is only 120
lines long, which makes it approximately sixty lines shorter than that
of Stertinius. Damasippus' representation of such views, moreover, is
neither pithy nor useful, both of which are necessary attributes of the
ideal advisor, nor does its one-sidedness invite the kind of conversational

---

[84] Muecke (1993) 130. One may recall that Horace criticizes the Stoics Fabius (cf. *S.*
1.1.13–14) and Crispinus (cf. *S.* 1.120–1) for being long-winded chatterboxes. See
Gowers (2012) 66 and 84 respectively for their association with this philosophical sect
(some of the evidence for Crispinus is taken from the *Satires* themselves).

exchange and observation that, in addition to being typical of
Horace's introductory satires, are also necessary for successful treatment (cf. *On Frank Criticism*, fr. 51.1–5: ἀκ[ού]σει ... θεωρῶν ἡμᾶς).
For his part, Damasippus is brimming with invective and does little or
no listening; if anything, his approach drowns the listener in a
relentless barrage of rhetorical questions designed to demoralize
without any perceivable benefit: "do you guard...?" (*S.* 2.3.123:
custodis . . .?); "lest you should be in want?" (123: *ne tibi desit?*);
"how small...?" (124: *quantulum...?*); "wherefore...?" (126: *quare
...?*).[85] Another consequence of his diffuse and badgering criticism of
vice that contributes to its overall uselessness is the apparent lack of
an audience or targeted victim: whereas Horace's persona's attacks on
vice are focused and intended to rebuke an interlocutor—if only a
fictional one—and provide admonitory advice for his friends and
patron,[86] his Stoic counterpart addresses the general folly of mankind
and thereby precludes the opportunity for intimate conversation and
correction (Horace himself is put under consideration only at the very
end). Damasippus' exaggeratedly long and comically inept attack on
vice, however, does not prevent Horace from cleverly transforming
his haughtiness into indirect self-examination, which, from the point
of view of the poet, does indeed serve a useful purpose.

It has been demonstrated in previous chapters that it is characteristic of Horatian satire to communicate a subtle, more directly personal message in an indirect and often paradoxical manner. Thus,
Damasippus' arrogant condemnation of the majority of society,
which reveals his ignorance, provides Horace with a suitable vehicle
for self-criticism and an opportunity to underscore his persona's
humble self-awareness. The Stoic zealot directs his final criticisms
toward the poet, who, having cleverly opened the way by means of the
seemingly innocuous question "from what vice of the mind am *I*
presently suffering?" (306–7: *quo me | aegrotare putes animi vitio*),
receives a threefold explanation effectively accusing *Horatius ethicus*
of being a complete hypocrite. More specifically, according to Damasippus the vices from which the poet suffers are the same ones he had
attacked in *Satires* 1, such as economic ambition (308: *aedificas*, "you
are building"). His rival's language here is, as mentioned above, most

likely a reference to the Sabine estate, which at the time Horace was apparently in the process of developing, and Edward Courtney even says that "Damasippus equates this with the lavish construction boom of the time, much deplored by moralists, including Horace himself" (citing *Ep.* 1.1.100: *aedificat*).[87] The Stoic critic also mentions lust (*S.* 2.3.325: *mille puellarum, puerorum mille furores*, "your thousand passions for lads and lasses"), which echoes *Satires* 1.2, and anger (323: *horrendam rabiem*, "your awful temper"; cf. the self-definition at *Ep.* 1.20.25: *irasci celerem, tamen ut placabilis essem*, "quick in temper, yet so as to be easily appeased"[88]), thus providing a connection to Horace's observations in *Satires* 1.3. The first accusation regarding Horace's ambition is bolstered by Damasippus' peculiar version of pictorial imagery (*S.* 2.3.320: *imago*), which, rather than encouraging his listener to observe clinically the likely consequences of his vicious habits in order to motivate reform, employs a traditional fable, which is in fact a modified translation of Babrius' original Greek version (28 = Perry 376) that is more a playful taunt (cf. 320: *abludit*) than a stern warning (cf. 314–20).[89] The point is that Horace's ambition and desire to imitate Maecenas not only contradict his earlier criticisms and therefore expose him for the hypocrite he is, but they also reveal his inconsistency and lack of a proper sense of decorum:

> "accipe: primum
> aedificas, hoc est longos imitaris, ab imo
> ad summum totus moduli bipedalis, et idem
> corpore maiorem rides Turbonis in armis
> spiritum et incessum: qui ridiculus minus illo?
> an, quodcumque facit Maecenas, te quoque verum est,
> tanto dissimilem et tanto certare minorem?"   (*S.* 2.3.307–13)

"Listen. First, you are building, which means, you try to ape big men, though from top to toe your full height is but two feet; and yet you laugh at the strut and spirit of Turbo in his armor, as though they were too

---

[87] Courtney (2013) 139. See also Kiessling–Heinze (1910) 227 and Muecke (1993) 165.

[88] Mayer (1994) 273, who interprets Horace's combination of the adjective and complementary infinitive in this passage as equivalent to the Greek ὀξύχολον, also cites *Odes* 3.9.23: *iracundior Hadria* ("[I am] stormier than the Adriatic").

[89] For Horace's more economic expression of the fable as well as the more vulgar version of Phaedrus (1.24 = Perry 376a), see Rudd (1966) 176–8. As Muecke (1993) 165 observes, the verb *abludo* is found nowhere else in Latin poetry and may be the negative of *adludo* ("to make playful allusion to").

much for his body. How are you less foolish than he? Is it right that
whatever Maecenas does, you also should do, so unlike him as you are
and such a poor match for him?"

This self-deprecating portrait of Horace's relationship with Maecenas,
which is appropriately viewed through the recent convert's Stoic lens,
highlights the poet's social ineptitude or, more precisely, his violation
of the Panaetian notion of "appropriateness" (*aequabilitas*).[90] Cicero
succinctly defines this trait in his treatise *On Duties*:

> Omnino si quicquam est decorum, nihil est profecto magis quam
> aequabilitas universae vitae, tum singularum actionum, quam conser-
> vare non possis si aliorum naturam imitans omittas tuam.   (1.111)

> If there is any such thing as propriety at all, it can be nothing more than
> uniform consistency in the course of our life as a whole and all its
> individual actions, which one would not be able to maintain by copying
> the personal traits of others and eliminating one's own.[91]

As one may recall, this same issue provides the impetus for *Satires* 1.6,
in which the poet addresses his limitations and sense of propriety by
disarmingly repeating the attacks of his envious detractors (cf. 46:
quem rodunt omnes).[92] By the time he had written the poem presently
under consideration, moreover, Maecenas had already rewarded him
with the Sabine estate, which undoubtedly would have provoked—at
least according to Horace's implication in *Satires* 2.3—a resurgence or
perhaps intensification of similar attacks. In all likelihood, therefore,
his vivid portrayal of Damasippus is intended to anticipate these
attacks by putting a face to potential detractors.

At the same time, the public nature of the overzealous interlocutor's criticism and exposure of Horace's faults in some ways reads like
a self-serving description of frankness gone wrong. It is characteristic
of the sage, for example, to promote self-knowledge by means of
communicating his own faults to other wise men and receiving correction, as Philodemus states in *On Frank Criticism* (col. 8b.11–14): καὶ
δή[ξον]ται δηγμὸ[ν] ἑαυτοὺς τὸν ἠπιώτατον καὶ χάριν ε<ἰ>δήσου[σι τῆς
ὠφελίας], "and they [wise men] will sting each other with the gentlest

---

[90] See Muecke (1993) 164–5 and Kemp (2009) 2–17.

[91] Horace actually advises against this within the context of patronage at *Ep.*
1.18.21–36, which Mayer (1994) 245–6 connects to Damasippus' criticism of Horace
as discussed above.

[92] For the importance of this for *Satires* 1.3, see Kemp (2009) 1–17.

of stings and will acknowledge gratitude for the benefit."[93] Plutarch, possibly inspired by the Epicurean tradition and perhaps even by Philodemus himself, makes a very similar observation in his treatise on flattery:

ὑπομιμνησκόμενος γὰρ ἄνευ μνησικακίας ὅτι τοὺς φίλους καὶ αὐτὸς εἰώθει μὴ περιορᾶν ἁμαρτάνοντας ἀλλ᾽ ἐξελέγχειν καὶ διδάσκειν, μᾶλλον ἐνδώσει καὶ παραδέξεται τὴν ἐπανόρθωσιν, ὡς οὖσαν εὐνοίας καὶ χάριτος οὐ μέμψεως ἀνταπόδοσιν οὐδ᾽ ὀργῆς.

(*How to Tell a Flatterer from a Friend* 72 f.)

For by being gently reminded, without any resentment, that he himself has not been accustomed to overlook the errors of his friends but rather to reproach and instruct them, he will be much more inclined to yield and accept correction as being a way to requite a kind and gracious feeling, and not blame or anger.

In *Satires* 2.3 this ideal of frank communication as practiced especially among Epicurean sages completely fails: the sage Damasippus, who employs *ad hominem* attacks (cf. 308–9), does anything but apply gentle and caring admonishment (cf. *On Frank Criticism*, fr. 26.6–7: κηδεμονικὴ νουθέτησις), while Horace is certainly not grateful for his overly harsh criticisms.[94] Instead, he underscores the relentlessness of the mad sage (cf. *S.* 2.3.326: *insane*) and his furious onslaught by posing as an exhausted victim, desperately crying out "enough already!" (323: *iam desine*), "hold it!" (324: *teneas*), and "spare me!" (326: *parcas*). Despite this humorous portrayal of frank criticism gone awry, in the end the poet still manages to "show his errors forthrightly and speak of his failings publicly" (*On Frank Criticism*, fr. 40.2–5: [δεικνύειν ἀνυ]ποστόλως τὰς διαμαρ[τί]ας καὶ κοινῶς εἰπ[εῖ]ν [ἐ]λαττώσεις), which, in addition to underscoring his self-awareness also disassociates him from the superficial righteousness of arrogant and ignorant zealots like Damasippus.[95] Indeed, H. B. Evans' observation concerning Davus in *Satires* 2.7 may rightly be applied to Damasippus' similar attitude toward the poet in this diatribe: "The joke, of course, is on the Mad Satirist who in his dogmatic

---

[93] Although the end of this statement reflects the conjecture of Olivieri (1914) 49, the importance of "benefits" in connection with frank criticism recurs in other, well-preserved passages of the treatise (e.g. frs. 20.4, 49.5 and col. 17b.10–11).

[94] For the concept of "cheerful admonishment" as Philodemus' preferred mode of correction, see Glad (1995) 120.

[95] Evans (1978) 307.

fervor lacks the wisdom, good sense and understanding which already characterize Horace's role in the satires."

In *Satires* 2.7 Horace presents his audience with a complementary self-examination of his own ethical credentials through the mouth of Davus, whose critical scrutiny of his master's faults is more focused and direct than that of Damasippus. In fact, Davus' ascription to Horace of vices the poet had systematically examined and condemned previously is foreshadowed by the final verses of *Satires* 2.3, which mention ambition, lust, and anger only in passing (323–5). Both poems are concerned with the seemingly all-inclusive condemnation of moral failings through extended diatribes, which Horace, in a spirit of parodic playfulness, attributes to their philosophical proclivities as Stoic sympathizers (although in the case of Davus this is not revealed until later). In a manner similar to that of Damasippus, the criticisms of Davus reproduce for his master the teachings of a Stoic authority (*S.* 2.7.45: *Crispini*; cf. *S.* 2.3.33: *Stertinius*), although twice removed (*S.* 2.7.45: *quae . . . docuit me ianitor*) and from a philosopher Horace had criticized earlier for being unreliable and loquacious.[96] Pseudo-Acro notes that Horace "also makes fun of Crispinus in the first book" (*ad* 45: *De Crispino et in primo iocatur*), quoting from *Satires* 1.1 (120: *Crispini scrinia lippi*, "the roles of bleary-eyed Crispinus"), but the poet also mentions him by name in *Satires* 1.3 (138–9: *ineptum . . . Crispinum*, "crazy Crispinus") and in *Satires* 1.4 (13–16: *Crispinus minimo me provocat*, "Crispinus challenges me at long odds"). And although Davus' report comes "somewhat garbled through the mouth of his fellow slave,"[97] his frank criticism is aimed exclusively at Horace and so encompasses in its entirety the topics of previous satires (whereas Damasippus had rather haphazardly directed his venomous invective toward society at large).[98] H. B. Evans notes that, "Because Davus concentrates on Horace alone, his speech to his master is more carefully focused and is reduced in length to approximately a third of Damasippus' rambling discourse."[99] Also worth considering here is the similar observation of Maria Plaza:

---

[96] For Horace's personal rivalry with Crispinus, who was also a poet and a moralizer, see Oltramare (1926) 129–37 and Stahl (1974) 44. The theme of ὑπομνήματα in this poem is discussed by Fiske (1971) 405.

[97] Muecke (1993) 215.   [98] Rudd (1966) 194–5. See also Hicks (2013) 189.

[99] Evans (1978) 307.

The difference from 2.3, another inverted poem where the satiric microphone is given to the persona's opponent (Damasippus), is that 2.7 is much more compact. Davus utters a lively *sermo* in the proper colloquial style, instead of abstract examples he constantly attacks Horace in person, and by being a slave accusing his master of enslavement he embodies the main theme of the satire.[100]

His speech and its topics, which are accompanied by vivid illustrations and examples pertaining to the poet himself, may be organized in the following manner: the inability to maintain constancy with regard to one's behavior (6–20), which corresponds to Horace's discussion of *aequabilitas* in 1.3; this first topic segues into the blaming of one's fortune and restlessness in general (22–9), which is introduced by the μεμψιμοιρία theme in *Satires* 1.1 (1–22); the topic of obsequiousness and subservience to Maecenas follows (29–42), which may be compared to Horace's emphasis on his passiveness and independence in 1.6 (cf. *Ep.* 1.7) as well as to his portraits of the toady in 1.9 and Ulysses in 2.5; sexual promiscuity and adultery are next (46–84), which easily contrast with the poet's condemnation of such vices in 1.2; finally, Davus criticizes his master for his refined palate and taste for luxurious foods (103–15), which contradicts his praise of meager fare in 2.2 and rejection of sumptuous feasting in 2.4 and 2.8.[101] In addition to providing "a sort of summary statement of Horatian satire . . . not at all unsuitable as one of the final poems,"[102] this critical review also provides Horace with another opportunity for self-revelation through the kind of public confession Philodemus recommends (cf. *On Frank Criticism*, fr. 49.2–7). Hans-Peter Stahl provides a striking description of the confessional nature of the poet's verses:

> Even if one refuses to acknowledge Horace as a precursor of authors like Goethe or Augustine, namely, as a writer of confessions, or is unwilling to recognize the self-revealing character of his poetry, nevertheless it is still possible in this passage to speak of a confessional element. Horace's verses likewise resemble those of a diary, a personal letter or some other

---

[100] Plaza (2006) 215.

[101] Rudd (1966) 194 has a similar organization, although, aside from some additional observations, I more closely follow that of Evans (1978) 308–9.

[102] Evans (1978) 312.

kind of private journal, as the poet himself suggests in *Satires* 2.1.30 ff., the last and definitive description of his model Lucilius.[103]

As in *Satires* 2.3, Horace's comic portrayal of a sermonizing "late learner" again exploits the Epicurean stereotype regarding Stoic harshness, cleverly transforming it into the means by which he emphasizes his willingness to disclose what is secret to his audience of close friends (cf. *S.* 1.4.73: *nec recito cuiquam nisi amicis, idque coactus,* "nor do I recite them to any save my friends, and then only when pressed," and *On Frank Criticism,* fr. 42.6–11: καὶ τῶν συνήθων δὲ [π]ολλοὶ μηνύσουσιν ἐθελονταί πως, οὐδ᾽ ἀνακρίνοντος τοῦ καθηγουμένο[υ δ]ιὰ τὴν κηδεμ[ονία]ν, "And many of the intimate associates will spontaneously disclose what is secret, without the teacher examining them, on account of their concern . . ."). As will be seen, the fact that Davus is one of Horace's "household members" (*familiares*) means that his criticisms are the result of frequent observations within a private setting, which, to a certain degree, provides the material for another humorous yet ultimately self-serving display of a Stoic's failure to administer properly frankness as the Epicureans understood and practiced it.

Horace's portrayal of himself as the master who receives criticism from his slave during the Saturnalia provides a suitable and distinctively Roman context for a comic engagement with the principles of frankness as Philodemus explains them. The circumstances related to this strange reversal of roles and Davus' identity as keen observer of another's faults are introduced without delay:

> "Iamdudum ausculto et cupiens tibi dicere servos
> pauca reformido." "Davusne?" "ita, Davus, amicum
> mancipium domino et frugi quod sit satis, hoc est,
> ut vitale putes." "age, libertate Decembri,
> quando ita maiores voluerunt, utere; narra." (*S.* 2.7.1–5)

Davus: "I've been listening some time, and wishing to say a word to you, but as a slave I dare not."

---

[103] Stahl (1974) 51–2: "Wenn man Horaz als vor-goetheschem und vor-augustinischem Schriftsteller den Konfessions- oder Bekenntnis-Charakter seiner Dichtung nicht hat anerkennen wollen, so kann man hier doch von einem Geständnis-Charakter sprechen. Auch seine Dichtung hat . . . Tagebuch-, Brief- oder kurz Privatcharakter, wie er selbst in der letzen und maßgeblichen Beschreibung seines Vorbildes Lucilius andeutet (sat. II I, 30ff.)." For the Epicurean practice of confession as a means of communal psychogogy, see especially Glad (1995) 124–32.

Horace: "Is that Davus?"

Davus: "Yes, Davus, a slave loyal to his master, and fairly honest—that is, so that you need not think him too good to live."

Horace: "Come, use the license December allows, since our fathers willed it so. Have your say."

To anyone familiar with Roman comedy, the vocabulary and colloquial tone in this opening passage make it perfectly clear that Horace intends to couch the following conversation within this same tradition. Not only is the opening verb *ausculto* mostly relegated to comic playwrights, being extremely common in Plautus and appearing eighteen times in Terence,[104] but the inclusion of distinctively comic and slave-related words like *mancipium* and *frugi*, as well as the conversational use of *age*, makes the same connection. One may add to this list the later appearance in the same poem of "scape-gallows" (22: *furcifer*), which is an abusive term commonly directed toward slaves by their masters in Plautus' works (it appears only twice in Terence, at *Brothers* 618 and *Eunuch* 129).[105] Indeed, the name "Davus" itself, which is probably taken from Terence's play *The Woman of Andros*,[106] appears to imply that Horace is being addressed by the *servus fallax* typical of comic plots. On the other hand, this particular version of Davus clearly indicates that, although restrained by the fear that normally motivates comic servants to deceive their masters (2: *reformido*), he wishes temporarily to abandon his apprehensions in order to address Horace as a social equal and candidly denounce him face to face:

Satires 2.7 is the richest of all the poems described thus far, because it features an additional perspective that is missing from the others. This perspective has to do with the switching of the usual roles between speaker and listener as sanctioned by the imagined setting of the Roman Saturnalia, in which equality between slaves and masters prevails or even the masters serve their slaves.[107]

---

[104] Cf. Courtney (2013) 155.   [105] Muecke (1993) 214.

[106] For the characterization of Davus in this play, see Plaza (2006) 216 and Karakasis (2013) 213–14.

[107] Stahl (1974) 43: "Die reichste unter den eben beschriebenen Satiren ist II 7, weil sie eine zusätzliche Perspektive besitzt, die allen andern fehlt: ich meine die Änderung der gewohnten Rollen zwischen Sprecher und Hörer, wie sie die hier fingierte Situation der römischen Saturnalien gestattet, wo zwischen Sklaven und Herren Gleichheit herrscht, oder gar die Herren ihre Sklaven bedienen."

Expounding on this interpretation, one may say that Davus wishes to employ the same "freedom of speech" (4: *libertate*) that is understood to be the satirist's prerogative, as Horace indicates elsewhere (cf. *S.* 1.4.103–4: *liberius si | dixero quid*, "if in my words I am too free . . . ").[108] In placing himself in the role of moral expert Davus closely imitates his master, adopting not only his expressions (6: *pars hominum*; cf. *S.* 1.1.61: *pars hominum*)[109] but also his concern with privately communicating advice to intimate associates and friends (2: *amicum*; cf. *S.* 1.4.73: *amicis*).

Despite the obvious irony and humor associated with such a reversal, there does appear to be a philosophical precedent for this relationship in the lives of individuals like Epicurus, whose servant named Mys, according to Diogenes Laertius, studied philosophy along with his master (DL 10.3): συνεφιλοσόφουν δ᾽ αὐτῷ . . . καὶ οἱ ἀδελφοί . . . καὶ δοῦλος Μῦς ὄνομα, "And Epicurus' three brothers practiced philosophy along with him, as did a slave of his named Mys."[110] As an individual who has shared living space with his master for an extended period of time, Davus has a proper understanding of Horace's habits and behavioral faults, which, despite the latter's apparent ignorance, have not gone unnoticed. On the contrary, as Philodemus explains, privacy and community life are so vital for the effective application of Epicurean frankness that even if a master does not disclose his vices, his slaves are nevertheless conscious of them (*On Frank Criticism*, col. 12a.5–8): ἐὰν δὲ μηδὲν μὲν ἐπιφέρωνται τῶν τοιούτων, συνοίδασιν ἄλλο[ι] τε καὶ [οἱ] οἰκέται, "But if they bring up no such thing, the slaves especially know . . . " Accordingly, Horace's attentive slave reveals that he has been quite observant in listening at the door (*S.* 2.7.1: *Iamdudum ausculto*), presumably while the poet recites his satires and condemns the same vices from which he himself is suffering, although Horace is intentionally obscure regarding what exactly Davus was listening to (which has prompted a variety of opinions from commentators[111]). The verb *ausculto*,

---

[108] See Stahl (1974) 45 and Cucchiarelli (2001) 157–8. Evans (1978) 309 and Sharland (2005) 104–5 discuss in more detail the significance of the reversal of the roles of satirist and listener in this poem.

[109] Other examples are given by Evans (1978) 310, Muecke (1993) 215, and Courtney (2013) 155.

[110] See Cucchiarelli (2001) 158.

[111] Palmer (1893) 356–7 offers five answers given by older scholars such as Richard Bentley, but ultimately agrees with the view of the ancient scholiasts, namely, that

which typically means "to hear or listen with attention" (*OLD* s.v. 1; cf. Plaut. *Stichus* 546: *ausculto atque animum advorto sedulo*, "I'm listening and paying very careful attention"), additionally may recall Philodemus' words concerning the important role of attentiveness in administering frank criticism (*On Frank Criticism*, fr. 51.1–5). By treating the *Satires* as an inadvertent confession of moral hypocrisy, Davus differs significantly from Damasippus, who criticizes the poet for his lack of productivity and for not being satirical enough (*S.* 2.3.1–16). But like Juvenal (1.1.1: *Semper ego auditor tantum, numquamne reponam...?*, "Am I always to be a mere listener? Will I never have the chance to respond?"), who was in all likelihood inspired by the opening of *Satires* 2.7,[112] Davus cannot remain silent for much longer while Horace continues to hold a double standard, and, in keeping with his character as a Stoic admirer, takes full advantage of the "license of December" offered by the Saturnalia in order to express his disgust without reserve. This ancient festival, which involved the loosening of traditional social restraints between masters and slaves,[113] likewise offers Davus the perfect moment in which to address Horace's intolerable hypocrisy and exercise frank criticism (this celebration also provides Damsippus with the opportunity to address the poet with impunity, cf. *S.* 2.3.4–5: *ipsis | Saturnalibus*). As previsouly mentioned, Philodemus discusses the importance of applying frank criticism in a cheerful manner and "at the opportune moment" (*On Frank Criticism*, col. 17b.3: κατὰ καιρόν),[114] which ideally is not hampered by social restraints and leads to mutual goodwill, but for Davus becomes the chance to unleash non-stop rebuke under the pretense of friendly intentions

---

Davus was listening to Horace scold some other slaves. Evans (1978) 309–10, probably inspired by the reversal-of-roles theme emphasized by Stahl (1974) 43, suggests that Davus was listening to Horace recite his satires. Courtney (2013) offers the same explanation. It is possible that he had overheard his master reading *Satires* 2.6, which would add to the humor of the last verses of this poem (117–18): *ocius hinc te | ni rapis, accedes opera agro nona Sabino*, "If you don't take yourself off in a jiffy, you'll make the ninth laborer on my Sabine farm."

[112] On the likelihood that Horace's opening in *Satires* 2.7 inspired that of Juvenal, see Evans (1978) 310 n. 15, Muecke (1993) 214, and Sharland (2005) 107.

[113] For the festival in general and the tradition of slaves playing "king for a day," see Sharland (2005) 103–20 and Scullard (1981) 205–7.

[114] See Gigante (1983) 68–9. Also Glad (1995) 142: "He [sc. the sage] should apply frank speech opportunely and cheerfully."

and altruism (cf. *S.* 2.7.2–3: *amicum* | *mancipium domino et frugi*, "a slave loyal [lit. friendly] to his master, and fairly honest"). This onslaught is perhaps foreshadowed by the strained tone of "for a long time now" (1: *Iamdudum*) as well as the rather emotional force of "desiring" (1: *cupiens*) and, in light of the intense diatribe to follow, the obviously ironic inclusion of "a few things" (2: *pauca*). It is quite possible, moreover, that in addition to allowing Horace to place himself under the scrutiny of a lowly slave, the extraordinary circumstances occasioned by this festive setting also entail or at least seem to suggest a self-inflicted inversion of the poet's satiric persona.

There are a number of important differences between Horace's self-justifying description of his upbringing in *Satires* 1.4, which establishes his ethical credentials and role as moralist at the outset of his satiric project, and his self-deprecating portrayal in 2.7, which seems to compromise this credibility through the exposure of his numerous vices. In the first instance, the poet is a youth whose impressionable mind (*S.* 1.4.128: *teneros animos*) is ready to be formed by his loving father's moral teachings (120–1: *sic me* | *formabat puerum dictis*), whereas by the time Davus approaches him with moral advice he is much older and stubbornly set in his ways. Horace's patience for such moralizing wears thin early on in the poem, as his demand to know the practical aim of his interlocutor's drivel reveals (*S.* 2.7.21–2): *non dices hodie, quorsum haec tam putida tendant,* | *furcifer?*, "Are you to take all day, you scape-gallows, in telling me the point of such rot?" (this kind of expression recurs in the diatribe satires as an expression of the practicality and usefulness of the poet's observations, cf. 1.1.14–15, 1.2.23, and 1.3.19–20).[115] Furthermore, in his youth his father's instruction resulted in the development of a good conscience (*S.* 1.4.133: *consilium proprium*), while, according to Davus, in his later years Horace's only proper attributes are his vicious traits (*S.* 2.7.89: *proprium quid*), which easily overcome his supposed moral and intellectual strengths (103: *virtus atque animus*). Of course, Horace's father had been concerned with preserving his son's reputation and financial stability (*S.* 1.4.116–19), which, in a manner consistent with Epicurean frankness, he attempted to achieve by taking advantage of the critical moment and admonishing him

---

[115] As Muecke (1993) 217 observes, the colloquial nature of such language adds to the overall conversational and comic element of this poem.

through vivid examples of the misery of others. In his own way, Davus also takes advantage of the opportune moment, namely, the Saturnalia, in order to address the poet. Instead of admonishment, however, which Philodemus describes as useful for preventing bad habits and associated with friendly and cheerful correction through examples (as a kind of τέχνη νουθετητική that adopts a gentle and philotropeic method of rebuke; cf. *On Frank Criticism*, frs. 72–3),[116] he deals out unrestrained rebuke, as if Horace were a stubborn and blindly vicious pupil. In other words, whereas Horace's father uses frankness in order to prevent his son from becoming vicious, Davus uses it to rebuke him on the grounds that he has in fact succumbed to the vices his father had so firmly condemned and is therefore thoroughly corrupt. Accordingly, his first application of frankness addresses Horace's fickle inconsistency and lack of integrity, which originate in his general discontentment with life:

> "laudas
> fortunam et mores antiquae plebis, et idem,
> siquis ad illa deus subito te agat, usque recuses,
> aut quia non sentis, quod clamas, rectius esse,
> aut quia non firmus rectum defendis et haeres
> nequiquam caeno cupiens evellere plantam." (*S.* 2.7.22–7)

"You praise the fortune and the manners of the men of old; and yet, if on a sudden some god were for taking you back to those days, you would refuse every time; either because you don't really think that what you are ranting is sounder, or because you are wobbly in defending the right, and, though vainly longing to pull your foot from the filth, yet stick fast to it."

Davus' initial evaluation of his master's disposition describes the overall failure to adhere to his father's core teaching, which was firmly centered on "living contentedly" (*S.* 1.4.108: *viverem uti contentus*) and placed the highest value on the "ancestral traditions" (117: *traditum ab antiquis morem*). As a consequence of having failed to live up to these moral standards, which are supposed to provide the justification for Horace's persona's criticisms, the poet's credentials are essentially revoked and he is given a taste of his own medicine: like the discontented masses in *Satires* 1.1 to whom a god offers an opportunity for

---

[116] See Gigante (1983) 78–82 and Glad (1995) 120. The distinction between admonition that is preventative and straightforward rebuke is mentioned by Michels (1944) 174 and Dewitt (1935) 313.

change (15: *si quis deus*), he too would refuse on account of his lack of independent resolve. Other scholars have observed that Horace is guilty of more than just μεμψιμοιρία: his main fault, according to Davus, is that he lacks independence (αὐτάρκεια), which he masks by means of clever poetry and the criticism of other people's vices.[117]

One of the many differences between Horace and the miser in *Satires* 1.1 is that the latter is ignorant of "the right" (107: *rectum*), whereas the poet fully appreciates the concept of rectitude but, according to Davus as quoted in the passage above, lacks the determination and moral strength to adhere to it steadfastly (*non firmus rectum defendis*). For this reason, Davus logically connects his master's discontentment and moral weakness to his false praise of meager fare:

> "si nusquam es forte vocatus
> ad cenam, laudas securum holus ac, velut usquam
> vinctus eas, ita te felicem dicis amasque,
> quod nusquam tibi sit potandum. Iusserit ad se
> Maecenas serum sub lumina prima venire
> convivam: 'nemo oleum fert ocius? ecquis
> audit?' cum magno blateras clamore fugisque." (*S.* 2.7.29–35)

"If so it be that you are asked out nowhere to supper, you praise your quiet dish of herbs, and, as though you were in chains when you do go anywhere, you call yourself lucky, and hug yourself, because you have not to go out for some carousal. Let but Maecenas bid you at a late hour come to him as a guest, just at lamp-lighting time: 'Won't someone bring me oil this instant? Does nobody hear me?' So you scream and bawl, then tear off."

This kind of inconsistency additionally seems to imply a certain degree of moral relativism, which, as Roland Mayer observes,[118] is very similar to that of the infamous Maenius in *Epistles* 1.15 (cf. *S.* 1.3.19–24), to whom the poet compares himself:

> nimirum hic ego sum; nam tuta et parvola laudo,
> cum res deficiunt, satis inter vilia fortis;
> verum ubi quid melius contingit et unctius, idem
> vos sapere et solos aio bene vivere, quorum
> conspicitur nitidis fundata pecunia villis. (*Ep.* 1.15.42–6)

---

[117] Muecke (1993) 217 and Rudd (1966) 189.   [118] Mayer (1994) 217.

Such a man, in truth, am I. When means fail, I cry up a safe and lowly lot, resolute enough where all is paltry: but when something better and richer comes my way I, the same man, say that only men like you are wise and live well—whose invested wealth is displayed in handsome villas.

Despite the poet's words here, the obvious difference between these two is that, unlike Maenius, who in *Satires* 1.3 overlooks his own faults, Horace has "confessed to a weakness, displaying honesty," and thereby "showed himself as skillful and confident enough to laugh at himself."[119] At the same time, however, the poet playfully suggests, both in the above epistle and in *Satires* 2.7, that he may in fact be, as Frances Muecke states, "a glutton and Maecenas' parasite, while claiming to be his friend."[120] Indeed, in *Epistles* 1.17 Horace gives the otherwise unknown Scaeva ironic advice on how to acquire favors such as "food" (48: *victum*) from a grateful patron,[121] and Davus even criticizes Horace's taste for dainty foods toward the end of his tirade. Here he interestingly employs the verb *captare* in order to brand the poet as a glutton and a freeloader,[122] just as Horace had done with Ulysses in *Satires* 2.2:

> tibi ingens
> virtus atque animus cenis responsat opimis?
> obsequium ventris mihi perniciosius est cur?
> tergo plector enim. qui tu inpunitior illa,
> quae parvo sumi nequeunt, ebsonia captas?
> nempe inamarescunt epulae sine fine petitae
> inlusique pedes vitiosum ferre recusant
> corpus. (*S.* 2.7.102–9)

Does your heroic virtue and spirit defy rich suppers? Why is it more ruinous for me to obey the stomach's call? My back, to be sure, pays for it. But how do you escape punishment more than I, when you hunt for

---

[119] Plaza (2006) 192.

[120] Muecke (1993) 218. Gold (1987) 130, however, states the following: "Some critics have detected in *Epist.* 1.17 and 1.18 a change of tone to disillusionment, bitterness, and alienation from Maecenas. Horace does not, however, show any bitterness at his own situation; rather, he uses an exploration of the bad forms of patronage to clarify his views, in a more general way than in previous works, on the proper and acceptable kind. Each example of repellant behavior here causes us to remember that it is not Maecenas who is under discussion."

[121] For the name, see Mayer (1994) 231 and cf. *S.* 2.1.53, where it also occurs.

[122] Cf. Kiessling–Heinze (1910) 333.

those dainties which cannot be bought at small cost? Why, that feasting, endlessly indulged, turns to gall, and the feet you've duped refuse to bear up your sickly body.

It would appear, therefore, that Horace is nothing more than an actor who, like the parasite, openly praises (cf. 22: *laudas* and 29: *tollis ad astra*) virtue before the wealthy Maecenas but only, as the passage immediately quoted above illustrates, in the hopes of getting a free meal (cf. 32–5). Part of this front with regard to the flatterer involves deflecting attention away from his own shortcomings, as Davus says when he accuses Horace of employing semantics for the purpose of obscuring his vices (*S.* 2.7.41–2): *insectere velut melior verbisque decoris | obvolvas vitium?*, "Would you presume to assail me, as though you were a better man, and would you throw over your own vices a cloak of seemly words?" Finally, Davus criticizes Horace for his insatiable lust by applying the Stoic paradox, "only the wise man is free and the foolish are slaves" (83: *quisnam igitur liber? sapiens*; cf. Cic. *Parad.* 5: *solum sapientem esse liberum, et omnem stultum servum*, "[they say that] only the wise man is free and all fools are slaves," and DL 7.121 [= *SVF* 3.355]: μόνον τ' ἐλεύθερον, τοὺς δὲ φαύλους δούλους, "[He said that the sage] alone is free, whereas lesser people are slaves"),[123] which, coming from the mouth of a household slave, clearly serves to underscore further the reversal of roles conceded by the Saturnalian privilege. As one may recall, Horace's father had attempted to prevent such a disposition by emphasizing the ruined reputation caused by chasing harlots as well as matrons (*S.* 1.4.111–15). Davus, however, explicitly accuses his master of being "captivated by another man's wife" (*S.* 2.7.46: *te coniunx aliena capit*), which, even if not equivalent to an adulterous affair (cf. 72: *non sum moechus*), highlights Horace's uncontrollable desire for illicit love.[124] Taking into consideration the Stoic point of view, as Edward Courtney does, it seems that Davus is "equating desire and accomplishment; remove fear of punishment and Horace will be as adulterous as the best of them."[125] By means

---

[123] See also Rudd (1966) 190 n. 45 and Muecke (1993) 219.

[124] One is reminded of Suetonius' account, probably inspired by *Satires* 2.3 and 2.7 as well as the *Odes* in general, of how Horace had surrounded his bedroom with mirrors so that he would be able to view his lovemaking from every possible angle.

[125] Courtney (2013) 157. Evans (1978) 310 n. 19 makes a similar observation. This is in some ways consistent with Horace's message in *Satires* 1.2, in which a healthy fear of punishment or a consideration of the negative consequences of adultery outweighs any foreseeable pleasure derived from such relationships, as Plaza (2006)

of these retrospective criticisms the poet shares with his audience a self-reflective summary of his literary persona, balancing, as it were, his positive self-portrayal in the programmatic satires in Book 1 by means of Davus' negative appraisal made in hindsight toward the end of the collection.

Despite his apparent familiarity with Horace's vices and sustained criticism aimed at exposing his master's hypocrisy, in the end Davus, in addition to being a *doctor ineptus*, is also a rather obnoxious interlocutor whose invective paradoxically only confirms the moral competence and confidence of the poet's persona.[126] Like Damasippus, whom Horace portrays as a clueless Stoic since he applies salubrious doctrines to everyone but himself, Davus is not even close to being the ideal sage: not only is he introduced by means of language better suited to the comic stage than to the observations of a Stoic philosopher, but he admits to being in the midst of an emotional quandary (1–2: *cupiens . . . reformido*) and anything but apathetic, which is certainly a humorous touch on the part of Horace. Even worse, Davus misunderstands the paradoxical antithesis concerning wise men and slaves, which, contrary to his preference for the comparative in issuing moral statements (e.g. 96: *peccas minus atque ego*), for the Stoics is absolute and thus does not admit of degrees of difference (cf. Horace's correct representation of this doctrine at *S.* 1.3.96: *quis paria esse fere placuit peccata*, "Those whose creed is that sins are much on a par").[127] Aside from his comic nature and philosophical incompetence, Davus also resembles Damasippus in the harshness and relentlessness of his frank criticism, which does not, as H. B. Evans explains, correspond to actual moral failings of the poet:

> Davus' experiment in satire is not completely successful; we regard it rather as a misguided attempt which merits the angry reaction of his master. To be effective satire should serve a purpose, and most of

211–12 explains: "Davus' argument that his master is only abstaining from adultery because of fear (2.7.72–77) is a shameful charge for a Stoic, but not for an Epicurean, to whom fear of subsequent suffering is an acceptable reason for checking his behavior. The 'misera formido,' wretched fear, imputed by Davus has in fact been used as a respectable (Epicurean) argument against seducing other men's wives throughout Horace's reasoning in satire 1.2." See also Hicks (2013) 193.

[126] Hicks (2013) 194: "Even if these accusations do prove true, however, it is hard to see how a little self-irony is going to overpower Horace's basic portrayal of the Stoics in general as going over the deep end."

[127] See Courtney (2013) 156.

Davus' does not. Indeed, after having read a similar and more long-winded diatribe within the same book in *S.* 2.3, we are pleased when Horace shouts down his slave after some hundred lines.[128]

And shout him down he certainly does, with hilarious threats of violence that have both comic and tragic tones (*S.* 2.7.116–17): *unde mihi lapidem ?. . . unde sagittas?*, "Where can I get a stone?. . . where can I find arrows?"[129] Similar to the ending of *Satires* 2.3, where Horace plays the overwhelmed victim of a moralizing Stoic's hard-hitting frankness, the poet once again reacts negatively to his interlocutor's observations. In the case of Davus, however, he seemingly places himself in the role of the recalcitrant pupil (although his reaction may have more to do with his servant's malignant approach), who, rather than accept correction in a docile fashion, as Philodemus explains, "vehemently resists frankness . . . and responds with bitterness" (*On Frank Criticism*, frs. 5.6–6.4: τὸ[ν σφοδ]ρῶς ἀντέχο[ν]τα παρρησίαι . . . τῶι δὲ καὶ [πικρ]ότητας ἀποδιδόντι).[130] Nevertheless, according to the Epicurean philosopher it is important for the one applying frankness to be persistent, for, even if the pupil initially despises the treatment, he will eventually, through multiple applications of this method, come to recognize his faults and become purified:

καὶ [τ]ότε συν[ε]χόμενος τοῖς ἐκχαυνο[ῦ]σι πάθεσιν ἢ κοινῶς ἀντικρούου-
σιν, εἶτα κουφισθείς, ὑπακούσεται. καὶ τότε τυχὼν τῶν διαστρεφόντων,
νῦν οὐ τεύξετα[ι]· καὶ πρότερον ἀν[τ]ιδοκε[ύ]ων, κα[ὶ] το[ῦ]το πλανω[δ]
ὡς οὐ πεπόηκεν, ὕστερο[ν] φωραθεὶς κα[ὶ] εὐφρονῶν ποήσει.]

(*On Frank Criticism*, fr. 66.6–16)[131]

Then, he was in the grip of plethoric or, generally, constipating pas-sions; but now, purged, he will obey; though then he had met with

[128] Evans (1978) 310.

[129] Muecke (1993) 226 cites Plaut. *Haunted House* 266 (*lapidem*) and *Odes* 1.12.24 (*sagitta*).

[130] See Gigante (1974) 41 and Glad (1995) 137–52 for "strong" students. Interest-ingly enough, Horace's outburst in verses 111–15 seems to be a reaction to Davus' observation that his master is a bad Epicurean, as the mention of enjoying *otium* and avoiding *cura* suggest (cf. *Odes* 3.1.40: *post equitem sedet atra cura*, "Dark Anxiety rides behind you, though you are a Roman knight").

[131] Glad (1995) 147–8 discusses this passage in more detail. As Konstan et al. (1998) 73 note, the verb ἀντιδοκέω, which they render "to be on the look-out," is unattested elsewhere. The translation adopted above is based on the suggestion of Gigante (1983) 79–80, which is also followed by Glad (1995) 147.

things that distorted him, now he will encounter them no longer. Then, he was contrary to your opinion and would not do it because he was wandering; now, caught red-handed [he will recover himself and do it.]

Philodemus observes that, through persistence, a stubborn pupil will learn to trust (πειθαρχήσει) the one criticizing frankly, eventually heeding (ὑπακούσεται) and even happily accepting the admonishment (εὐφρονῶν) after having been purified (κουφισθείς; the process of relief or κούφισις is also described in terms of "purification" in fr. 46.4–5: καθάρσεως).¹³² It is abundantly clear from the final exchange between Horace and Davus, however, which resembles the burlesque ending of *Satires* 2.3, that purification and final acceptance are by no means the end-products of his household interlocutor's critical approach. For this reason, Davus' attempt to motivate correction through frankness completely fails, and, despite his overly negative description of Horace's bad habits being based on personal experience, one is left doubting both his motives and his overall trustworthiness as a moralist. As H. B. Evans puts it, "Since Horace has already treated these failings within his two books, one is left wondering whether it is worth listening to Davus at all."¹³³ If anything, this third-rate philosopher seems more concerned with using the festive license in order to unload his bottled-up hatred than with bringing about any serious moral reform (a fine friend, indeed). In accordance with Horace's premeditated approach, the intended result of his failure is the same as in *Satires* 2.3: the overbearing and silly slave, in the process of venting his disgust for vice through a Stoic diatribe, actually becomes the means by which Horace applies disarming criticism to himself and thus displays his good cheer and sense of moral honesty, which is a portrayal his audience of close friends would have understood and appreciated.

Horace's self-portrayal as a well-disposed and virtuous friend of Maecenas, who, despite the critical observations of his detractors, consistently draws from the ethical views of Epicurean contemporaries like Philodemus in order to dodge the criticism and maintain the moral high ground, is in many ways too good to be true. But the fact that his creation of a morally upright and philosophically coherent persona reflects an obvious concern with issues such as friendship and the management of wealth, and that this concern is in many ways

---

¹³² See Glad (1995) 155.　　¹³³ Evans (1978) 311.

framed by Epicureanism, suggests that early in his career as a poet Horace was very attracted to the teachings and way of life advocated by the Garden. Of course, scholars and critics have always detected the presence of philosophical doctrines in the *Satires*, but this presence has rarely been considered an essential or unifying component of these poetic observations of vice. The preceding study has endeavored to offer an interpretation that will hopefully lead to a deeper appreciation of the presence of Epicureanism in the *Satires*. At the very least, it attempts to encourage readers of Horace's earliest works to consider these underlying doctrines in the light of an author whose writings are not widely known and whose influence has consequently not been taken into account seriously enough. Philodemus' ethical treatises obviously cannot, on their own, address every aspect of Horatian satire or provide an answer to all of the questions scholars may have. They can, however, serve as a useful source or tool for viewing these poems from a new angle, or even as a road-map that can guide readers through the many twists, turns, and apparent dead ends of Horace's two books of *Satires*.

Bibliography

Acosta Méndez, E. 1983. "PHerc. 1089: Filodemo 'Sobre la adulacion.'" *Cronache Ercolanesi.* 13: 121–38.

Allen, J. 2001. *Inference from Signs: Ancient Debates about the Nature of Evidence.* Oxford: Oxford University Press.

Allen, W. 1938. "On the Friendship of Lucretius with Memmius." *Classical Philology* 33: 167–81.

Allen, W. and De Lacy, P. H. 1939. "The Patrons of Philodemus." *Classical Philology* 34: 59–65.

Alföldy, G., Hölscher, T., Kettemann, R., and Petersmann, H., eds. 1995. *Römische Lebenskunst: interdisziplinäres Kolloquium zum 85. Geburtstag von Viktor Pöschl: Heidelberg, 2.–4. Februar 1995.* Heidelberg: Winter.

Amoroso, F. 1975. "Filodemo sulla conversazione." *Cronache Ercolanesi* 5: 63–76.

Anderson, W. S. 1982. *Essays on Roman Satire.* Princeton: Princeton University Press.

Anderson, W. S. 1995. "*Horatius Liber*, Child and Freedman's Free Son." *Arethusa* 28: 151–64.

André, J. 1967. *Mécène: Essai de biographie spirituelle.* Paris: Les Belles Lettres.

André, J. 1981. *L'Alimentation et la cuisine à Rome.* Paris: Les Belles Lettres.

Angeli, A. 1990. "La critica filodemea *all'Economico* di Senofonte." *Cronache Ercolanesi* 20: 39–52.

Angeli, A. and Colaizzo, M. 1979. "I frammenti di Zenone Sidonio." *Cronache Ercolanesi* 9, 47–133.

Annas, J. 1989. "Epicurean Emotions." *Greek, Roman and Byzantine Studies* 30: 145–64.

Armisen-Marchetti, M. 2006. "*Ex insano insanior*: La parodie de la consolation dans la *Satire* II, 3 d'Horace." In Champeaux and Chassignet, eds., 343–54.

Armstrong, D. 1964. "Horace, *Satires* 1.1–3: A Structural Study." *Arion* 3: 86–96.

Armstrong, D. 1986. "Horatius Eques et Scriba: *Satires* 1.6 and 2.7." *Transactions of the American Philological Association* 116: 255–88.

Armstrong, D. 1989. *Horace.* New Haven: Yale University Press.

Armstrong, D. 1993. "The Addressees of the *Ars Poetica*: Herculaneum, the Pisones and Epicurean Protreptic." *Materiali e discussioni per l'analisi dei testi classici* 31: 185–230.

Armstrong, D. 1997. Review of R. O. A. M. Lyne, *Horace: Behind the Public Poetry*. *Phoenix* 51: 393–405.

Armstrong, D. 2004a. "Horace's *Epistles* 1 and Philodemus." In Armstrong et al., eds., 267–98.

Armstrong, D. 2004b. "Introduction." In Armstrong et al., eds., 1–22.

Armstrong, D. 2010. "The Biographical and Social Foundations of Horace's Poetic Voice." In Davis, ed., 7–33.

Armstrong, D. 2011. "Epicurean Virtues, Epicurean Friendship: Cicero vs the Herculaneum Papyri." In Fish and Sanders, eds., 105–28.

Armstrong, D. 2014a. "Horace's Epicurean Voice in the Satires." In Garani and Konstan, eds., 91–127.

Armstrong, D. 2014b. Review of V. Tsouna, *Philodemus, On Property Management*. *Bryn Mawr Classical Review* 2014.03.13.

Armstrong, D. 2016. "Utility and Affection in Epicurean Friendship: Philodemus *On the Gods* 3, *On Property Management*, and Horace *Sermones* 2.6." In Caston and Kaster, eds., 182–208.

Armstrong, D., Fish, J., Johnston, P. A., and Skinner, M. B., eds. 2004. *Vergil, Philodemus, and the Augustans*. Austin, Tex.: University of Texas Press.

Armstrong, D. and McOsker, M. *Philodemus: On Anger*. Forthcoming.

Armstrong, D. and Ponczoch, J. A. 2011. "[Philodemus] *On Wealth* (PHerc. 1570 cols. VI–XX, PCC. 4–6A): New Fragments of Empedocles, Menander and Epicurus." *Cronache Ercolanesi* 41: 97–138.

Arnott, W. G. 2010. "Middle Comedy." In Dobrov, ed., 279–332.

Arrighetti, G. 1955. "Sul valore di *ΕΠΙΛΟΓΙΖΟΜΑΙ ΕΠΙΛΟΓΙΣΜΟΣ ΕΠΙΛΟΓΙΣΙΣ* nel sistema epicureo." *Parola del passato* 10: 404–15.

Asmis, E. 1984. *Epicurus' Scientific Method*. Ithaca, NY: Cornell University Press.

Asmis, E. 1990. "Philodemus' Epicureanism." *Aufstieg und Niedergang der römischen Welt* 36.4. 2369–406.

Asmis, E. 1991. "Philodemus' Poetic Theory and *On the Good King According to Homer*." *Classical Antiquity* 10: 1–45.

Asmis, E. 1995. "Epicurean Poetics." In Obbink, ed., 15–34.

Asmis, E. 2001. "Basic Education in Epicureanism." In Too, ed., 209–39.

Asmis, E. 2004. "Epicurean Economics." In Fitzgerald, Obbink, and Holland, eds., 133–76.

Asmis, E. 2011. "The Necessity of Anger in Philodemus' *On Anger*." In Fish and Sanders, eds., 152–82.

Atherton, C. 2009. "Epicurean Philosophy of Language." In Warren, ed., 197–215.

Augoustakis, A. and Traill, A., eds. 2013. *A Companion to Terence*. New Jersey: Wiley-Blackwell.

Auvray-Assayas, C. and Delattre, D., eds. 2001. *Cicéron et Philodème: La polémique en philosophie*. Paris: Rue d'Ulm.

Avallone, R. 1962. *Mecenate*. Naples: Libreria scientifica editrice.

Axelson, B. 1945. *Unpoetische Wörter: ein Beitrag zur Kenntnis des lateinische Dichtersprache*. Lund: C. W. K. Gleerup.

Bagnall, R. S., ed. 2009. *The Oxford Handbook of Papyrology*. Oxford: Oxford University Press.

Bailey, C. 1926. *Epicurus: The Extant Remains*. Oxford: Clarendon Press.

Bailey, C. 1947. *Titi Lucreti Cari De Rerum Natura Libri Sex*. 3 vols. Oxford: Clarendon Press.

Bailey, C. 1964. *The Greek Atomists and Epicurus: A Study*. New York. Russell & Russell.

Balch, D. L. 2004. "Philodemus 'On Wealth' and 'On Household Management': Naturally Wealthy Epicureans against Poor Cynics." In Fitzgerald, Obbink, and Holland, eds., 177–96.

Baldwin, B. 1970. "Horace on Sex." *American Journal of Philology* 91: 460–5.

Bandiera, E. 1996. "Baio." In Mariotti, ed., 1.658–9.

Barbieri, A. 1976. "A proposito della *Satira* II, 6 di Orazio." *Rendiconti della classe di scienze morali, storiche e filologiche dell'Accademia dei Lincei* 31: 479–507.

Barnes, J., Brunschwig, J., Burnyeat, M., and Schofield, M., eds. 1982. *Science and Speculation: Studies in Hellenistic Theory and Practice*. Cambridge: Cambridge University Press.

Barsby, J. 1999. *Terence: Eunuchus*. Cambridge: Cambridge University Press.

Barsby, J. 2001. *Terence*. 2 vols. Cambridge, Mass.: Harvard University Press.

Bassi, D. 1914. *Herculanensium voluminum quae supersunt, collectio tertia*. Milan: Ulrico Hoepli.

Beck, J.-W. 2003. *Mempsimoirie und Avaritia: Zu Einheit und Programm von Horaz' Satire 1, 1*. Göttingen: Duehrkohp & Radicke.

Bellandi, F. 1996. "Tillio." In Mariotti, ed., 1.917–18.

Beloch, G. 1926. "Mithres." *Rivista di filologia e d'istruzione classica* 54: 331–5.

Boll, F. 1913. "Die Anordnung im zweiten Buch des Horaz' Satiren." *Hermes* 48: 143–5.

Bond, R. P. 1978. "A Discussion of Various Tensions in Horace, *Satires* 2.7." *Prudentia* 10: 85–98.

Bond, R. P. 1980. "The Characterization of Ofellus in Horace, *Satires* 2.2 and a Note on v. 123." *Prudentia* 14: 112–26.

Bond, R. P. 1985. "Dialectic, Eclectic and Myth (?) in Horace, *Satires* 2.6." *Antichthon* 19: 68–86.

Bond, R. P. 1987. "The Characterization of the Interlocutors in Horace, *Satires* 2.3." *Prudentia* 19: 1–21.

Bonner, S. F. 1977. *Education in Ancient Rome: from the Elder Cato to the Younger Pliny*. Berkeley: University of California Press.

Bourgey, L. 1969. "La Doctrine épicurienne sur le rôle de la sensation dans la connaissance et la tradition grecque." In *Association Guillaume Budé*,

306 *Bibliography*

Actes du VIII Congrès, Paris, 5–10 avril 1968. Paris: Les Belles Lettres:
252–8.

Bowditch, P. L. 2001. *Horace and the Gift Economy of Patronage.* Berkeley:
University of California Press.

Bowditch, P. L. 2010. "Horace and Imperial Patronage." In Davis, ed., 53–74.

Boyencé, P. 1959. "Portrait de Mécène." *Bulletine de l'association Guillaume*
Budé 3: 332–44.

Bradshaw, A. 1989. "Horace *in Sabinis*." *Latomus* 206: 160–86.

Branham, R. B. and Goulet-Cazé, M., eds. 1996. *The Cynics: The Cynic Move-*
ment in Antiquity and its Legacy. Berkeley: University of California Press.

Braund, S. M., ed. 1989. *Satire and Society in Ancient Rome.* Exeter: Exeter
University Press.

Braund, S. M. 1996. *The Roman Satirists and their Masks.* London: Bristol
Classical Press.

Brink, C. O. 1963. *Horace on Poetry: Prolegomena to the Literary Epistles.*
Cambridge: Cambridge University Press.

Brown, E. 2002. "Epicurus on Friendship (*Sententia Vaticana* 23)." *Classical*
Philology 97: 68–80.

Brown, P. G. McC. 1992. "Menander, Fragments 745 and 746 K-T, Menander's *Kolax,* and Parasites and Flatterers in Greek Comedy." *Zeitschrift für*
Papyrologie und Epigraphik 92: 91–107.

Brown, P. M. 1993. *Horace, Satires I.* Warminster: Aris & Phillips.

Brown, R. D. 1987. *Lucretius on Love and Sex.* Leiden: Brill.

Brunschwig, J. 1986. "The Cradle Argument in Epicureanism and Stoicism."
In Schofield and Striker, eds., 113–44.

Brunt, P. A. 1988. *The Fall of the Roman Republic and Related Essays.*
Oxford: Clarendon Press.

Bushala, E. 1971. "The Motif of Sexual Choice in Horace, Satire 1.2."
Classical Journal 66: 312–15.

Caini, C. 1939. *Sui papiri ercolanesi 222, 223 e 1082. (Filodemo, Περὶ*
κολακείας). Naples.

Cairns, F., ed. 1981. *Papers of the Liverpool Latin Seminar.* vol. 3. Liverpool:
Francis Cairns Publications.

Cairns, F. 2005. "*Antestari* and Horace, *Satires* 1.9." *Latomus* 64: 49–55.

Capasso, M. 1989. "Primo supplemento al Catalogo dei Papiri Ercolanesi."
Cronache Ercolanesi 19: 193–264.

Capasso, M. 2001. "Les livres sur la flatterie dans le *De vitiis* de Philodème."
In Auvray-Assayas and Delattre, eds., 179–94.

Casolari, F. 2003. *Die Mythentravestie in der griechischen Komödie.* Münster:
Aschendorff Verlag.

Castaldi, F. 1928. "Il concetto della ricchezza in Epicuro." *Rendiconti della*
classe di scienze morali, storiche e filologiche dell'accademia dei Lincei 6:
287–308.

Caston, R. R. and Kaster, R. A., eds. 2016. *Hope, Joy, and Affection in the Classical World*. Oxford: Oxford University Press.

Cataudella, Q. 1950. "Filodemo nella satire 1.2 di Orazio." *La parola del passato* 5: 18–31.

Cèbe, J. 1966. *La caricature et la parodie dans le monde romain antique: des origines à Juvénal*. Paris: E. de Boccard.

Champeaux, J. and Chassignet, M., eds. 2006. *Aere perennius: hommage à Hubert Zehnacker*. Paris: Presses de l'Université Paris-Sorbonne.

Champlin, E. 1989. "*Creditur vulgo testamenta hominum speculum esse morum*: Why the Romans Made Wills." *Classical Philology* 84: 198–215.

Champlin, E. 1991. *Final Judgments: Duty and Emotion in Roman Wills 200 B.C.–A.D. 250*. Berkeley: University of California Press.

Chandler, C. 2006. *Philodemus on Rhetoric, Books 1 and 2*. New York: Routledge.

Christenson, D. M. 2013. "Eunuchus." In Augoustakis and Traill, eds., 262–80.

Cichorius, C. 1922. *Römische Studien: Historisches, epigraphisches, literargeschichtliches aus vier Jahrhunderten Roms*. Leipzig: B. G. Teubner.

Cipriani, G. 1992. "Sintassi e semantica nella satira I, 9 di Orazio." *Aufidus* 18: 75–104.

Citroni Marchetti, S. 2004. "I precetti paterni e le lezioni dei filosofi: Demea, il padre di Orazio ed altri padri e figli." *Materiali e discussioni per l'analisi dei testi classici* 53: 9–63.

Classen, C. J. 1978. "Horace—A Cook?" *Classical Quarterly* 28: 333–48.

Clay, D. 1983. "Individual and Community in the First Generation of the Epicurean School." In Macchiaroli, ed., 255–79.

Clay, D. 2004. "Philodemus on the Plain Speaking of the other Philosophers." In Fitzgerald, Obbink, and Holland, eds., 55–71.

Codoñer C. 1975. "Precisiones sobre las sátiras diatríbicas de Horacio." *Emerita* 43: 41–57.

Cody, J. V. 1976. "Horace and Callimachean Aesthetics." *Latomus* 147.

Coffey, M. 1976. *Roman Satire*. London: Methuen & Co.

Corbeill, A. 1996. *Controlling Laughter: Political Humor in the Late Roman Republic*. Princeton: Princeton University Press.

Courtney, E. 1994. "Horace and the Pest." *Classical Journal* 90: 1–8.

Courtney, E. 2013. "The Two Books of Satires." In Günther, ed., 63–168.

Crönert, W. 1906. *Kolotes und Menedemos, Texte und Untersuchungen zur Philosophen- und Literaturgeschichte*. Leipzig: E. Avenarius.

Crook, J. A. 1967. *Law and Life of Rome*. Ithaca, NY: Cornell University Press.

Cucchiarelli, A. 2001. *La Satira e il poeta: Orazio tra Epodi e Sermones*. Pisa: Giardini.

Cucchiarelli, A. and Traina, A. 2012. *Publio Virgilio Marone, Le Bucoliche: Introduzione e commento*. Rome: Carocci.

Curran, L. 1970. "Nature, Convention and Obscenity in Horace, *Satires* 1.2." *Arion* 3: 220–46.

Damon, C. 1997. *The Mask of the Parasite*. Ann Arbor, Mich.: University of Michigan Press.

Davis, G., ed. 2010. *A Companion to Horace*. New Jersey: Wiley-Blackwell.

De Falco, V. 1926. "Appunti sul '*Περὶ κολακείας*' di Filodemo. Pap. erc. 1675." *Rivista indo-greco-italica di filologia, lingua, antichità* 10: 15–26.

De Lacy, P. 1958. "Epicurean *ΕΠΙΛΟΓΙΣΜΟΣ*." *American Journal of Philology* 79: 179–83.

De Lacy, P. H. and De Lacy, E. A. 1978. *Philodemus: On Methods of Inference*. Naples: Bibliopolis.

De Sanctis, D. 2015. "Questioni di stile: osservazioni sul linguaggio e sulla comunicazione del sapere nelle lettere maggiori di Epicuro." In De Sanctis et al., eds., 55–73.

De Sanctis, D., Spinelli, E., Tulli, M., and Verde, F., eds. 2015. *Questioni epicuree*. Sankt Augustin: Academia.

Deichgräber, K. 1930. *Die griechische Empirikerschule: Sammlung und Darstellung der Lehre*. Berlin: Weidmannsche Buchhandlung.

Del Mastro, G. 2000. "Secondo supplemento al Catalogo dei Papiri Ercolanesi." *Cronache Ercolanesi* 30: 157–241.

Deiss, J. 1985. *Herculaneum: Italy's Buried Treasure*. New York: J. Paul Getty Museum.

Della Corte, F. 1969. "Vario e Tucca in Filodemo." *Aegyptus* 49: 85–8.

Della Corte, F., ed. 1982. *Prosimetrum e spoudogeloion*. Geneva: Istituto di filologia classica e medievale.

Desideri, P. 1996. "Stertinio." In Mariotti, ed., 1.906.

Desmond, W. 2008. *The Cynics*. Berkeley: University of California Press.

Dessen, C. W. 1968. "The Sexual and Financial Mean in Horace's *Serm.*, 1.2." *American Journal of Philology* 89: 200–8.

DeWitt, N. W. 1935. "Parresiastic Poems of Horace." *Classical Philology* 30: 312–19.

DeWitt, N. W. 1936. "Epicurean Contubernium." *Transactions and Proceedings of the American Philological Association* 67: 55–63.

DeWitt, N. W. 1939. "Epicurean Doctrine in Horace." *Classical Philology* 34: 127–34.

DeWitt, N. W. 1954. *Epicurus and His Philosophy*. Minneapolis: University of Minnesota Press.

Diggle, J. 2004. *Theophrastus: Characters*. Cambridge: Cambridge University Press.

Dobrov, G. W., ed. 2010. *Brill's Companion to the Study of Greek Comedy*. Leiden.

Dorandi, T. 1982. *Filodemo, il buon re secondo Omero*. Naples: Bibliopolis.

Dorandi, T. 1991. *Filodemo, storia dei filosofi: Platone e l'academia (PHerc. 1021 e 164)*. Naples: Bibliopolis.

Dorandi, T. 1994. *Filodemo, storia dei filosofi: la stoà da Zenone a Panezio (PHerc. 1018)*. Leiden: Brill.

Dorandi, T. 2016. "Modi e modelli di trasmissione dell'opera *Sulla Natura* di Epicuro." In De Sanctis et al., eds., 15–52.

Dorandi, T. and Spinelli, E. 1990. "Un libro di Filodemo sull'avarizia?" *Cronache Ercolanesi*: 53–60.

Duckworth, G. E. 1952. *The Nature of Roman Comedy: A Study in Popular Entertainment*. Norman, Okla.: University of Oklahoma Press.

Dudley, D. R. 1974. *A History of Cynicism from Diogenes to the 6th Century A.D.* New York: Gordon Press.

Dufallo, B. 2000. "Satis/Satura: Reconsidering the 'Programmatic Intent' of Horace's *Satires* 1.1." *Classical World* 93: 579–90.

DuQuesnay, I. M. Le M. 1981. "Vergil's First *Eclogue*." In Cairns, ed., 98–103.

DuQuesnay, I. M. Le M. 2009. "Horace and Maecenas: The Propaganda Value of *Sermones* I." In Freudenburg, ed., 42–101.

Edwards, C. 1996. *The Politics of Immorality in Ancient Rome*. Cambridge: Cambridge University Press.

Erler, M. 2011. "Autodidact and Student: On the Relationship of Authority and Autonomy in Epicurus and the Epicurean Tradition." In Fish and Sanders, eds., 9–28.

Essler, H. 2011. "Cicero's Use and Abuse of Epicurean Theology." In Fish and Sanders, eds., 129–51.

Evans, H. B. 1978. "Horace, *Satires* 2.7: Saturnalia and Satire." *Classical Journal* 73: 307–12.

Evenpole, W. 1990. "Maecenas: A Survey of Recent Literature." *Ancient Society* 21: 99–107.

Fairclough, H. R. 1913. "Horace's View of the Relations between Satire and Comedy." *American Journal of Philology* 34, 183–93.

Fairclough, H. R. 1991. *Horace: Satires, Epistles, Ars Poetica*. Repr. Cambridge, Mass.: Harvard University Press.

Fantham, E. R. 1989. "Mime: The Missing Link in Roman Literary History." *Classical World* 82: 153–63.

Feeney, D. 2009. "Becoming an Authority: Horace on his own? Reception." In Houghton and Wyke, eds., 16–38.

Ferguson, J. 1990. "Epicureanism under the Roman Empire." *Aufstieg und Niedergang der römischen Welt* 36.4. 2263–5.

Ferrario, M. 2000. "La nascita della filologia epicurea: Demetrio Lacone e Filodemo." *Cronache Ercolanesi* 30: 53–61.

Ferri, R. 1993. *Il dispiacere di un epicureo*. Pisa: Giardini.

Ferriss-Hill, J. 2011. "A Stroll with Lucilius, *Satires* 1.9 Reconsidered." *American Journal of Philology* 132: 429–55.

Ferriss-Hill, J. 2015. *Roman Satire and the Old Comic Tradition*. Cambridge: Cambridge University Press.

Fish, J. 1998. "Is Death Nothing to Horace?: A Brief Comparison with Philodemus and Lucretius." *Cronache Ercolanesi* 28: 99–104.

Fish, J. 2004. "Anger, Philodemus' *Good King*, and the Helen Episode of *Aeneid* 2.567–89: A New Proof of Authenticity from Herculaneum." In Armstrong et al., eds., 111–38.

Fish, J. 2011a. "Not all Politicians are Sisyphus: What Roman Epicureans were Taught about Politics." In Fish and Sanders, eds., 72–104.

Fish, J. 2011b. "On Orderly Symposia in Homer: A New Reconstruction of *De bono rege* (Pherc. 1507), col. 19." *Cronache Ercolansei* 41: 65–8.

Fish, J. and Sanders, K., eds. 2011. *Epicurus and the Epicurean Tradition.* Cambridge: Cambridge University Press.

Fiske, G. C. 1971. *Lucilius and Horace.* Repr. Madison, Wisc.: University of Wisconsin.

Fitzgerald, J. T., ed. 1996. *Friendship, Flattery and Frankness of Speech: Studies on Friendship in the New Testament World.* Leiden: Brill.

Fitzgerald, J. T., Obbink, D., and Holland, G. S., eds. 2004. *Philodemus and the New Testament World.* Leiden: Brill.

Fordyce, C. J. 1961. *Catullus.* Oxford: Clarendon Press.

Fraenkel, E. 1957. *Horace.* Oxford: Clarendon Press.

Frank, T. 1933. *An Economic Survey of Ancient Rome.* 5 vols. Baltimore: Johns Hopkins University Press.

Frede, M. and Striker, G., eds. 1996. *Rationality in Greek Thought.* Oxford: Oxford University Press.

Freudenburg, K. 1993. *The Walking Muse: Horace on the Theory of Satire.* Princeton: Princeton University Press.

Freudenburg, K. 2001. *Satires of Rome: Threatening Poses from Lucilius to Juvenal.* Cambridge: Cambridge University Press.

Freudenburg, K., ed. 2005. *The Cambridge Companion to Roman Satire.* Cambridge: Cambridge University Press.

Freudenburg, K. 2005. "Introduction: Roman Satire." In Freudenburg, ed., 1–30.

Freudenburg, K., ed. 2009. *Oxford Readings in Horace: Satires and Epistles.* Oxford: Oxford University Press.

Freudenburg, K. 2010. "Horatius Anceps: Persona and Self-Revelation in Satire and Song." In Davis, ed., 271–90.

Freudenburg, K., Cucchiarelli, A., and Barchiesi, A., eds. 2005. *Musa pedestre. Storia e interpretazione della satira en Roma antica.* Rome: Carocci.

Frischer, B. 1995a. "Horazens Sabiner Villa: Dichtung und Wahrheit." In Alföldy et al., eds., 31–45.

Frischer, B. 1995b. "Fu la Villa ercolanese dei Papiri un modello per la villa sabina di Orazio?" *Bollettino del Centro Internazionale per lo Studio dei Papyri Ercolanesi* 25: 211–29.

Furley, D. J. 1967. *Two Studies in the Greek Atomists*. Princeton: Princeton University Press.

Garani, M. and Konstan, D., eds. 2014. *The Philosophizing Muse: The Influence of Greek Philosophy on Roman Poetry*. Newcastle: Cambridge Scholars.

Gargiulo, T. 1981. "PHerc. 222: Filodemo sull'adulazione." *Cronache Ercolanesi* 11: 103–27.

Gerhard, G. A. 1909. *Phoinix von Kolophon*. Leipzig: B. G. Teubner.

Giannantoni, G. 1984. "Il piacere cinetico nell'etica epicurea." *Elenchos* 5: 25–44.

Giannantoni, G. and Gigante, M., eds. 1996. *Epicureismo greco e romano: Atti del Congresso internazionale, Napoli 19–26 maggio 1993*. Vol. 2. Naples: Bibliopolis.

Gibson, R. 2007. *Excess and Restraint: Propertius, Horace, and Ovid's* Ars Amatoria. London: Institute of Classical Studies.

Gigante, M. 1974. "Motivi paideutici nell'opera filodemea 'Sulla libertà di parola.'" *Cronache Ercolanesi* 2: 59–65.

Gigante, M. 1975. "'Philosophia medicans' in Filodemo." *Cronache Ercolanesi* 5: 53–61.

Gigante, M. 1979. *Catalogo dei papiri ercolanesi*. Naples: Bibliopolis.

Gigante, M. 1983. *Ricerche filodemee*. Naples: Gaetano Macchiaroli.

Gigante, M. 1992. *Cinismo e epicureismo*. Naples: Bibliopolis.

Gigante, M. 1993. *Orazio, una misura per l'amore: Lettura della satira seconda del primo libro*. Venosa: Osanna.

Gigante, M. 1995. *Philodemus in Italy*. Trans. Dirk Obbink. Repr. Ann Arbor, Mich.: University of Michigan Press.

Gigante, M. 1998. *Altre ricerche filodemee*. Naples: Gaetano Macchiaroli.

Gigante, M. and Indelli, G. 1978. "Bione e l'Epicureismo." *Cronache Ercolanesi* 8: 124–31.

Gigon, O., ed. 1978. *Lucrèce*. (*Entretiens* 24). Geneva: Fondation Hardt.

Gillespie, S. and Hardie, P., eds. 2007. *The Cambridge Companion to Lucretius*. Cambridge: Cambridge University Press.

Glad, C. 1995. *Paul and Philodemus: Adaptability in Epicurean and Early Christian Psychagogy*. Leiden: Brill.

Glad, C. 1996. "Frank Speech, Flattery and Friendship in Philodemus." In Fitzgerald, ed., 21–59.

Glidden, D. K. 1983. "Epicurean Semantics." In Macchiaroli, ed., 185–226.

Glidden, D. K. 1985. "Epicurean Prolepsis." *Oxford Studies in Ancient Philosophy* 3: 175–217.

Gold, B. K. 1987. *Literary Patronage in Greece and Rome*. Chapel Hill, NC: University of North Carolina Press.

Gold, B. K. 1992. "Openings in Horace's *Satires* and *Odes*: Poet, Patron, and Audience." *Yale Classical Studies* 29: 162–85.

Gordon, B. 2012. *Invention and Gendering of Epicurus.* Ann Arbor, Mich.: University of Michigan Press.

Gosling, J. C. B. and Taylor, C. C. W. 1982. *The Greeks on Pleasure.* Oxford: Oxford University Press.

Gowers, E. 1993. *The Loaded Table: Representations of Food in Roman Literature.* Oxford: Oxford University Press.

Gowers, E. 2003. "Fragments of Autobiography in Horace, Satires I." *Classical Antiquity* 22: 55–92.

Gowers, E. 2009a. "A Cat May Look at a King: Difference and Indifference in Horace, Satire 1.6." In Urso, ed., 301–16.

Gowers, E. 2009b. "The Ends of the Beginning: Horace, Satires 1." In Houghton and Wyke, eds., 39–60.

Gowers, E. 2012. *Horace: Satires Book I.* Cambridge: Cambridge University Press.

Graziosi, B. 2009. "Horace, Suetonius, and the *Lives* of the Greek Poets." In Houghton and Wyke, eds., 140–60.

Greenberg, N. A. 1955. "The Poetic Theory of Philodemus." Dissertation: Harvard University.

Greene, W. C. 1920. "The Spirit of Comedy in Plato." *Harvard Studies in Classical Philology* 31: 63–123.

Griffin, J. 1984. "Augustus and the Poets: Caesar qui cogere posset." In Millar and Segal, eds., 189–218.

Griffin, M. 1996. "Cynicism and the Romans: Attraction and Repulsion." In Branham and Goulet-Cazé, eds., 190–204.

Griffin, M. 2001. "Piso, Cicero and their audience." In Auvray-Assayas and Delattre, eds., 85–100.

Grilli, A. 1983a. "*ΔΙΑΘΕΣΙΣ* en Epicuro." In Macchiaroli, ed., 93–109.

Grilli, A. 1983b. "Orazio e l'epicureismo ovvero *Serm.* 1,3 ed *Epist.* 1,2." *Helmantica* 34: 267–92.

Grimal, P. 1993. "Recherche sur l'épicurisme d'Horace." *Revue des Études latines* 71: 154–60.

Guidobaldi, M. P. and Esposito, D. 2012. *Herculaneum: Art of a Buried City.* New York: Abbeville Press.

Günther, H.-C., ed. 2013. *Brill's Companion to Horace.* Leiden: Brill.

Hadot, I. 1969. "Épicure et l'enseignement philosophique héllenistique et romain." *Association Guillaume Budé, Actes du VIII Congrès, Paris, 5–10 avril 1968*: 252–8. Paris: Les Belles Lettres.

Hall, C. M. 1935. "Some Epicureans at Rome." *Classical Weekly* 28: 113–15.

Hanchey, D. 2013. "Cicero, Exchange, and the Epicureans." *Phoenix* 67: 119–34.

Hanslik, R., Lesky, A., and Schwabl, H., eds. 1972. *Antidosis: Festschrift für Walther Kraus zum 70. Geburtstag.* Vienna: Böhlau Verlag.

Harrison, S. J. 1965. "Horace's Tribute to his Father." *Classical Philology* 60: 111–14.

Harrison, S. J., ed. 1995. *Homage to Horace: A Bimillenary Celebration.* Oxford: Clarendon Press.

Harrison, S. J. 2007. *Generic Enrichment in Vergil and Horace.* Oxford: Oxford University Press.

Harrison, S. J., ed. 2007. *The Cambridge Companion to Horace.* Cambridge: Cambridge University Press.

Heinze, R. 1889. *De Horatio Bionis imitatore.* Bonn: University of Bonn.

Henderson, J. 1999. *Writing Down Rome: Satire, Comedy and Other Offenses in Latin Poetry.* Oxford: Oxford University Press.

Hendrickson, G. L. 1900. "Horace, 1.4: A Protest and a Programme." *American Journal of Philology* 21: 121–42.

Hendrickson, G. L. 1918. "An Epigram of Philodemus and Two Latin Congeners." *American Journal of Philology* 39, 27–43.

Hense, O. 1969. *Teletis reliquiae.* Leipzig: B. G. Teubner.

Herter, H. 1970. "Zur ersten Satire des Horaz." In Korzeniewski, ed., 320–64.

Hicks, B. V. 2013. "The Satiric Effect in Horace's *Sermones* in the Light of His Epicurean Reading Circle." Dissertation: University of Texas at Austin.

Hiltbrunner, O. 1972. "Einladung zum epikureischen Freundesmahl." In Hanslik, Lesky, and Schwabl, eds., 168–82.

Holzberg, N. 2002. *The Ancient Fable: An Introduction.* Bloomington, Ind.: Indiana University Press.

Hopkins, K. 1983. *Death and Renewal.* Cambridge: Cambridge University Press.

Horsfall, N. 1995. *A Companion to the Study of Vergil.* Leiden: Brill.

Houghton, L. B. T. 2004. "The Wolf and the Dog: (Horace, *Sermones* 2.2.64)." *Classical Quarterly* 54: 300–4.

Houghton, L. B. T. and Wyke, M., eds. 2009. *Perceptions of Horace: A Roman Poet and his Readers.* Cambridge: Cambridge University Press.

Hubbard, T. K. 1981. "The Structure and Programmatic Intent of Horace's First Satire." *Latomus* 40: 305–21.

Hudson, N. 1989. "Food in Roman Satire." In Braund, ed., 69–88.

Hunter, R. L. 1985a. "Horace on Friendship and Free Speech (*Epistles* 1.18 and *Satires* 1.4)." *Hermes* 113: 480–90.

Hunter, R. L. 1985b. *The New Comedy of Greece and Rome.* Cambridge: Cambridge University Press.

Hutchinson, G. O. 2013. *Greek to Latin: Frameworks and Contexts for Intertextuality.* Oxford: Oxford University Press.

Indelli, G. 1988. *Filodemo: L'ira.* Naples: Bibliopolis.

Indelli, G. 2004. "The Vocabulary of Anger in Philodemus' *De ira* and Vergil's *Aeneid.*" In Armstrong et al., eds., 103–10.

Indelli, G. and Tsouna-McKirahan, V. 1995. *[Philodemus] [On Choices and Avoidances.]* Naples: Bibliopolis.

Isnardi, P. 1966. *Techne: Momenti del pensiero greco da Platone a Epicuro.* Florence: Nuova Italia.

Jaeger, W. 1957. "Aristotle's Use of Medicine as Model of Method in his Ethics." *Journal of Hellenic Studies* 77: 54–61.

Jensen, C. 1907. *Philodemi Περὶ οἰκονομίας qui dicitur libellus.* Leipzig: B. G. Teubner.

Jensen, C. 1923. *Philodemos über die Gedichte, fünftes Buch.* Berlin: Weidmann.

Jocelyn, H. D. 1977. "The Ruling Class of the Roman Republic and Greek Philosophers." *Bulletin of the John Rylands Library, University of Manchester* 59: 323–66.

Karakasis, E. 2013. "Masters and Slaves." In Augoustakis and Traill, eds., 211–22.

Keane, C. 2006. *Figuring Genre in Roman Satire.* Oxford: Oxford University Press.

Kemp, J. 2009. "Irony and *aequabilitas*: Horace, *Satires* 1.3." *Dictynna* 6: 1–17.

Kemp, J. 2010a. "A Moral Purpose, a Literary Game: Horace, *Satires* 1.4." *Classical World* 104: 59–76.

Kemp, J. 2010b. "Flattery and Frankness in Horace and Philodemus." *Greece & Rome* 57: 65–76.

Kemp, J. 2016. "Fools Rush In: Sex, 'the Mean' and Epicureanism in Horace, *Satires* 1.2." *Cambridge Classical Journal* 62: 130–46.

Kenney, E. J. 1970. "Doctus Lucretius." *Mnemosyne* 23: 366–92.

Kernan, A. 1959. *The Cankered Muse.* New Haven: Yale University Press.

Kiessling, A. and Heinze, R. 1910. *Q. Horatius Flaccus Satiren.* Berlin: Weidmannsche Buchhandlung.

Kilpatrick, R. S. 1986. *The Poetry of Friendship: Horace, Epistles I.* Alberta: Alberta University Press.

Kilpatrick, R. S. 1996. "*Amicus Medicus*: Medicine and Epicurean Therapy in *De Rerum Natura*." *Memoirs of the American Academy in Rome* 41: 69–100.

Kindstrand, J. F. 1976. *Bion of Borysthenes: A Collection of the Fragments with Introduction and Commentary.* Uppsala: Almquist & Wiksell.

Klein, S. V. 2012. "Performing the Patron–Client Relationship: Dramaturgical Cues in Horace's *Sermones* 2.5." *Illinois Classical Studies* 37: 97–119.

Kleve, K. 1963. *Gnosis Theon: Die Lehre von der natürlichen Gotteserkenntnis in der epikureischen Theologie.* Symbolae Osloenses 19. Oslo: Universitetsforlaget.

Kleve, K. 1989. "Lucretius in Herculaneum." *Cronache Ercolanesi* 19: 5–27.

Klingner, F. 1970. *Horatius: Opera.* Leipzig: B. G. Teubner.

Knorr, O. 2004. *Verborgene Kunst: Argumentationsstruktur und Buchaufbau in den Satiren des Horaz.* Hildesheim: Olms-Weidmann.

Kondo, E. 1974. "Per l'interpretazione del pensiero filodemeo sulla adulazione nel PHerc. 1457." *Cronache Ercolanesi* 4: 43–56.

Konstan, D. 1973. *Some Aspects of Epicurean Psychology.* Leiden: Brill.

Konstan, D. 1996. "Friendship, Frankness and Flattery." In Fitzgerald, ed., 7–19.

Konstan, D. 1997. *Friendship in the Classical World*. Cambridge: Cambridge University Press.

Konstan, D. 2011. "Epicurus on the Gods." In Fish and Sanders, eds., 53–71.

Konstan, D., Clay, D., Glad, C. E., Thom, J. C., and Ware, J. 1998. *Philodemus: On Frank Criticism*. Atlanta, Ga.: Society of Biblical Literature.

Körte, A. 1890a. "Augusteer bei Philodem." *Rheinisches Museum* 45: 172–7.

Körte, A. 1890b. *Metrodori Epicurei Fragmenta*. Leipzig: B. G. Teubner.

Korzeniewski, D., ed. 1970. *Die römische Satire*. Darmstadt: Wissenschaftliche Buchgesellschaft.

Kroll, W. 1918. "Demetrios." *Realencyclopädie der classischen Altertumswissenschaft Supplementband* 3: 329–30.

Kroll, W. 1921. "Kolax." *Realencyclopädie der classischen Altertumswissenschaft*: 1069–70.

La Penna, A. 1996. "Mecenate." In Mariotti, ed., 1.792–803.

Labate, M. 2005. "Poetica minore e minima: Mecenate e gli amici nelle *Satire* di Orazio." *Materiali e discussioni per l'analisi dei testi classici* 54: 47–63.

Laks, A. and Schofield, M., eds. 1995. *Justice and Generosity: Studies in Hellenistic Social and Political Philosophy*. Cambridge: Cambridge University Press.

Landolfi, L. 1982. "Tracce filodemee di estetica e di epigrammatica simpotica in Catullo." *Cronache Ercolanesi* 12: 137–43.

Last, H. M. 1922. "The Date of Philodemos *de Signis*." *Classical Quarterly* 16: 177–80.

Laurenti, R. 1973. *Filodemo e il pensiero economico degli epicurei*. Milan: Cisalpino—Goliardica.

Leach, E. W. 1971. "Horace's *pater optimus* and Terence's Demea: Autobiographical Fiction and Comedy in *Sermo* I.4." *American Journal of Philology* 92: 616–32.

Leach, E. W. 1993. "Horace's Sabine Topography in Lyric and Hexameter Verse." *American Journal of Philology* 114: 271–302.

Lee, G. 2008. *Catullus: The Complete Poems*. Oxford: Oxford University Press.

Lefèvre, E., ed. 1975. *Monumentum Chiloniense: Studien zur augusteischen Zeit: Festschrift E. Burck*. Amsterdam: Adolf Hakkert.

Lefèvre, E. 1975. "*Nil medium est*. Die früheste Satire des Horaz 1.2." In Lefèvre, ed., 311–46.

Lefèvre, E. 1981. "Horaz und Maecenas." *Aufstieg und Niedergang der römischen Welt* 31.3: 1987–2029.

Lejay, P. 1966. *Oeuvres d'Horace. Satires*. Repr. Hildesheim: Georg Olms.

Lejay, P. and Plessis, F. 1915. *Oeuvres d'Horace. Texte latin: publiées avec une étude biographique et littéraire, une notice sur la métrique et la prosodie dans les "odes" et "épodes," des notes critiques, un index des noms propres et des notes explicatives.* Paris: Hachette.

Lomiento, L. 1993. *Cercidas: testimonia et fragmenta.* Rome: Gruppo Editoriale Internazionale.

Long, A. A. 1971. "Aesthesis, Prolepsis and Linguistic Theory in Epicurus." *Bulletin of the Institute of Classical Studies* 18: 114–33.

Long, A. A. 1986. *Hellenistic Philosophy: Stoics, Epicureans, Sceptics.* Berkeley: University of California Press.

Long, A. A. and Sedley, D. N. 1987. *The Hellenistic Philosophers.* 2 vols. Cambridge: Cambridge University Press.

Longo Auricchio, F. 1986. "Sulla concezione filodemea dell'adulazione." *Cronache Ercolanesi* 16: 79–91.

Longo Auricchio, F. and Capasso, M. 1987. "I rotoli della Villa ercolanese: dislocazione e ritrovamento." *Cronache Ercolanesi* 17: 37–48.

Lowrie, M. 2007. "Horace and Augustus." In Harrison, ed., 77–89.

Ludwig, W., ed. 1993. *Horace, l'oeuvre et les imitations: un siècle d'interprétation.* (*Entretiens* 39). Geneva: Fondation Hardt.

Lyne, R. O. A. M. 1995. *Horace: Behind the Public Poetry.* New Haven: Yale University Press.

Macchiaroli, G., ed. 1983. *ΣΥΖΗΤΗΣΙΣ: Studi sull'epicureismo greco e romano.* Naples: Gaetano Macchiaroli.

MacKay, L. A. 1942. "Notes on Horace." *Classical Philology* 37: 79–81.

Mader, G. 2014. "Figuring (Out) the *Avarus*: Ethics, Aesthetics and Counter-Aesthetics in Horace, *Satire* 1.1." *Classical Journal* 109: 419–38.

Mangoni, C. 1993. *Filodemo: Il quinto libro della Poetica (Pherc. 1425 e 1538).* Naples: Bibliopolis.

Mansbach, A. R. 1982. "*Captatio*: Myth and Reality." Dissertation: Princeton University.

Manuwald, A. 1972. *Die Prolepsislehre Epikurs.* Bonn: Rudolf Habelt.

Marchesi, I. 2005. "Traces of a Freed Language: Horace, Petronius and the Rhetoric of Fable." *Classical Antiquity* 24: 307–30.

Mariotti, S., ed. 1996–8. *Orazio: enciclopedia oraziana.* 3 vols. Rome: Istituto della Enciclopedia Italiana.

Martindale, C. 1993. "Introduction." In Martindale and Hopkins, eds., 1–26.

Martindale, C and Hopkins, D., eds. 1993. *Horace Made New.* Cambridge: Cambridge University Press.

Maslowski, T. 1978. "The Chronology of Cicero's Anti-Epicureanism." *Eos* 62: 55–78.

Mayer, R. 1994. *Horace: Epistles, Book I.* Cambridge: Cambridge University Press.

Mayer, R. 1995. "Horace' Moyen de Parvenir." In S. J. Harrison, ed., 279–95.

Mayer, R. 2005. "Sleeping with the Enemy: Satire and Philosophy." In Freudenburg, ed., 146–59.

Mazurek, K. T. R. 1997. "Self-parody and the Law in Horace's *Satires* 1.9." *Classical Journal* 93: 1–17.

Mazzoli, G. 1968. "L'epicureismo di Mecenate e il Prometheus." *Athenaeum* 46: 300–26.

McKeown, J. 1979. "Augustan Elegy and Mime." *Proceedings of the Cambridge Philological Society* 25: 71–84.

McNeill, R. L. B. 2001. *Horace: Image, Identity, and Audience.* Baltimore: Johns Hopkins University Press.

Mette, H. J. 1961. "'Genus tenue' un 'mensa tenuis' bei Horaz." *Museum Helveticum* 18: 136–9.

Michels, A. K. 1944. "*Parrhesia* and the *Satire* of Horace." *Classical Philology* 39: 173–7.

Milanese, G. 1990. "Il poeta, la materia: Lucrezio, Orazio, Filodemo e altri." *Aevum Antiquum* 3: 187–201.

Militello, C. 1997. *Filodemo, memorie epicuree (Pherc. 1418 e 310).* Naples: Biliopolis.

Millar, F. and Segal, E., eds. 1984. *Caesar Augustus: Seven Aspects.* Oxford: Clarendon Press.

Millet, P. 1989. "Patronage and its Avoidance in Classical Athens." In Wallace-Hadrill, ed., 15–47.

Mitsis, P. 1988. *Epicurus' Ethical Theory: The Pleasures of Invulnerability.* Ithaca, NY: Cornell University Press.

Moles, J. 1985. "Cynicism in Horace Epistles 1." *Papers of the Liverpool Latin Seminar* 5: 33–60.

Moles, J. 2007. "Philosophy and Ethics." In Harrison, ed., 165–80.

Momigliano, A. 1973–4. "Freedom of Speech in Antiquity." In Wiener, ed., 2.252–63.

Mommsen, T. 1880. "Inschriftbüsten 1. Aus Herculaneum." *Archäologische Zeitung* 38: 32–6.

Mommsen, T. 1887. *Römisches Staatsrecht.* 3 vols. Leipzig: S. Hirzel.

Monet, A. 2001. "La *Flatterie* de Philodème et l'organisation des *Vices*." In Auvray-Assayas and Delattre, eds., 195–202.

Montiglio, S. 2014. *From Villain to Hero: Odysseus in Ancient Thought.* Ann Arbor, Mich.: University of Michigan Press.

Morris, E. P. 1931. "The Form of the Epistle in Horace." *Yale Classical Studies* 2: 81–114.

Muecke, F. 1993. *Horace, Satires II.* Warminster: Aris & Phillips.

Muecke, F. 2007. "The *Satires*." In Harrison, ed., 105–20.

Müller, R. 2013. "Terence in Latin Literature from the Second Century BCE to the Second Century CE." In Augoustakis and Traill, eds., 363–79.

Musurillo, H. A. 1964. "Horace and the Bore: The *character dramaticus* of *Sat.* 1.9." *Classical Bulletin* 40: 65–8.

318 *Bibliography*

Natali, C. 1995. "*Oikonomia* in Hellenistic Political Thought." In Laks and Schofield, eds., 95–128.

Newman, J. K. 1967. "Augustus and the New Poetry." *Latomus* 89.

Nisbet, R. G. M. 1987. *Cicero: in L. Calpurnium Pisonem Oratio.* Oxford: Clarendon Press.

Nisbet, R. G. M. and Hubbard, M. 1970. *A Commentary on Horace: Odes Book 1.* Oxford: Oxford University Press.

Nisbet, R. G. M. and Rudd, N. 2004. *A Commentary on Horace: Odes Book 3.* Oxford: Oxford University Press.

Nussbaum, M. 1986. "Therapeutic Arguments: Epicurus and Aristotle." In Schofield and Striker, eds., 31–74.

Nussbaum, M. 1994. *The Therapy of Desire: Theory and Practice in Hellenistic Ethics.* Princeton: Princeton University Press.

O'Connor, D. K. 1989. "The Invulnerable Pleasures of Epicurean Friendship." *Greek, Roman and Byzantine Studies* 30: 165–86.

O'Keefe, T. 2001. "Is Epicurean Friendship Altruistic?" *Apeiron* 34: 269–305.

Obbink, D., ed. 1995. *Philodemus and Poetry: Poetic Theory and Practice in Lucretius, Philodemus, and Horace.* Oxford: Oxford University Press.

Obbink, D. 2007. "Lucretius and the Herculaneum Library." In Gillespie and Hardie, eds., 33–40.

Oberhelman, S. and Armstrong, D. 1995. "Satire as Poetry and the Impossibility of Metathesis in Horace's *Satires.*" In Obbink, ed., 233–54.

Oliensis, E. 1998. *Horace and the Rhetoric of Authority.* Cambridge: Cambridge University Press.

Olivieri, A. 1914. *Philodemi Περὶ παρρησίας libellus.* Leipzig: B. G. Teubner.

Oltramare, A. 1926. *Les Origines de la diatribe romaine.* Geneva: Imprimeries Populaire

Pace, N. 2000. "La rivoluzione umanistica nella Scuola epicurea: Demetrio Lacone e Filodemo, teorici di poesia." *Cronache Ercolanesi* 30: 71–80.

Palmer, A. 1893. *The Satires of Horace.* London: Macmillan.

Pasquali, G. 1920. *Orazio lirico.* Florence: Felice le Monnier.

Pennacini, A. 1982. "Bioneis sermonibus et sale nigro." In Della Corte, ed., 55–61.

Perret, J. 1964. *Horace.* Trans. B. Humez. New York: New York University Press.

Perry, B. E. *Aesopica.* 2 vols. Urbana, Ill.: University of Illinois Press.

Philippson, R. 1881. "De Philodemi libro qui est Περὶ σημείων καὶ σημειώσεων et Epicureorum doctrina logica." Dissertation: Berlin.

Philippson, R. 1909. "Zur Wiederherstellung von Philodems sog. Schrift Περὶ σημείων καὶ σημειώσεων." *Rheinisches Museum* 64: 1–38.

Philippson, R. 1911. "Horaz' Verhältnis zur Philosophie." *Festschrift König-Wilhelms- Gymnasium zu Magdeburg.* Magdeburg: K. Peters.

Philippson, R. 1916. "Philodems Buch über den Zorn. Ein Beitrag zu seiner Wiederherstellung und Auslegung." *Rheinisches Museum* 71: 425–60.

Bibliography   319

Philippson, R. 1929. "Zu Philodem und Horaz." *Philologische Wochenschrift* 47: 894–6.

Philippson, R. 1938. "Philodemos." *Realencyclopädie der classischen Altertumswissenschaft* 19: 2444–82.

Pigeaud, J. 1990. "La Folie dans la satire II, 3 d'Horace." *Orphea Voce* 3: 7–43.

Plaumann, G. "'Εταîροι." *Realencyclopädie der classischen Altertumswissenschaft* 6: 1374–80.

Plaza, M. 2006. *The Function of Humor in Roman Verse Satire: Laughing and Lying.* Oxford: Oxford University Press.

Ponczoch, J. A. 2009. "*PHerc.* 1570: A Treatise on Poverty and Wealth." *Cronache Ercolanesi* 39: 141–60.

Powell, J. G. F., ed. 1995. *Cicero the Philosopher: Twelve Papers.* Oxford: Clarendon Press.

Powell, J. G. F. 1995a. "Introduction: Cicero's Philosophical Works and their Background." In Powell, ed., 1–35.

Powell, J. G. F. 1995b. "Cicero's Translations from Greek." In Powell, ed., 273–300.

Price, T. D. 1932. "Restoration of Horace's Sabine Villa." *Memoirs of the American Academy in Rome* 10: 135–42.

Purcell, N. 1983. "The *Apparitores*: A Study of Social Mobility." *Papers of the British School at Rome* 51: 125–73.

Radermacher, L. 1920–1. "Die Zeit der ersten Horazsatire." *Wiener Studien* 42: 148–51.

Rawson, E. 1985. *Intellectual Life in the Late Roman Republic.* London: Duckworth.

Reckford, K. J. 1959. "Horace and Maecenas." *Transactions and Proceedings of the American Philological Association* 90: 195–208.

Reinhardt, T. 2016. "To See and be Seen." In Williams and Volk, eds., 63–90.

Ribbeck, O. 1884. "Kolax: eine ethologische Studie." *Abhandlungen der philologisch-historischen Classe der königlich sächsischen Gesellschaft der Wissenschaften* 9: 1–114.

Rich, N. M. A. 1956. "The Cynic Conception of Aytarkeia." *Mnemosyne* 9: 23–9.

Rimell, V. 2005. "The Poor Man's Feast: Juvenal." In Freudenburg, ed., 81–94.

Ringeltaube, H. 1913. *Quaestiones ad veterum philosophorum de affectibus doctrinam pertinentes.* Göttingen: Officina Academica Huthiana.

Rist, J. M. 1972. *Epicurus: An Introduction.* Cambridge: Cambridge University Press.

Rist, J. M. 1974. "Pleasure: 360–300 B.C." *Phoenix* 28: 167–79.

Roberts, M. 1984. "Horace *Satires* 2.5: Restrained Indignation." *American Journal of Philology* 105: 426–33.

Roskam, G. 2007. "*Live Unnoticed*," *Λάθε βιώσας: On the Vicissitudes of an Epicurean Doctrine.* Leiden: Brill.

Rostagni, A. 1923–4. "Filodemo contra l'estetica classica." *Rivista di filologia e d'istruzione classica* 51: 401–34.

Rudd, N. 1961. "Horace's Encounter with the Bore." *Phoenix* 15: 79–96.

Rudd, N. 1966. *The Satires of Horace.* Cambridge: Cambridge University Press.

Rudd, N. 1986. *Themes in Roman Satire.* London: Duckworth.

Rudd, N. 1989. *Horace: Epistles Book II and Ars Poetica.* Cambridge: Cambridge University Press.

Saller, R. P. 1982. *Personal Patronage under the Early Empire.* Cambridge: Cambridge University Press.

Saller, R. P. 1989. "Patronage and Friendship in Early Imperial Rome." In Wallace-Hadrill, ed., 49–62.

Sallmann, K. 1970. "Satirische Technik in Horaz' Erbschleichersatire (s. 2.5)." *Hermes* 98: 178–203.

Samuelsson, J. 1900. "*Ultra non etiam silere* quid significat?" *Eranos* 4: 1–10.

Santoro, M. 2000. "Il pensiero teologico epicureo: Demetrio Lacone e Filodemo." *Cronache Ercolanesi* 30: 63–70.

Sbordone, F. 1965. "Nuovi frammenti dei papyri ercolanesi." *La parola del passato* 103: 307–13.

Scarpat, G. 1964. *Parrhesia: storia del termine e delle sue traduzioni in latino.* Brescia: Paideia.

Schiesaro, A. 1984. "*Nonne vides* in Lucrezio." *Materiali e discussioni per l'analisi dei testi classici* 13: 143–57.

Schlegel, C. M. 2000. "Horace and his Fathers: Satires 1, 4 and 1, 6." *American Journal of Philology* 121: 93–119.

Schlegel, C. M. 2005. *Satire and the Threat of Speech: Horace's Satires, Book 1.* Madison, Wisc.: University of Wisconsin Press.

Schmid, W. 1978. "Lucretius Ethicus." In Gigon, ed., 123–57.

Schmidt, E. A. 1997. *Sabinum: Horaz und sein Landgut im Licenzatal.* Heidelberg: Winter.

Schofield, M. 1996. "*Epilogismos*: An Appraisal." In Frede and Striker, eds., 221–38.

Schofield, M., Barnes, J. and Burnyeat, M., eds. 1980. *Doubt and Dogmatism: Studies in Hellenistic Epistemology.* Oxford: Clarendon Press.

Schofield, M. and Striker, G., eds. 1986. *The Norms of Nature: Studies in Hellenistic Ethics.* Cambridge: Cambridge University Press.

Schrijvers, P. H. 1993. "*Amicus liber et dulcis*: Horace moraliste." In Ludwig, ed., 41–90.

Schroeder, F. M. 2004. "Philodemus: *Avocatio* and the Pathos of Distance in Lucretius and Vergil." In Armstrong et al., eds., 139–56.

Schulze, W. 1904. *Zur Geschichte lateinischer Eigennamen.* Berlin: Weidmannsche Buchhandlung.

Scott, W. 1885. *Fragmenta herculanensia.* Oxford: Clarendon Press.

Scullard, H. H. 1967. *The Etruscan Cities and Rome*. London: Thames & Hudson.

Scullard, H. H. 1981. *Festivals and Ceremonies of the Roman Republic*. London: Thames & Hudson.

Sedley, D. N. 1973. "Epicurus, *On Nature* Book XXVIII." *Cronache Ercolanesi* 3: 5–83.

Sedley, D. N. 1982. "On Signs." In Barnes et al., eds., 239–72.

Sedley, D. N. 1998. *Lucretius and the Transformation of Greek Wisdom*. Cambridge: Cambridge University Press.

Sedley, D. N. 2011. "Epicurus' Theological Innatism." In Fish and Sanders, eds., 29–52.

Shackleton Bailey, D. R. 1976. *Two Studies in Roman Nomenclature*. New York: Interbook Inc.

Shackleton Bailey, D. R. 1985. *Q. Horati Flacci Opera*. Leipzig: B. G. Teubner.

Shapiro, S. O. 2014. "Socration or Philodemus? Catullus 47 and Prosopographical Excess." *Classical Journal* 109: 385–406.

Sharland, S. 2005. "Saturnalian Satire: Proto-carnivalesque Reversals and Inversions in Horace, *Satire* 2.7." *Acta Classica* 48: 103–20.

Sharland, S. 2009a. "Soporific Satire: Horace, Damasippus and Professor Snore (Stertinius) in *Satire* 2.3." *Acta Classica* 52: 113–31.

Sharland, S. 2009b. *Horace in Dialogue: Bakhtinian Readings in the Satires*. Oxford: Peter Lang.

Shearin, W. H. 2014. *The Language of Atoms: Performativity and Politics in Lucretius' De rerum natura*. Oxford: Oxford University Press.

Sider, D. 1987. "The Love Poetry of Philodemus." *American Journal of Philology* 108: 310–24.

Sider, D. 1995. "Epicurean Poetics: Response and Dialogue." In Obbink, ed., 35–41.

Sider, D. 1997. *The Epigrams of Philodemos*. Oxford: Oxford University Press.

Sider, D. 2009. "The Special Case of Herculaneum." In Bagnall, ed., 305–14.

Sider, S. 1990. "Herculaneum's Library in 79 A.D.: The Villa of the Papyri." *Libraries & Culture* 25: 534–42.

Smith, W. S. 2005. "Advice on Sex by the Self-defeating Satirists: Horace *Sermones* 1.2, Juvenal *Satire* 6, and Roman Satiric Writing." In Smith, ed., 111–28.

Smith, W. S., ed. 2005. *Satiric Advice on Women and Marriage: From Plautus to Chaucer*. Ann Arbor, Mich.: University of Michigan Press.

Snyder, H. G. 2000. *Teachers and Texts in the Ancient World: Philosophers, Jews, and Christians*. London: Routledge.

Stahl, H.-P. 1974. "Peinliche Erfahrung eines kleinen Gottes: Horaz in seinen Satiren." *Antike und Abendland* 20: 25–53.

Stanford, W. B. 1954. *The Ulysses Theme: A Study in the Adaptability of a Traditional Hero*. Oxford: Basil Blackwell.

Starks Jr., J. H. 2013. "*opera in bello, in otio, in negotio*: Terence and Rome in the 160s BCE." In Augoustakis and Traill, eds., 132–55.

Storey, I. C. 2003. *Eupolis: Poet of Old Comedy*. Oxford: Oxford University Press.

Striker, G. 1977. "Epicurus on the Truth of Sense Impressions." *Archiv für Geschichte der Philosophie* 59: 125–42.

Sudhaus, S. 1906. "Eine erhaltene Abhandlung des Metrodor." *Hermes* 41: 45–58.

Swain, S. 2013. *Economy, Family, and Society from Rome to Islam: A Critical Edition, English Translation, and Study of Bryson's Management of the Estate*. Cambridge: Cambridge University Press.

Syme, R. 1939. *The Roman Revolution*. Oxford: Oxford University Press.

Tait, J. I. M. 1941. "Philodemus' Influence on the Latin Poets." Dissertation: Bryn Mawr College.

Talbert, J. A. 1984. *The Senate of Imperial Rome*. Princeton: Princeton University Press.

Tarrant, R. 2007. "Horace and Roman Literary History." In Harrison, ed., 63–76.

Tate, J. 1928. "Horace and the Moral Function of Poetry." *Classical Quarterly* 22: 65–72.

Taylor, C. C. W. 1980. "All Perceptions are True." In Schofield, Barnes, and Burnyeat, eds., 105– 24.

Tepedino Guerra, A. 1977. "Filodemo sulla gratitudine." *Cronache Ercolanesi* 7: 96–113.

Tepedino Guerra, A. 1978. "Il primo libro 'Sulla ricchezza' di Filodemo." *Cronache Ercolanesi* 8: 52–95.

Tepedino Guerra, A. 1985. "Il PHerc. 1678: Filodemo sull'invidia?," *Cronache Ercolanesi* 15: 113–25.

Thomas, R. 2007. "Horace and Hellenistic poetry." In Harrison, ed., 50–62.

Toher, M. 2005. "Tillius and Horace." *Classical Quarterly* 55: 183–9.

Too, Y. L., ed. 2001. *Education in Greek and Roman Antiquity*. Leiden: Brill.

Tracy, V. A. 1980. "*Aut captantur aut captant*." *Latomus* 39: 339–402.

Traill, A. 2013. "Adelphoe." In Augoustakis and Traill, eds., 318–40.

Trapp, M. B. 1997. *Maximus of Tyre: The Philosophical Orations*. Oxford: Oxford University Press.

Tsakiropoulou-Summers, T. 1995. "Philodemus' Περὶ ποιημάτων and Horace's *Ars Poetica*: Adapting Alexandrian Aesthetics to Epicurean and Roman Traditions." Dissertation: University of Illinois at Urbana-Champaign.

Tsakiropoulou-Summers, T. 1998. "Horace, Philodemus and the Epicureans at Herculaneum." *Mnemosyne* 51: 209.

Tsouna, V. 1993. "Epicurean Attitudes to Management and Finance." In Giannantoni and Gigante, eds., 701–14.

Tsouna, V. 2003. "'Portare davanti agli occhi': Una technica retorica nelle opera 'morali' di Filodemo." *Cronache Ercolanesi* 33: 243–7.

Tsouna, V. 2007. *The Ethics of Philodemus*. Oxford: Oxford University Press.

Tsouna, V. 2009. "Epicurean Therapeutic Strategies." In Warren, ed., 249–65.

Tsouna, V. 2011. "Philodemus, Seneca, and Plutarch on Anger." In Fish and Sanders, eds., 183–210.

Tsouna, V. 2012. *Philodemus, On Property Management*. Atlanta, Ga.: Society of Biblical Literature.

Tsouna, V. 2016. "Epicurean Preconceptions." *Phronesis* 61: 160–221.

Turolla, E. 1931. *Orazio. Biografia*. Florence: Felice Le Monnier.

Turpin, W. 2009. "The Epicurean Parasite: Horace, *Satires* 1.1–3." In Freudenburg, ed., 127–40.

Urso, G., ed. 2009. *Ordine e sovversione nel mondo greco e romano*. Pisa: Edizioni ETS.

Van Rooy, C. A. 1973. "Imitatio of Vergil, Eclogues in Horace, *Satires*, Book 1." *Acta Classica* 16: 69–88.

Verde, F., ed. 2010. *Epicuro: Epistola a Erodoto*. Carocci: Rome.

Verde, F. 2013. *Epicuro*. Carocci: Rome.

Vischer, R. 1965. *Das einfache Leben. Wort- und motivgeschichtliche Untersuchungen zu einem Wertbegriff der antiken Literatur*. Göttingen: Vandenhoeck & Ruprecht.

Vooys, C. J. 1934–41. *Lexicon Philodemeum*. Amsterdam: Purmerend.

Wallace-Hadrill, A., ed. 1989. *Patronage in Ancient Society*. London: Routledge.

Wallace-Hadrill, A. 1989. "Patronage in Roman Society: From Republic to Empire." In Wallace-Hadrill, ed., 63–88.

Warren, J. 2002. *Epicurus and Democritean Ethics: An Archaeology of Ataraxia*. Cambridge: Cambridge University Press.

Warren, J., ed. 2009. *The Cambridge Companion to Epicureanism*. Cambridge: Cambridge University Press.

Wehrli, F. 1951. "Ethik und Medizin: Zur Vorgeschichte der aristotelischen Mesonlehre." *Museum Helveticum* 8: 36–62.

Welch, T. 2008. "Horace's Journey through Arcadia." *Transactions of the American Philological Association* 138: 47–74.

White, M. L. 2004. "A Measure of *Parrhesia*: The State of the Manuscript of PHerc. 1471." In Fitzgerald, ed., 103–32.

White, M. L. 2009. "Ordering the Fragments of *PHerc*. 1471: A New Hypothesis." *Cronache Ercolanesi* 39: 29–70.

White, P. 1978. "*Amicitia* and the Profession of Poetry in Early Imperial Rome." *Journal of Roman Studies* 68: 74–92.

White, P. 1993. *Promised Verse: Poets in the Society of Augustan Rome*. Cambridge: Cambridge University Press.

White, P. 2007. "Friendship, Patronage and Horatian Sociopoetics." In Harrison, ed., 195–206.

Wickham, W. C. 1912. *Q. Horati Flacci Opera*. Rev. H. W. Garrod. Oxford: Oxford University Press.

Wiener, P. P., ed. 1973–4. *Dictionary of the History of Ideas: Studies of Selected Pivotal Ideas*. 5 vols. New York: Charles Scribner's Sons.

Wigodsky, M. 2009. "Horace and (not necessarily) Neoptolemus: The 'Ars poetica' and Hellenistic Controversies." *Cronache Ercolanesi* 39: 7–27.

Wilke, K. 1914. *Philodemi Epicurei De ira liber*. Leipzig: B. G. Teubner.

Williams, C. 2012. *Reading Roman Friendship*. Cambridge: Cambridge University Press.

Williams, G. D. 1995. "*Libertino patre natus*: True or False?" In Harrison, ed., 296–313.

Williams, G. D. and Volk, K., eds. 2016. *Roman Reflection: Studies in Latin Philosophy*. Oxford: Oxford University Press.

Wimmel, W. 1962. *Zur Form der horazischen Diatribensatire*. Frankfurt am Main: Vittorio Klostermann.

Wojcik, M. R. 1986. *La Villa dei Papiri ad Ercolano: Contributo alla ricostruzione dell'ideologia della nobilitas tardorepubblicana*. Rome: L'Erma di Bretschneider.

Wright, F. A. 1921. "Horace and Philodemus." *American Journal of Philology* 42: 168–9.

Wurster, S. 2012. "Reconstructing Philodemus: The Epicurean Philosopher in the Late Republic." Dissertation: University of Melbourne.

Zetzel, J. E. G. 2009. "Horace's *Liber Sermonum*: The Structure of Ambiguity." Repr. in Freudenburg, ed., 17–41.

Zetzel, J. E. G. 2016. "Philosophy is in the Streets." In Williams and Volk, eds., 50–62.

Zoepffel, R. 2006. *Aristoteles Oikonomika: Schriften zu Hauswirtschaft und Finanzwesen*. Berlin: Akademie Verlag.

Index Locorum

HESIOD
Works and Days
  778 91

HIPPOCRATES
Epidemics
  6.3.12 67
  12 87 n. 42
  17.5 87 n. 42
  17.7 87 n. 42
  17.8 274

HOMER
Iliad
  2.182–206 223
  3.216–224 223
  18.535 197–8 n. 16
  20.443 191
  24.261 193 n. 9
Odyssey
  1.346–7 32 n. 44
  5.291 152 n. 61
  7.216 255
  8 32
  9.19–20 215
  11.100–37 208
  20.13 255
  22 32

HORACE
Art of Poetry
  25–6 174
  26 148
  40–1 174–5
  41 148
  58–9 69 n. 135
  70–2 147–148
  93–4 135
  231 147
  234 147
  248 186 n. 157
  309 173–4
  333–6 140
  335–6 78–9
  438–44 17 n. 9
Epistles
  1.1 167
  1.1.4 154 n. 68
  1.1.24–6 133, 245 n. 134
  1.1.65 218
  1.1.78–9 220
  1.1.94–7 188–9
  1.1.100 285
  1.1.106–8 252

1.2.17–31 209
1.2.26 260 n. 31
1.2.28–9 258
1.2.46 99 n. 73
1.2.55 107
1.4.15–16 7 n. 23, 17, 258
1.4.26–30 42
1.4.39 43 n. 70
1.7 167
1.7.12 165, 192
1.7.15 179, 242
1.7.35–49 243 n. 128
1.7.37 178
1.7.44–5 242
1.7.45 241 n. 120
1.10.1–2 280 n. 75
1.12.20 270
1.14 241
1.14.37–8 205 n. 40
1.15 7 n. 23
1.15.24 258
1.15.40 219–20
1.15.42–6 296–7
1.15.43–4 181
1.16.1–16 241
1.17 156
1.17.13–32 90
1.17.17 99
1.17.18 14–15, 75
1.17.20–1 99
1.17.24 99
1.17.29 75
1.17.32 75
1.17.41 212
1.17.43 212
1.17.48 297
1.18 156
1.18.1 212
1.18.1–2 196
1.18.1–8 14–15
1.18.5–8 75
1.18.10–14 193–4
1.18.21–36 286 n. 91
1.18.44 212
1.19.1 192
1.19.11 280
1.20.25 285
2.1.49–52 211
2.1.59 131
2.1.124 174
2.1.128 174
2.2.49–52 169, 266 n. 43

General Index

Actium, battle of (30 BC) 202
adultery
  desire equated with act 298–9
  objections to 110 n. 100, 113–14,
    117–18, 298–9 n. 125
Aesop 88 n. 45
Alcaeus 92 n. 59
Alcubierre, Roque Joaquín de 22 n. 22
Alexander the Great 32
Allen, Walter, Jr. 32 n. 46, 47–8 n. 80,
    50 n. 86, 66
Amafinius 146
ambition, condemned 171–2, 175–6,
    179–81, 183–6, 211
Amoroso, Filippo 25, 230 n. 90
Anacreon 32
Anderson, W. S. 2, 15, 130 n. 4, 191,
    197 n. 16, 201, 250 n. 2, 281
anger 119–28
  excessive 125–6
  physical symptoms 126–7
ant, as symbol of industry/
    prudence 89–90, 91–2, 95, 265–6
Antigonus Gonatas 32–3, 172, 187
Antipater 237
Antisthenes 209
Apuleius 70 n. 137
Archilochus 5 n. 14
Aristius Fuscus 280 n. 75
Aristophanes 131, 208
Aristotle 14, 32, 253
  concept of "natural wealth" 37–8
  doctrine of the mean 153–4
  influence on *Satires* 109
  Nicomachean Ethics 18, 161–2
Armstrong, David 7 n. 25, 10–11, 16–17,
    25 n. 32, 26, 34 n. 53, 42 n. 68, 45, 46,
    51 n. 90, 67 n. 128, 73, 113 n. 109,
    128 n. 147, 136, 140 n. 31, 141 n. 32,
    159, 160 n. 81, 180–1, 186 n. 157,
    246–7, 281
Arrius 277
The Art of Poetry (Horace), dedication 10
Asmis, Elizabeth 43, 62, 66 n. 125,
    85 n. 38, 125 n. 141, 159 n. 79,
    162 n. 86, 258

Augustus, Emperor *see* Octavian
avarice, condemned 40 n. 65, 82–4,
    93–5, 102–6, 259–61, 271–6

Bacchylides 32
Bailey, Cyril 147 n. 50, 155 n. 69
Barbieri, Aroldo 9, 242 n. 123, 251 n. 3
Bentley, Richard 164–5, 292–3 n. 111
Bion of Borysthenes 32, 75, 80, 83,
    84, 88–9, 94 n. 61, 95 n. 63, 98,
    108, 151, 172, 183 n. 152, 187,
    188 n. 163, 209, 275
  On Anger 59 n. 113, 281
  On Apathy 127–8 n. 147
  stylistic borrowings from 127–8
Bond, R. P. 251 n. 6, 252–3
Bowditch, Phoebe 43 n. 70,
    235, 241
Boyancé, Pierre 175
Brink, C. O. 9, 140 n. 31

Callias 52
Callimachus 109 n. 99, 115, 116, 224
Capasso, Mario 16, 23, 25 n. 31
captatio (legacy hunting) 207–8,
    208 n. 47, 210–11, 210–11 n. 58, 297
Castaldi, Francesco 33 n. 50, 34 n. 53
Cataudella, Quintino 9, 109 n. 99,
    117 n. 123
Catullus 2 n. 6, 51 n. 91, 110, 166,
    169 n. 107, 190, 240 n. 119, 244–5
Cèbe, J.-P. 270, 282 n. 81
Cercidas of Megalopolis 116–17
Champlin, Edward 218
choices/avoidances, philosophical
    concept 107–8
  centrality to Epicureanism 138–9
  and hedonic calculus 28–9, 149, 181
  motivations 79, 254
Chrysippus 14, 59 n. 113, 87 n. 42, 209,
    237, 279, 281
Cicero 5, 10, 11, 67
  attacks on Cynics 79
  commentary on Epicureanism 161,
    175 n. 128
  on flattery 54–5

Muecke, Frances 5, 211 n. 59, 217, 224
    n. 80, 234 n. 97, 250 n. 2, 251 n. 6,
    253 n. 14, 266, 268, 277–8, 280, 281,
    283, 285 n. 87, 294 n. 115, 297
Musurillo, Herbert 191, 194
Mys (servant of Epicurus) 292

"natural wealth" 37–8, 40, 236–7
neologisms 147–8
New Comedy 131, 182–3
Nisbet, R. G. M. 165

Obbink, Dirk 10–11, 25
Oberhelman, Steven 136
Octavian (later Emperor Augustus) 6,
    60, 167
    appearance in *Satires* 2.1 202–4
Odes (Horace) 9, 17–18, 174, 204
    publication date 204 n. 36
Oliensis, Ellen 3, 5, 93 n. 60, 171, 195,
    198, 217, 234, 244
Olivieri, Alessandro 23, 25, 118–19, 187
    n. 160, 287 n. 93
Oltramare, André 102, 139 n. 27, 182
    n. 147, 264, 267 n. 45
Origen 113–14, 115
overindulgence, condemned 253–9,
    256–7 nn.21, 22, 276–8
    see also sexual activity
Ovid 70 n. 137

Palmer, Arthur 250 n. 2, 292–3 n. 111
Panaetius of Rhodes 14, 119–20, 125
    n. 140, 145
Pasquali, Giorgio 7–8, 114 n. 111
patronage 12, 45–8, 52–6, 164–89,
    207, 232
    disengagement from public life 175–9
    and frankness 53–4, 186–9
    (Greek) development of system 31–4,
    52–4, 166–7
    mutual benefits 77–8
    overlap with true friendship 167–8,
    177–9, 184–5, 187–8
    reasons for seeking 31–4
    risk of destruction by flattery 169–71,
    54–6, 167, 182–4
Persius 145
persona of Horace
    contrasted with protagonists of the
    Satires 192–4, 197–8, 207–8,
    211–12, 232–3, 248, 287–8, 296–7

criticised by interlocutors 279–80,
    283–301
Cynical touches 108
Epicurean basis 1–7, 12, 51, 81, 201
    moral worth 12, 18, 128, 154–5, 163,
    189, 232, 301–2
    self-deprecation/self-parody 132,
    168–9, 206, 211, 294
Philip II of Macedon 32
Philippi, battle of (42 BC) 169
Philodemus of Gadara 7–8
    accusations of flattery 21, 55, 167,
    185, 192, 207
    archaeological finds 21–3
    biography 18–21
    collections of works 24–7
    condemnation of avarice 83–8
    condemnation of Cynicism 74–5, 78
    Cynic influences on 73–4, 79–80
    depictions of anger 73–4, 79–80
    diatribes 73–5
    on economics 34–51, 84–5, 87–8, 180
    on frankness 9, 27, 55–9, 61
    on friendship/intimacy 158
    influence on Horace 8–9, 11, 60–1,
    67, 77–8, 156–7, 159–60, 209–13,
    229–32, 301–2
    methodology 63–7
    relationship with Piso 20–1, 48–51,
    165, 182, 185, 192
    Roman influences on 44–5, 54–5
    studies of 10–11, 19 n. 12, 23–4
    see also economics; flattery
Philippson, Robert 4 n. 13, 7, 7 n. 27, 19
    n. 12, 64 n. 123, 67 n. 128, 139 n. 26
Piaggio, Antonio, Fr 22, 25
pig, significance in Epicurean
    imagery 17 n. 11
Pindar 32
Piso 19–21, 34, 48–51, 141 n. 33, 165,
    182, 185, 192
Plato 5, 5 n. 14, 32, 282 n. 82
    quoted/paraphrased by Horace 14, 15
Plaza, Maria 281 n. 78, 288–9,
    298–9 n. 125
pleasure *see* hedonic calculus
Pliny the Elder 255
Plotius Tucca 6–7, 16–17, 200
Plutarch 33–4
    *How to Tell a Flatterer from a
    Friend* 56 n. 105, 218
Polyaenus of Lampsacus 31, 35